The Christ Letters.

Christ Returns
Speaks His Truth

The Recorder

Audio Enlightenment Press

Giving Voice to the Wisdom of the Ages

Printed in the United States of America

0 1 2 3 4 5 6 7 8 9

ISBN 978-1-941489-39-0

www.AudioEnlightenmentPress.com

www.MetaPhysicalPocketBooks.Com

First Printing April 2018

This expanded edition is an exact duplication of the original Christ Letters, Christ Articles including all the proper formatting as stipulated by the Recorder, as well as the 2007 and the 2014 Special Messages from Christ.

CHRIST RETURNS – SPEAKS HIS TRUTH

FOREWORD

First, I would like to explain why I have used the title of recorder in place of my real name.

There was never the slightest doubt in my mind, whilst writing these LETTERS, that they emanated from Christ. I have described my reasons for being so sure of this, in my short biography.

During the writing of the LETTERS, I was clearly told to leave myself out of the picture that CHRIST'S LETTERS must stand entirely on their own. People must decide for themselves whether the Letters rang true or whether people felt they were fake. I had written down what I had received, I would try to get them out for public scrutiny and whatever happened after that was strictly between the reader of the LETTERS and Christ Consciousness.

Christ promised in the LETTERS that they would form a link between the reader's mind and Christ Mind and help would be given in understanding the deep meaning hidden behind the words.

Many people have reported experiencing that contact. Many people have been aware of an inflow of insight.

Therefore, just as a secretary's name is unimportant in a business transaction, so is my name and my identity unimportant. What is truly important is whether the reader can feel this is the authentic Christ who has risen in spiritual consciousness to the very portals of the Equilibrium whilst still retaining individuality in order to remain in contact with the world of individuality.

Secondly, there has been division in opinion regarding the sometimes strange formatting of the LETTERS.

I would like to explain that as Christ impressed my mind with words or pictures, which made it necessary for me to build up what I saw in words, I also felt the emotions (to a certain degree) that Christ felt when going through the events he is describing at this time. By dropping back into the vibrations of that time, Christ entered into those times, and relayed them through my mind. There was no way that the LETTERS could have been written in plain print or just using italics. So often, when a new wonderful insight was put through my mind, I wondered 'How can I get this across?' You will know what I mean as you read the LETTERS.

And so, to show that some powerful statement had come from Christ's mind into mine, I used italics, dark print and capitals. People have complained that this unconventional formatting interferes with the flow of reading. But this is just the point. These Letters are not meant to be read. They are meant to be PONDERED and this means you have to stop on the words in print which hold up the flow of words and THINK about what the words are trying to convey to you. You must remember at all times that when Christ tries to reach your human intelligence, he is relating truths which go way beyond your own experience in life in this world. You have to reach into the infinite dimension in order to try to understand what you are being told. And so, if you spend half-an-hour pondering a paragraph with weird formatting, it is half-an-hour well spent if gradually, your mind opens up to new possibilities beyond your present thinking. As you reach up in consciousness to Christ Consciousness, asking for illumination, it will surely be given you. Not necessarily at that moment but perhaps, – wham, – when you least expect it, the answer will come shafting into your mind and you will KNOW that – 'YES, THIS IS IT!' – THIS IS THE TRUE ANSWER.

Introduction

Christ Says:

'I have come to rectify the misinterpretations placed on the teachings given when known as 'JESUS' in Palestine, 2000 years ago.'

Christ also says:

'Because people are on the threshold of a world crisis of enormous proportions, it is vital for survival that **I, the Christ**, should reach all who will listen. You know little of the true processes of creation in which you, yourselves, play a major role. It is imperative you should understand them sufficiently to enable you to embark on the implementation of a higher vision for all humanity.

'It is impossible for my spiritual consciousness to take on human form; to enable me to speak to you directly, I have de-programmed and prepared a receptive, obedient mind to receive my Truth and frame it in words. She is my 'recorder'.'

Recorder: Before reading **Christ's Letters**, you may want to know how this spiritual exercise of transmission of consciousness was achieved.

The work of preparing me to become Christ's recorder began 40 years ago, when as a committed Christian, encountering grievous difficulties as a farmer, and asking Christ for help, an unexpected forceful answer caused me to re-examine and discard all religious dogma. Enlightenment followed and clearly led in new directions of work and study, I founded a business dealing with people, which flourished. For seven years I enjoyed success and much happiness. To grow in spiritual understanding, I then went through diverse very traumatic human experiences and after much suffering, painfully and gainfully learnt their lessons then transcended them spiritually.

One evening, in response to prayer for guidance, the presence of Christ became a reality, who gave me irrefutable proof of his identity. He spoke to me for an hour, sending strong waves of Cosmic Love through my body and gave me a brief description of what I was to be taught and eventually achieve. A fortnight later, he led me through a transcendent experience of Conscious Union with 'God'. I became a healer and instrumental in some instantaneous healings.

From 1966-1978, at important points of my life, in response to questioning, Christ instructed me in spiritual-scientific principles, now explained by Christ in his **Letters**. In 1975, I experienced a night of visions describing events between 1983 and 1994, all of which came true. I was again told there would be work for me to do in the future.

Eventually, after many and varied vicissitudes, always alleviated by my strong connection with Christ and my deepening understanding and personal experience of 'First Cause', I was brought to my present home. Here, I have lived an increasingly solitary life in the past twenty years, sometimes in clear and close contact with Christ and sometimes left to strengthen my faith and patience in the spiritually dry periods. In the past four years I have been led through mental/emotional purification, reaching my goal of perfect inner peace and joy.

Christ has put me through a gradual but very clear refining process. When perfectly empty of self, malleable and receptive – the Voice began its dictation and the Letters began to take shape. **These Letters are entirely the work of Christ**. Nothing in them has been derived from other literature, although in recent years, certain writers have obviously drawn much of their own inspired insight from Christ's conscious radiation of Truth. All those who are in harmony with his Consciousness are greatly blest. I am merely the 'Recorder' – nothing more.

Expanded Contents

Letter 1. Christ speaks of his reasons for returning to dictate these **Letters**. Says that mankind brings their own woes upon them through their thoughts and actions. Explains why his true mission on earth was not recorded properly. Says there is no such thing as 'sin against God'; neither is our true **Source of Being** understood. Describes his six weeks in the desert and what really took place – what he learnt and how the knowledge changed him from rebel to Master and Healer.

Letter 2. Continues the story of his life on earth, his return to his mother in Nazareth and reception! His first public healing and the tremendous response. Choosing disciples. His true teachings.

Letter 3. Continues life incidents, teachings, his awareness that his time on earth was to be cut short by crucifixion. The things he did to arouse the anger of the Jewish Religious Leaders. What really took place and was said at the 'Last supper', the disciples' attitudes, and the truth concerning his 'ascension'.

Letter 4. **Christ** gathers up the threads of his teachings in Palestine and says that he and Muhammad, Buddha and all other Masters have continued to develop spiritually until they have all ascended into **CHRIST CONSCIOUSNESS**. Christ speaks of the truth of the sexual relationship, saying that the attitude between men and women will eventually change. Spiritual progress will take place and children with new spiritual potential will be born.

Letter 5 & 6. Christ begins to explain the true processes of creation. He touches on what science and religious doctrines have believed, rejects them and defines the **TRUTH of BEING. He** touches on the truth regarding the human ego, – the means of earthly individuality and therefore necessary, but also the source of all suffering.

Letter 7. **Christ** describes the truth concerning the sexual act – what really takes place spiritually and physically. How children are born on different levels of consciousness. He explains men and women's place in the world order.

Letter 8. **Christ** explains the reality of men and women, how to live within the **LAWS of EXISTENCE** and come into a state of harmonious blessed state of being in which all things are abundantly provided, health is restored, and joy becomes a natural state of mind. Every individual can reach this interior state of blessedness, and peace will then become the norm.

Letter 9. **Christ** ties up loose ends of his other **Letters** and tells people plainly how to overcome the ego, gain true self-esteem and experience the joy of perfect inner peace. He touches on racism and a personal message of encouragement and love to all who are drawn to his **Letters**.

Christ Returns, Speaks His Truth

The Christ Letters

LETTER 1

I, the **CHRIST**, take this opportunity to speak directly to YOU.

I have come to rectify the misinterpretations placed on the teachings given when known as 'Jesus' in Palestine, 2000 years ago.

They are being put through one who, during the past forty years, has been spiritually sensitive and dedicated enough to receive my words and act on them.

These LETTERS ARE TRUTH.

They transcend all religious doctrines in the world.

--These LETTERS will LIBERATE you.

They are for all people who are searching for meaning to existence, purpose in their lives, strength to face the daily struggle to live and endure hardship, sickness, despair, and inspiration for those who aspire to greater spiritual awareness in their daily lives.

You might say that these **Letters are a MASTER's COURSE** for those who are ready to put foot to the path which I travelled when on earth in Palestine.

You may doubt that the above words are true. As you read these pages and go into the facts I am giving you concerning existence and the origins of personality, you will realize that this truth could only have come from the highest source.

Those who have difficulty in understanding the **LETTERS** should read them a page at a time, then put them aside and meditate. Gradually, the meaning will seep into your consciousness for these pages are a link between your consciousness and my transcendent consciousness.

Come to these **LETTERS** with a mind as free of ideas and beliefs and prejudice as a very little child before it is indoctrinated with human belief.

Bring me your uncluttered mind, a seeking mind, and I will fill it with true treasure, the treasure of highest knowledge which, as you absorb it, will lighten your daily load and lead you into 'green pastures of brightest light', signifying abundance, joy, rapture and fulfillment of every need. You will

3

come to know how it feels to be abundantly blest with all that exists beyond your present human comprehension.

These **LETTERS** are sent to all people throughout the world with my compassion and love. As you read them, you will feel the love and the compassion and will come to realize that your daily struggles with existence were never intended for you. There is no need for you to experience pain and stress when you understand, absorb and practice the **TRUTH OF EXISTENCE** consistently.

THE PURPOSE BEHIND THESE LETTERS.

They are intended to bring enlightenment to the world generally, to enable humanity to construct a NEW CONSCIOUSNESS during the next two thousand years. These **LETTERS** are the seeds of the future spiritual evolution of humankind.

Note well:

It is the spiritual evolution of the 'human consciousness' that brings about the mental and physical evolution in your personal and global lives and brings humanity into ever more harmonious states of well-being.

If you find this hard to believe, reflect on the past two thousand years and see what has been accomplished since I last spoke to people in person.There has been a gradual evolutionary trend towards the **brotherly love** I constantly preached to the Jews.

When I walked the earth, there were no such humanitarian organizations as you have now. Ambition, greed, and self-gratification were regarded as normal behavior.

There was little brotherly love even amongst the Jews whose prophets, for generations, had exhorted them to love their neighbors as themselves.

As humanity has developed its capacity for brotherly love so has humanity made life more pleasant and comfortable for itself in the form of mutual consideration, courtesy, kindness and in the provision of hospitals, child welfare societies, care of the aged, human rights movements, and many other institutions devoted to the improvement of the human condition. All these have been born in the hearts and minds

of those who sincerely heeded my original words spoken in Palestine urging people towards brotherly love and compassion for their fellow men.

This form of spiritual caring and brotherly love gained tremendous impetus in the 19th century, when my words were preached with renewed sincerity and intensity from pulpits and gladly received by earnest and sincere congregations. Preachers and congregations were, by that time, spread world-wide on every continent. The Sabbath was truly regarded as a day of rest and the thoughts of the majority of Christian people were lifted to the contemplation of the power of God. **Such a world-wide cessation from normal duties and occupations, meant that a 24-hour long elevation of 'conscious thought' towards the Divine Creative Power created a regular and powerful 'human/Divine' consciousness underpinning and inter-threading human lives. Human petition drew the Power of the Divine into the human consciousness and human experience and led directly to growth and expansion in every facet of human life.**

However, people did not yet know how **to mentally direct Divine Power into spiritual rather than 'ego' channels of creativity**. Consequently, the expansion of 'collective consciousness' brought 'evil' results arising out of the 'ego power' as well as the 'good' results produced by the 'spiritual consciousness' of inspired and enlightened people.

N.B. FOR THIS REASON .... I have come expressly to explain to you a vitally important fact of existence. Please read carefully.

It is this:

* Your personal **consciousness** is entirely responsible for whatever comes into your life and personal experience. It is your personal **consciousness** which brings you good or evil. *

*In your sub-conscious, you bring through strongly imprinted but hidden recollections of past traumas/emotions of past life/lives which can erupt and color your present consciousness. *

 * Your specific and impassioned prayer for alleviation of some kind, may be answered but it will avail you little in the long term **if your mind and heart continually operate in contravention of the Universal Laws of LOVE and you live in a mindset of constant criticism.** *

5

Universal Laws of Existence relate ONLY to 'activities of consciousness' .... and are exact and undeviating .... they are NOT rewards or punishment from 'God'.

I repeat: are not 'PUNISHMENT FROM GOD' – they relate to the 'Causative Factor of Consciousness' which attract/magnetize electrical particles that thus bond together and appear to the world as outer visible solid forms and experiences.

N.B. Sometimes, people make **powerfully prayerful contact** with the **DIVINE REALITY** behind and within all creation, **It responds** and **Its activity** is shortly revealed as necessary improvements within the personal and national life – and people may exclaim 'This is a miracle!'

But – in the long term, – **the state of the Personal or National consciousness will again re-assert itself in their experiences and will re-produce the same negative effects in health or affairs as they did previously**.

You cannot effect permanent changes in your lives unless you change your consciousness. Therefore people must pray and strive at all times to achieve unconditional **Love**.

For in the 20th century, human mental abilities out-stripped their spiritual development.

Scientists thought they could explain away the origins of creation and ascribe them to accident. As a direct result = people ditched morality and began to give way utterly to self-will.

They set in motion a new momentum of menace in the world, for they began to create a new form of 'world ego-consciousness' directly in opposition to the NATURE of the Divine – UNCONDITIONAL LOVE. The human consciousness blocked the inflow of the Divine.

NOTE WELL: The ever-increasing lurid imaginings of a few people, which would have been contained locally, a century ago, now became a

CONTAGIOUS MENTAL INFECTION
glorified in literature, films, theatre

spreading world-wide, creating a global '**Human Consciousness**' similar to their own, expressed as sexual excesses, violence, and perversions. This **MENTAL INFECTION** first manifests as egocentric modes of living and the creation of technical devices – which have created serious health disorders, climatical changes, crop failures, environment deterioration, extinction of living creatures, and wholesale slaughter of human beings.

Mental Infection manifests in the human personality as deranged and destructive behavior, drug-taking, abominable cruelty and depravity, gangster operations, and sexual excesses. Thus has a vicious circle of malignancy and perversions of thought and activities been created by entertainment and media magnates. The purpose – to capture egocentric public vested interest.

Your TV and Cinema screen has become the new Bible of human behavior.

Personal tragedies unknown to human kind a century ago, have become rife and people live in fear of walking the streets. Households are barricaded behind high walls. Family and social problems are taken into regular public debate – and so the saga of human misery is perpetuated.

This is the **BEAST** stalking your lands and feeding a **miasma of beastliness** into innocent minds.

It will be perpetuated until my **Christ Knowledge is acknowledged, accepted and lived by the majority of people on earth. Because this knowledge will show you how to get back on the true PATH OF LIFE in order to start creating the kind of lives you truly desire.**

Because I am unconditional LOVE I am speaking the TRUTH which many spiritual minds suspect but which is rejected by those who are spiritually blind – at the moment.

These words are not spoken to threaten or punish you – but to alert you to the source of all the unspeakable horrors which daily fill your newspapers and TV screens.

It is only my love for all people that forces me to descend through the various levels of consciousness to reach the dimension of human depravity to warn you of its consequences in your present lives.

NOTE WELL – IMPORTANT

You wonder from whence has come the HIV virus which attacks man's precious self-defence system – the immune system, and also targets his abilities to procreate?

This virus, if left to spread unchecked – (not by drugs) – by SPIRITUAL AWARENESS – will wipe out the unwary. The Enlightened will avoid these and other pitfalls of existence.

Wake up! Realize! Your own strong 'consciousness impulses' are life impulses.They are highly creative electro-magnetic impulses!

When they are of a **virulent – violent – aggressive – murderous nature – they emit electrical particles of virulent, violent, aggressive, murderous CONSCIOUSNESS** which take form as virulent viruses in the air, spreading from one innocent person to another.

What is born and nurtured in the diseased mind eventually takes on form in the physical world. This is not punishment from 'God' as the churches may teach you. It is, a **SCIENTIFIC FACT OF EXISTENCE**. Therefore, it is a matter of extreme urgency for all spiritually minded people to set aside 'infantile' imaginings to perceive, clearly, the **TRUTH of creation & existence.**

My MESSAGE to all CHURCHES.

I, the CHRIST, have come expressly to tell you **the truth about the origins of the 'human personality'**. I will explain exactly why and how mankind has been given a natural inbuilt propensity for self-will and a controlling desire for self-gratification and self-defense.

This is not sin – but part of the natural creative processes. There is no 'punishment' from on high!

Men, through the willful and harmful exercise of their 'Ego-Power', draw to themselves their own punishment.

NOTE WELL: For this reason, just as scientific school text-books become redundant as the human mind discovers and absorbs more advanced scientific knowledge, so should the present form of 'Christianity', built upon spurious doctrines centred around my crucifixion, be allowed to die a natural death.

N.B. Your present global crisis, introducing a new break down of International Law and laying the foundation for future global terrorism, clearly indicates that no religion in the world possesses the requisite knowledge and effective leadership to initiate changes in human mental patterns – which will lead directly to peace and prosperity.

THE TRUE SPIRITUAL LEADER will be able to show their congregations how and why modern mindsets have created the calamities and horrors which have been created in 'consciousness' and are only just beginning to make themselves fully felt in your midst as diverse forms of pestilence and earthquakes, floods, famines, wars, revolution and other tragedies. Be assured! No evil which comes to your earth is a 'natural disaster'. Everything inimical to your perfect welfare is bred first in your 'human consciousness' and then given form within your global experience. **This is what I tried to tell the Jews when I walked the earth – and WEPT – when they laughed and refused to believe it. They called me a madman.**

Let not the churches make the same mistake!

Because the churches have been moribund, cemented into rituals and dogmas, their priests and pastors have been unable to meet the evolving spiritual needs of ardent seekers of Truth. As a result, the churches are emptying. **If they are to endure, the churches must put aside their differences and have the humility to accept that inspiration does not necessarily come to earth in ways acceptable to themselves. They must remember that I, the Christ, was not acceptable to the Jews.** The churches must keep open minds and hearts to receive whatever they intuitively feel is a Higher Truth than that to which they presently cling ... and to abandon the old beliefs which have permitted the **BEAST** to take control of human thought.

Pray sincerely, with all your souls, minds, hearts – for **true enlightenment** – rather than a re-iteration of old and false beliefs. Wake up and accept that these rituals and past beliefs have not fulfilled my words to mankind, when I promised that 'greater things than I did' would you do.

Meanwhile, until true enlightenment comes to you – (after much meditation and prayer) – teach, demonstrate and live:

BROTHERLY LOVE
with all the strength of soul, heart and mind
minute by minute in your daily lives.

Because – to combat the global destructive consciousness forces, humanity must make every effort to move on swiftly to the next stage of its development.

URGENT NEED FOR A HIGHER VISION

It must be widely accepted there is a HIGHER VISION to strive to implement in your daily lives.

It is only by reaching for a higher vision that the physical world will be rescued from wholesale annihilation.

Without the vision either for the self or for the world, there can be no spiritual evolution or the achievement of those things greatly desired. At the present time, your perception of life is one of travail and deprivation. These beliefs are shockingly depicted and re-inforced by your TV viewing. They later bring upon you the misery you hope will never happen to you.

Therefore, to save you from your own folly expressed through the media and TV, the 'human consciousness' must be SPEEDILY uplifted to see **what I saw in the desert** –

the **Reality of Love** behind and within all existence.

N.B. When this great truth is both perceived and warmly acknowledged, the **Reality of Love** will begin to manifest Itself in multiple ways in every living thing and in the environment itself.

The experience of abundance and joy will re-inforce the consciousness of abundance and joy. **And so a spiritual spiral of ever more exalted and wondrous living will be set in motion.**

When the TRUE nature of 'Being' is fully understood – humanity will move on to the next rung of spiritual evolution and will put into motion a new and blessed form of human endeavor and personal experience. To achieve these goals, humanity must first gain insight into:

WHAT and WHO you are

A new and important question is already coming into people's consciousness. 'Who are you – really – behind the facade you present to the world?' What does it take to be **REAL?**

It is this question of 'Who you really are' which is answered, on every level of your being, within these pages. **And if you can accept as your own guidelines for daily living – all that I understood during my six-weeks 'desert' experience – you too will eventually become WHOLE and REAL even as I became WHOLE and REAL before I commenced my ministry of healing and teaching.**

Since there are few people in the world who would regard themselves as **WHOLE** at this present time, you must surely recognize that there is the most urgent necessity for me to **intrude into your minds** to lead you into a new way of thought and feeling. Such a change in consciousness will bring you into Divine harmony with **Reality** and better living conditions and security.

To be able to do this work of 'reconstruction' within your 'consciousness, I must first impress on your minds – and you must accept – there was much that I taught in Palestine which men were not yet ready to receive.

Significantly, it has never been publicly questioned **why** there is no record of my early life as a young man. What was the true reason for such an all important omission?

Equally significantly, although I spent six weeks in the desert after my baptism, and emerged from that experience as a TEACHER & HEALER, not one writer has even attempted to describe what actually took place during that time other than that I was 'tempted of the devil' and 'was with the wild beasts' and the 'angels were with him'. There is not the slightest 'hint' as to what happened to me in the desert which would enable me to come back to towns and villages proclaiming the 'Kingdom of God is within!' and to speak in the synagogues with such authority that the Jewish elders were astonished.

The truth regarding my human state was, by common consent of my disciples, suppressed to give greater credence to my supposed 'Divinity' and ministry.

According to the gospels, it was said of me that I was the 'only Son of God'. Why then, did I frequently refer to myself as the 'Son of Man'? I specifically made these statements to counter-act the prevalent beliefs in my 'divinity' and to impress on people's minds that I was of the same physical origins as themselves. I intended them to understand that what I could do, they could also do if they only had my knowledge and followed my instructions for right thinking and right action.

So many myths have arisen around my earthly person and my SPIRITUAL CONSCIOUSNESS that it is time to be rid of them as completely as possible, since they are preventing people from evolving spiritually.

You, who have been indoctrinated with religious teachings, must try to understand that when describing my life, my disciple gospellers related only what they personally remembered which fully supported their account of my 'supernatural' activities. They also included much that had been spoken of me by others, during the thirty odd years following my death.

After such a lapse of time and inevitable embroidery of truth – how could they possibly write an authoritative 'biography' of me and of what really happened or properly explain my true spiritual perceptions which gave birth to my words and 'miracles'?

Only one person can write from this standpoint – and that is myself. Therefore, these Letters will bring you my Truth in a way that no spectator could possibly tell it, no matter how well they thought they understood my thinking.

(For this reason, over forty years, my 'recorder's' mind has been systematically cleansed of all orthodox teachings and the system of communication between us has been perfected.)

If my **Truth** expressed in these **Letters** differs from much written in your New Testament, is it to be wondered at or rejected for that reason?

Therefore, I am descending in consciousness briefly, as near as necessary, to your plane of consciousness to describe my life and teachings 2000 years ago.

12

MY PLACE IN HISTORY

I must first point out that my life and person were briefly referred to in the 'History of the Jews' written by Josephus for the Roman Governor, and presented to the Roman Emperor.

Josephus briefly noted that Jesus, who attempted to overthrow law and order and the governance of the Romans was punished and crucified.

It has been argued that this was some other Jesus recorded by Josephus. But this is not so. I, who later became the **CHRIST** who performed so-called miracles of healing and materialisation, was the insurrectionist. But – I was no 'rabble rouser'. I did not deliberately stir people up to defy the Romans and disrupt law and order.

I was a rebel against existing Jewish traditions and because, when I emerged from my six weeks sojourn in the desert, **I saw a better way to – think – and – live – and I tried to pass on my knowledge to my fellow Jews with little success.**

It is important you should understand that the pressure of public opinion weighed with my followers. Whilst, they truly believed I had brought a 'soul-saving' message to the Jews and was the Messiah, the 'Son of God', they were also of the world, trying to relate to the world as best they could. Therefore, although they knew my reactive feelings towards the Jewish beliefs, they were not happy to dispense with the Old Testament altogether, since it had supported and kept the Jews together throughout their history. In the interests of preserving what they thought to be valuable in the old dispensation, they suppressed any description of the 'person' I was.

My disciples and Paul built their own edifice of 'sacred beliefs' on what they wanted to preserve from my life and teachings. They only taught, and consolidated what they deemed to be valuable to people – Jews and Gentiles – alike – at that time and in the future.

Consequently, they distilled what they could use and they 'let go' most of what I termed the 'secrets of the Kingdom of God' for they never understood them.

Nor found them desirable in the creation of a new perception of the **'Divine'** – the **'Father'**.

To preserve the Jewish belief in 'salvation from punishment for sins' by means of sacrifice in the Temple – the 'person of Jesus' was adopted as the 'supreme' sacrifice who had paid for men's sins by my crucifixion. This belief served many purposes at that time.

It gave my death on the cross – a valid and heroic reason. It proved to the people that I was the 'Son of God' who had carried out a specific mission to the very end of my life.

This belief also proved to be of great comfort to Jews when their Temple was destroyed by the Romans – and led to many converts taking place.

Many sects of Jews – and Gentiles also – did not believe in life after death. Consequently, it was greatly comforting to hear that 'Jesus Christ' had overcome death and retained his body. To much human thought at that time, life was not possible without a body. Therefore, life after death could only mean the resurrection of the body.

It also kept my name constantly alive in the minds of people. I was the 'historic figure' who had valiantly died to ensure that men should be freed of all fear of hell and damnation. Providing they believed in 'me', they could walk as 'freed men'.

It is only because my 'name' has been kept alive to this very day that I am now able to come to you and give you of the **TRUTH** I so dearly wanted to share with people 2000 years ago.

MY EARLY LIFE and EXPERIENCES IN THE DESERT

I was born in Palestine. My mother was convinced that I would be a Messiah. Contrary to popular belief, I was not a saintly child.

When taken to the Temple, aged twelve years old, to be interviewed by the Chief Priests to determine whether I would be fit to enter Jewish Religious Training, I was rejected as being too opinionated.

Bitterly disappointed, my mother took me home again and did her best to raise me in the sanctity which marked her own demeanor at all times. This was an impossible task for I was, above all things, an individualist and unruly in behavior. I resented my mother's guidance and her attempted discipline. As a youth, I became unmanageable – a true rebel!

I rejected my mother's staunch adherence to the Jewish faith and traditions, preferring laughter to sanctimonious attitudes. I refused to learn a trade which would have bound me down to routine. I chose to mix with all and sundry of the poorer classes, drank with them, knew prostitutes, and enjoyed talking, arguing, laughing, and being bone idle. When I needed money, I went into the vineyards for a day or two or took other jobs paying me enough to eat and drink and give me the leisure I craved.

For all my many shortcomings as a human being, my careless, easy, indolent attitudes, my self-will and ego-centric determination to think my own thoughts irrespective of what others might try to tell me, I cared about people very deeply. **I was deeply emotional. In your present speech forms, you would call me 'over-reactive', 'over-emotional'. I had a warm, compassionate, empathetic heart. I was deeply moved in the presence of sickness, affliction and poverty. I was a staunch supporter of what you call the 'under-dog'. You might say I was a 'people's person'. I lived with them closely, in a spirit of comradery; I listened to their woes, understood, and cared.**

It is important to understand my true origins and my early youthful characteristics because these were the goads which pushed and prodded me into eventual Christhood.

What I most strongly detested and resisted was the misery – the sickness and poverty – I saw around me.

It infuriated me – and I became passionately, vociferously angry to see people dressed in rags, thin and hungry, diseased, crippled, yet heartlessly browbeaten by Jewish leaders who burdened them with meaningless traditional laws and observances, threatening them with Jehovah's punishment if they did not obey. I declared to all who would listen to me that these poor people had enough to bear without being crushed by senseless measures restrictive of pleasure. What was the point of life at all if we were not born to be happy?

I refused to believe in a 'just' God according to Jewish traditions. The biblical prophetic warnings of Jehovah's 'judgment and anger' against people, disgusted me. People were human, after all, doing whatever their human natures prompted them to do. They had been born sinful – so why should they be judged and condemned to lives of suffering and poverty because they had broken the Ten Commandments? Where was the sense in such statements?

To me, this Jewish belief depicted an illogical, cruel "God", and I wanted nothing to do with "Him". It seemed to me that if such a 'deity' existed, it followed that mankind was doomed to eternal misery. The simplicity and freedom I found on the hillsides, the plains, the lakes and the mountains, refreshed my inmost spirit and quietened my angry murmuring against the Jewish God. Consequently, I refused to believe a word that the Jewish Elders tried to teach me.

However, during my middle twenties, a new line of questioning took possession of my thoughts. As I walked ever more frequently alone in the hills, my rebellion was gradually replaced by an all-consuming longing to know and understand the true nature of **THAT** which must surely inspire and respire through creation.

I reviewed my lifestyle and saw what suffering my actions had caused my mother and many other people. Although I felt such deep compassion for the weak and suffering, my rebellious nature had prompted much thoughtless and selfish behavior towards my family. My underlying love for them now welled up in me and I found myself becoming equally rebellious against my past behavior. I heard talk about John the Baptist and the work he was doing amongst the Jews who came to listen to his words even from Jerusalem. I decided to visit him to be baptized myself.

On my way to the River Jordan, I felt exhilarated at the prospect of being baptized and starting a new life.

I knew that, despite my unruly emotionalism, I had also been born with a keen intelligence and a gift for insightful, impressive debate which I had used willfully and negatively, leading people into unruly arguments. I had thrown my talents away by pursuing a life of self-will, idleness and pleasure. As a result, I had forfeited all respect from others; neither did I possess any self-respect. For the first time, I found this to be intolerable. It occurred to me that, in the future, I could and must put my natural gifts to better use. Instead of just making a noise, perhaps I could find a way to lighten the burdens of those whom I so deeply pitied. Up to that time, I had been of little practical use to anyone.

MY BAPTISM

When I entered the water in the River Jordan to be baptized by John, I expected to feel nothing more than relief that I had, for once, taken a positive step in reforming my behavior. I expected to feel a new determination to go home and astonish my mother and neighbors with my new kindly attitudes towards them.

What really happened when John baptized me was an experience completely different to anything I had ever thought possible.

I felt a great wave of tremendous energy surge through my body. I was literally stunned by it. As I staggered out of the river, I felt myself elevated in consciousness in a most extraordinary way. A great inflow of glowing happiness uplifted me to a state of ecstasy. I was enraptured and aware of a great Light.

Stumbling, I moved away from the river and walked and walked, not knowing where I was going. I continued on, unseeingly, into the desert.

Please note! MY SIX WEEKS IN THE DESERT were a time of total inner cleansing of my human consciousness. Old attitudes, beliefs and prejudices were dissolved.

The time has come for me to share with receptive people all that I felt, 'saw', realised and understood.

(To help people abandon the age-old imaginative pictures of a biblical 'deity' I will avoid referring to 'God' by that word and will use a terminology designed to stretch your minds to embrace what 'really is' beyond all earthly form, color, sound, emotion, and comprehension.

This terminology will become ever more meaningful as you persevere in meditation and prayer.)

WHAT I FELT WHEN IN THE DESERT

I was uplifted into inner radiant light and felt vibrant and wondrously alive with power. I was filled with ecstasy and joy and I knew beyond all doubt that THIS POWER was the true Creator out of which all created things had been given their being.

This glorious interior harmony, peace, and sense of perfect fulfillment, needing nothing more to be added to that beautiful moment, was the very nature of the Reality – the Creative Power – giving Life to creation and existence.

What I 'saw', realized, perceived when in the desert.

I was lifted into another dimension of conscious perception, which enabled me to see the TRUTH concerning life and existence. I saw, lucidly and clearly, what was real and what was false in man's thinking.

I realized that this 'Creative Power' I was experiencing was infinite, eternal, universal, filling all space beyond sky, oceans, earth, and all living things. I saw IT was MIND POWER.

IT was the CREATIVE POWER of MIND.

There was no point where this 'DIVINE CREATIVE POWER OF MIND' was not.I realized that human mind was drawn from DIVINE CREATIVE MIND but was only a candle lit by the sun.

At times, my human sight was so spiritually heightened, I could see through rocks, earth, sand. These now appeared to be only a 'shimmer of tiny `motes'.

I realized that nothing was really solid!

When I had moments of doubt that this could be so, the changes in the phenomena stopped taking place, and much later, I discovered that: my thoughts, if strongly imbued with CONVICTION could effect changes in the 'shimmer of motes' (what science presently calls electrically charged particles) and therefore produce changes in the appearance of the rock or whatever I was studying.

It was at this point, that I came to realize the powerful effect that CONVICTION or unwavering FAITH had on the environment when stating a command or even a belief.

What was even more startling was my mind-opening, 'cosmic consciousness' realisation that all I had been witnessing was really the **'Creative Power'** of **Divine Mind** Itself made visible in the 'shimmer of tiny motes'.

Not only this, its **appearance** could be profoundly affected by the activity of human thought.

I realized there was nothing solid in the universe, everything visible was manifesting a differing 'state of consciousness' which determined the composition and form of the 'shimmer of motes'.

Therefore, all outer form was an expression of the inner consciousness.

LIFE and CONSCIOUSNESS, I realized, were one and the same thing.

It was impossible to say 'This is LIFE' and 'That is CONSCIOUSNESS'.

Consciousness was Life, and Life was Consciousness and was the **'Creative Power'** of both; **DIVINE UNIVERSAL MIND'** beyond, within and behind the universe.

I realized that people placed highest importance on **individuality and form.** They could not imagine mind or intelligence operating in any effective way other than through the medium of individual form. Because of this, the Jews had created a mental image of a vast supreme being, having all the attributes, positive and negative, of a human being. Thus was it possible for prophets to believe in – and speak of – Jehovah's anger, threats of punishment, visitations of sickness and plagues in response to human waywardness. But these mental images, I realized were myths. They did not exist.

I perceived that, in any dimension of existence, it was the MIND – the intelligence exhibited – which was the all-important factor relating to creation and man, himself. Therefore, Genesis should be rewritten: Before creation – was **UNIVERSAL MIND – Creative Power behind and within creation itself.**

Having 'seen' so clearly, beyond all dispute, that the Creative Power of UNIVERSAL MIND was everywhere, within the infinity of the skies and active within earthly forms as well, I was inwardly directed to look around me and saw only gravel and rock. Then, suddenly I was presented with a picture of a beautiful land in which were growing every conceivable plant, shrub and tree, even birds flitted in the trees, and animals grazed the grass.

Watching this vision with amazement, I 'saw' that plants and trees, every one of them – and yes, even birds and animals, in reality, were composed of hundreds of communities of infinitely tiny entities (your modern scientists

19

call them 'cells') working continuously, in an entirely harmonious spirit of cooperation, to produce the substance and various organs of the inner system and the outer appearance of the completed living entity.

I contemplated this wonderful activity for a long time, although time was no longer of any importance to me. As I gazed and gazed, I thought, 'Who would have guessed that within the outer covering of fur, feather, skin, there was such intense activity within tiny communities of entities, working together to give life, form, nutrition, healing, protection, endurance to the bodies of so many different species.

It was the intelligently performed WORK which attracted my attention.

Therefore, **WORK**, I realized was an integral part of the **Creative Power Activity** from the very least 'entity' (cell) within living systems to the most advanced entity in the universe – man himself. In the systems of all living things, all the labor was under the direction, ultimately, of the **Divine Creative Power,** in whom were the plans and designs of creation. I saw that these plans and designs were, in reality, 'consciousness forms' and could be termed WORDS, since each WORD signifies a very special 'consciousness' form.

Hence the original WORD in '**Creative Power Consciousness'** becomes manifested in the visible world. The WORD, and therefore the '**Consciousness Pattern'** remains within the **DIVINE CREATIVE MIND** continually bringing forth its own.

I could 'see' then, that everything in the universe, did 'live, move and have its being' in the **Creative Power** of **UNIVERSAL MIND** which was infinite and eternal and was the only true **Reality** behind all manifestations of individualized form.

I was filled with praise that everything in the world was out of, and yet within this superlative **Creative Power of Divine Mind**. I marvelled at all this secret activity forever taking place in all living things, including human bodies, and wondered how it was that such infinitely small units worked intelligently according to specified plans to produce, unerringly, the proposed form – tree trunk, leaf, flower, fruit, insects, birds, animals and human bodies.

I then realized, even more clearly, that the '**Creative Power'** was the very **Source** of all '**intelligent activity' in the universe.**

If mankind possessed intelligence, it was only because he had drawn it from the **'Universal Source of All Being'**.

Furthermore, I was shown that the **Divine Creative Power** always worked according to certain fundamental and exact principles of construction.

I was shown that:

Just as men have clear characteristics and a well-defined 'nature' in their self-presentation to the world at large, so did the CREATIVE POWER possess a clearly defined 'Nature' – distinct characteristics – which could be clearly recognized in the manner that all living things, plants, animals, birds, men, were constructed and maintained.

I 'saw' that these 'principles' and 'characteristics', clearly observable in the process of creation, were set, invariable LAWS governing all of existence.

These LAWS are so much part of life that they are never questioned. They are undeviating and consistent – but there would be no such laws if there were no **Creative Intelligent Power** manifesting Itself through the universe. These 'principles' of creation, the characteristics of the Creative Power Itself, are as follows:

(I am translating them into your present tense because these 'principles' are eternal.)

1. The 'Nature' of the 'Creative Power' is GROWTH.

Everything living always grows.

GROWTH is a universal characteristic, an undeviating principle of existence.

2. The 'Nature' of the 'Creative Power' is NUTRITION and NOURISHMENT. Nutrition and Nourishment are a normal and marvelously organized process within bodies which is evident to all who take the trouble to consider them. Nutrition is provided for all living things according to individual preferences and the food is digested to promote health and well-being. When little creatures are born, milk is already supplied within the mother, ready and waiting for the newborn. This too is a mystifying principle of existence none can deny.

21

No science can explain why such a fortuitous function within the system ensuring survival of the species, should have originally come into being. The actual function itself may be understood but not the 'why' and the mainspring of the function.

3. The 'Nature' of the 'Creative Power' is HEALING.

Healing is a natural characteristic of existence and can be said to be a natural 'Perfecting Process', which takes place to ensure individual comfort but none can explain what prompts the activity of healing.

4. The 'Nature' of the 'Creative Power' is PROTECTION.

Protection is an integral characteristic of Creative Power and all of Its seeming 'miraculous' activity in the world is geared towards protection. (Today, your medical text books describe the various protective systems in your body but when I was in the desert I 'saw' the characteristic of Protection inherent in the Intelligent Creative Power in the following way.)

As plants, birds and animals were presented to me for inspired observation, I could see how every 'need of protection' in bodies has been lovingly supplied, with the greatest attention to detail.

5. This characteristic of 'Protection' is combined with the other dynamic characteristic of FULFILMENT OF NEED.

This was made clearly apparent in the provision of hair, fur and feathers to protect the skin of living creatures and to provide warmth in the cold and shelter in the heat. I saw that the tender endings of important and sensitive fingers and toes were all provided with appropriate protection of hoof and nail. Eyebrows protected eyes from sweat, eyelids and lashes protected eyes from dust and damage. I realized that those animals which attracted flies were equipped with the kind of tails which would most speedily get rid of them.

What a happy, joyous kind of love and caring were expressed in these small physical attributes which seemed so small and inconsequential and yet had such a profound bearing on the comfort of all living things. These physical luxuries, added to the basic physical design, were clearly the product of an Intelligence which intended creation to be comfortable and

happy – free of the stress which would have been experienced by man and beast if these 'luxury items' had not been given them!

Even the natural functions were so intelligently and comfortably designed as to call forth thanksgiving. Everything tucked so neatly out of sight. How blest, how fortunate was mankind to be born into a life so wonderfully provided for! Again my praises soared and I was lifted on an inner golden light of rapturous wonder – for I now 'saw' that, in addition to freedom from stress, living creatures were also meant to express the exuberant loving **NATURE** of the **Creative Power**. For this reason, they were equipped with limbs: arms, hands, legs and feet, fingers and toes, to enable them to move about, run, leap and dance, to be able to express their inmost thoughts and feelings. I even felt that if mankind longed to fly and grow wings and believed with all their hearts they could do so; eventually they would begin growing something additional to enable them to fly.

It was at this point of understanding of the **NATURE** of the '**Creative Power**' that I came into the full consciousness of the **LOVE** directing the **WORKS** of the **Universal Intelligent Creative Power**.

As I pondered this **LOVE**, I realized that the 'mother' in creation, nourishes, protects, fulfills the needs and tries to promote healing of offspring; this is the activity of **LOVE**.

6. The innate characteristic of the LOVING INTELLIGENT CREATIVE POWER which has given creation its individual form and 'being' is WORK.

It works for us, in us, and through us.

Its 'work' is always, always, always, prompted by LOVE.

This cosmic revelation filled me with joy and astonishment. What a wonderful world we lived in! It was the culminating point in my enlightenment and my overall view of the **TRUTH** concerning the **SOURCE of ALL BEING.**

I had already 'seen' the reality of the physical bodies composed of various communities of identical 'infinitely tiny entities' working in a spirit of co-operation and harmony to produce the various components of the body – flesh, bone, blood to eyes and hair.

The only difference between these communities **lay in the type of work** demanded by their common goals. Surely the **DIVINE IMPULSE** behind all this intelligent, purposeful activity in the body, was both the inspiration and foundation of man's own conduct when people worked in unison to produce a planned objective? They drew intelligence and purpose from the **Creative Power yet how very different was man's behaviour when engaged in earthly construction or any other communal project for it was inevitably characterized by arguments and dissension.**

I was brought to a realization of the **INFINITE POWER** of the 'Intelligent Creativity' ever active within creation, maintaining order, co-operation, harmony, daily productivity, unequalled by man anywhere, at any time.

7. SURVIVAL was a natural characteristic of the 'Creative Power'. In every case, the most wonderful provision had been made for all living things to grow, be healed of illnesses and injury, nourished in order to keep the body healthy, and to produce its own kind in order to ensure survival on this earth. This was the only reality mankind could be absolutely sure of and Its activity was consistent, year in and year out. The sun, moon, stars, all remained in their places for millennia and it was recognized that they all possessed their own paths of movement – this phenomena was all part of the grand scheme for survival in creation.

If this was so, how could there not be survival of the eternal flame of: Loving Intelligent Creative Power hidden within the created entities of every kind in the universe? Therefore, this world was but a shadow and image of the hidden worlds of Loving Intelligent Creative Power beyond this dimension. The Reality of the entirety of creation lay beyond this visible world.

8. The inherent characteristic of Loving Intelligent Creative Power was RHYTHM. I saw that there was a RHYTHM in operation in the world.

Everything was subject to seasons which gave a blossoming and burgeoning of life, a growing season coming up to the ripening and harvest, and the production of seeds which ensured the survival of plant life. Then there was the gradual dying away and rest period of winter. But nothing created and living was allowed to become extinct. The sun and moon expressed these characteristics within the universe. This rhythm could even be seen in the females of living things.

Therefore, everything in creation had its due time for appearance and harvest. It followed that man himself was subject to tides of growth and success and tides of dormancy.

9. The inherent characteristic of the Loving Intelligent Creative Power was LAW AND ORDER.

The undeviating order and reliability apparent in creation, even governing the tiny entities ('cells') within the body, were astonishing and far transcended any human endeavor. Therefore, the entire universe was operating under a system of perfect LAW & ORDER.

I realized on ever higher and higher levels of spiritual exaltation that the 'creative power' exhibited intelligent purposefulness and loving concern for all living things. I realized that life was not something nebulous or amorphous but an intelligent loving creative power which I could actually feel within myself as a tremendously heightened state of being, perception, radiance, ecstasy, joy, love. I knew myself to be one with it – filled with it – and I was one with everything around me and one with the sky and stars.

And – most wonderful and glorious of all – **the very 'Nature' and 'Function' of this 'Father – Creative Power'** was to work in order to create joy, beauty, and comfort to ensure mankind's well-being, to work within mankind to provide interior joy, health and comfort, and to work through mankind, inspiring him with new realization and understanding.

Wonderful vistas of glorious creativity came to mind. Once we became truly 'at one', purified channels and instruments of the **'Intelligent Creative Power'**, we could gradually ascend in consciousness until we truly expressed through our minds and hearts the very **'NATURE'** of the **'Universal Creative Power'**. Then 'life on earth' would indeed become a 'state of heaven' at all times and we would enter into a state of eternal life!

This must surely be the true goal behind creation, I thought. And it came to me with a surge of elation and loving joy, that this was the purpose for which man had been evolved and developed!

But – even at this present time, although mankind was so very imperfect in his behaviour, absolutely nothing was impossible to him in the future, since, despite his wrongdoing, he was one with the "Creative Power' and the

'Creative Power' was within him, giving him life, limb, and everything else he needed.

All of this realization lifted me to the heights of rapture, elation and sublime ecstasy, so that I was scarcely able to bear it. I felt my body must dissolve with the expansion of Power within me. I was irradiated with **LIGHT** and could see **IT** all around me illuminating the desert scene.

My heart sang in praises. How wonderful and beautiful was the Loving Creative Power which worked in, through and for us, unceasingly!

What a MIRACLE was creation!

I cried out loud:

'**YOU** are the **SOURCE of all BEING,** both creator and also manifested within and through the created: there is nothing in the entire universe which is apart or separate from the limitless, eternal infinity of **DIVINE LIFE, Creative Power Consciousness** – that you are – how then is it possible that mankind is so sinful – and why do people suffer disease, misery and poverty? Tell me, o loving **loving 'Father' Creative Power**, because I have been heavily burdened with the pain of their miserable lives.'

Then I was shown the reality of the 'earthly condition' of all living things.

I felt immense excitement because, at last, I would be able to understand how it was that such a loving **Divine 'Creative Power'** could allow Its creation to endure such misery.

I was shown that every living thing in creation should be radiantly healthy, cared for, nourished, protected, healed, maintained in peace and plenty, prospered within an orderly society of 'beings' extending only love to each other.

(However, at the moment of creation, two BASIC IMPULSES came into being, ensuring individuality, and it was these which controlled mankind's consciousness.

These IMPULSES were explained to me in detail but this knowledge is reserved for a future Letter when you will be better able to understand it).................................

I was shown the following vivid vision.

First of all, I saw a new-born babe as 'light', a life-form of 'Creative Power'.

As the baby grew into childhood, then manhood, I saw the pure LIGHT of the 'Creative Power' gradually dimmed and then obscured altogether in him, by a dense wrapping of chains and thongs.

I questioned the meaning of the vision and there came to my mind a clear understanding which may be expressed in the following words:

'From birth to death – people believe and insist that their five senses of sight, hearing, touch, smell and taste, correctly predicate the 'reality' of themselves and the universe around them. Therefore, because they draw their mind power direct from Divine 'Creative Power', it is done to them according to their beliefs.

Each thong represents a person's habitual thoughts, responses to people and events, prejudices, hates, animosities, anxieties, sorrows, all of which bind him down and shut out the Light from his inner vision drawn from the 'Creative Power'. Thus he enters into darkness but does not know it. He believes he is growing up and becoming mature in the ways of the world which will enable him to forge ahead and make 'good' – become successful – the aim of most people on earth.

In fact, the more mature he becomes and versed in worldly ways, the more densely do his chains and thongs imprison him within the grip of the twin IMPULSES of 'Bonding-Rejection'.

Furthermore, each chain is forged out of selfish and deceitful desires, greed, aggression, violence and rape. These chains hang heavy around him and burden the psyche, which is the 'creative consciousness power' deep within him. Chain and thong will bind him tighter with every passing year until he realizes what he is doing to himself and sincerely repents each thong and chain and makes due restitution to others whom he has harmed.

With this vision I learnt a most valuable aspect of existence. Man himself is born with all the potential to make a beautiful life for himself but he, himself, by indulging his selfish desires and hatreds, creates a prison of misery for himself from which there was no escape until such times as he realizes the **TRUTH OF EXISTENCE.**

All the problems of harsh existence lay within the thought processes of man himself!

Only people's 'consciousness forms', their thoughts, words, feelings, actions created a dense barrier between their consciousness and the Universal Creative Consciousness interpenetrating the universe in every leaf, tree, insect, bird, animal and human being.

I was also shown the LAWS OF EXISTENCE controlling the human ability to create new circumstances and environment, relationships, achievement or failure, prosperity or poverty.

Whatever man profoundly **BELIEVES** himself to be, good or bad, that will he become.

Whatever man **FEARS** others will do to him, so will they do.

Whatever man **HOPES** that others will do to him, he must first do to them, since he is then creating a 'consciousness pattern' which will return to bless him to the extent he has blest others.

Whatever disease man **DREADS** so will he become prey to it for he will have created a 'consciousness pattern' of the very thing he least wants to experience.

Whatever is sent forth from man's mind and heart – returns to him in due course in some form or another, but remember that like always breeds like. Strongly emotional thoughts are 'consciousness seeds' planted within a man's own orbit of consciousness. These will grow, bearing a like harvest for his reaping.

These are the fruits of free will.

There is no way that man may escape what he thinks, says or does – for he is born of the Divine Creative Consciousness power and is likewise creative in his imagining.

Those who long for good for themselves must first give it to others. Let their very existence be a blessing to others.

When such people are in harmony with all others, they are then perfectly attuned to the universal creative consciousness power and they are brought into the flow of the Father 'nature' which is growth, protection, nourishment (physical, mental, spiritual) healing, fulfillment of need, within a system of law and order.

How can I describe for you, my inner glow, my transcendent brightness and brilliance of joy and powerful feelings of love which possessed and inflated my entire being with their intensity until I cried out with the pressure within my mind and heart. It was so powerful it seemed it would entirely dissolve my bodily form. As I received all this supreme, sublime understanding of the Reality, our Source of Being, and the true nature of creation itself – and of mankind, I was uplifted in spirit and my body became light as air.

At that time, when I was thus elevated within the **Divine Creative Power Itself,** I was indeed almost a 'Divine Person' myself, experiencing a high degree of the **'Nature'** of the **'Father-Creative Power'** within me and feeling Its own drive and caring concern for all humanity. Therefore, I could later say with truth: **"Only I know and have seen the 'Father'.**

In that moment how I yearned to teach, heal, comfort, uplift, feed, take away the people's pain and misery.

I longed to release them from their fear of a mythical 'avenging god'!

When I returned to tell them the truth, How I would emphasize the **'reality'** of the **'Father-Creative Power'** – **PERFECT LOVE** – supplying their every need All they had to do was 'Ask, seek, knock' and all their needs – of whatever kind – would be bestowed upon them.

How joyously I would tell them the 'good news' that 'redemption from suffering' lay within their grasp if they only took the necessary steps to cleanse their minds and hearts of the TWIN IMPULSES of manifested 'being'.

This should be simple enough, I thought, one only needed understanding and self-control.

(- I have descended towards your vibrations to refer back to my actual state of mind during the time I was in the desert.It will help your own understanding immeasurably if you try to enter my 'state of consciousness' at that time. So many things, such as my works of healing and 'walking on water' will become clear to you.. They will be seen to be a natural consequence of my new understanding of the **'Father-Creative Power'**.

If you read the gospels of Matthew and Mark, their records will have new meaning for you.-)

To return to my final hours of enlightenment, – there I was in the desert, possessing the clear understanding that man himself – (through no fault of his own) creates the barrier to attunement to the **'Father-Creative Power'**, and now I was longing to hurry back and teach, heal, comfort, dry the tears of those I so greatly pitied.

Yet I was reluctant to leave this 'hallowed' place where I had been so illumined and transformed in spirit. On the other hand what a wonderful future lay ahead of me!

I would walk through all the cities, towns, villages and tell everyone I met – the GOOD NEWS! 'The Kingdom of Heaven', that place where all sickness disappeared and every need was supplied was within them! Because I knew that the 'Father' and I were 'one', now that my mind had been cleansed of the old thoughts and ideas, I would direct healing at their illness and disease. I would teach them how to relieve their poverty.

When the **FATHER CONSCIOUSNESS** within me began to dim, and I gradually returned to human consciousness I became aware of gnawing hunger and also a return of my human conditioning and thought.

My reactions to my six weeks' experiences began to change. My usual human awareness of 'me' and my desires, took over my thoughts.

'Why, the most amazing and completely unexpected thing has happened to me!' I exulted. 'I have been given knowledge beyond any yet given to any other man.'

I was jubilant with the realization that, at last, my doubt and rebelliousness against the avenging 'god' of the Traditional Orthodox Jews was vindicated. I had been right after all!

Who had ever suspected the human mind could be so highly creative, that a strongly-held thought or desire would actually manifest itself in the visible realm? I realized that Moses must have known something of this, because he had accomplished some strange things when the Israelites were in dire need.

He became a leader and changed the course of the Israelites previously enslaved in Egypt. I could return now and free my people from the rigid control of their own Teachers.

My hunger pains now became intense. It occurred to me that I could turn stones into bread to satisfy my longing for food because I remembered that the '**Father-Creative Power**' worked through my mind and therefore, everything in the universe would be subject to my command.

I was about to speak the 'word' which would change stones into bread but something in me halted me abruptly.

It came to me, strongly, that the '**Father-Creative Consciousness**' was perfect protection, nourishment, fulfillment of need, and so the hunger would be taken care of, if I asked the 'Father' for relief.

I realized that if the little 'i', the human me, in my need, used the 'Creative power' for selfish reasons, I would be erecting a barrier between the 'Father-Creative Consciousness' and myself, and everything I had just learnt might well be taken away from me.

This frightened me, and swiftly I asked the '**Father-Creative Power**' for new strength to carry me back to habitations and Nazareth again**. I also asked for relief of hunger in the form that would be right for me.** Immediately, the hunger pangs subsided and I felt a surge of energy flow through my entire body. Thus I proved that all I had seen, heard and understood was '**reality**' and not some vain imagining born of my time in the desert, fasting and alone.

My new energy enabled me to make haste over the rough tracks on my way out of the desert.

On the way, I met a well-dressed man of sweet and pleasing countenance. He greeted me warmly, expressing concern on seeing my rough, unkempt appearance and loss of condition.

Gladly, he sat me down on a rock and shared his excellent meat and bread with me. I wondered why he was in such a desolate place and where he had come from. In response to my questioning, he only smiled and seemed not the

31

least surprised when I said I had been in the desert for so many days I had lost count of time. I explained how I was enlightened as to the true nature of the Creator of the world and shown the natural **Laws of Existence**. He only smiled and nodded.

'I am going back to my people to teach them everything I have learnt.' I said joyously. 'Why I will be able to heal them and bring them release from every sickness and trouble.'

The stranger replied sadly: 'It will take many millennia.'

I was about to rebuke his lack of faith when I realized he was gone.

I knew then that a Divine messenger had come to succor with good bread and meat – and compassionately give me warning that I might not find my mission so simple, despite my enthusiasm. I was deflated by his word of warning. My enthusiasm waned. The way to the first village on my road seemed endless. How a change in human thought produces a change of mood!

It came to me that I could further prove the truth of all I had been shown by jumping over the edge of a precipice which would greatly shorten my journey. As I was about to do this, it came to me forcibly that I was trying to 'prove' my time of enlightenment was real. If I required such proof, then I was in a state of doubt and I would probably kill myself, besides I had been shown that in every eventuality I could lift my thoughts up to the '**FATHER-CREATIVE CONSCIOUSNESS**' and ask for a solution to every problem. How quickly I forgot the **Truth!**

So I prayed, passionately asking forgiveness for being weak enough to indulge my own fantasies and seeking my own way of doing things.

Again, the answer came in renewed strength and a greater sureness of foot as I scrambled over the rough ground. I found, too, that I was covering long distances so quickly that it seemed that I had stepped outside normal time reckoning, and I was in a lighter dimension where human experience was lifted above its heavy thralldom of exhausting expenditure of energy. Walking was so easy it was now invigorating. I exulted in the fact that I had found the key to 'more abundant life'!

A while later, feeling so much at ease, my mind began to wander and I thought about my meeting with the stranger and the kindness he had shown me. But I also remembered his warning and again my old nature re-asserted itself and I felt deeply rebellious that he should presume to tell me how my work would go. I decided he knew nothing about my future and set his warning aside.

'Why,' I thought, 'with my knowledge I could accomplish things no man has ever done before. Instead of struggling in a difficult life, I could begin to accumulate wealth easily, attract followers wherever I went, and share my knowledge with them to make their lives easier also. I could take away all pain and suffering.'

As I contemplated the many places I could visit so easily, I felt myself skimming the surface of the ground and rising until I reached the highest peak of a steep mountain overlooking the countryside below.

There it was, all laid out before me. I felt my previous enthusiasm return. Why, it would be so simple to round up the people and share all my knowledge with them. I would become powerful, even famous as the man who rescued mankind from all their sickness and troubles. I would gain their admiration and respect and would no longer be remembered as an idle worthless fellow.

With a tremendous shock, all I had been taught so recently, but a few hours ago, returned to mind with great force and clarity.

Had I not been taught that the only way I could ever prosper was to abandon my self-will and turn to the 'FATHER' for assistance in everything I undertook?

Then I remembered that creation had its own special purposes to fulfill. The individualizing process had created the 'pull and push', the 'give and take' in human behavior. Although these human characteristics caused people great anguish in their lives, was it not the anguish which forced them to seek better ways to **live** in order to find true happiness? I realized that the ills of mankind had their place in the human scheme of existence.

Was it right for me to bring privileged information to people in order to nullify the effects of the 'individualizing process'?

I realized I had been thinking from the 'central point' of my individuality, the 'ego', and it was the ego drive which built barriers between mankind and

'Father-Creative Consciousness'. Therefore, my 'Central point of human desiring' would have to be conquered if I was to live in perfect harmony with my **'Father'** as was my sincere intention. And so I continued on my way, pondering what might lie ahead and how I might best overcome the impulses governing my humanhood in order to remain in the Flow of 'Father Consciousness' from which I would draw inspiration, guidance, answers to problems, my daily nourishment, daily health, daily protection. In fact, I realized that whilst I remained within this daily Flow of Father Consciousness', no harm could ever come near me and my every need would be met. And more importantly: the 'Father Consciousness' working through me would do whatever was required for people in dire need of healing and comfort.

At all times, I must overcome my rebelliousness against the harsh realities of existence and listen to the 'inner voice' and conform to the 'Higher Will' of the 'Father'. This 'Higher Will' was 'Perfect Love' directed entirely at promoting my highest good. It would be extremely foolish, I realized, to continue along the path of 'self-will' which had dictated my behavior to that time.

It was then that I was inspired to speak in parables to the people. Those who were ready to receive the knowledge would understand and make good use of it.

But, as it turned out, even my disciples could not rid themselves sufficiently of Jewish doctrine to enable them to understand either the principle of consciousness or the activity of the **Divine 'Creative Power'** within creation. (Until this time, it has remained a mystery to all except the spiritually enlightened.)

Even the spiritual words of enlightenment cannot be immediately, fully comprehended by the human mind; therefore these **Letters** must be read slowly and accompanied by much meditation and prayer to be properly understood.

Remember, unless you can become as a **'child'** – (getting rid of a useless clutter of beliefs, prejudices, resentments, ambitions, and ego-drive) with a mind filled with wonder and utmost faith, you will not be able to absorb these pages as you should.

To become a'child', you must make an effort to shed all past mental conditioning.

If you are mentally/emotionally/physically suffering, it is only because whatever have been your most sincere beliefs, they have not been helpful to you; they have not promoted your well-being.

It is time to examine your **MINDSET**. Are you happy with it?

You can make choices, and as you make them, you can call upon the 'Father' to help you make the changes, and the help will surely be given you, – providing'you do not doubt.

I therefore urge you to continue to read and absorb the following pages. I want to impress on you the strength of your mindset – which is the sum total of all your conscious and subconscious programming.

It is essential you should understand that none of this human mindset has its origins in the spiritual dimension.

It is entirely earthly and probably filled with mythical ideas, prejudices, misconceptions, resentments, buried memories of past hurts, and habitual methods of dealing with the ups-and-downs of life. Your human mindset (including any religious ideas or beliefs) determines your world, your relationships, experiences, successes, failures, happiness and misery. It is even responsible for your sickness, disease and accidents. Nothing happens by chance. Everything is woven out of the inner threads of your personal consciousness – thoughts, expectations, beliefs in life, fate, "God". You live in a world of your own making. This is why children raised in the same environment turn out differently. Each one has its own individual Mindset constructed according to inherent character traits.

If, from birth, you had no developing Mindset, you would be as unconscious as a statue, devoid of feeling, responses and thought. Vacantly, you would stare at the world, and whilst there might be a great deal of activity around you, nothing would impinge on your consciousness, since you would be devoid of reaction. Nothing would make you happy or miserable, even if a bomb exploded in your vicinity.

Without a mindset, you have no life, no development, no evil, no good. Your TYPE of mindset determines the quality of your life. This is the very first

Truth of Existence I want you to realize and understand fully. Furthermore, for as long as you live you carry your mindset with you wherever you go.

There is no escaping it, and day after day, it will continue to create for you the type of existence you have experienced in your past. Many people go through their entire lives believing they are unfortunate. They think that other people have been mean, unkind, ugly to them, and have made their lives thoroughly unhappy.

They believe that 'other people' quarrel with them and constantly make difficulties whilst they are absolutely innocent of any provocation.

On the contrary, 'other people' are not to blame. It is the personal mindset which is attracting to them their negative conditions.

Many people shy away from the suggestion that they alone are responsible for their troubles. It is more difficult for some people to face up to their inadequacies than it is for those who have the inner strength and self-confidence to look at themselves fairly and squarely.

Sincere Prayer draws the 'Father-Creative Consciousness' into the mind, quietly, secretly, it cleanses the human consciousness of all that the seeker no longer feels comfortable with. It is, of necessity, a very gradual process of inner cleansing and development.

EMOTIONAL PATTERNS

Your emotional patterns can be as damaging to your overall welfare as your mindset. Your mindset together with your emotional patterns are your creative tools.

These together create the necessary outlines for future possessions, events and circumstances. These CREATIVE TOOLS work in your life whether you intend them to or not.

It is far more difficult to discover your deep-seated emotional attitudes either conscious or subconscious than to recognize your mental conditioning.

People can be possessed by negative emotional patterns and be quite unaware of them, since they are covered by the moment-to-moment emotions arising from the daily routine.

To discover what your emotional patterns really are, ask yourself questions along the following lines, and be totally honest with yourself. To try to hide from the truth of your emotional patterns is merely to deceive yourself and hold yourself back from achieving the joyous state of existence you were intended to enjoy.

How do you really feel about LIFE? I want you to write yourself a warmly compassionate letter, telling yourself exactly how you feel as you answer the following questions:

Are you happy to be alive or would you prefer to be able to cease to live? If your truthful answer is the latter, then you have a negative attitude towards existence and are at war within yourself at a deep level. You know, consciously, that you have to continue your daily life but at your deepest level you would like to quit. The interior war prevents you from attracting all that you could be experiencing with a positive emotional pattern.

How do you really feel about your relatives? Is there any buried hostility which you do not want to admit or that you did not realize existed?

How do you feel about your employment, colleagues, entertainment, other races.etc. Write down all your discoveries about yourself and lock it away in a safe place.

This work you have done for yourself is for yourself – only for your benefit. You have not done it to make you a better person, or to please 'God' or to win approval from other people. You have done this work to remove existing inner blocks to your spiritual development and ultimate happiness.

If you decide to change your life by reading these Letters daily, I urge you to put your dated letter in a safe place. Re-read it in a year's time and rejoice in the great changes which you will see have taken place in your mindset. You will also see that there have been changes in your circumstances.

Remember that prayer and meditation focused entirely on your Creator will bring you new strength and insight which, in turn, will bring changes to your feelings and environment.

When praying – Never focus on your problems – always – ask for the right remedy. Let your Creator bring you the right solutions which your human mind is incapable of thinking up.

For instance – never tell your Creative 'Father' how ill you are. Concentrate on the Power you are receiving immediately into your condition (although your consciousness may be too densely human to feel it) and give thanks for your swift recovery and believe in it.

When you 'give thanks' you are accepting, acknowledging, believing, impressing in your own consciousness the realization that your prayer now lies within the 'Father Love Consciousness' and is being 'processed' for visible manifestation in due course at the right time. When in Palestine, I constantly gave thanks for the work before it was accomplished.

Never pray and then go out of your room and tell people how ill you feel, or how terrible the personal or national situation is. If you have asked the Father Creator to solve your problems, finances or poor health, what an insult to the Father Creator to continue to bring up past negative conditions? You immediately undo the work the Father Creator is engaged in.

If, in your mind, after prayer, the old conditions have not become past negative conditions, then return to prayer until you can dismiss them from your mind and really believe that all is being Divinely taken care of – right that minute. Return again and again to giving thanks for the benefits you have asked for. They will surely materialize.

There are many thousands of people in your world today, consistently relying on the Universal Father Creator to fulfill their every need and witnessing to the manifold blessings in their lives.

Abandon fears, they have availed you nothing. Now turn to the universal 'Father' Creator – as the **SOURCE OF YOUR BEING**, conception, growth, development, nutrition, regeneration, healing, fulfillment of your every need, **PROTECTION**, all within a system of **SPIRITUAL LAW & ORDER.**

Realize that all this wonderful work is constructive, purposeful, orderly.

You truly have a **MASTER MIND** behind you, your family and living conditions. **TRUST IT**.

Do not allow your thinking to spoil the Divine Creative Operation!

Remember, above all – that **I, the CHRIST**, only performed my so-called miracles because I realized that the 'Kingdom of God' was within me and that I could always rely on my **Creator 'Father'** to do the work in and through me.

Remember that you only have an individual consciousness because you have drawn it from the **Creative 'Father' Consciousness'**.

When your personal consciousness is fully cleansed of negativity, you will discover that you, too, have become a purified channel of Creative 'Father' Consciousness. You will also be a joyous source of growth, nutrition, healing, nurturing, protection, fulfillment of need, within a system of good organizational law and order to all who come within your orbit. This powerful influence will be extended through your mind to your families, friends, neighbors, farm lands and your animals and crops.

Even as electricity passed through your hands will light a Bunsen burner in a laboratory, so will your **LIFE FORCE** radiations benefit all who come within your radius of influence.

This was the intention behind creation. You were intended to **express Universal Creative Consciousness** through your mind and heart. I, the **CHRIST**, have come at this time to show you how to do this.

First of all, consider my 'state of consciousness' when I performed my so-called miracles.

I did not pray a set prayer. I simply asked the **Creative Father** radiating through my own consciousness, for whatever was needed:

I strongly realized and visualized the '**Father Creative Consciousness**' was a dynamic operating Force which manifested itself through the visible world as:

Creativity,intelligent design, growth, nutrition and nourishment, protection, healing, regeneration, fulfillment of every need – all within a system of law & order.

I realized that the '**Creative Father Consciousness**' would **radiate all Its Nature** through my consciousness to enter the consciousness of those who had asked for healing and sincerely believed they would receive it. I also knew that if they did not have 'faith and expectancy of healing', this type of negative consciousness would not be influenced by the inflow of the **NATURE** **of 'Father Consciousness'** and no healing would take place.

I also realized that the healing work done by the **Creative Father Consciousness** was really **Love made visible** on earth.

I also realized that all the work done by the **Creative Father Consciousness** within the visible world was love made manifest – and gave thanks.

I realized that out of **Universal Consciousness** had come all the substance of the universe – and gave thanks.

I realized that **'Father Creative Consciousness'** was the '**worker**' and that **It** was eternal and infinite and nothing – nothing except the human mind could stop it from doing its work.

Therefore, I rid my mind of any human feelings and thoughts, and I knew that I was a perfect channel of '**Father love**' and knew that the perfect will of '**Father love**' would be accomplished in the person who needed healing.

But note this: I also knew that whatever in that person's consciousness had brought about his crippled, or maimed, or diseased condition had been erased in his body for the time being. The question was: would his normal 'consciousness' bring about a return of the condition divinely erased from his body?

Therefore I said to the person who had received healing: 'go your way and sin no more'

I want you to know and believe with all your hearts that my state of consciousness when on earth, described to you in the above paragraphs, is the 'state of consciousness' to which you should also aspire with all your mind and heart.

My experiences of enlightenment in the desert enabled me to achieve the **CHRIST CONSCIOUSNESS** to a large extent whilst on earth. But you can follow in my steps if you have the will to do so, and I will surely be at hand to help you on your journey. You may feel my presence if you are sufficiently sensitive to do so. But if for some time, you feel nothing, do not be cast down, because as you do the work of changing your consciousness, you can be absolutely certain you will be tuning into my **CHRIST CONSCIOUSNESS** and I will be aware of all that is happening to you.

KNOW that your purpose on earth is to ascend in spiritual consciousness until you transcend all the humanhood which presently holds you back, until, eventually, you, too, can control the elements and become a master.

Realize too that when **world consciousness** is fully attuned to '**Father Creative Consciousness'**, all things inimical to the perfect well-being of man will disappear. There will be no more malaria bearing mosquitoes, locusts to strip your crops, severe climatic conditions, infections, viruses, and everything else which presently cause problems for living things. You will live within a cloak of universal protection. When your own consciousness is perfectly attuned to and in harmony with **Father Love** – then you too will be divinely protected and will become channels of: Creative design, growth, nutrition and nourishment, protection, healing, regeneration, fulfillment of need, law & order.

FATHER LOVE will be operational within your mind, heart, body and your affairs. It will be operational in all those to whom you direct its power.

LETTER 2

I am the **CHRIST**.

Whilst I operate from the highest realms **of DIVINE CREATIVE CONSCIOUSNESS**, my influence encircles your world.

Speaking metaphorically, I am as distant in 'consciousness' from your world as your sun is distant from earth. Yet if you call on me sincerely, I am as close to you as is necessary to help you.

There will be many who will be unable to receive these **LETTERS**. Such people are not yet ready for them.

There will be those who will try to stifle their existence, since the teachings will be threatening their livelihood or religion. They will not succeed. These **LETTERS** will be strengthened by opposition.

There will be those who will receive these **LETTERS** with joy, since in their souls they have known that beyond the religions of the world has been **TRUTH – the REALITY** of existence. These are the people who will prosper and will eventually save the world from self-annihilation.

I will now take up my 'autobiography' from where I left off in my last **LETTER**.

My purpose in giving you some of the biographical details of my entrance into public life as teacher and healer is to bring alive for you, my youthful attitudes and behaviour, the circumstances of my attaining my own state of spiritualised humanhood.

It is important you should be able to visualise Palestine as it was when I was on earth and clearly see the inner conflicts which my teachings aroused in the people indoctrinated in the Jewish beliefs and Traditional Rites.

These conflicts lie at the heart of the gospellers' inability to record, accurately, all that I tried to teach them.

In the gospels are frequent references to my parables describing the reality of the Kingdom of Heaven or Kingdom of God, whichever term the gospellers used but **nowhere has any attempt been made to reach into the words themselves, explore the figures of speech, or lift out the spiritual meaning of the Kingdom of God or the Kingdom of Heaven.**

As I speak of my true sermons given to the people, you will, in the light of my experiences in the desert and of your own knowledge of scientific facts, be able to understand, at last, a little of what I was attempting to teach at that time.

Since I was largely unsuccessful, it is imperative another attempt should be made to do so, at the beginning of this age, this millennium, **since it is on my privileged, highest spiritual knowledge and insight that the next age will be founded and developed.**

It was – and is – essential for a Teacher such as I and others have been, super-sensitive and wholly committed mentally and emotionally to a search for **Truth of Existence,** to come to earth to **COIN WORDS** to describe to people on earth, imprisoned in words, what lies in the **CREATIVE UNIVERSAL DIMENSION** in an unformed state. Were it not for such inspired Teachers, people on earth would have remained in ignorance of all that lies beyond the earth – **ready for contact, to be personally experienced and absorbed to promote future spiritual evolution.**

Not only this – the Bible is said to be the most widely read book in the world. In its present form it has served its purposes.

The New Testament, as it stands, with all its baggage of misinterpretation is a deterrent to spiritual evolution. It is now time to move forward into a new realm of mystical perception and understanding.

Since it is impossible for me, to descend into human body again to speak to the world, and I have other dimensions to whom I minister, I have trained a sensitive soul to receive and transcribe. It is the nearest I can do to talking to you personally. I hope you will be able to receive and accept this.

Whatever is erroneous is erased. You may be sure of this.

The incidents and healings related in the following pages are not important. They happened but they are given only to enable you to understand their true spiritual significance.

I want you, as you read, to relate the conditions of 2000 years ago to your present life and times. I want you to regard the persona of 'Jesus' as an 'icon' of what can eventually be achieved by every human being who is ready and willing to become a founder member of the 'kingdom of heaven' on earth. Although people of your present world are what you call sophisticated, big-headed in their modern

'knowledge and learning', versed in contemporary manners, and in new ways of relating one to another, basically, the people all those years ago were the same as yourselves.

They were controlled and motivated entirely by their TWIN IMPULSES
of Bonding–Rejection
Desires–Repulsions
even as you are.

They loved, hated, criticised, condemned, slandered and gossiped, possessed ambitions to rise to the top of society, despised those who were failures in life, secretly 'slept around' as you call it, and taunted those who were different in any way to themselves.

To help you fully understand and enter into my time on earth, my 'consciousness has descended to your plane of earthly existence to experience yet again the 'persona' of 'Jesus' and the emotions and events in which I was involved.

****

When I left the desert and put foot to the road leading to my village of Nazareth, I was still elated, exuberantly joyous in the knowledge so gloriously revealed to me in the desert. I focused my thoughts entirely on all that **I had learnt** and if my thoughts strayed to my former negative forms of thought, I swiftly turned to the **'Father'** for inspiration and determination in overcoming them. In this way, I returned, constantly, to the **Light of awareness and understanding.**

Some people looked at me askance, seeing my joy and also my dirty, unkempt appearance. Was I happy with drink, they wondered? Others looked at me with abhorrence. Instead of reacting with anger as in the past, I remembered that I had been blest with visions and knowledge they could not even begin to imagine. I blest them and prayed for their inner vision to be similarly opened, and continued peacefully along the road to my home.

There were villagers, however, who viewed my pitiful state with compassion and hurried into their houses to fetch me bread and even wine to help me on my way. There was always someone who offered shelter for the night. The '**Father Life**' indeed supplied all my needs and gave me protection as needed.

All this time, I said not a word about my weeks in the desert. I felt that the time was not yet ripe. Eventually, I reached my home town, Nazareth, and the villagers openly scoffed, pointing at my filthy self and tattered clothes.

'Dirty lazy layabout' were some of the kinder words thrown at me.

I came to my mother's door with a feeling of dread, since I knew she would be more shocked than her neighbours when she saw me stand in front of her: thin, bones showing through skin, eyes sunken and cheeks hollowed out, face burnt black and lips blistered with the sun, and beard grown long and straggly. My clothes! She would be outraged when she saw my clothes – their original colour wholly obscured by desert dust and the cloth torn and ragged.

I mounted the steps and braced myself to endure the heat of my mother's fury. When I knocked, my sister came to the door. She looked at me, open-mouthed, wide-eyed and frightened, then slammed the door in my face. I could hear her running to the back of the house, screaming:

'Mother, come quickly, there is a dirty old man at the door.'

I could hear my mother muttering crossly to herself, hurrying to the door. Flinging it open, she stood, rooted in shock. I smiled but for a moment, she looked me up-and-down with increasing horror as she realised this dreadful creature was indeed her wayward son, Jesus.

I held out my hand to her, saying:

'I know I cause you much pain but can you help me?'

Immediately, her expression changed and drawing me inside, she secured the door.

'Quick,' she said to my frightened sister. 'Stop that noise and put water on to boil. Your brother is starved. It doesn't matter what trouble he has got into, he belongs to us. He must be looked after.'

Gently, she helped me take off my clothes and bent me over a large container of water and scrubbed me clean. She washed and trimmed my hair and beard, and lightly covered the sores on my body and lips with a healing salve. Neither of us broke the silence.

I savoured the love she showed me and tried to show my gratitude by a more gentle and sensitive approach.

Having helped me put on a clean robe, she sat me down to a frugal meal of bread, milk and honey. Reluctantly, she gave me wine, to pick up my strength, but it was obvious she thought that wine had been the cause of my shocking plight.

Then she led me to a bed and placed a cover over me. I slept for several hours and woke refreshed to a morning, bright with sunshine seen through the window.

I was now longing to talk to my mother, to tell her that I was indeed a Messiah but not the kind the Jews imagined. I could save people from the bad results of their 'sins'. I could help them find health, abundance, fulfilment of their needs, because I could now teach them exactly how the world had been created.

As I tried to tell her, she started off by being excited and delighted. She jumped to her feet and wanted to rush out to tell the neighbours her son was indeed the Messiah – they should hear how nicely he now talked – and he had been fasting in the desert!

But I stopped her from doing this. I said that I had not yet told her what had been revealed to me. One of the most important things I had learnt was that the Orthodox Jews were entirely wrong in their belief in an avenging 'god'. There was no such thing.

This frightened and upset her and she exclaimed, 'How then will Jehovah govern the world and make us good and listen to his prophets, if He does not punish us? Are you now so big that you are going to tell the High Priests their

47

own business handed down to them from the time of Moses? Are you going to bring more shame on this house?'

She began to cry, saying with anger: 'You've not changed a bit. You've only changed in what you're saying. You have brought me nothing but grief. How could I have ever believed you would be a Messiah? You will only lead people into greater torment then ever before, with your strange ideas.'

My brothers heard her wailing and came running, wanting to turn me out of the house. Because I did not want a disturbance, I offered to leave peacefully.

If this was how my mother reacted, I could be sure that everyone else would react in the same way to what I wanted to tell them. I realised I needed a quiet time of absolute rest and silence in which to collect all my thoughts and experiences together. I would have to pray for inspired guidance on how best to approach the Jews with my message of 'good news'. I was sure that the **'Father Life' would meet my need**, and I would find the right accommodation somewhere. My mother, although furious with my seemingly 'big-headed attitudes', was, nonetheless, torn with her feelings of love and compassion for my emaciated condition. She rejected everything I appeared to stand for – rebelliousness, contempt for the Jewish Religion, high-handed attitudes towards authority, my self-will and arrogance, but she still loved me and was deeply afraid that I would eventually land up in greater trouble than I had ever thought possible.

She admonished my brothers, telling them to hold their noisy arguments and turned to me. 'You can stay here until you are better,' she said. 'Perhaps whilst you are here, I can talk some sense into you. I can tell you now, if you go out into the streets and begin talking as you have to me – you will end up in an even worse state than ever. Good people will spit and throw their rotten rubbish over you. You are a disgrace to your family.'

So, despite her anger, I laughed and thanked and kissed her warmly. Gladly, I remained with her, knowing very well that underneath her anger, she was deeply anxious for me. She fed me well and made me good new clothes. I appreciated all she did towards improving my appearance, as I knew that to move freely between rich and poor, I must be acceptably clad in decent garments.

At times, there were food shortages in the home. Drawing on the power of my 'Father', I replenished them saying nothing. Neither did she. I knew she wondered sadly whether, to all my other bad habits, I had now added that of thief.

Then she caught me with a freshly baked loaf in my hands and knew that I had not been out of the house to buy it and neither had the stove been in use that day.

She said nothing but gave me a long pondering look. I could see her attitudes change at that moment. She was no longer sure of her ground. She was beginning to question her own attitudes towards me and also the truth of my statements:

'What really happened to him out in the desert? How could he make a loaf of bread without fire, flour and yeast? What does it mean? Is he the Messiah?'

Then my brother cut his hand. He was in much pain when it festered. He allowed me to put my hands on his wound and quietly pray. I could see that he felt the **'Power'** flow into his hand because he looked at me strangely.

'The pain has gone' he said briefly. He was surly as he walked away, and I knew that whilst he was relieved to be free of pain, he did not like me for having been able to help him. I sensed his jealousy.

My sister scalded her hand and another brother often complained of bad headaches. I was able to cure them both.

My brothers and sisters began to joke about my 'magic powers'. They questioned what 'evil' I might do to them if they angered me. The tension in the home deepened and I felt sadness for my mother who longed for peace in the house.

But she saw changes in my behaviour and was comforted. I was quieter, visibly controlled likely outbursts, reined in my energy, curbed impatience, no longer argued. I became more caring, listened to her womanly grumbles, helped her in the house by repairing broken furniture and walked the hills to distant farms to find the fruit and vegetables she wanted.

I came to love her tenderly and compassionately as a mother should be loved. One day, she ventured to ask me: 'Do you still say that Jehovah is a myth?'

'Job said that if Jehovah were to withdraw his breath, all flesh would collapse together. That is the 'Jehovah' **I believe in and saw.'**

49

'No one has seen Jehovah!' she said firmly.

'I saw **THAT Which has brought all things into being**,' I replied quietly. 'I call **IT** the '**Father**' because **IT** is **PERFECT LOVE; LOVE** more perfect than a mother's' I added, smiling at her. '**IT** works in, through and for all **ITS** creation. It is the '**Father**' in me which has brought you the things you needed in the house and healed my brothers and sisters so swiftly.'

I could see she was beginning to understand a little of what I said.

'What of 'sin'?' she asked.

'There is no 'sin' as we understand it. We are born to behave as we do. We have to find a way to overcome our human thoughts and feelings for they separate us from the protection of the 'Father' and bring us our sickness and misery. When we have learnt how to overcome the 'self' we will enter the Kingdom of Heaven.'

My mother turned away silently, obviously pondering what I had said to her but no longer angry. I knew she was thinking about my statements and realised they would be turning her safe and well-known world upside down. Without her belief in a Jehovah threatening dire vengeance if mankind was unruly, she would feel lost and insecure. She would wonder how the world would ever manage if it was left entirely to men to control the evil doings of themselves and others. Even kings and governors were wicked in their actions. Without Jehovah to rule and punish sinners where would it end?

Whilst regaining my strength, I studied the Scriptures diligently to enable me to meet Pharisees and Scribes with confidence. It was also imperative I should know what had been written of the Messiah because I was convinced I was 'he' of whom the prophets had spoken. I could indeed rescue – save – people from misery, sickness and poverty, even restore them to health and prosperity by showing them the truth concerning the Kingdom of Heaven and the **Reality** of the '**Father**'.

When I felt I was sufficiently prepared to go out and teach and heal, to please my mother, I agreed to go, one Sabbath, to the synagogue in Nazareth, and speak to the congregation.

As was customary, I stood up, and was handed Isaiah to read. I chose the passage prophesying a Messiah would come who would release the Jews from every type of bondage:

"The Spirit of the Lord is upon me, because he has anointed me to preach the good news to the poor, He has sent me to proclaim release to the captives and recovering of sight to the blind. To set at liberty, those who are oppressed, to proclaim the acceptable year of the Lord."

Then I sat down, saying: 'Today, you have seen this prophecy fulfilled in me.'

There was shock and amazement on the men's faces but I continued to speak, knowing that the 'Father' would tell me what to say. The words came without hesitation.

I spoke about my experience in the desert and related my vision of the baby growing into manhood, all the while, all unknowingly, wrapping himself around with mental thongs and chains, thus blinding and imprisoning himself in interior darkness and **shutting himself off from God**.

I explained that in so doing, they exposed themselves to oppression from conquerors, slavery, poverty and disease.

'For God is LIGHT' I said. 'And LIGHT, is the substance of all visible things. **And LIGHT is LOVE which makes all things for man to enjoy.'**

'All blessings of abundance and health were freely available to him, who loved God with mind, heart and soul and lived strictly according to the Laws of God.'

When I had finished, there was complete silence in the synagogue. I felt that the congregation had experienced something strange and powerful and had been lifted to a higher plane of thought and wanted nothing to disturb the transcendent tranquility of that moment.

Then the whispering started amongst themselves. They were wondering who I was! Some were convinced that I was the person, Jesus, whose family was known in the village, but others could not accept this, since I had spoken as one having authority.

Unfortunately, I felt my old reactions to these religious men returning. I knew they had despised me in the past and so I expected rejection. I slipped back

51

into my old challenging attitudes and thoroughly angered them. Through my own human reactions, I invited disaster. And disaster I almost got.

The younger men, urged on by their elders, rushed at me and dragged me to the highest cliff top to hurl me to my death but I prayed to my '**Father**' for deliverance. Suddenly, it seemed they were so stirred up they hardly knew what they were doing, and turned on each other, I was able to slip from their midst and escape.

It was strange. They seemed not to notice my going.

Badly shaken by my experience, I managed to send a message to my mother, saying I was leaving Nazareth immediately and was going down to Capernum, a gracious town by the sea of Galilee.

At first, I thought to join old acquaintances but I felt, intuitively, this was not the right thing to do. So, all the way down and on entering the town, I prayed for the '**Father's**' direction and help in finding accommodation. I had no money and would not beg.

As I walked the street, a woman of middle years came towards me, heavily laden with baskets on her arms. Her countenance was sorrowful. It seemed she had been crying. On impulse, I stopped her and asked where I might find accommodation. She said, briefly, that she would normally offer me a bed but she had a very sick son at home. She added that she had been to buy provisions to feed the 'comforters' who had already gathered to mourn when her son died.

My heart grieved for her but also rejoiced. Straightway, I had been led to someone I could help. I expressed my sympathy and offered to carry her baskets to her house.

She looked at me for a moment, wondering who I might be, but was apparently satisfied by my appearance and demeanour. On the way, I said that I could probably help her son.

'Are you a doctor?' she asked.

I replied that I had received no medical training but nonetheless I could help him.

On reaching her house – large, and well-built of stone, indicating social standing and prosperity, she took me to her husband, saying, 'This man says he can help our son.'

He nodded morosely but said nothing. The woman, Miriam, drew me away saying he was distressed and very angry.

'The boy is our only son amongst many daughters and he is blaming God for giving the child the sickness.' Miriam wept. 'If he speaks like this against God, what other troubles will be heaped upon us, I wonder?'

'Take comfort,' I said. 'Shortly, your son will be well again.'

She looked doubtful but led me to the room in which the boy lay. It was hot and stifling, and filled with gloomy, talkative 'well-wishers'. I asked the mother to clear the room but the visitors were resistant. They wanted to see what would be done and only left reluctantly when Miriam called her husband to speak to them. I could hear them arguing with the father in the next room.

What did he think this man could do, if the doctor had been unable to help the boy? The father came into the room to see for himself.

His son was deathly pale and had a high fever. The mother explained he could not keep his food down, and had loose bowels. He had been like that for several days and had lost so much weight, the doctor had said nothing more could be done for him. He would probably die.

I placed my hands on the boy's head and prayed, **knowing and silently giving heartfelt thanks that the 'Father' LIFE** would flow down through my hands and into his body. Thus the healing work would be accomplished. I felt extreme heat and a tingling vibration in my hands, and the **Power** pouring into his frail body. I was overcome with joyous thanksgiving. How great, how wonderful was the **'Father Life'** when released to do **Its** natural work of healing!

His mother and father, looking anxious, wondering what would happen next, held each other's hands and watched intently. As they saw their son's colour gradually change from white to a more healthy glow, they exclaimed in astonishment and delight. After some time, the boy looked up at me, saying brightly: 'Thank you. I am well now. I am hungry and want something to eat.'

His mother laughed with happiness and held him close, but also looked apprehensive.

'I cannot give you food, my son. The doctor will be angry.'

She had been warned to starve him of all but water. I smiled and said: 'He is cured. You can give him bread and wine, and he will keep it down.'

His father, Zedekiah, was all amazed joy and gratitude. After embracing his beloved boy, he turned to me and wrung my hands warmly. He kept patting my shoulder but shaking his head, unable to speak for the tears which were running down his cheeks.

When he had largely recovered his composure, he went through to the living room and said to the people there: 'My son, almost dead, has been returned to fullness of life again!'

His words were met with a great clamour of jubilation, excitement, disbelief, questioning, laughter and congratulations. The boy's mother stood there, her face wreathed in smiles.

After that, there was no question of needing accommodation. When Zedekiah told the astonished 'comforters' that the boy was cured, and the youth, himself, appeared smiling at the door, and asked, yet again, for food, the 'well-wishers', one and all, gathered around me and invited me to their homes. However, I preferred to remain with the boy's father, who now said he had many questions to ask me; he hoped I could answer them.

After food and wine were placed on the table and everyone was invited to eat their fill, Zedekiah sat down and asked his first question.

He said: 'You have done something no priest or doctor could do. Healing only comes of God. Although you are a stranger, I perceive you must come from God.'

'Yes.' I said. And the people murmured, wonderingly.

'This illness which has come upon my son. Was this a punishment for something I have done wrong in the past? And how could I commit so grievous a sin that God should want to take my only son from me?' Many of the people nodded when they heard these words.

'You have asked the question I most want to answer, Zedekiah. **God gives us LIFE and being.** He would not snatch these away as a man will snatch some treasure from another man because he is angry with him. This is the way that mankind behaves. Not God. And God is not placed on a throne in some part of the sky like human kings sit on thrones and govern their people. This is the human way, and a human belief – not truth. The way of God is far beyond anything the human mind can devise or dream about. I alone have 'seen' **'That which has brought us into being'**, and I know that **IT** is not the kind of 'God' taught by the Rabbis. I saw that **IT** is **'Perfect Love'** and for this reason I would rather speak of the **'Father'**, for I have seen that **It works** within every living thing, keeping them in a good state of health even as a human father works to keep his children well fed, clothed and protected within the shelter of a home. I have 'seen' **IT** within everything in the world.

'How can that be?' a man asked doubtfully.

'It is not possible for an individual 'being' of any kind to be everywhere at once. But the air is everywhere although we cannot see it. Nonetheless, we know – and do not doubt – it is very real and very important to our existence. If there were no air and we could not breathe it, we would die. The movement of air, which we call wind, we cannot see but we see it agitate the leaves, and drive the clouds across the sky, so we know the air is around and above us and is strong. And now I will ask you, what is the most real and valuable part of a man – his body or his mind?'

Some answered it was the body, otherwise he would have no place on earth, could not work, could not be seen, would not be known. Others said they thought that his mind was more important than his body. And I answered: 'His mind is the most important part of him since without his mind, he could not power his body. He would not eat, drink, sleep, move, plan, or live. Yet, we cannot see mind. We can only know we have a mind because of the thoughts it produces and because the thoughts fashion some kind of action in our lives. We believe mind works through the brain. Yes, it does. For how could brain, born of flesh, produce thoughts, feelings, ideas, plans? And now it should be clear to you that this is how the **'Father'** is present within all things; **It** is the directing **'mind'** behind the human mind, working **Its** great works within every living thing. We know this is so, for we see the marvels it brings about. We see the growth of children, we see the food they eat miraculously changed into another substance which nourishes and makes them grow. How this happens, we do not begin to know or even imagine.

55

Even if we did know, we would still not know what set such an important life process to work in living bodies of every species. See how wonderfully, the bodies of each species is fashioned and created purposefully, expressly to transform the kind of food they eat, into nourishment to grow bone, blood and flesh.'

'Now you show us these things, we can see they are truly marvellous.' A young man exclaimed. 'They are! They are! We see the young bodies going through their various stages of development, and we see their minds keeping pace with their physical development until the youths and maidens begin to long to find a spouse and to become parents themselves. Then the great work of conception is accomplished and the growth of the seed within the womb continues, until it comes forth as a full term child. Think! Who determines all this steady, orderly growth within the woman, from whence come the plans which govern the right development of head, body, and limbs and are unvarying from one woman to another, and from one species to another? Who decides the exact moment when birth shall begin – the physical means by which the child shall be brought forth from the womb, the provision of milk for the child? Think – is it the mother? No, it is not the mother, she is but witness of all that takes place in her from the moment her husband has been to her and planted his seed to join with hers. Does God do all these things from afar? Do his thoughts reach out to each man and woman and decide when these things shall take place?

No, all this work is accomplished by the '**Creative Mind Power**', the '**Intelligently Loving Life**' within every living thing. We see the parents' love of their young, be they bird, animal and man. Where does this love come from? It is drawn from the '**Creative Mind Power**' – **Perfect Love** – of the 'Father' within us. It is because the 'Father' does the work within the plants, the trees, the birds, animals and man himself, that we are here today, living, breathing, eating, sleeping, having children, growing old and then dying to pass on to some more happy place. All of this is the work of the '**Father**' active within us. How can you possibly deny the truth of all I have said tonight? Today, you saw a dying youth brought back to fullness of life again within a short time – was it I who healed him? Not at all. Of myself I can do nothing. It was the **LIFE** that is the 'Father' active within all things, which came in full force to repair an ailing body and bring it back to full health again because I believed It would and did not doubt.'

There were sighs of satisfaction in the room. New light, new interest, even new gentleness showed in their faces.

'Why then, does man suffer so grievously?' Miriam asked.

'Because when man is begotten, when **LIFE** takes on form within the seed, **IT** takes on the humanhood which separates **IT** from every other individual in the world. To make **IT** single, a lone figure, joined to none other, solitary, private, **ITS** own person, **IT becomes subject to – is controlled** by two mightily strong impulses in his earthly nature – to hold fast to all those things he greatly desires and to reject and push away all that he does not want. These two most basic impulses in man underlie every single thing he ever does throughout his life, and are entirely responsible for the trouble man brings upon himself. Although the '**Father' is active within man, IT** has nothing of *humanhood* in **IT**.

Therefore the 'Father' holds nothing, rejects nothing, condemns nothing, does not even see 'wrongdoing'. All that man does which man calls 'sin' is only of this world and is only punished within this world – for it is a Law of Earthly Existence, as you know, that whatever you sow you will reap as a like harvest. Because he draws LIFE and MIND from the 'Father', man himself is creative in thought, words and deeds. Whatever he thinks, says, does, and believes, returns to him in like form, some time later. There is no punishment from the 'Father' – whatever ills come to mankind is of their own making entirely.'

People murmured that this was a new teaching altogether, and yet it made greater sense than all they had been taught before.

Several voices urged me to tell them more.

'I tell you, in me you have seen the LIFE active as healing; follow me and you will hear of the PATH you must walk to find happiness; in my words will you find the TRUTH of Existence never yet revealed by any other man.

'It has been said of the Messiah he will utter secrets hidden from the beginning of creation. I tell you truly, these secrets you will hear from me. If you listen carefully and grasp their meaning, and practice their truth, and hold fast to their laws, you will be made new and will enter into the Kingdom of Heaven.'

After I had spoken, the people were quiet for a moment and then there was a clamour of excited talk but Zedekiah stood up and said it was time for the household to settle down. His boy needed sleep and his wife and daughters, too, were weary after all their weeping.

It was arranged that, the next morning, I should go down to the harbour and sick people would be brought to me. Thus, I was able to launch my mission and everything was speedily arranged for me in the best possible way. It seemed that if I did not heal, there would be no interest in and no acceptance of all I had to tell them. Healing demonstrated the truth of what I wanted to teach, and my teachings would explain the reasons why I was able to bring them healing from the **'Father'**.

When I woke the next morning, I felt joyously alive with the expectation of wondrous things to come.

After I had broken my fast, I set out with Zedekiah towards the town harbour, my heart aglow with love for everyone I passed. I greeted them warmly, telling them I had 'good news' for those who wanted to hear it. When I reached the jetty, I found men, women and children seated on the ground, awaiting my arrival. Some held out their hands to me imploringly. These looked very ill, some were crippled, many were covered in sores.

My heart still ached for their pitiful state but now I could also rejoice because I knew that it was not the **'Father's Will'** they should be like this. Quite the contrary! The **'Father'** was **Itself** all healing, all health, all fitness. I had proved this the night before and in my home. I exulted that I would be able to demonstrate this wonderful truth to the crowds now gathering around me.

One sad old face caught my attention. She was wrinkled and thin and crooked. I went to her and kneeling beside her, I placed my hands on her head and immediately felt the flow of **'Father Power'** through my hands, vibrating through her head until her whole body shook with the **Life Force** energising her limbs. People, watching this were astonished and wondered what I might be doing to her, but others quietened their objections. Gradually, her limbs began to unbend, lengthen, straighten; her face became alive with the joy of returning strength. I helped her to stand up, then she stood proudly by herself. She was so overcome with happiness; she began to weep then laughed and danced, calling out to the people: 'Praise God' she said, 'Praise God' and others standing there took up the refrain. They were all deeply moved by what they had seen.

The crush of people pressing in against my person was so great, Zedekiah offered to control them. In orderly fashion, assisted by other eager onlookers, he marshalled the sick towards me, that I might attend to them according to their deepest need.

At last, feeling tired, my host invited me back to his house to dine. He sent away those whom I had not been able to heal for lack of time. He assured them I would return the following day.

It was a festive evening – so much to talk about – so much to celebrate – so much to teach – so much to learn – all of it certainly 'good news', the people agreed. I knew that by many, I was accepted as speaking truly of what I had 'seen' in the desert.

And so it continued for many days. People came to see me from far and wide. Zedekiah and other of his friends helped me to control the crowds to enable me to heal and teach. The people listened gladly. They were talking amongst themselves about the '**Father**' and were eager to learn more about the 'thongs and chains' which bound people in misery.

The crush became so great, I soon realised I would have to find my own helpers on whom I could rely to assist me. It was time for Zedekiah to return to conduct his leather business which he had been neglecting.

I went away to the hills to pray about choosing 'disciples'. When the conviction came to me that I would be guided as to whom to choose, I returned to Capernum. I felt a strong inclination to go down to the water front to speak to some men I had seen listening intently to my teachings.

Whether they would leave their fishing nets to join me, remained to be seen. But when I called them, Simon, Andrew, James and John, they came immediately, happy to help in my work of healing and teaching. Others also joined me as I began my work amongst the people.

I left my host, Zedekaih's house with his warm assurances I could return at any time.

Thus it was that I commenced my mission as a teacher and healer wandering wherever needed through towns and villages. Before setting out, I gathered together the young men who had consented and were eager to help me. They would be listening to my teachings and would be mystified by much that I wanted to say. It was vital I should first explain the background to all that had been revealed to me in the desert.

I told them that despite my previously lazy way of life, I had always had a profound compassion for people. It was my compassion that made me turn from the 'God' taught by the Rabbis. When I spoke of my total rejection of a punishing Jehovah, I could see the doubt and shock in their faces.

At considerable length, I explained that I questioned how it was possible to speak of a 'good' God, when there was so much suffering endured by innocent children. As I spoke, I saw their faces gradually relax. I continued to voice my previous doubts and anger until I saw their expressions change into those of acceptance and then full agreement. I discovered I had put to them their own doubts and questions which, previously, they had never had the courage to put into words.

As we spoke together, I could sense their relief that they were no longer alone in their secret resistance to the rabbis' teachings.

I told them there came a time when I began to realise ever more clearly that I was wasting my life. I wanted to change and felt very strongly I should go to John the Baptist as a starting point, as it were, to the commencement of a new way of living.

I described what happened during the baptism and my six weeks in the desert. I explained that all my previous thoughts and beliefs, attitudes, arrogance, rebelliousness were gradually cleansed from my consciousness whilst I was going through the deep revelations and visions showing me the '**Reality**' I now called the 'Father'. I explained the nature of the '**Father**' and that this '**Divine Nature**' also constituted the '**Divine Will**'. I told them that it was man himself, who, through wrong thinking and wrong behaviour, shut himself off from the '**Father**' within him, and man alone, by first repenting and then by mental-emotional cleansing, could find his own way back to full contact with the '**Father**'. **When this was accomplished, the full Nature of the 'Father' would be released into the person's mind, heart, body, soul and his life environment and experiences. As this happened, such a person would enter into the Kingdom of Heaven ruled by the 'Father' and also, the Kingdom of Heaven would be established within the**

consciousness of the person. He would then have attained the purpose behind his existence.

As I spoke to my disciples, I saw their reactions reflected in their faces. All doubt had gone, there was now a light of dawning comprehension and joy. These young men became enthusiastic believers and exclaimed: 'This is indeed good news!'

However, after their first acceptance of all I said, there were times when they wondered whether all I said could be true. I understood this. To be prepared to rid themselves of the image of 'Jehovah' so deeply imprinted in their minds took a great deal of courage.

There were times when they spoke amongst themselves and questioned who was this man claiming such marvels? Supposing they came along with me and it turned out that I was really a messenger from Satan? What then? They would be severely punished by Jehovah.

They had much to lose – their standing in society as sober, hardworking young men, their reputation as tradesmen and artisans, their loss of income, and biggest obstacle of all, the probable anger and rejection by their families. What would they receive in return?

I told them I could not promise them any earthly reward for their help in spreading the 'gospel of good news'. I had no doubt at all that wherever we went we would be given food and shelter and would be well received by the people. I could only promise them the **Truth** that the **'Father' knew their needs and would fulfill them and keep them healthy. I could also promise them that as they turned to the 'Father' and trusted the 'Father' every step of the way, they would be happy in a way they had never been happy before. They would experience the Kingdom of Heaven themselves to the extent they set aside the demands of 'self' and served other people. They would witness the healings, and these would increase their faith and give them the courage to endure any discomforts of the journey.**

And this was how we came to start on our mission of spreading the 'GOOD NEWS' of the 'GOSPEL OF THE KINGDOM'.

I sent these young men ahead of me into the town we were to visit. As they entered it, they told the people to gather together to hear the 'Good News of the Kingdom of Heaven'. The people were astonished and wanted to know

61

more but the disciples urged them to fetch their friends and neighbours and they would be told all about it 'when Jesus arrived', and there would be healing of their sick people. Excitedly, many ran to help spread the 'good news' and soon they were gathered together in a huge crowd.

I, who had so deeply and passionately rebelled against the long-faced religious homilies threatening violence, punishments and damnation to sinners, now walked with joy to meet these crowds.

I had my 'good news' to share with them to brighten their day, and healing of ailments and afflictions to gladden their lives.

Whereas, before, I moved amongst people selfishly and empty handed, taking their goodwill and sometimes their hand-outs with little gratitude, I came now with an abundance of life-giving possibilities for everyone who was prepared to listen to my words and take action to improve his quality of life.

I want you who are reading these pages, to fully understand my position at that time, my state of consciousness after my illumination in the desert, and the persona I presented to my countrymen as 'Jesus'. There have been so many conjectures that I am about to give you the truth.

I was born to have, when mature, a fine physique, strong aquiline features, a remarkable intellect and a love of mimicry and laughter – but, like so many of you today, I took no care of my earthly talents. At the time of going into the desert, my face and manners were what you might call 'down-graded' from what they should have been. Whilst I had begun to examine and rebel against what I had become, my intellect had also suffered from mis-use, constantly engaged in arguments and dissensions over religion and indulging in flippant speech. I made people laugh. I was liked by the men and women I mixed with, but certainly not respected. Hence the astonishment of those who had known me, when I spoke to them in the synagogue in Nazareth.

Whilst my mother nursed me back to good health, I made powerful use of the knowledge and enlightenment given me in the desert. This restored me to the man I was meant to be.

When I started my mission, I was fully aware that I was the only one with the supreme knowledge of the secrets of creation and existence itself. Therefore, I could say with perfect confidence, "No one has 'seen' the 'Father' but me".

I knew that all that men believed in so wholeheartedly was false – not real.

I knew that I had been specially fashioned and designed by the 'Father' for this mission. I had been blest abundantly with the physical energy, vitality of speech and the ability to devise meaningful parables, to enable me to pass on the message successfully and in a form that would never be forgotten.

Besides which I understood my fellow men so well from long association with them that I knew their fondest hopes, their most desperate fears; I knew what made them laugh and prompted them to mockery and derision of the rich and pompous; and I knew, also, how deeply, so many, young and old, suffered silently and bravely. I knew and experienced deep compassion for the populace which lived in fear of – or endured – the verbal whiplash of Pharisees, and bowed down to the tax laws of the Romans. I knew how their proud Jewish spirit was bruised by the conquering gentiles whom they were forced to honour with their lips and hand and knee salutations, yet whom they despised behind closed doors. I knew and fully understood the lives and thinking of the populace. I had previously thought their thoughts, felt their resentments, endured their kind of anxieties in times of lack, felt powerless in the grip of the Roman governance.

I now knew that none of this suffering was really necessary. Knowing as I did, the *Reality* of existence, the *Reality of Universal 'God'*, I could clearly perceive the foolishness of the Jews in authority, who were imposing a burdensome way of life upon the populace which was wholly erroneous and in direct contradiction of the *Truth of Being*. The situation made me deeply angry.

Therefore, I knew I had been perfectly fashioned and honed to become a purified instrument of Divine Action in Palestine – driven by my passion for TRUTH and driven by my compassion for my fellow human beings. Hence I called myself 'Son of man' because I knew exactly what mankind was up against in their daily lives.

Furthermore, I had perfect confidence I could achieve my objectives of bringing Truth to the people and thus be instrumental in changing the quality of their lives. For that reason, although I knew right at the outset of my mission there would be a penalty to pay for all I proposed to do – turn the known Jewish world upside down and inside out – I was prepared to face up to it, go through it, could not evade it, because I loved people with 'Father'

LOVE flowing through my heart and being. For 'Father' LOVE is the essence of GIVING – giving Itself into visible being and visible existence and growing, protecting, nourishing, healing, and fulfilling all the needs of all creation made visible.

I knew I was the 'Father's' gift of salvation to the people – to the world – NOT –

as they supposed and taught down the centuries – salvation from the punishment meted out by an angry God to 'sinners' –

BUT –

to save people from the daily repetition of the same mistakes in wrong thinking – <u>wrong thinking which created their misfortunes, poverty, sickness and misery.</u>

Because I loved the human race so deeply, I was prepared to teach and heal in defiance of the Jewish Priests. I was prepared to die on the cross for what I had truly 'seen' in the desert, knew with all my heart, and wanted to share to the last drop of my ability to do so.

****

THIS IS THE TRUTH BEHIND MY CRUCIFIXION AND ALL THE REST YOU'VE HEARD IS MAN- MADE CONJECTURE ARISING OUT OF THE JEWISH PRACTICE OF BURNT OFFERINGS IN THE TEMPLE.

****

I was a gift from the 'Father' to mankind to help them surmount their ignorance of the Laws of Existence, and find the true Path of Life leading to the joy, abundance and perfect wholeness of the Kingdom of Heaven.

These were the perceptions, the desires, the intentions and goals and the thoughts which I bore within my mind and heart. This was the earthly mental-emotional framework clothing my spiritual consciousness hidden within the head and figure of 'Jesus'.

It was my spiritual consciousness channelled into the above forms of thought and feeling which impelled me to set out on a three year journey to bring the people, what I fully believed, was final rescue from their own blind thinking and feeling which were creating their own troubled lives. I truly believed that if only the people could be shown all that had been given to me to understand, they would realise their past folly and would make every effort to change their thinking and put foot to the Path of Life leading to the Kingdom of Heaven. To this end, I was prepared to give my life.

Because of the wrong interpretation placed on my mission by Jewish teachers, my true message has been distorted out of recognition and the purpose of these Letters is to bring to the people of this New Age, the truth of what I really spoke to the crowds in Palestine.

Therefore, returning to my recounting of those days, let me take you back to a special day which bore fruit amongst my listeners and made a lasting impression in the minds of my disciples.

Hence, for me also, it was a particularly meaningful day.

I took time off from the pressure of people, to go into the hills to pray and meditate to recharge my spiritual batteries by making a deep, strong, more powerful connection with the **'Father'** within me. This connection was so rapidly obscured within my consciousness when I was busy amongst the crowds that I was exhausted. Arriving in the cave I used when in that area, I pulled out the pallet hidden under a rock and lay down to sleep. Instead of sleep, however, I felt the immediate inflow of **Divine Life,** the **'Father'**, and the tiredness was dissolved as my body was charged with the **Power** which is the **Creative Source of All Being**.

I was lifted in consciousness into golden Light, and as I was travelling upwards within this Light, It suddenly changed to purest white and I knew that, in consciousness, I was now at the portals of the Equilibrium which is the Eternal, the Universal, the Infinite dimension beyond all conception of human mind.

I observed the LIGHT but was not of IT, nor was IT powerfully within me, since this was the 'God' dimension of the void, the no-form of the Universal Equilibrium. But IT communicated with me and infused me with Its glowing LOVE. It impressed in me, yet again, that IT was the

LOVE

governing all existence.

I knew that wherever there was lack there would eventually be fulfilment, even as waters flow to fill a lake.

Where there is misery, there would be joy because it was the NATURE of the Universal to move into any living thing in need, to bring fulfilment and joy.

I knew that where there was no growth, circumstances would arise to promote the growth.

I knew that where there was a sense of failure, challenges would be provided to spur people into success and self-confidence.

I 'saw' that this LOVE WORK constantly initiated by the 'Father' in the lives of overburdened people, might not be recognised as a 'gift of LOVE' by the recipients. They might be so sunk in their apathy, feelings of failure, their belief that nothing good could ever come their way, they would fail to see anything in their lives beyond their own beliefs and feelings! Hence, they would remain rooted in their own self-created hell.

There was no need to feel sorry for anyone. The only need was a compassionate heart and a determination to bring Truth to heal their ignorance.

The greatest gift a man could give to another was the enlightenment of ignorance of existence and its cosmic laws, for the TRUTH was:

Every single soul was embraced within the UNIVERSAL and the degree of UNIVERSAL INPUT via the 'Father' LOVE WORK in their lives depended entirely on the individual's receptivity.

I realised that what people needed urgently to hear was what I had just been told.

They needed to 'see' and fully realise the intention and the purpose and the potential of LOVE, which was the very substance of their being.

Because of their disbelief, they might cast the 'Father' LOVE WORK aside as being more 'pain-inducing challenges' and thus lie down in their failure forever.

I now saw, even more clearly, I was sent to awaken people to all the possibilities for self- development, prosperity and the achievement of joy and happiness, but it would be up to them to wake up and take advantage of what was offered them.

I remember that this upliftment lasted all night, and in the morning **I rose feeling alive** as never before. My message had been clarified. I had seen, even more clearly, the **Reality** of the **'Father'** and knew that I would be able to go out that day and meet the crowds and transmit to them, the power and the life of what had been shown me.

As I climbed down from the cave, I came to a large rock overlooking a steep precipice. When I sat, I was able to look down over the town we were to visit that day.

I could feel that 'Perfecting Process' – that 'Making Whole' Impulse – **the 'Father'** – surging through me and I longed to share It with others before the problems of daily living should swamp **It**, and **It** should lose its power and driving force within my human consciousness.

My disciples joined me a short while later. On entering the town, they spoke to the people and directed the gathering crowds to move on to sloping ground beyond the dwelling places. Standing on a large rock in their midst, I began to speak.

I found that the passion and the joy – the yearning, longing, and conviction were all spontaneously poured into the words I spoke to them.

'You are sorely pressed down and weary. Your tasks grow heavier as you get older, your bellies are often empty, your clothes get threadbare, people make you angry, and you feel there is no end to your trouble and heaviness of spirit.

'But this is not the truth concerning your existence. Your lives were intended to be very different. 'If you could only see beyond your feelings – if you could only lift your minds to make contact with the 'Father' within you, you would be able to 'see' and **know** what your state of existence should be. You would realise that you were created to enjoy abundance, protection, good health, and happiness.

'But because, daily, you live in fear of 'good and evil' and **believe** and **expect** these more than you believe that the **'Father'** is abundant **LIFE** and **LOVE** within you, supplying you with all things necessary for health and well-being, it is your most feared 'good and evil' experiences you attract into your lives and bodies. Your beliefs in 'good and evil' obscure – CLOUD OVER – all that the **'Father'** has in store for you if only you will believe in **'Father LOVE'!**

'You judge your todays and expect of your tomorrows what you have experienced in the past. Therefore, are the ills of your yesterdays continually repeated in the future.

'You are enslaved by your memories and your undeviating belief that what was past must return again and again to burden and wound you.

'You do not need to heal your bodies or try to make your lives better, you need to heal your beliefs!

'I have told you there is nothing solid under the sun.

'If you could heal your beliefs, bring your beliefs into line with the **'Father'** **true Intention** for you, the wrong beliefs governing your bodies and lives, would dissolve like mist in the sun.

'Your every circumstance would immediately come back to the **Divine Intention** behind all creation.

'You would find that for every difficulty, for every lack of every kind, there is always a means to end the difficulty, there is always a filling of your basket to meet your need.

'What do you think happens when the sick come to me and I lay my hands upon them?

'Am I thinking about the illness, am I wondering if the person will be healed, am I afraid the 'Father' may be sleeping or is so far away I cannot be heard?

'No, if these were my disbelieving thoughts, there would be no healing.

'When a person approaches me for healing, I immediately rejoice because I **know** that the **Power** which is the **'Father'** is within me, ready and waiting to heal the moment I ask. I give thanks because I **know** that the '**Father's Will'** is **health**, not sickness. Therefore, I pray that the '**Father's Will'** be done in the sick person. **As I remove the belief in sickness from the sick person's body and KNOW that the 'Father's Will' of health is flowing into his system, so does the appearance – the appearance – of sickness change into the reality of 'Father Health' and the body is made whole once more.**

'Sickness is nothing more than a lowering of vitality – a reduction of LIFE – within the affected part. Restore 'Father Life' to the true Intention and Plan of your system and the entire system functions as it should.

'You have been told that God sends sicknesses, plagues, famine, destruction to nations when they do not keep his laws, you have been told that you yourselves are punished by an angry God for sins you have committed. **What is punishment but evil-doing under the guise of goodness?** I say to you that evil does not come from God. How can God be of two parts – good and evil?

'It is only in your minds that you conceive good and evil, only in your hearts do you think and feel it. These thoughts and feelings have nothing to do with the true God which is the '**Father**' within you, bringing you every good thing if you will but believe this is so.

'It is your belief in good and evil, and the good and evil in your hearts, which brings you sickness.

'In reality, you live within the Kingdom of Heaven, and the Kingdom of Heaven is within you, and you are governed by the '**Father**', but because you believe in the punishments from God, believe that only sacrifices in the Temple will save you, believe that you are heir to sickness, poverty, misery, you create with your minds, the very things you do not want.

'Be not downcast – rejoice and be glad and **know** that those who experience lack, far from being punished and abandoned by God, even though they have sinned, are truly blest.

'The man who has nothing is rich in the **Power** of the **'Father'** if he will but heed **It**, trust **It**, and live within **It**.

'For when your bellies are filled, and your bodies know ease, and your minds and hearts are comfortable, you have no urgent and present need of the **'Father'** to become active within you to fulfill your needs. You believe by your own thoughts and hands do you fulfill your own needs easily, so when you speak of 'God' you can only speak of what you have heard spoken by others – you, yourself, have no direct experience of 'God'.

'Consider the rich. They are sunk, bound, bogged down in their own riches. They get up in the mornings and go about their daily business, knowing nothing about the **Power of the 'Father'** within them. They think the thoughts which will increase their riches, the thoughts which will boost the 'self', they send out commands which will burden those who serve them, they live their lives according to their own choosing. Therefore, because they draw their limited life only from their own limited human thinking arising from their bodily minds and hearts, they get sick and experience as much misery as does the man who has nothing. They do not realise they are only half alive because they are not in touch with the **SOURCE OF LIFE**, the 'Father' within them. Neither do they ever 'see' that much of the good which has come into their lives is not of their own devising but is the **LOVE WORK** of the '**Father**' hidden within them.

'The religious leaders are at ease in their own comforts of positions of authority. They have no need of anything beyond their own physical satisfactions. Because they have no personal knowledge of God, they must read, from their Holy Books, the words of holy men spoken a thousand years ago, and tell the people what they think the words mean.

'But all they speak is drawn from their own little minds which are imprisoned in the comforts of their lives, sunk in the expectations of what they shall eat and drink and what apparel they will wear to impress the people. They know nothing of the inspiration which gave birth to the words spoken by the prophets all those centuries ago. Neither do they know whether those words are what you really need to hear at this moment, for times have changed.

'Believe me, the rich men and the religious leaders are strong in earthly things and do not want to be moved on from all that they regard as secure and everlasting in their traditions and observances. Any deviation will shake the foundations of their beliefs and therefore of their lives, and so they build mental defences against the inflow of the **Power** of the 'Father'. They too, get sick, and they, in their own way, know misery as do you who have no earthly comforts.

'There is no difference between you who have little in life and those who have it all, for rich and poor alike get sick, make enemies, find themselves alone.

'But the potential for you gaining more than the religious and rich can ever hope to gain, in health, happiness, good fellowship, achievement in your chosen way of life, is enormous. And when it is all accomplished, you will **know that the opportunities, the ability, the inspiration** all came from the 'Father' within, because you will **know** you could never have done such things if you had not asked the **'Father'** within you to help you use all your talents, to put plenty of food in your cupboards, and clothes on your back and happiness and a good life for your children.

'All these things will the **'Father' do** for you, if you will but ask – and believe – and know – and remember at all times – that it is the **'Father Nature'** to create and then provide abundantly for all **Its** creation.

'Just as you would not wilfully deprive your children of the things they need, so will your **'Father'** never wilfully deprive you of all you need for a happy life. If you are poor, it is because you have not yet understood the **nature** of the 'Father'; nor have you understood that you must work **with** the **'Father'** to fulfill your own needs. You must immediately grasp the **divine opportunities** presented to you to help you forward.

'If only I could show you and make you see and **believe** that when you mourn, your sadness is known to the 'Father'. In time, your sadness will be changed to joy, if you will but turn to the **'Father'** and watch the work the **'Father Love'** is doing in you. You will find comfort beyond anything you thought possible.

'How blessed you are when you are hungry and when you are thirsty, for your needs are known to the **'Father'**. Shortly those needs will be satisfied if you cease to wail and begin to pray to the **'Father'** and ask – believing you will receive.

'How can you believe that to eat and be properly clothed you must first go to the Temple and offer burnt sacrifices of the **'Father's'** own living creatures to pay for your sinning? Can you not see that the living things you burn have been created to enjoy life even as you have been created to enjoy life? They have been created to be a blessing and blest on this earth even as you have been born to be both blessing and blest, for this is the nature of **'Father Love'** revealed in **Its** creation.

'If you remember that 'what you truly believe', is what you get, can you not see that this Jewish belief in Temple sacrifices of living things will bring you nothing but misery?

'Believe in punishment and punishment is what you will get. Believe in killing and destruction as being the right way to reach God, and that is what you will experience – killing and destruction.

'If you are hungry and thirsty, it is because you are turning away from the **'Father'** within you.

'By indulging your fearful thoughts, anxieties and feelings of hopelessness, **you** are creating the very conditions you want to rectify. You are doing all these bad things to yourselves.

'Therefore, even more blest are you when you hunger and thirst for goodness and for contact with the **'Father'** within you, because then you will surely be filled up a hundred times over.

'Blessed are you when you are attacked and robbed because you will see 'God-in-action' when you stand still in perfect trust and see deliverance taking place.

'Blessed are you when you are caught up in conflict, yet you can still care about your fellow man and be the peace maker. You carry the love in your heart which is of the **'Father'** and you are truly a child of the **'Father'**.

'Blessed are you when you have been deeply wronged by another yet can forgive and can show mercy, abstaining from seeking justice or the means to persecute him. You put yourself directly in harmony with the love which is 'God-active-within you' and even so will you be spared in times of trouble.

'Most blessed of all are the pure in heart, for such as these have rid themselves of all anger, hatred, vindictiveness, unkindness, envy,

72

hardness of heart – and stand before the world as Love- made-visible. They will know the Reality called 'God' and they will know the Reality is the 'Father' within them.

'How can I help you see this great truth? How can I help you see the reality of the Kingdom of Heaven, the Kingdom of God?

'You do not have to look up at the sky because that is not where you will see the activity of the '**Father**' so clearly that it must surely re-inforce your faith. This is where people, down the centuries, have made the big mistake of turning in towards their dreaming, their imagination, and creating for themselves a Jehovah which does not exist. You will not find the '**Father**' some place in the heavens above you. The '**Father**' is in no special place but everywhere around you and within everything.

'You can see the '**Father's**' marvellous work. Look around you at the growing things, the wheat, the grass, the flowers, the trees and birds, and in every living thing, you will see the mysterious and wonderful work of the 'Father' ceaselessly active. It is here that the 'Father' is perfectly in control. You can see that there is perfect law and order, growth, development, and eventually the harvest to bless both man and beast and birds.

'Consider the way that a man after tilling his fields, will scatter seed over the earth and cover it over. He packs up his tools and goes home, content that eventually, if there is sufficient rain; there will be food for him to feed his children. For many days, he sleeps and wakes and does nothing more to his plants, but when he visits them he will see the blades of green pushing through the soil. Later, he will return and see the growth of stalks and leaves, and later on again he will see the forming of the seed, and then one day he will see that the grain is plump and golden and ready to harvest. Meanwhile, all this growth has taken place without any help from him. The wheat has grown in a marvellous way that he cannot explain. Is it magic? **No, it is the work of the 'Father', the Power, Loving Intelligence** throughout the universe, which inspires the work and respires through it; it is the activity of the '**Father' which is the INTELLIGENT LIFE OF THE UNIVERSE.**

'When you enter the Kingdom of God, you have a good feeling. You feel happy and joyous. Can you imagine how a woman would feel if she lost a large sum of money and wondered how she would feed her children? The woman of the house would be in tears and would sweep the house so thoroughly that there would not be a speck of dust – then – hidden in a dark corner she finds the treasured piece of silver and immediately her tears are dried, she begins to smile and then feels so alive and so joyous that she rushes out of her house to call in her neighbours to have a celebration party. Where she had thought she had lost everything, she was now rich after all.

'So is it when you find the Kingdom of Heaven – the Kingdom of God. Instead of tears and fears, and hunger and sickness, you find the peace, joy, plenty, and health of the Kingdom of God. You will never experience any kind of lack again.

'The Kingdom of God can also be likened to a very rich man who was a dealer in pearls. All his life, he had wanted to find a special pearl which would outshine all others, it would be flawless and perfect and he would be the envy of every other dealer. One day, he found such a pearl, beautiful beyond imagining, perfect beyond all others. He sold everything he owned, he abandoned all that he had accumulated, to buy this pearl and was happy beyond all dreaming.

'What does this mean? It means that all the things he had previously valued in his life – his richly furnished house, his valuables, his way of life, plenty of food and drink, he gladly gave them all up in order to possess the treasure beyond price – **the knowledge** leading him into the **Kingdom of God** <u>where happiness is a state of mind which cannot be touched by the outer world with all its cares and worries.</u>

'The 'Kingdom of God' is within you, you enter the 'Kingdom of God' when you realize fully that the 'Father' is active at all times within you. It is a state of mind, of perception and understanding that the Reality behind and within all things visible, is the 'Father' and is beautiful and perfect and that all the things which are contrary to beauty, harmony, health, abundance are the creations of man's wrong thinking.

'How I have grieved over you who suffer, but you do not need to suffer if you listen to what I have to tell you. But I must warn you that the Path leading into the Kingdom of Heaven is difficult to follow because it means that – first – you have to deal with your 'self'.

'Why is it the 'self' you have to deal with? Because out of your desire to protect and promote your own personal good come all your selfish thoughts, words and actions.

'You will probably ask 'Why should I have to worry about these? If what you say is true, that there is no punishment, that 'God' sees not our evil – then why should we be concerned about the way we behave?'

'There is so much here to be learnt that I hardly know where to begin.

'As I have explained you draw your LIFE from the 'Father', therefore, you draw your capacity to think and love from the 'Father'. Even as 'Father Intelligence' is creative, so is your consciousness creative. With your minds and hearts you actually form the plans of your own lives and experiences.

'And what kind of lives do you plan and form in your minds? If someone annoys or hurts you, you retaliate in some way or another, you believe that if your eye is taken, you must expect the adversary's eye in return. You believe that whoever kills should be killed as punishment and compensation, you believe that whoever robs you should pay the price, that whoever steals your wife, should be stoned along with your wife. You believe in the extraction of payment for every evil thing that comes your way. Since it is human nature to hurt others, and you have been taught to retaliate, your lives are a continual scene of warfare, warfare in the home amongst husbands, wives, children, and neighbours, and public figures and between nations. Your **'Father'** knows nothing of this warfare in your lives, but knows the stress in your minds and bodies arising from this warfare but can do nothing – nothing to ease your pain – until you yourselves stop the warfare. You yourselves must cease your fighting and live in peace with your family, neighbours, employers, public figures and other countries.

'Only then, can the 'Father' LOVE WORK take place in your minds, hearts, bodies, and lives.

'Only then will you be able to recognise and see the Love Work being done in you – and for you by the 'Father'.

'Remember also the great LAW 'YOU REAP EXACTLY AS YOU SOW'.

'You cannot pick figs from brambles, or grapes from thorn trees, or harvest wheat from weeds. Think about this and understand this parable because it is very important to you – not only today – but also throughout all your days and years to come, even into eternity.

'So, if you want to change your lives – change your thoughts,

Change your words arising from those thoughts,
Change your actions arising from the thoughts.

'What is in your minds will create all your experiences, your sickness, poverty, unhappiness and despair.'

A man shouted out to me: 'Tell us, Teacher, how do we remain peaceful with our neighbours when they, themselves, will give us no peace?'

I said to him, smiling: 'When your neighbour comes to you and says he has to travel some distance away and does not want to go alone and asks you to go with him – what do you do?'

The man laughed. 'If my neighbour wanted to take me away from what I was doing, I would not be pleased. I would tell him to find some one else to go with him as I was busy.'

'And how would your neighbour feel?' I asked. The man shrugged. 'I don't know.'

'And next time you needed him to do you a favour, how will he respond to your asking?' The man was no longer laughing. He did not reply.

Another man said: 'He will swear at him and tell him to go elsewhere for help.'

I said to the people: 'He has answered rightly. And how will he feel?' I pointed to the man who had first spoken, smiling at him.

A woman shouted above the laughter: 'He will tell everyone he meets what a selfish and miserable neighbour he has. Perhaps he will want to hurt him in some way.'

There were shouts of agreement and I nodded: 'Yes, he will have forgotten that he was once asked by his neighbour to walk one or two miles with him and he refused. He will not see the LAW of REAPING and SOWING at work in his life. He set it in motion when he refused to go a mile with his neighbour and now he is reaping of his attitudes and actions. Of what use to be angry when he has created the situation all by himself?'

The people laughed and nodded and spoke to one another. Never before had they heard such knowledge of human behaviour. Here was an entirely new teaching.

I said to them: 'I advise you, when your neighbour comes to you asking you to walk a mile with them or anything else that will make him more at ease and happy, first think about what you would like him to do for you if you also have a need? How would you like him to respond to your request?'

A murmur swept through the crowd and I could see that they understood what I was telling them.

'In fact, if your neighbour asks you to go one mile, do it with a happy, easy agreement and be prepared to go on to do two miles if necessary. When you refuse people, you do not realise it, but you tighten up your minds and bodies ready to protect yourself from being forced to do something you do not want to do. You tighten up your minds and bodies and the **'Father'** is tightened up also and cannot do **Its LOVE WORK** within you, and out of this tightening comes sickness.

'Again, you may meet someone sorely in need, who is cold and unhappy. He may ask you for your coat. Don't pass him by, glaring at him.' Some people laughed. They knew this was what they would do. 'No, give him your coat, and if he is really cold, give him your cloak also. Go your way, rejoicing.'

'Rejoicing?' A disbelieving voice asked.

I laughed and said: 'Yes, my friend, – rejoicing! Firstly, because you had a coat and a cloak to give, and then rejoicing because you realise that now you have a lack of a coat and cloak yourself, your **'Father'** within you will shortly return the coat and cloak to you in some surprising way. If, however, you give him coat and cloak and then continue walking, grumbling to yourself – 'Now why did I do that? I was foolish. Now I will be cold instead of him, and people will laugh at me because I have given my coat and cloak and left myself with nothing – and what will my wife say when I get home?'

The people were nodding and laughing, enjoying the picture of the man who gives away coat and cloak and then remembers what an evil thing he has done to himself. I knew that very often, they did deprive themselves to help others – and then regretted their generosity afterwards.

I waited a moment and then shouted in a loud voice to get their full attention: 'But have I not told you that you REAP as you SOW? Have I not told you clearly that your thoughts, words, actions create your future circumstances? So what do you want to SOW to REAP after you have given your coat and cloak to the stranger? Do you want your gifts restored to you – or do you want to be without coat and cloak for a long, long time, because that is what will happen to you if go on your way, angry and upset because you gave away your coat and cloak. Your words and actions will seal, make hard like rock, the poverty you have brought upon yourself by giving away your coat and cloak.'

The people were no longer smiling and laughing, they were very quiet and listening intently.

'Remember, first do to others what you would have them do to you, then there will be peace and contentment in your minds and hearts and the '**Father**' will be able to do **Its LOVE WORK** within your bodies, minds and hearts. Give and give abundantly, and rejoice that you have gifts to give to those in need, because as you give so will your gifts be restored to you in the way that you most need them. Give with happy hearts, give in the faith and knowledge that where there is lack in your lives, so will the '**Father**' do **Its LOVE WORK** abundantly in you – and for you.

Do nothing with heavy heart because a heavy heart is what you will continue to have.

Give everything with joyous spirit, that everything in your life may bring to you only joy and spiritual insight.'

A man commented: 'This is against man's nature. It is natural to be anxious about the future. Clothes are expensive, food is not easily come by. Life is a constant struggle.'

I answered him in a loud voice because he was only saying what I knew most of my listeners were thinking.

'But you do not know for sure that tomorrow you will be struggling to live. You do not know that tomorrow you won't have a splendid job, or any other wonderful thing come your way. You do not know this – but you are making very sure for yourself that there will not be a marvellous job, or some other wonderful opportunity in your life – because you are creating the circumstances of your tomorrows.'

He was angry. 'I am? How am I doing that?'

'Have I not just told you?' I turned to the people laughing. 'Tell me, how has this man, up front, in the red cloak, created his tomorrows?'

The crowd was silent, then a very young man, Mark, shouted to me: 'I know. He said he would be struggling to buy food and clothes. You have told us that what we think and talk about is what we will get.'

'Exactly,' I said. 'You are a very clever boy. You have understood. Take care that you do not create for yourself the things you do not want. And I will be happy for you to become my disciple when you are older and your parents will let you go.'

Some of the people laughed – but some did not. I could see that they did not believe a word I was saying.

'You will never enter the Kingdom of Heaven by being anxious. If you are having a hard time today, why moan about it? Will it make you feel better if you go about complaining, will your crying brighten your day? And if you are anxious about your tomorrows, you are making your tomorrows burdensome and weary even before you get to them. Why do it? What good will it do for you? When did anxiety ever accomplish anything for you? You might as well try to make yourself taller by being anxious that you are short.

'No, do not dwell on the things you do not have. Dwell on the things **which can be yours** if you turn to the '**Father**' within you and ask in perfect faith, believing you will receive – and I tell you without fear of contradiction, that you will receive. But you must ask properly – believing. You will receive nothing if you ask, but, at the same time, wonder whether you have been heard or whether the '**Father**' will **feel** like giving you what you want. This is the human way of giving, but not the way of the '**Father**' which gives abundantly and fulfills your needs.

'The '**Father**' always pours **Its** gift out upon you, gifts of food in plenty, clothes, house, friends, providing you yourself have a clean heart and mind, and providing you constantly rely on the '**Father**' as your moment-by-moment support.

'If you pray and do not receive, do not, for one moment, think it is because there is no '**Father**', or the '**Father**' does not listen to you, rather, you must ask yourselves **what is in you** that is preventing the '**Father**' LOVE WORK being done in and for you.

'If you go to the altar to pray or offer a gift, and on the way there you remember that you have quarrelled with someone, turn around and go to that person and make your peace with him. Then, when you approach the '**Father**' in prayer, **you will have a clean and pure mind**, and you will be heard by the '**Father**' and the '**Father**' will be able to respond, giving you all you need, in the peace and quietness of your being.

'If you still cannot believe that the '**Father**' cares for its creation, look about you at the radiant flowers in the fields, how beautiful they are! Consider the brilliant thought which has gone into their design, their beauty! Where will you find the colours that you see in their petals? With all his wisdom, Solomon himself was not able to have such beautiful clothes made for himself. See the way the flowers attract the bees and the bees help to bring next seasons' seeds, to make your world beautiful and to give you food. Why can you not believe and trust in the '**Father**' when the world around you is planned, designed and cared for in such a wonderful way?

'But remember – these living plants and trees, unlike mankind, cannot complain about their lot, and see themselves as hungry and naked, and so they do not 'undo' the work the '**Father**' does in them.

'It is you with your continual complaining and talking about what you lack, your aggression towards each other, your insistence on retribution, your criticism and slandering, which makes your lack – and your sickness – consistent, day after day.

'I have told you all these things to prepare you, who are sick, for healing. You cannot be healed unless you believe with all your hearts that healing will take place. Remember that sickness of the body arises from an illness within the mind, such as your bad temper, resentments, angers, hatreds.

'Father Love' is the source of all health, therefore all thoughts and feelings contrary to **'Father Love'** bring sickness.

'Just as all your evils and sickness begin in the mind – **so does your good**.

'Have as much care for your neighbour as you have for yourself.

'Bless your neighbour when you have an argument, pray for him when he is harsh with you, help him out in any way you can at all times, even if he turns his face from you, because then you are constructing good in your mind and thoughts, and good will be the harvest of your sowing. Not only this – you are bringing your mind into harmony and attunement with the **'Father'** within you, which is **Perfect Love. Under these conditions, the 'Father' can do Its perfect LOVE WORK in you.'**

When I had finished speaking, the people brought their sick to me and according to their faith were they healed.

****

LETTER 3 will describe more of **Christ's teachings** and explain the events leading to his crucifixion and death. He describes in poignant detail, his last Supper with his disciples when he found himself alone in spirit because his disciples, till the last, refused to believe he would be crucified. Repeatedly, he was misunderstood, and he realised again how little he had managed to teach anyone during his three years of **missionary work**. He was glad to be leaving!

LETTER 3

(Since these Letters take you into a spiritual-mental dimension transcending the human plane of activities and concerns, they will be best absorbed if preceded by a time of stillness and relaxation. Quieten your minds, if possible, going into a state of inner silence of thought. It is only when you are in this completely receptive state that these Letters will penetrate your human thought with their reality.)

My BOUNDLESS CELESTIAL LOVE impels me to return again and again to write to mankind, with the intention that finally – as many of you who are ready to receive it – will possess the knowledge which will enable you to transcend your humanhood and merge into 'Father Consciousness' – the true 'Love Consciousness' in which are realised all things bountiful and beautiful.

As I have said previously and want to repeat, my entire mission on earth was prompted by LOVE and was directed ONLY at teaching the Truth of Existence, for without this knowledge, there is no hope of redemption from the travail which mankind is born to endure.

I know this statement will bring much grief to sincere and dedicated followers of the Christian religion, and those who have centred their entire faith on the person of 'Jesus'. But I tell you truly; to succeed in ridding yourselves of the humanhood which holds you back from the full realisation of UNIVERSAL TRUTH, and the understanding of the true nature of the *'spiritual-human' condition* I termed the 'Kingdom of God', *you must turn away from the old dogmas of 'salvation by the blood of the lamb', the Trinity, and other beliefs, and come with perfectly open receptive minds to the* TRUTH *of* EXISTENCE.

No other salvation is possible. 'God' cannot 'save' you, since, in ignorance of the facts of existence, mankind will continue to make the same earthbound mistakes till the end of time, thus creating his own sickness and misery.

Furthermore, no matter what a man's belief may be in regard to 'salvation from sins', this is a human fallacy, since the Law of Cause and Effect is imponderable and an intrinsic – inherent – natural characteristic of existence. You cannot divorce effects from causation, nor can you erase causation and still have effects. In every level of Being this is Truth.

You may now be sufficiently advanced in your thinking to be able to receive the following fundamental truth concerning your earthly existence.

The Law of 'Cause and Effect', 'Reaping and Sowing' is the visible effect of what you call 'electromagnetism', and no one who has any knowledge of science would expect 'God' to set aside the laws of electromagnetism, which are those of 'activity-bonding-rejection'.

'Activity-Bonding-Rejection' or 'Movement-Attraction-Repulsion' are the fundamental IMPULSES of EXISTENCE and of HUMAN CONSCIOUSNESS itself, which have brought about your visible forms in life, and are the only 'instruments' or 'tools' of creation. They are responsible for the formation of substance or 'matter' and also for the development of individualised forms and finally of personality itself in all living entities.

Since these Laws are fundamental to your individualised existence, it is impossible to set them aside. Therefore, you cannot ignore the problems inherent in your individualised existence and believe that 'God' will save you from them. Your only hope of final escape, of stepping off the treadmill of human experience, is to recognise and acknowledge them and then work minute-by-minute to transcend them and eventually merge, in purity of mind, heart and action, and become 'one' with Universal Love Consciousness – the 'Father' which does the LOVE WORK.

At the same time, as you grow in awareness of the true NATURE of the 'Father' 'within you and transcending you, and all around you', you will come to have undeviating faith that, in every circumstance, you can draw upon the inspiration, power, and upliftment directly from the 'Father' within and around you.

You will come to KNOW it is really the 'Father' which supports and guides you into the Kingdom of 'Father Love Consciousness'.

It will become abundantly clear to you that whilst the 'Father' is universal, It is also individual for you. It knows you, is aware of your thinking and your problems. Within the 'Father Love Consciousness' are the perfect solutions awaiting your recognition. When you recognise them, you will be released from pain when you become pliable and willing to listen.

Until you are willing to listen, you will never be filled with the 'Father Love Consciousness'.

I will tell you a parable. Imagine a child screaming and kicking because he wants ice cream.

All the time, he is making this noise, his father is waiting patiently at the door of his room to show him that he has brought him ice cream and _fruit._

You may think this parable is improbable, nonetheless it is true. Mothers will remember times when children have been inconsolable over something, refusing to listen to what mother is trying so hard to tell them, and yet mother has the solution waiting for them the moment they stop making a noise and dry their tears.

I can see the travail of people and their crying and weeping and my compassion is boundless.

You are heard but within the context of your present consciousness, there is little I can do for you. I cannot penetrate the thongs and chains of your years of ignorant thinking and acting.

I see the pain perpetuated in the churches, in services and pulpits by ignorant sermons. I see nations and their people trying so hard to grapple with the difficulties arising from their traditional values, cultures, and religious beliefs. I see the limitations in their daily living, the lack of fulfilment of their needs and purposes, and the suffering emanating from relationships of every kind.

The collective consciousness emanating from the world is a miasma of fears, resentment, angers, emotional turbulence of passionate desires, revenge and exhaustion,inter-threaded with compassion, determination to uplift world consciousness, dedication to the search for unconditional love by those who have received inspiration and a degree of enlightenment.

I come close to people who call on me and work with them to relieve their distress, but their mindset and beliefs are so strongly imprinted in their brains, that my Truth cannot reach through and bring new knowledge to their minds. Many people have heard, albeit briefly and imperfectly, but have lacked the courage to accept new ideas and speak out. Furthermore

the time has not been right to reach through barriers of human consciousness to teach you.

But now the time is right. You have moved into a new dispensation of vibrational frequencies which will enable you to more easily rise from the materiality of the previous age. This may sound a strange statement, but there is a universal store of knowledge regarding energies you do not begin to understand. At this time, there is no earthly mind capable of understanding. It is only possible for you to 'imagine' the spectrum of energy, which is not truth.

It will help you, therefore, if you can accept my statements, taking them on trust, because they are true. You are moving into new frequencies of vibration pertaining to 'human consciousness' which will enable you to move forward into the spiritual-mental development I described in Letter 1.

Since I have diverged, I must now repeat: You can no more escape the most fundamental **Laws of Existence** regarding your thinking and feeling – sowing and reaping – than you can escape the laws of electromagnetism in your material world, for electromagnetism is the IMPULSE producing the Law of sowing and reaping just as electromagnetism produces form within the fundamental field of energy particles.

Therefore it is not possible to continue to believe in Christian dogma and also try to follow these Letters because dogma, relating to 'salvation by my death on the cross', the Trinity, physical resurrection from the dead, and use of incense and set forms of prayer, are fallacious and the facts now presented to you in these Letters are Truth. The dogma and the sacramental trimmings are, what you would term 'red herrings', to gain your attention and allegiance but obscuring the Truth of my teachings.

Therefore, these Letters had to be written.

The only way I could reach the world at this present time when it is poised to enter a new mind/emotional dispensation, was by using a receptive, obedient and deprogrammed mind to receive the instruction and do the manual work for me.

These Letters offer the only true means by which people will find the path to the spiritual dimension in which all human error fades away and only love remains.

Anything else which may be said is purely human rationalisation and reason – and these are not TRUTH.

People are seeking new ways to resolve old problems, particularly in America, but until they understand the true nature of LIFE, the ego, and the Laws of Existence, they will but strengthen the pull of the 'ego' and their pain will continue.

Remember, as I record for you in the following pages, the simple Truth I spoke two millennia ago, this Truth remains constant and consistent.

Therefore, it is only possible to deepen your understanding of Truth, not to alter it.

Have you realised as you have read the first two **Letters**, that all I spoke to the people of Palestine was a direct outcome of my having perceived the **'reality of existence'** in the desert – **that nothing was solid?**

Have you remembered that, in my transcendent state, as I looked at the rocks, sand, mountains, water below me in the Dead Sea, all appeared to be as a **'shimmer of motes'?**

Rock, sand, mountains, water were differentiated one from the other, only by the difference in the intensity of the 'shimmer of motes' and by the apparent density of motes within the shimmer. There is no other way I can describe what I saw when on earth or convey the facts concerning the true substance of 'matter' and the apparently solid fabric and construction of your world.

In modern speech, you would probably call the 'shimmer of motes', a vibration of particles.

Perhaps you could combine the two terms and describe the most fundamental visible 'reality', as a **'shimmer of particles'**. This conveys the sense of the 'light glow' in which I saw the particles dance. Having said all the foregoing as introduction to my account of my activities in Palestine, let me take you to another day, two thousand years ago, when the sun shone, and the sky was a clear, clear blue, and I started to climb the hills 'with my disciples, in an effort to retire to rest, meditate and pray.

But this was not to be. We had thought to escape, but despite telling the people of our intentions, we were first followed by a few who then shouted to others that we were going into the hills.

Although we begged them to return to their homes, the few eventually grew into a great concourse of people tagging along behind us. They were insistent that I should speak to them.

You may wonder why they were so anxious to listen to me.

Intuitively, they knew that I spoke words of LIFE to them.

Always, I showed them the activity of the '**Father**' around them and this gave them hope and helped them to see the world with new vision.

I spoke to them of **LOVE** and they felt comforted.

This was why I could say to them, knowing that they would understand and agree with me:

'Come unto me, you who are weary and heavy laden and I will give you rest. My yoke is light and my burden easy.'

They knew that when I spoke these words, as I frequently did, I was comparing the rules and laws of the Jewish leaders with the Truth I was presenting to the people.

So it was, that when I was besought by the people to teach them, what could I do but sit down on a rock above them – and teach.

I was determined that, if they had come this far to hear me, they would hear something they would remember and possibly speak about all their lives.

I knew that despite all I had told them about the '**Father**' and '**Father Love**', they were still apprehensive of rejection by 'God'. Although I had tried to help them understand that the '**Father**' of which I spoke, was not the personalised 'God' which they worshipped, I knew very well that they were confused. Although I had told them again and again that the '**Father**' was within them, they were still worried that they might incur punishment from on high by believing my words.

What should I teach them that day, I asked the **'Father'**? Then I noticed the goats and sheep feeding on the hillside under the vigilant care of their shepherd and my message for the day entered my mind. I stood up and shouted so that my voice would carry to the back of the crowds:

'You see these sheep and goats feeding on the hills. The sheep are in one place and the goats in another.

'Consider the sheep. They are patient and non-aggressive towards each other even when huddled tightly in a corner of their pen. They feed quietly, never claiming ground which is not theirs, leaving the pasture closely cropped but not damaged, allowing the grass to recover after they have passed over it. Most importantly, they listen to their shepherd's voice. Therefore, he takes good care of them. He guides them into the best pastures and he sleeps with them at night that they may not be threatened or attacked by dogs or robbers.

'Look at the goats, how they scramble and leap over the rocks and get themselves into awkward or dangerous places. They tear at the brambles and the foliage of trees. They are despoilers. Were it not for their use to mankind, there would be no place for them other than to be tethered all day or put out into the desert.

'I look at you below me, and I know that amongst you are many sheep – and, also among you are many goats.'

There were a few angry murmurs but, on the whole, people good-naturedly jostled and ribbed one another, pointing out the 'goats' and laughing and nodding. It was good to see them laughing and so I continued.

'You can tell the sheep by their homes, the way they treat their neighbours, and the way they are regarded by all in their community. You can likewise tell the goats – are they likely to have many friends?' There was a loud roar from the crowd: 'No-o-o-o!' followed by much laughter.

'Does the shepherd follow after the goats and care for them – or must they look after themselves and come home by themselves to be milked at night?'

Again the crowd laughed and shouted various replies, some of them very amusing and witty.

'And so is it with you who are sheep and those of you who are goats – you are protected by the '**Father**' if you are sheep, and you are not protected by the '**Father**' if you are goats, because you are obstinately following your own desires every day and possibly leaving a trail of destruction behind you. Tell me – can the '**Father**' protect the people who are goats?'

The crowd was silent but listening intently.

'Will you say then, that the '**Father**' is angry with the goats and will not protect them, or will you rather say that just as the shepherd cares for his sheep and would care for the goats if they would allow it, the '**Father**' loves sheep and goats equally but is powerless to protect equally because of the goats' natural behaviour?'

'Also, consider the feeding habits of sheep and goats. Sheep are content to eat grass only, for which their stomachs are perfectly designed, but the goat will eat anything he comes across, having no respect whatever for his constitution. So is it with people who have no regard for what they will feed their minds with, since they have no fixed goal or clear purpose. Like goats, they do not recognise when mental food is harmful or is taking them in the direction they should not go in their daily lives or whether it will lead them into harmful myth or dangerous fallacy.

'They roam, picking up the mental equivalent of brambles, old shoes, bits of cloth, leaves, thistles, weeds, for they lack good sense.'

A man called out to me: 'Master, what if a person who is a sheep, makes a mistake, and gets himself into trouble, will the '**Father**' then abandon him?'

I asked him a question by way of answering him: 'What does the shepherd do when one of his sheep falls into a pit, or tumbles over a cliff, or gets caught in brambles? I will tell you. The shepherd leaves his flock and swiftly seeks out the missing sheep and will not leave it until he has brought it to safety. So is it with the '**Father**' – not even a sheep can avoid doing wrong in one way or another, but rest assured that the '**Father**' **immediately responds to its bleating and rescues it. And if a goat should begin to behave like a sheep and heed the shepherd's voice, then he too will come under the protection of the shepherd and will be cared for even as sheep are cared for.**

'So it is with you and the **Kingdom of Heaven – the Kingdom of 'God'.'**

Several voices called out, asking me to tell them what I meant by the **'Kingdom of God'**.

'What I am telling you is unlike anything you have yet heard from any prophet at any time.

'**Do not try to understand what I am saying by thinking of what you have been told by your Teachers. They can only repeat from the scriptures and have no personal knowledge of the Kingdom of God or Heaven.**

'**God is not contained within any one place but is everywhere as are the heavens and air above you.**

'**The Holy Word spoke truly when it says "In God you live, move and have your being".**

'**For the Kingdom of God is above, around and also within you – and you can enter the Kingdom of God.'**

People shouted impatiently: 'But what is it?'

'**It is a state of mind and heart which is fully possessed by 'God' – your 'Father'. When you are in this state, the 'Father' is the head of your body and directs everything you do and all of your life.' Some of the people grumbled. 'How can that be?'**

'**It is possible to be so emptied of self – of selfish desires, enmities, angers, jealousies, greed, vindictiveness that only 'God' is left in control within your mind and heart.'**

'**What happens then?' asked a woman.**

'**Then you enter into the 'State of Being' which is 'God-directed'. It is altogether beautiful and glorious. It is love, it is generosity, it is caring for other people as you care for yourself, it is non- judgmental since you accept other people exactly as they are, knowing that they too are 'God' children and are equally in the 'Father' care. It is happiness beyond measure, beyond description, it is joy in the beauty of the world, it is life unlimited and increased energy, it is health and it is the fulfilment of your every need before you even know that you have such a need.'**

91

'Why do the Rabbis not tell us these things?' several voices complained.

'Because I alone have seen the 'Father', I alone know how the world has been made and the laws of existence. And because I know all these things, you have but to come to me and ask and I will reveal all that has been given to me. I tell you truly – as many of you as believes – and understands – and seeks to put my words into daily practice – will be saved from the tribulation that mankind endures. You suffer because you do not understand how you have been created, and the true purposes for which you were born.

'You were born to be sons and heirs of the 'Father', you were born to enjoy all that the 'Father' is in Itself, and all that It can give you. But you turn your backs on all the glory of the kingdom and try to find pleasures in earthly things. Whilst you do this you will never find the Kingdom of God nor enter into the Kingdom of Heaven.'

'How shall we enter the Kingdom?'

'I have already told you. You enter the **Kingdom of Heaven** when you repent of all that you are in your heart and mind. When you take your evil to the 'Father' and ask forgiveness and pray for the strength to be cleansed of your evil thoughts, words and deeds, and you finally get rid of them, then you may be sure that you are about to find the **Kingdom of Heaven**. When you have accomplished this, you will find that your attitudes towards others are changing, for the '**Father**' will be doing Its Love Work within you. You will be free of the chains and thongs of evil desires and deeds which previously bound you and made you a captive in the world. More than this, you will find that the '**Father**' does satisfy your every need.'

A woman shouted: 'I have a need at this very moment, Master, I am hungry'.

The people laughed but then several voices joined in, saying: 'We have been with you many hours, you made us walk and walk before you would consent to teach us. We have shown you we are the good sheep. Will you not help us and satisfy our hunger?'

I realised that they spoke the truth and felt deep compassion for them. They had followed after me not just for healing but because they longed to know the **Truth** as it had been given to me by the '**Father**'. I had told them that the '**Father**' satisfies their needs. This would be an opportunity to show them the power of faith and the **Power** that is 'God'. I would prove to them that nothing is impossible when you truly believe as I believed and perceived.

I called my disciples to me and told them to find out if there were any present who had food. They found a young boy with loaves and fishes and brought them to me.

I withdrew some way from the crowd and quietly contemplated the loaves and fishes, **knowing** that they were but **'God' Mind Power'**, the substance of all 'matter', made visible.

I **knew** that **'God' Mind Power'** was limitless and powerfully active within my consciousness.

I knew that the **nature** of the **'Father'** is the fulfilment of need.

As I blest the food, I felt the **POWER** flow fully through my mind, body and hands and I **knew** the people's hunger would be satisfied. I did not know how this would be, I just knew it would.

I then took the baskets of food and told the disciples to distribute it, **feeling** absolutely certain that everyone would have as much food as they needed.

As it was broken and passed around, so did it multiply itself until all the throng were fed and satisfied. There were several baskets of left-overs.

In this way, I demonstrated that:

matter' – whatever is visible within the universe – is **mind/consciousness made visible through the vibration of the 'motes'** (which science terms particles) changes in the 'vibration of motes', hence changes in 'matter', take place as a result of a powerfully directed, disciplined, focused movement/imagery in **mind/consciousness energy when one acts purely out of a 'love consciousness' to accomplish good for others, the only limits to the 'Father' Love Work' within the world, ARE THE LIMITS WHICH MAN'S MIND SETS UPON THAT WORK such changes in 'matter' can only take place when the consciousness of 'man' is perfectly in harmony and united with 'Father Universal Consciousness'.**

Although there was amazement amongst the people and my disciples, when the people were fed in this way, **not one of them understood** how such a thing was accomplished.

They could only conclude this was the greatest miracle they had ever seen. It also confirmed their belief that I was the Son of God.

Another day, I was sitting under a tree outside Bethesda, surrounded by people who had brought their sick to be healed. As always, they marvelled at the return of life and health to these people and wondered how such miracles could be done.

Again, I tried to make them understand the **Power of Faith**.

In the gospels, it has been stated I said that if a man had faith the size of a mustard seed he would be able to move mountains.

This statement is a misinterpretation of what I truly said and it reveals how little my disciples and gospellers understood my teachings when we were on earth.

If a person were to have 'faith' the size of a mustard seed – what does that mean? How can you measure faith in such a way?

Faith is faith.

It is a 'power of total conviction' in the mind, possessing the mind and cannot be restricted in 'size'.

Faith, arising out of your need to believe in something, because such a belief will serve your purposes in some way, can be powerful and strong, but never could it be estimated in 'size'!

Belief is even stronger. Belief is the offspring of hearsay and logic. Because you have heard something and been convinced that what you have heard or read is true, you develop a deep belief in what you have heard. You believe it to be true. You believe in a total, complete way which defies contradiction.

I was constantly telling the people: 'Believe you will receive – and you will receive'.

However, I knew at the time, that it would be well nigh impossible for the people to ever have the faith which would cause miracles to happen, since no matter how much I might explain Truth to them, they would still never have the intense knowing given me in the desert.

But now, as I relate, in small measure, the story of my sojourn on earth in Palestine, it is with the intention that you, my reader, will begin to perceive and understand the knowledge I was given during my enlightenment.

My intention is to give you **knowledge**. Hearsay is when you are told something but you cannot really prove it is true. **Knowledge is when you are told something – or read something – and because what you have now heard or read complies logically and realistically with all related items of knowledge already in your mind, and you can understand and believe it in a realistic, logical way, the new information becomes knowledge. <u>You KNOW that what you now 'know' is TRUE.</u> You have a sense of 'conviction'.**

Up to this time, some of you have had faith in 'Jesus Christ' but you have been like precocious children. Your faith has been partially blind and accepting, yet interwoven with much doubt. Therefore, whatever you needed to be done for you, you depended on 'Jesus' for the work to be accomplished. Whereas, in fact, much of what you believe you have derived directly from 'Jesus' has been your own 'faith in Jesus' made visible in the form of things asked for.

Whilst this child-like 'faith' is very important to your well-being, those of you who are capable of moving onward on the spiritual path to perfection, must now reach a deeper level of true knowledge of the relation between mind and 'matter'. Without this foundation, people will continue to flounder in religious myths and will be locked into the misery of the human condition.

When I was on earth, I spoke **Truth** to the people, but it was continually misinterpreted. What I really said regarding **faith**, was this:

'You see this great big tree. It has grown out of the tiniest seed imaginable. See the vast trunk and branches and foliage. **All that enormous growth has come out of a small seed.**

'How did such a thing come about? From whence came all the wood in the tree and the foliage which adorns it! Is not this as much a miracle as are the miracles I perform for you, day after day? Is not the growth of this tree as much the work of the '**Father**' as the healing which takes place in sick people?

95

'I ask you – what is a seed? Can you tell me? No – you cannot. But I will tell you.

'It is a tiny entity of 'consciousness knowledge'. It is the 'consciousness knowledge' of what it will become. It is a fragment of 'consciousness' drawn from 'Divine Creative Consciousness'.

'It is a fragment of mind power drawn from 'Father Mind Power' ... which, when planted in the earth and watered by rain, will begin to clothe itself with the visible 'matter' of which it possesses knowledge, deep within itself. This knowledge is true, it is firm, it is strong and undeviating. This self-knowledge embodied in the seed, is a conviction in 'consciousness'.

'All of life forms arise out of this one-pointed self-knowledge – a 'conviction in consciousness'. This 'conviction in consciousness' is what separates the inanimate soil and rocks from all that lives and grows upon the face of the earth. Where there is no 'conviction of consciousness' or 'knowledge of identity' there is no growth. The consciousness within soil and rocks remains 'consciousness' in a dormant form.

'Therefore, if you could believe in what you ask for,
as powerfully as does a mustard seed know its own identity,
you would be able to do anything you wanted to do.

'If you could carry within your mind, a seed – the perfected plan of your most heartfelt goals, and know beyond all doubt, that it can grow and come into perfect fruition, you would see this wonderful seed take on a life of its own which would presently manifest in your life.

'And you could surely move the mountains in your lives – those mountains which stand across your path and prevent you from achieving all that you would like ... mountains which, in times of recklessness and evil thinking have been created by yourselves.

'If you only understood creation and existence, you would be able to live lives of total freedom, limitless achievement and transcendent joy.

'Seek to understand and you will find that little by little, understanding will come to you.

96

'Knock on the door of the universe giving access to 'God' – the 'Universal Father Consciousness' and eventually, you will find the door swinging open, and you will have entrance to the secrets of the world.

'Only believe and you will receive.'

I also reminded them at all times:

'Only those with pure minds and hearts will accomplish these mighty things.

'The wicked may flourish for a while, as have kings and marauding armies and others hoarding iniquity in their minds; they have been permitted to do their work for a while, since certain good would also arise out of the evil, but eventually they fail and their names are reviled by the rest of the world.

'Therefore, as many of you as would succeed, examine your motivations. Desires born solely of selfish longing for wealth or comfort eventually end in disappointment, sickness and death.'

And I say to you who read these words – let no one dare to deny the Truth I speak until they too, have walked the Path of Self Renunciation which I walked on earth and reached the same union with the 'Father' and the heights of incontrovertible knowledge and understanding as I possessed. When you have achieved all this, you will no longer have any desire to deny the truth I speak to you but will be unable to restrain yourselves from joining 'me' in teaching your fellowmen. Until that time, hold your peace, and let no man know your ignorance.

How often, throughout the world, people gladly embrace my teachings as being highly moralistic and the most perfectly formulated guidelines to good behaviour and daily living. However, they add, quickly, that the stories of miracles should be discounted since such aberrations of natural laws of the universe are not possible.

This type of thought is building barriers to the future progress in spiritual-scientific development of which the human mind is capable.

In fact, I did not come to earth to introduce a new religion or higher moral code than that given by Moses in the Ten Commandments. My purpose was to bring a new perception of 'God' as creator and

understanding of existence itself. Out of that knowledge would come a new way of life.

The correct attitude towards my mission on earth, in this third millennium, is to acknowledge that the 'miracles' I performed are beyond the capabilities of the average human being at this time. However, such 'miracles' were examples of what can be achieved in the future when people's minds are fully imbued with the true knowledge of existence and are also, through faith, meditation and prayer, fully attuned to and imbued with 'Universal Life/Love Consciousness'.

Was it really true I **'walked on water'** when my disciples boarded a boat to cross the lake?

If you have read the biblical account of this incident, you will realise that the disciples had left me behind. I yearned for an opportunity to withdraw from all human contact, retire to the hills, and once more enter into a profound meditation to allow my consciousness to merge into the universal dimension of 'God Consciousness'.

Whilst in this spiritual state transcending human consciousness, all awareness of physicality disappeared, and ecstatically I was lifted into the Universal Stream of Life and knew that the UNIVERSAL LIFE was all, LIFE was the reality of my beingness, and all else were but temporary changing appearances of UNIVERSAL LIFE made visible I KNEW, I felt, I was LIFE ITSELF, and as I slipped beyond earthly consciousness into the universal LIFE CONSCIOUSNESS, the laws governing my physical being were transcended and no longer applied to the flesh and blood of my human body.

I longed to move about in this new transcendent state, and found myself floating out of my cave. I could see my disciples on the lake and knew they were in distress. Effortlessly, I floated down over the hill towards the shore and as I began to regain contact with my normal human concerns – in this case, my disciples – I found myself coming to rest on the waters. However, I was still in that condition where I realised fully that I, Myself, was LIFE individualised, and therefore, my body was suffused with LIFE POWER which continued to lighten and transform the atomic structure of my physical state.

You must understand that hearing and thinking in the human consciousness state – and the ascension into the TRANSCENDANT REALISATION of UNIVERSAL LIFE, when the personal consciousness is now withdrawn from the bodily condition and wholly merged in 'Universal Father Consciousness', belong to two entirely different dimensions of being.

The human consciousness can receive inspiration from the 'Universal Father Consciousness' but the inspiration received mingles with the human condition and is frequently misinterpreted according to the store of knowledge already controlling the brain and therefore the mental processes themselves. Unfortunately, the inspiration you receive is contaminated and distorted by your present strongly maintained beliefs.

Whereas the TRANSCENDANT PERCEPTUAL and REALISATION STATE rises out of, emerges,from the physical condition. The brain is no longer in control. It no longer has any influence on the Transcendent Perceptual state which is Truth itself.

It is no longer controlled or affected by human belief.

It is in a state of 'What Really Is' back of visible manifestation and existence, instead of in the human dimension of 'What It Believes Existence to be'.

It is in the Transcendent State of Consciousness that 'miracles' are but normal working of Universal Law.

Before I continue with this account of my life on earth, I want to stress again that everything in the universe is a particular and individualised STATE OF CONSCIOUSNESS made visible.

I have had to descend from my present STATE OF CONSCIOUSNESS of UNIVERSAL LOVE, in order to experience again my life on earth which remains indelibly imprinted within the consciousness energy of the world itself, dating back to the time of its moment of creation.

You must understand that when I left my body in Palestine, I left everything pertaining to that life behind me.

I had fulfilled my mission. Therefore, when I died on the cross, I was set free, I was lifted into glorious **LIGHT** to partake of that **LIGHT**, to *be* the

LIGHT, and rejoice in the **LIGHT** which is **Universal Love, Life, Beauty, Harmony, Joy and Rapture. MOVING BETWEEN DIFFERENT LEVELS OF 'CONSCIOUSNESS'** is no easy or pleasant assignment. It is only because my mission on earth was not completed when I died in Palestine, that I now return to help you prepare to enter a new age, a new phase of individualised existence on earth.

You may gain some understanding of what I mean by the 'discomfort of this enterprise' when you remember the times you have recalled some deep sadness in your life and you find yourself reacting with almost the same degree of tension and emotional stress as you did when the sadness actually took place.

Reflecting on past suffering and sorrow will make you want to cry. You will feel a return of the original depression and anguish as you relive that time in your imagination. You may want to withdraw from people because your 'consciousness' has now descended from your former state of happy, peaceful equilibrium, to experience, yet again, the 'lowered consciousness vibrations and consciousness forms' you created at the initial time of your suffering.

Changing moods indicates a change in your consciousness energies. A lift in your consciousness vibrations gives you a physical, emotional and mental lift, making you feel happy. A drop in your consciousness energies will depress the functioning of your entire system and you will feel the onset of depression – or at the very least, a drop from the former buoyancy you were enjoying.

I am describing for you **a fact of existence.**

Your entire universe manifests the differing frequencies of vibrations of consciousness energy particles. As these frequencies move up or down from one level to another, **so do the visible and physical structures manifest differing levels of energy and there is a change of mental patterns and emotions and appearance.**

To descend from my state of consciousness to re-enter the conditions of my time on earth, is prompted only by <u>my love for mankind</u>.

For two thousand years, 'Christians' have been reliving the trauma of my crucifixion.

Some people have even experienced the stigma which is nothing more than a hysterical and morbidly emotional response to what they believe I endured. People have worked themselves up into an emotional pitch akin to frenzy whilst imagining the anguish of my suffering before my death. Their emotional gratitude for what I endured sends them into a state of physical distress. This is being written on your Good Friday, and I have come specially to talk to you about my crucifixion and to tell you that you must abandon all the drama associated with the remembrance of this day. I died – and that was, for me, a wondrous release.

It is time that people wake up from their long, long dream and come to understand existence as it really is – and the truth concerning my crucifixion, which has been hidden till this time.

On Good Fridays, year after year down the centuries, you have created a contaminated traumatic 'consciousness state of being' throughout the world as far removed from the spiritual dimension of **UNIVERSAL CREATIVE CONSCIOUSNESS** as hell is removed from heaven.

Now that I have chosen to relive my life on earth in the persona of 'Jesus' through the mind of the one who is receiving my words, in order to help the world move on to a new phase of spiritual/mental development, I ask those who can receive my words, to give up this practice of remembering my death and exercising physical 'self-denial' during your Lenten fast to commemorate my 40 days in the desert. As you must realise from this narrative, my time in the desert was one of great joy and blessedness of spirit.

888888888888888888

Many events of great spiritual significance took place just prior to my death which are excellent examples of the great **Cosmic Laws** in action within your dimension of existence. I am now giving you a brief account of those important events since it is my purpose to enlighten your minds wholly – to give you knowledge beyond any knowledge yet received by any other person in your universe.

When I began to prepare my disciples for my approaching death, it was an immensely difficult task. They could scarcely contain their shock and astonishment. The thought of my being crucified as an ordinary felon was repellent beyond words **and neither did they want to lose me from their**

midst. I had called them to follow me and leave behind lives which had been fairly prosperous. They had left their families and homes to re-build their lives around me and my work. They had taken pride in my progress through the towns. They had been willing to be associated with me and be known as my disciples despite the rejection and harsh criticism of their Religious Leaders. Furthermore, they loved and respected me, both for the way I lived my own teachings and the way I had compassionately healed so many people and brought them comfort in their unhappy lives. They truly believed I was the Son of God. How could the **Son of God** end up on the cross, they asked each other. Their horror increased with every question. It was unthinkable. They felt a tremendous void opening up in front of them – a void in their lives and a huge crater in the earth on which they walked and a vast expanse of instability and lack of purpose within themselves. **What I told them about my future crucifixion they dared not contemplate. Such an event would destroy everything they had believed in with all their hearts.**

Consequently, my disciples loudly and volubly resisted what I tried to tell them and stated again and again that such a thing could never be. When I stood firm against their stubborn denials, they were eventually forced to quieten their arguments and **outwardly** accept that such a thing might be possible. I told them that after my death, they would see me again and that I expected them to carry on the work I had started.

The pain and argumentativeness I had aroused in my disciples also affected me, deeply. It was no easy undertaking to go to Jerusalem where my fate awaited me. More than anything, I wondered how I would measure up to this great challenge of my endurance. Would I be able to transcend the physical condition and enter into **Universal Father Consciousness** and remain there until I died? At times, I was deeply frightened of the ordeal but I dare not reveal this fear to my disciples.

Therefore, I began my last journey towards Jerusalem with powerfully mixed feelings. On the one hand, I was weary of healing and talking and teaching people who listened with open mouths and had no real understanding of anything I was trying to tell them.

I had thought that my knowledge would enable people to climb out of their misery and, at the very least, make contact with the **'Father'** and gain a glimpse of the **'kingdom of heaven'**.

102

There had been no evidence of such a spiritual awakening even amongst my disciples.

My disappointment and sense of failure made me glad to be moving on from the earth life to the glorious existence I knew awaited me after my death.

At the same time, I wondered how I would endure the pain of the crucifixion.

Throughout my mission, I had lived in a more or less consistently peaceful – frequently exalted – state of mind, with my thoughts focused on the 'Father Love Consciousness', author of all being, knowing that I had but to ask and what I asked for would swiftly manifest itself.

Would I be able to keep my equanimity when brought before the Council, when led out to my crucifixion, when nailed to the cross with my weight hanging from my hands?

Because I was now giving way to doubts and fears, the normal level of my consciousness frequencies were dropping. They were taking me down into the frequencies of the earth plane consciousness. I became a prey again to my old aggression, prompting me to unreasonable actions I would never have contemplated earlier when in my former state of total harmony with the **'Father Love Consciousness'**. My doubts and conflicts externalised in my life as human emotions and impulses which contravened the **Cosmic Law of Love.**

First, there was the episode of the Fig Tree. I was hungry and went to the tree not really expecting to find fruit because it was not the right season for figs. When my search was 'unfruitful', I cursed the fig tree. Twenty four hours later, it was shrivelled to its roots.

It was a shocking experience. It was the first time my words had caused harm to anything.

However, it clearly demonstrated, for my disciples, the power of THOUGHT for good or evil. It showed them that the more spiritually evolved a person is, the greater is the impact of their words on the environment.

I took the opportunity to point out to my disciples that I had thoughtlessly behaved as does the average man or woman *who – when having high expectations – cannot get what they want.*

They usually react with anger, tears, hostility, and even sharp words which might or might not amount to a kind of 'ill-wishing' or cursing of the person who has denied them their heart's desire. They had now seen for themselves what my cursing had done to the fig tree.

They should now be able to understand that whilst a strong conviction would bring about anything they might desire and imagine, they must also be constantly aware of their own mental- emotional condition. *They must not harbour resentment against others but must swiftly forgive, otherwise they could do much damage to those they resented ... which damage would return to them, in due course, as a harvest of their sowing.*

Furthermore, as one sows so does one reap. I knew that what I had done to the fig tree would inevitably return to me in one form or another.

I took my disciples to the Temple. It was many years since I had been there, and I knew my visit would serve to set in train the events which would lead to my crucifixion. Some of the people recognised me and in response to their requests, I began to teach them. More people gathered and crowded the money lenders who began to complain. Their shouting and loud complaints broke my train of thought as I was teaching.

Suddenly my wrath was aroused. Here were people earnestly gathered around me, wanting to hear the words of **LIFE** which soon I would not be able to speak to them, and there were the money lenders who made their living by selling livestock for sacrifices which did the people no good whatever. These men only brought people into debt and misery. I felt a rush of blood to my head and I pushed the tables over, scattering their money, and I drove the money-hearted men out of the Temple.

Now there was a great commotion of shouting and screaming. Some people were scrambling to pick up the money. The money lenders were calling down curses on my head, denouncing me as evil, as one doing the work of Beelzebub and a thousand other devils. The Priests and Pharisees and all the people who set great store by the sacrifices in the Temple, came running together to find out the cause of the noise and confusion.

On hearing the money lenders' story, they were so outraged by my actions, they launched into vociferous condemnation of me and lamentations to impress the Priests, each one making louder protest than their neighbours to demonstrate their horror at what I had done. Such a thing had never been seen in the Temple before.

Even those who had previously listened to me were now disturbed at my wilfulness and wondered what kind of man I might be.

They were standing close together, watching the proceedings, when they were noticed and approached by the Priests and Pharisees who persuaded them I was trying to destroy all they had believed in, preaching a false 'God' entirely unlike anything they had ever heard about in their synagogues. The Priests passed on their own outraged anger to the people and convinced them that my sin would contaminate them also if they persisted in listening to my madness.

Gradually, the people were persuaded I was an evil influence and should be removed before I could disrupt the peace of the country and bring down the wrath of the Roman Governor on the entire country of Palestine.

My disciples ashamed of what I had done, quietly left the scene and hid amongst the alleys some way from the Temple. When they returned to me later, they clearly showed they were also sorely tried by my actions. They wondered whether I had taken leave of my senses, gone mad, prophesying my death and then doing those very things which would probably be the cause of it.

It was at that time that Judas, who had never fully shed his Jewish beliefs, began to doubt whether I was the Messiah after all. Three years I had taught the people and there was no lessening of the Roman rule. Three years and people were no nearer the happiness I had promised them. And now it seemed that I was about to become a disturber of the peace – bringing down the wrath of Rome on their heads.

He heard that the Jewish High Priest wanted to get rid of me and so he offered his services to identify my person when required to do so.

When it was time for me to eat the Passover with my disciples, I arranged we should eat it all together in a large supper room. I knew it would be the last time I would eat any food on earth. I do not want to return deeply to the consciousness of that night.

I felt **great** sadness to be leaving my disciples who had served me so well. With my sadness came a return of all my fears and conflicts. I had moments of deep emotional self-pity. I felt that no one understood all I had tried to do for my people and the sacrifice I was prepared to make for them.

John was giving a vivid account of the story of the Israelites' last night in Egypt before they escaped into the desert. He spoke of Moses' instructions to the head of each family to kill an unblemished lamb, to cook it in a certain way and paint its blood on the doorposts of all Israelite dwellings, because that very night, angels would come and slaughter all the first born children of the Egyptians and their livestock. With great relish, he recalled the outcry made by the Egyptians when they woke to find the bloodied first- born in every home. None was spared.

It was the kind of horrible story I rejected as having any value for anyone seeking higher spiritual Truth. I wondered how much my disciples had really understood when I spoke of their '**Heavenly Father**' and His love for all mankind. How could they relish the thought of 'angels' killing the Egyptian first-born when I had clearly told them that 'God', the '**Father**' was **Love.**

But the Jews had always been pre-occupied with the shedding of blood to atone for their sins.

Even Abraham, the founder of the Israelite nation, had been convinced he should take his only son into the desert and kill and offer him as a sacrifice to God. A pagan and revolting thought!

I thought of the animal sacrifices in the Temple. Loving all the wild things of creation as I did, the practice was an abomination to me. And now I was about to be put to death because I had dared to speak the words of Truth. And when I considered how little I had achieved in passing on my knowledge, I wondered why I had been sent on such a mission!

I felt a momentary spasm of resentment and anger inter-threading my usual feelings of love for these men.

With some cynicism, I wondered what effective token of remembrance I could leave with them, to bring back to their minds all my teachings when I was no longer with them. If they could so swiftly forget all my teachings on the '**Father's Love**' and enjoy the horrible story of the Passover, whilst I was still in the room with them – how much would they remember when I had died as a 'felon' on the cross, the most despicable of deaths?

Then it came to me that since they were so moved by the 'shedding of blood', I would give them blood to remember me by!

With these ironical reflections, I took up a loaf of bread, broke it and passed it to my disciples and told them to eat it. I likened the brokenness of the bread to the future brokenness of my body and asked them to repeat this 'breaking of bread and distribution' as a means of remembering the sacrifice of my body to bring them the TRUTH – the Truth about God and the Truth about life, the Truth about Love.

Realising I was in a strange mood, they stopped eating, listened, took the bread and ate it silently.

Next, I took up my goblet of wine and passed it around, saying that they must each drink from it for it was a symbol of my blood which would shortly be shed because I had dared to bring them the **Truth of Existence.**

I saw that the edge in my voice had reached some of them. Soberly, each one took a sip and then passed the goblet to his neighbour. But still, they said nothing. They sensed I was in earnest and would not tolerate any more argument.

Then I told them that a certain man amongst them would betray me.

(Privately, I understood his motives and knew that he was a necessary part of the future sequence of events. He was but playing a role which his nature had prompted him to do. I knew that he would suffer greatly and I felt compassion for him. But these thoughts I kept to myself.)

When I mentioned that one of them would betray me and told Judas to leave and do what he had to do quickly, the disciples came alive, wondering if this was really their last meal with me.

Now there was a great deal of emotional distress, questions, even recriminations for having led them into such a trap. Again, they wondered what they would do with their lives after I had gone. They asked what kind of standing they would have in the community if I were crucified. They would be an object of derision, they argued. No one would ever again believe a word they spoke.

Deeply saddened by their self-centred response to my predicament, I assured them they had no need to fear for their own safety. They would abandon me and would not be connected to my crucifixion. After my death, I suggested they should disperse and return to Galilee.

This touched Peter deeply and he reacted, vehemently denying that he would ever abandon me – but of course he did.

All the love that I had felt for my fellow men, all that I had longed to accomplish for them – in this moment of my own need – still met with blank non-comprehension, even resistance. Their only concern was what would happen to them. There was no word of kindness, offering of help, anguish for my future ordeal.

How hard was the human heart, I thought. How many weary centuries would pass before mankind would be able to move beyond their own hurt and pain to feel even a glimmer of love and compassion for other unfortunates in a worse situation than themselves?

And so – although deeply disappointed – even hurt – by their selfish reactions, I also understood them and attempted to give my disciples courage to face the future and assured them that I would always be with them even when I was hidden from their sight.

The work I had started would be promoted from the life beyond. I would not leave them alone. They would know and feel my presence and this would be a comfort to them.

I told them to cling to their memories of my time with them. I warned that there would be many who would continue in the knowledge I had given them, but there would be outsiders who would seek to add the voice of tradition and reason to my teachings. My words would be so distorted that, eventually, they would no longer reveal the original Truth I had brought the world.

When I told them that this would happen, they were upset – even panic stricken. I was relieved to see that my teachings had not been in vain after all – they had not entered totally deaf ears. They asked me to tell them more – but I raised my hands and said that that was all I could say.

At this point, I felt I had said all I ever wanted to say whilst on earth, that my speech with men had been accomplished. All I greatly, deeply desired was to retreat into silence and find peace and comfort in my contact with the **'Father'**.

We left the supper room and walked to the Mount of Olives, but the mood of my disciples was one of inner conflict, fear and doubt. Most of them left to join their families and friends who would be still celebrating their own Passover.

In the garden, there was a special boulder, shaped like a little cave. I liked to shelter in it from the wind. And so I sat and meditated and prayed, seeking a way into the exalted harmony I had enjoyed in the past. I knew that when I moved into attunement with the 'Father Love', my fears would dissolve and I would be in a state of total and absolute peaceful confidence again. As I felt the Power of Love move into me and possess my human consciousness, so did the strength to endure what lay ahead, possess my heart. I would be able to remain within the Love and give the Love to others to the very end.

And so it was.

I will not even attempt to re-enter into the trial and crucifixion state. It is of no consequence.

When I finally died on the cross and my spirit withdrew from my tortured body, I was lifted into ineffable and radiant **LIGHT**. I was enclosed in the warmth and comfort of **LOVE**, such as I had never experienced before. I had a sensation of enveloping praise, a powerful assurance of work well done, of ecstasy in universal strength to continue the work, and joy and rapture which is far beyond any that the earthly condition can ever know. I moved into a new and wondrously beautiful way of life but I still descended in consciousness to remain in touch with the people I had left behind. I was able to show myself to those who were sufficiently sensitive to be able to see me. However, the story of Thomas who supposedly fingered my wounds is nonsense.

My disciples did not know that I had secretly arranged with Joseph of Aremathea to take my body to his own unused tomb after my death, where he would anoint it according to custom before the sun set. Then, when darkness had fallen and the Sabbath was being observed by everyone in Jerusalem, assisted by two mounted trustworthy servants, he would take my body secretly by during the night, and by out of sight tracks during the day, to a mountain side outside Nazareth, in Galilee. There, further assisted by my family, if he followed my directions, he would find a small, hidden cave which had given me shelter from storms and a refuge from people when I was young, unhappy and rebellious, and at odds with the world. Joseph promised to find the cave from a map I had given him and to leave me there after further embalming. He would build up the small entrance to thoroughly block it from intruders. There, my body has rested, free from molestation.

It has been said of me that 'my body rose from the dead'. What an absurdity conjured up by earthly minds which were at a loss to satisfactorily explain my death as a felon on a cross!

What need would I have of an earthly body to continue existence in the next dimension?

How could such a ridiculous myth persist even into the 21st century? It has been a measure of the lack of understanding of 'Christians' that they have blindly accepted such a dogma to this very time.

Think about this carefully. Having been released from an earthly body and after my experience of the ecstasy and glorious rapture of passing into a higher dimension of **UNIVERSAL CONSCIOUSNESS**, why would I want to return to the earthly dimension to enter my body again? Of what use would it be to me in your world or in mine? Whilst the 'physical substance' of my body might be spiritualised when perfectly attuned to the '**Father Love Consciousness**' whilst I still lived on earth, would not my body be an encumbrance and a deterrent to my subsequent journeys within the highest Spiritual Kingdoms? Visible things are but a manifestation of specific frequencies of vibration in consciousness which produces a 'SHIMMER OF MOTES OR PARTICLES' giving an appearance of solid 'matter'.

Each visible substance possesses its own unique vibrational frequency. A change in the rate of vibration produces a change in the appearance of 'matter'. As consciousness energies change so do the appearances of 'matter' change.

Therefore, it was possible for me to focus and lower my frequencies of consciousness to that point where my form became visible to the human eye. I could return to my disciples and be seen by them. And I did so. I loved them more than ever before, and owed them as much comfort and support as I was able to give them after my death. Not only this, it was necessary to direct my own power into their minds in order to give them the impetus and courage to continue the work I had started.

However, I want you to know that the 'individualised consciousness' which has ascended in vibrational frequencies to the very portals of the **Universal Creative Dimension** becomes **LIGHT INDIVIDUALISED**, an **INDIVIDUALISED CONSCIOUSNESS** which needs no body in which to express and enjoy all that the **GLORIOUS CONSCIOUSNESS** can devise in the highest **SPIRITUAL REALMS**. It is a supreme and enraptured state of being having none of the needs, desires, impulses experienced by those who have not fully mounted high beyond and above the ego.

Whilst living on earth, your minds remain anchored within certain parameters of vibrational frequencies, imprisoned in bodies which have their own needs. If your consciousness were to truly soar beyond these parameters, your earthly self would disappear. When I was trapped in a body, I was also largely confined to these parameters of vibrational frequencies and consciousness.

Furthermore, imagination alone can soar no further than your previous experiences and therefore you are confined to your past which you project into your future.

However – little by little – you will be led by those minds which are sensitive enough to access the higher spiritual dimensions and can thus move beyond your present consciousness boundaries. They will record for you those wondrous experiences and states of being beyond your own, to which you yourselves will then be able to aspire. In this way, you go forwards in levels or steps of spiritual development.

Each step brings you a higher vision of what can be achieved and out of this vision you formulate a new goal. With this goal ever before you, you work to cleanse yourself of the contaminating influence of the 'bonding-rejection' impulses of your earthly existence. Step by step you transcend your ego.

When you transcend your ego and it dies within your consciousness, you are now abundantly alive within the **'Father Love Consciousness'** and find the reality of the kingdom of heaven in your lives, within yourself and in your environment.

To enable YOU to reach these pinnacles of love, joy, harmony and rapture, I lived, worked and died in Palestine and I have come to you now in these **Letters.**

Let not my work be in vain this second time. As you read these pages, seek, meditate and pray for inspiration, you will come to feel the **'Father's'** response and if you listen every day attentively, you will hear the **'Father's' Voice.**

This Voice is ever with you. Dismantle the barriers created by self-will. Open yourselves to receive strength, power, inspiration and love direct from the '**Father Love Consciousness'.**

Read and re-read these **Letters** that they may eventually become absorbed into your consciousness. As you do so, you will be journeying towards **LIGHT**, and you will radiate **LIGHT** to others. Such **LIGHT** is not just 'light' as is electricity but is the very nature of **UNIVERSAL CONSCIOUSNESS** which I described to you in my **Letter 1**.

Therefore, as you radiate the **LIGHT**, you will radiate unconditional love. You will promote the growth and spiritual development of every other living entity. You will yearn to nourish and nurture, you will work to promote protection and healing and education. You will long to assist in the establishment of loving law and order in which all will be able to live harmoniously, successfully and prosperously. **You will be in the Kingdom of Heaven.**

At the same time, let there be no illusions.

As steps are taken to introduce these **Letters** to the outside world, there will be exactly the same recriminations, the same condemnation, the same talk of Satan, the devil, as there was when I first taught in Palestine. Take heart, pray for courage. Those who endure to the end will rise above the turmoil and violence and will rest in the peace and joy of the kingdom.

****

LETTER 4

I, the CHRIST, have come – in my love for you – to make a summary of all that I perceived during enlightenment in the desert and tried to teach the Jews in Palestine 2000 years ago. Some details of my earthly life have been related in **Letters 1, 2 and 3.**

If you have read these, you will know it is of the utmost importance to your well-being to understand that – whilst my followers eventually created a religion they called 'Christianity' founded on reports of my life and teachings – I am not dictating these **Letters** to teach and confirm what my followers have taught. Christianity is a formal religion which, **purely** for reasons of expediency, took on many beliefs contrary to the spiritual Truth of our **SOURCE of BEING.**

What has the 'spilling of blood' to do with UNIVERSAL SPIRIT?

As you must now realise, my teaching from the very beginning of my mission on earth in Palestine, has always been born of the highest spiritual **Truth of Existence**, having nothing to do with human concepts and rationalisations as taught by human minds.

Therefore, I repeat emphatically, whilst my persona on earth two thousand years ago was that of **JESUS**, the purpose of my presence, the **CHRIST PRESENCE,** within these **Letters** is to reach sensitive and inspired souls to teach them how to draw on **Divine Assistance** during the future horror in which the world will ultimately be embroiled. For this reason, my powerful longing to rescue those who can receive me has been crystallised in the form of **TRUTH OF EXISTENCE** within these **Letters**. Know this – heed it.

I would have you know – **and take particular note** – that I came to the Jews in Palestine 70 years before Jerusalem was razed to the ground.

I came to the Jews to warn them that their code of conduct would be of no value to them when the future time of travail came upon then, sending them out into a hostile world. It is recorded in a gospel that I wept in despair, lamenting the fact that I would have gathered the people as chicks beneath a mother hen's breast, to protect them in their time of destruction but the people would not heed me. Instead, their religious leaders put me to death.

But after the dispersal of the Jews, when their Temple was taken from them, did they learn from their experiences? Did they wonder why such a catastrophe had overtaken them? No, they continued in their old traditions and belief in their superiority, although repeatedly, historical events proved to them that they were subject to disasters as were other people. At this very time, they have chosen to ignore the **TRUTHS of EXISTENCE as I taught them in Palestine**, and are bringing upon themselves the self- same conditions as followed my earthly life in Palestine.

No matter where they may reside, their materialistic values, their **head**-for-an-**eye** traditions, are drawing to them the human sorrow they have created for others down the ages by their arrogance and greed. Everything they have endured, they have brought upon themselves.

This also applies to those who, through expediency, have allied themselves with Jews because of their financial power within world financial spheres and world markets. Who is it keeps the vast majority of the world population hungry when there is sufficient food stockpiled to feed people adequately if 'profit as motive for existence' were abandoned? Given the will, financial leaders could formulate and embark on plans to distribute the surplus of goods to the under-privileged. If they were to do so, they would find the entire universe responding with blessings, world economy would flourish and peace would become a world condition.

Before this can happen, **what has already been created in consciousness and by aggressive, debased actions, WORLD-WIDE**, must first be drawn into materialised human experience – not as retribution but as a natural working of the **LAWS of EXISTENCE**.

Rest assured that countries who resist the 'evil' of others, are only resisting the consequences of their own 'seeds of consciousness and actions' in years gone by. Therefore, 'bully-boy' tactics, the ferocious attack of the mighty upon the weak, no matter how intransigent the weak may appear to be, can only bring even greater times of trouble for the bullies. Where they experienced a pin-prick, they are stock-piling in consciousness, the future devastation they are presently dumping on others. Perhaps they should regard the 'pin-prick' from the weak as a bugle call to alert them to their downward slide into moral decadence.

Because such people are constantly breaking the **LAWS of EXISTENCE** and drawing destruction of an unparalleled magnitude upon cities and earth, it is my intention in this **Letter** not only to summarise all that I taught and lived in Palestine but to spell out clearly the underlying causes of your approaching world crisis which I did not cover when last I came to mankind in speech.

These LETTERS have been written prior to the most crucial time in your history, and when the travail is truly upon you, you will wonder why I did not warn you earlier.

But, I have to tell you, through receptive minds, I have been trying to alert the world for the past twenty five years, but neither media, nor publishing house, nor TV, was prepared to listen and give me the opportunity to speak to you through my agents.

Politicians could reach you – but I, the Christ, could not do so because of the hardness of your hearts and your refusal to concede that I, the living Christ, could return at this time through de- programmed and dedicated minds to warn nations of what they were creating for themselves in the future.

The churches, who claim to believe in my existence, have been as self-absorbed in their own humanly conceived religious traditions as have the materialists. Now, at the Eleventh Hour, when fear has descended on the masses, and they are prepared to heed my words, the doors must surely open or again my efforts for humanity will have been in vain.

I have come to say there will indeed be a sorting of the 'goats' from the 'sheep' as has been recorded in the gospels in the Bible. The 'sheep' refer to those souls who can peacefully receive the highest spiritual truth yet dispensed on earth. The 'goats' refer to those who do not have the capacity to listen to anyone or anything because they have too great a rebellious spirit and ego- drive.

Why will they be separated at this time? They will be separated because those who are able to receive the truth contained within these pages, and to live by the guidelines of the Laws of Existence will find that although the next period of world history will be bitter indeed, they will continue in comparative peace and protection, fulfilment of need and upliftment of spirit.

The 'goats', unfortunately, will have to endure all the horrific force of their innate rebellious consciousness.

This is NOT a punishment from Someone on High – but a natural working out of the Law of Existence: what you carry in your minds and hearts will eventually externalise in your body, life and environment. When you resist and rebel, life offers resistance to you in the fulfilment of your desires.

I have long since ascended to the highest frequencies of consciousness vibration in the Celestial Kingdoms and am Divine Consciousness Itself individualised. My Consciousness can encircle the globe to whoever calls on me.

So is it with all the great Teachers who have lived on earth, and were enlightened and perceived the REALITY of the SOURCE of all BEING, and have taught people from their exalted level of enlightenment.

They were lifted in spiritual Power to penetrate the dense veil of human consciousness and perceive what truly lay beyond the world of 'matter' – they saw, as clearly as previous mental conditioning would permit, the basic unity of creation, within the realm of Creativity Itself.

One and all have, after transition into the next dimension of existence, escaped the treadmill of re- incarnation and moved on into ever higher realms of individual pure spiritual consciousness to the portals of **UNIVERSAL CONSCIOUSNESS** Itself. They have become Individualised **DIVINE CONSCIOUSNESS** possessing the power and the insight of **Divine Consciousness.**

They, too, share in the CHRIST CONSCIOUSNESS as I said in an earlier Letter. They combine the heights of Intelligent Love with the heights of Loving Intelligence, combining the Power of Will with the Power of Purpose. They are equally male and female in their drives. They are the perfect demonstration of strength and nurturing.

They are the perfect EXAMPLE of what all men – and women – should be striving to attain.To attain to such perfection of being, the human spirit must set aside all divisions and rivalry. Whoever may be your acclaimed Prophet, you can be assured that he is LIFE ITSELF and powerful within the Brotherhood of all great Teachers. Each

Prophet, each Teacher has perceived the same **REALITY** and lived in such a prayerful way as to ensure he will eventually achieve the goal of every man – perfection in Paradise.

It is vitally important you should understand this and realise that the divisions you make between your Teachers are wholly erroneous, because we are all united in our common **SOURCE of BEING.** We are a **Brotherhood of Beings of Life, each** manifesting through our individuality the highest **TRUTH** of our **SOURCE of BEING.**

We are equal in purity, power, beauty, grandeur of spirit and love.

THEREFORE, the 'sheep' of every religious persuasion – those who have sufficiently evolved in spiritual understanding of the fundamental unity in your SOURCE of BEING – should swiftly seek to unite in equal brotherhood in your towns and countries and reach out and bond with your spiritual brethren world-wide, irrespective of all that is taking place in the external world. You should transcend all religious differences, Christian, Muslim, Sufi, Jew, Israeli, Palestinian, Hindu, Buddhist, etc and regard yourselves as all being equally within the safe haven of Universal Love and Universal Intelligent Protection – at peace with yourselves, with each other and with those who are determined to fight to a finish.

ONLY IN THIS WAY WILL YOUR PLANET SURVIVE THE TURMOIL WHICH LIES AHEAD OF YOU.

I have also returned to all those who are neither Muslim nor Christian, Buddhist nor Hindu. I have come to those who desire, nay long, to know the **Reality** behind all existence.

I have told you that I came – in the persona of Jesus – to the Jews in Palestine. I might well have said that I came to the Arabs in the persona of Muhammad, since Muhammad and I are of one spirit.

To divide us into 'persona' having different names – **JESUS and MUHAMMAD**, or **MUHAMMAD and JESUS** is the same as giving identical twins different surnames because one teaches literature and the other teaches maths.

We are both of **CHRIST CONSCIOUSNESS**, both individualisations of **DIVINE CONSCIOUSNESS.**

When on earth, we both spoke of a God of Love and Mercy according to the way in which our humanity permitted us to perceive our inspired knowledge from God.

You must bear in mind that we were both human beings who had been deeply conditioned by our traditional beliefs inherited down the ages. Therefore, our inspiration came to us through minds already possessed by other ideas.

As I have previously told you, inspiration, unless directed into a clean, deprogrammed mind, will always take on the overtones of convictions derived from early childhood conditioning. The rational mind which takes over when the inflow of inspiration ceases, begins to explain the new knowledge and insight in terms of what is already accepted by the human mind.

But, as I have already told you, I was a rebel almost from the outset of my life and could not accept the Judaic beliefs. I was a clean, eagerly receptive, open-minded vessel into which the **TRUTH OF EXISENCE** could be poured in the desert, enabling me to see **UNIVERSAL CONSCIOUSNESS clearly.**

Now our perceptions are of the very highest order – we are of one MIND, one LIFE, one LOVE, reaching out equally to Muslim and Jew and Christian, Buddhist and all people, atheist or agnostic. Our only motive in calling to them is to bring them inspired heart-changing insight which will enable them to recognise their essential underlying brotherhood in spirit, encourage them to think new thoughts, relate to each other peacefully with forgiveness in their hearts, and thereafter live their lives differently, drawing LIGHT from their **SOURCE of BEING.**

We would both speak of UNIVERSAL CONSCIOUSNESS to you who are living in this present scientific age because you have travelled far into scientific understanding and can now receive what we both have to say.

Together we say with one voice – heed, listen: WE – and you on earth – are all one at the very roots of our being.

Whatever destruction you hand out to others, you are also handing out to yourselves.

I – WE – must make it clear that **WE** have come to all people of good sense, good will and good heart, irrespective of their present race and religious beliefs. **WE embrace, love, draw you all into our consciousness mantle of protection and safety.**

WE are aware of your problems on earth at this present time.

WE are aware of the centuries-old conflict between Judaism and Islam.

But this rift has nothing to do with US. Your squabbles leave us unmoved. Why jeopardise your own good, your own future felicity by fighting over some concept which is meaningless and therefore without value? In reality, you adhere to your chosen religions because, in the depths of your heart, you are all reaching out to the **SOURCE OF YOUR BEING**, although you call your **SOURCE of BEING** by different names.

We are both aware of the struggles of individual Jews to live a 'good life', and of individuals of Islam to truly reverence and venerate Allah throughout the day, attributing all they do and achieve to his power working on their behalf, and of Christians immersed in their beliefs of Salvation by the blood of Jesus – you are all striving to attain 'goodness' but will never do so whilst you remain divided by your beliefs.

Once the maelstrom of the present world consciousness of mutual aggression has been fully spent – the day will surely come when Muslim, Jew, Christian, Buddhist and Hindu will gather together, rejecting their differences in religious beliefs and mingling as one people, to give thanks to **DIVINE CONSCIOUSNESS** out of **WHICH** they have drawn their being, and from WHICH will come all future boundless blessings of beautiful, inspired and caring lives.

Together you will rebuild on old foundations and will say: 'Let such a thing never happen between people again for now we know that at the roots of our existence, we are truly one. When I make you suffer, I too am lessened in **Divine Life**, and my own suffering will follow.' **WE**, and the **BROTHERHOOD** within **CHRIST CONSCIOUSNESS** are also fully aware of Buddhists and Hindus, followers of Tao, the spiritual adepts in the Philippines, and every other sect and religious discipline in every country, which is aimed at reaching and touching, even momentarily, the equilibrium of their **UNIVERSAL SOURCE of BEING**.

119

We are aware of ALL. YOU are all encompassed within our Universal Love, Compassion and Caring. YOU are all important to us, irrespective of your beliefs, for you are all ONE at the grass roots of your being – your souls are unified in Divine Consciousness.

One and ALL, you are unified and one at soul level within your SOURCE of BEING.

If you catch a drop of rain in the palm of your hand, can you say that because the droplet of rain has landed in YOUR hand, and because it has separated from the rain that is falling to ground, that the droplet is different in 'being', chemical composition, and quality of purity or strength from the rest of the rain presently falling around you?

You may touch your droplet with green dye, and make it green, but can you say that that green droplet is entirely different to the rest of the rain falling at that very moment?

You of good sense, good will, and good heart, sincere and true, will be able to reply – no, the rain is not different. It is exactly the same in quality and being as the rest of the rain; the only difference is that green, or red, or blue dye has been added. Therefore, it has become something more than the rain falling around us, but the droplet of rain in the palm of my hand is **basically** the same as the rain.

Every one of you, no matter who you are, what colour skin you may possess, what kind of hair adorns your head and protects it from the sun, the shape of your head or body, the language you speak, the thoughts you think, the kind of words you use, the actions and deeds you perform as a result of your beliefs and your thoughts – no matter what your PHYSICAL AND HUMAN CONSCIOUSNESS DIFFERENCES – you are ALL, exactly the same as each other, of the same quality, begotten of the same **SOURCE OF BEING,** having the same potential in infinity, the same spiritual capacities in infinity in every respect. The only difference between everyone of you, Muslim Arab, Russian Jew, American Christian, Tibetan Buddhist, Indian Hindu, are the additives which have been pumped into each of you as a result of your genetics derived from your parentage and race, environment, family upbringing, family resources poor or wealthy, education, and opportunities in life.

BUT – these are ALL superficials. They are additives masking your **Reality** you call your soul even as dye will mask the truth concerning the drop of water in the palm of your hand. Your soul comes directly from **Divine Consciousness** and remains itself, pristine and pure, and unified in **Divine Consciousness** with all other souls, despite all the additives which have covered and corroded it since birth.

You must also realise that everyone is born with differing **human** capacities to make use of the additives pumped into them at birth. The human capacities to be utilised by each soul depend on the spiritual progress it made in previous lives.

Some people climb out of deep holes of disadvantages, depression and despair and achieve high positions of trust and respect, wielding much influence over others – and some people fall from dizzying heights of advantage, wealth, opportunity, and talents, into black holes of despair and depression, drug taking, murder, rape, and whatever.

Nevertheless, for all that you have each made – or not made – of your opportunities or your lack of them, you all remain fundamentally and basically of the same 'beingness' and potential. You are ALL able to rise up, little by little, from whatever spiritual level of consciousness you presently occupy to the heights of **DIVINE CONSCIOUSNESS** within the Celestial Kingdoms.

As you accept these **Letters** as being the **TRUTH of EXISTENCE** and seek, daily, to live the guidelines which will bring each of you into harmony and contact with **THAT WHICH GAVE YOU BEING** – you will surely move towards and achieve the highest spiritual goals you have set yourself at this present time. You can all rise to the point where you fully accept the **TRUTH**, work to purify your personal consciousness in order to absorb **DIVINE CONSCIOUSNESS** and become individuals filled with – and radiating – **the Power of Divine Consciousness** in your immediate surroundings and eventually throughout the world.

YOU are ALL important within your immediate environment.

The parent who feels that all that is done for the family is not appreciated, who feels that he/she does not make an impact on family life, is never heard, respected, loved, who feels that outside the home or in the workplace he/she is of no consequence and will not be missed, is lacking insight. Such a person, be they male, female, father, mother, friend, worker, employer, all make an impact on their environment. If they were removed from it, there would be a hole in the fabric of the environment, there would be loss, and it would take time for that gap to be filled in with the arrival of someone else and by new activities of those left behind.

A void is left by the biggest Power and Voice, Doer of good, or the most menial worker sweeping the floor or garden paths. Each one inhabits a special place in the whole environment. Each one brings their own talent, their own character, their own way of doing things, their own impact on the people they speak to, to the place where they live or work. They are vital in their own niche.

No one can rob a person of their importance, except the person himself by his denial of his value.

No matter if a person is born handicapped – they still have their unique place of importance in the family, the environment. Sometimes, they occupy a greater position of importance than if they had been born whole and perfect. Their achievements arouse wonder and respect.

The impact they make on the environment depends entirely on their will to be, their will to act, their will to radiate good will, their will to make the most of their opportunities, their will to be special for people by making other people feel better than they did before the contact took place.

Every condition arises out of the WILL which is exercised at all times.

Some have been born with great willpower, others with less, but the moment that a person fully realises that all **WILLPOWER** has been drawn from **UNIVERSAL CONSCIOUSNESS** and **WILLPOWER** can be increased by calling on one's **SOURCE of BEING** for increased willpower, so does the person begin to realise that willpower is not limited after all. It can be drawn, according to the magnitude and strength of one's faith, from **UNIVERAL CONSCIOUSNESS** Itself.

Each and everyone of each gender, every race, nation, religion, every level of resources and income from pauper to king, is equally important in the moment of NOW, in the moment of end of day.

True differences only arise from what each person gives of himself to this moment, the next moment, and the rest of the day.

A King or Prime Minister can be remembered for his goodness, the benefits he brought his country, or for the misery he imposed on the people. Similarly, a man born into an impoverished family, who may not have developed his abilities to any high level, **but who gave his all in his service to his environment,** will eventually be as revered by kin and friends – and in the next life reap of his sowing as does the King or Prime Minister.

Such a person will have contributed 'life' to his environment, because the nature of life force is unconditional love and service, work and harmony, giving whatever is necessary for the fulfilment of the needs of another.

If, each day, your life-force is spent in just giving a cup of tea to people who are sick, then let that life- force be spent in its highest form: as eager willingness to walk to the patient with a warm smile, and hand over the tea with kindness, goodwill, and a desire for the healing of the person.

In such a way, a tea giver can become a radiant medium of healing and upliftment.

The more frequently the tea-giver calls silently for an inflow of **Divine Consciousness** into her own consciousness, the greater and more penetrating will be her radiated life-force to the patient. The sick person may not be aware of what is happening, but a room of sick people attended by such a tea-giver, or carer, will recover more swiftly than those who receive their tea from one who hands it to them without a glance of recognition, without a word, without a kindly thought.

No, each job, each moment, can be sacred and beautiful, radiant with the inflow of **Divine Consciousness** life force, uplifting, healing to the self and others, if a person takes time to realise he/she is a channel of **Divine Consciousness** which is itself all healing, all protection, all fulfilment of a person's every need.

One person, even one who cleans the floors and empties bed pans, possessing such a realisation can enter a room and become the most important – perhaps, the only – distributor of good amongst six people handing out bed pans. Such a person can leave behind a legacy of increased strength in every patient. **Every single person who realises that from their eyes is radiated potent** life-force to those at whom the vision is directed, can know that their glance, that penetrating look, that smiling gaze has benefited the one who received it.

For everything we – yes, you and **I, the CHRIST**, think and do is an act of consciousness – and consciousness is life-force. With the activity of our minds, yours and **mine**, we shape our consciousness, our life-force into different forms which will bless or curse the environment.

The only difference between you and Muhammad and myself, known on earth as Jesus, is the kind of thought and feeling that Muhammad and I radiate to others. We both radiate life-giving consciousness energy to the world.

What are you radiating in your world?

Remember again, how, during a time of great stress during my time in Palestine, I cursed the fig tree, and it shrivelled to its roots. Not long afterwards I was also roundly cursed by Roman soldiers and Jewish priests alike. I, too, was shrivelled to my roots before I died on the cross. Beware what you hand out to others; make certain that you would like to receive the same.

A cup of water handed to someone with love can bless and uplift that person or, if handed out with ill-feeling can make the recipient feel small and of no account – a little weaker and more depressed.

What part are you playing in your environment? Are you honoured and recognised for the love and goodwill you distribute the moment you set foot in your work place? Have you caught a vision of what is really important in life?

Have you set yourself a spiritual plan, a spiritual goal to be achieved before you pass on into the next beautiful dimension?

Will you be sufficiently purified and committed to unconditional loving to move into the higher levels of spiritual consciousness –

or will your goals still be those of your earth plane?

Ask yourself: What part do you really want to play in your environment? What is your spiritual destination?

Just as importantly, what are your attitudes towards other people – superiority and exclusivity – or an awareness that most people are doing the best they can with whatever talents they possess?

To reach your full potential you must realise that neither position nor wealth can limit the power you exercise in the world. Your only limitations are your attitudes and thoughts arising from your attitudes.

The life-force radiated from the mind of king, prime minister, general, or lowly servant, or soldier, is equally powerful and productive of good in the environment, providing each one disciplines his thoughts to become attuned to the spiritual frequencies of unconditional love and Divine Consciousness. Furthermore, such thoughts enter and enhance the world consciousness force itself. Each person adding their spiritual thought to world spiritual thought strengthens it.

The only factor which determines the degree of imparting of life-or-sickness propensities is the level of realisation and spiritual understanding that a person has drawn from the **SOURCE of BEING.**

Therefore, the man who happily removes the neighbourhood refuse with a good heart and a blessing on all whom he meets, is a bright light shining in his little world, and the moneygrasping, ill-tempered man of wealth and substance emerging from his mansion to go to his office, is a pool of darkness which can be felt negatively by those who venture near him.

No matter what you do, what you possess, the position you occupy in life, there is no limit to your potential development for good. There is no limit to the potential grandeur and glory of your being. Your only limitation is the amount of time and energy, you are prepared to devote to meditating on your **SOURCE of BEING** and opening your human consciousness to enter into **IT** and receive **IT** into your mind.

Therefore, religious leaders, revere your congregations, because you do not know what spiritual insight and progress is taking place in the minds of those who may appear to be very humble and of no account socially.

Religious leaders, cease your criticism of other religions because you do not know the heights of spiritual knowledge, insight and enlightenment their adherents may have attained.

Religious leaders, realise that you, yourselves, are only as spiritually advanced as is your personal perception of **Reality.**

If you have no perception of what lies beyond the veil of your material world – you may be religious, but you do not have a spiritual consciousness.

This is the true ideal, the true aspiration, the highest goal – to understand and experience the Reality behind and within all things giving them their individual being.

You may call the Reality – God, Allah, Jehovah, Infinite Intelligence, Divine Mind or Divine Consciousness or the Tao. All these names mean the SOURCE of your BEING – your CREATIVE ORIGINS.

YOU CAN HAVE NO HIGHER ASPIRATION THAN THIS – to understand and experience the Reality behind and within all things – giving, maintaining and sustaining all individual being.

This was the goal presented to you by every enlightened Teacher who has come to earth.

They all shared the same vision, the same realisation and understanding. Such Teachers were held in high esteem, but few of their followers understood what they were being taught. Each man placed his own interpretation on the Teacher's words. Each man's interpretation arose out of his personal conditioning and bias.

In your personal lives, remember at all times, that your thoughts, words, deeds, not only have a bearing on your future life, but also affect the people with whom you are relating at any moment.

What are you, employer or employee, personally contributing to the successful operation of the business in which you earn your daily bread – be it factory, farm, shop or professional office? What are you giving to your employees or fellow workers in well-being and good feeling, what are you doing for the entire building?

'For the building'? you may ask in amazement.

But I repeat – what are you doing for your building, your vehicles, your entire business venture? Everything, bricks, mortar, steel, glass, paper,

126

metal, tyres, engines and petrol, is permeated with the consciousness you exude as you go about your daily affairs. This is the reason why some people leave a trail of destruction behind them because they have an ill-humoured, irritable, critical, destructive consciousness and others keep their possessions intact and looking new for years because they appreciate and cherish them daily.

Everything on your earth is the energy of consciousness made visible – be it in the form of 'solid' inanimate matter or living plasma. With your thoughts, you feed or destroy whatever is in your environment.

What are you doing to your family, home, and environment?

Are you grumbling, denigrating, destructive in thought towards your work and other people? Then rest assured, you are leaving a little trail of destructive consciousness behind you which will help erode all that it penetrates and imbues.

If you focus on the desire to love, to accept, to work with gladness in your heart, then everywhere you go you are shedding a consciousness of strength, blessing and growth.

When I was on earth in Palestine, I was dealing with Orthodox Jews who believed in and upheld codes of conduct so rigid they bordered on cruelty; their traditional laws were inhibiting, depressing, confining and ridiculous. I brought to these people a new vision of an eternal **'Father'** which was both transcendent to themselves – and yet everywhere present – ever aware of their needs, and of such universal love that they could rest assured it was always the **'Father's Will'** to fulfill those needs.

I told the people to look around them, look at the countryside, at the hills where sheep and goats grazed in peace, at the lakes filled with fish, and at the birds flying in the air and resting and nesting in trees, and the flowers so gorgeously clothed in many colours. I told them: 'Look – understand what you are seeing. You are seeing a world where everything has its needs, and everything has those needs fulfilled. How can you doubt when you see the sheep living entirely on grass? What does the grass contain that it feeds fleece, bone, blood and flesh and produces young? Are you not witnessing a marvel of supply? Look at the needs of birds how wonderfully they are provided for. They have shelter in trees and seeds for strength. As for people who have their needs of housing, food and clothes, the '**Father**' has given them the entire world from which to fulfill their needs.'

Muhammad, after enlightenment perceived the same indwelling universal Spirit, both existent and active in all things. **We – Muhammad and I** spoke to our fellow countrymen of the same inspired **Truth** and asked them the same kind of questions. 'Is such an all-knowing '**Father**' - '**Allah**' - **Divine Consciousness** not also aware of your deeper needs – your needs of love, health, and prosperity? How can you doubt this? Only have faith, and your needs will be supplied according to your faith'.

It is your lack of faith which withdraws energy from the natural flow of 'Father' - 'Allah' - Love in your bodies, relationships and lives.

So often in despair, when on earth in the person of Jesus, I exclaimed: 'Would that I could tell you and show you and make you **see** how it is that the '**Father**' knows your needs. Would I could show you how you, yourselves, contribute to the making of your own tomorrows, and the tomorrows of all those who surround you. If only I could help you see that you truly reap as you sow! If only you could see the **truth of existence** as I saw it when in the desert in Palestine. You would know then that your thoughts and actions grow in magnitude and strength, day by day, and take on outer form exactly as the seeds of plants go into the earth and grow, taking on ever greater outer form of stems, leaves and fruit, as each day passes after another.

'I would I could show you how important you are every second of the day, in the fabric of your home, your work and your country.

'I long to help you see how your thoughts are the origin of all your good and evil. They are the very ground of your good and evil. If it be that evil comes to you, do not look at your neighbour to see from whence has come that evil – look within your own hearts and see when last you were at odds with someone, destructively – by slander, falsifying truth, rejection, criticism. That was the moment of the birth of your present grief!

'You have been told that you must wrest an eye from whoever takes your eye but I tell you that this is foolish. If you have your eye gouged from its socket, and you likewise take your opponent's eye, you will probably find yourself shortly without a hand and leg. Better to stand stock still, raise your mind and heart to the '**Father**' - '**Allah**' - **Divine Consciousness** and pray for help and healing and protection from any greater calamity!

128

'And pray too for your adversary because any ill-feeling you have towards him, will only draw more pain and distress towards yourself. Forgive him, pray for him, and you will bring into being, blessings for yourself. Not because you have 'pleased' the '**Father' - 'Allah'** – and 'done the right thing' – but because your consciousness will attract blessings into your experience. You will be truly blessing yourself as you pray for blessings for others. But let not this be your motive, otherwise the blessing is tainted by your self- regard.

'Always, in any situation when you are threatened – stop, stand, turn and call on the '**Father' – Divine Consciousness** for help – and watch the deliverance. It will surely come.

'I tell you beyond all fear of contradiction that if any of you will live in the protection of the '**Father' - 'Allah' - Divine Consciousness** by radiating goodwill and love to everyone in your life and country, and even your so-called enemies, you will never be attacked, you will never know sorrow, you will never be subject to any of the human ailments and misfortunes which the human consciousness creates.

'You will be enfolded in a mantle of **Light and Love ... Divine Consciousness** will flow into your mind, your body and your life. People may be falling ill around you, felled by an attack, or 'drowning' in an agony of fear, but you will walk the same path conscious that no one has the least **human** power against the **POWER** – the **SOURCE of your BEING** – which has given you your own being and life on earth.

'Not one may dare deny this statement, since none who would want to deny it, has reached the level of spiritual consciousness where such protection is a normal occurrence. Therefore how can they deny this statement?'

And I speak the self-same **truth** to those who have reached the level of spiritual consciousness which perceives the universality of the '**Father'** - '**Allah' - Divine Consciousness,** and **Its** abundant love radiated to all and everyone. Such spiritual adepts strive to live within and radiate that love – and will gladly confirm that this is a truth I have stated. They will have experienced the miraculous protection and fulfilment of need and will know they can relax in the 'sun' of the '**Father' - 'Allah' - Divine Consciousness** goodwill and love. They will also be happy to accept that **Divine Consciousness** called by any other name – God, Jahveh, the Absolute, Infinite, Allah, always remains the universal inter- penetrating

Divine Consciousness despite all the differing terminologies used by various nations. They will have reached that level of spiritual awareness when they can perceive that behind all colour, language, beliefs, actions of whatever kind, all people – all creation itself – is one at the grass roots of their being. Man and ant share the same origins within the equilibrium of **UNIVERSAL CONSCIOUSNESS.**

THIS IS TRUE FREEDOM. The only freedom.

Until you are prepared to realise and accept that your **SOURCE of BEING** within you, and above and around you, can indeed flow into your mind and body DIRECTLY IN RESPONSE TO PRAYER, you will be subject to all the ailments of the earthly and human consciousness.

When you steal, you will lose things also. When you fight, and wound, maim and kill, you will be maimed, wounded or killed in body and or spirit. When you start a war, it will be a long and bitter struggle. Everything evil you endure, you have been the original cause of it.

Yours is the ability to choose the way you wish to live in future. You choose the way you will live by changing your consciousness from antagonism to love and acceptance of every one equally.

If you imagine the damage and hurt you would like to inflict on another, your thought will reach your enemy and will erode their strength according to the intensity of your intention.

Do not think that your thought has dissolved and is no more. It rests in electro-magnetic strength, taking on form until it rebounds to harm you also.

You can do much damage with your thinking and feeling. Damage to others and damage to yourself.

Therefore, guard them – the tools of your creativity – well, and at all times turn to the **'Father' - 'Allah' - Divine Consciousness**, and ask for relief from any thought which is contrary to true unconditional love. According to the power of your prayer and the sincere faith in which you raise your mind to **Divine Consciousness**, your thoughts will be imbued with new life and love.

What We – the Brotherhood of Illuminates – the Enlightened Ones – in CHRIST CONSCIOUSNESS – are about to tell you is of vital importance to the world generally. We speak equally – to Christian, Judaism,

130

Muslim, Hindu, Buddhist and to every religion, and every race of the world.

We speak to all – because each and every one in the world needs this instruction to make it possible for you to move on to higher levels of spiritual awareness.

Your personal and sexual relationships between men and women are of far more importance to your overall well-being than you can presently even imagine.

We deal with these relationships at length in the following pages, only because it is absolutely imperative – vital – for you men and women to wake up to the basic reality of your male or female individuality – and identity – and true source of gender differences.

You must fully understand the true origins of your male and female bodies and characteristics. They are not just bodies created with differing physical organs and modes of sexual expression in order to create children. They draw the origins of their masculinity or femininity from their very SOURCE of BEING – from within the equilibrium of UNIVERSAL CONSCIOUSNESS.

(I am telling you this before you read **Letter 5** so that you will study that **Letter** bearing in mind what I am telling you now about your sexuality.)

Therefore, if the sexuality of a man and woman is not used in conformity with the **Divine Consciousness Intention** expressed in the original act of creativity at the time of the 'Big Bang', it is obvious that although the sexuality may produce children, it will not bring to men and women the unity of being and personal fulfilment and joy it was meant to bring. In fact, the reverse is true; eventually the sexual act itself brings disappointment and satiation, after which any 'love' previously felt by partners, drains away. With knowledge and understanding, spiritually based men and women will make every attempt to transcend their present state of consciousness in regard to male-female relationships of any kind, no matter what those relationships may be, sexual or otherwise. They will strive to express within their minds and hearts the purposes for which they were created in different forms. They will understand the origins of their differing innate impulses, temperaments, and modes of self-expression and will value them. **They will use their differences to enhance the well-being of each other**. Competition

131

will disappear. As this happens, they will tune into **Divine Consciousness** ever more easily. As they tune into **Divine Consciousness** ever more easily, so will they ascend into higher levels of spiritual consciousness.

At the moment your approach to your sexuality is your barrier to your ascension in consciousness.

It roots you in your humanhood.

I – We – cannot emphasize sufficiently that you have not discovered the Truth of your existence until you have fully understood and sought to implement in your daily lives, in your homes and workplace, your full comprehension of the true meaning of 'man' and 'woman'.

You have been told that you must not commit adultery. But I tell you that when you desire your neighbour's wife or husband, you are making pictures in your thoughts which will affect the thinking of your neighbour's wife or husband. He or she will begin to think about you in the same way – or will feel uncomfortable in your company, feeling your sexual need, and will avoid you in future.

What is in your mind will surely come into being in the world. So do not fool yourself that you can daydream and conjure up pictures pleasing to yourself which will damage no one else. For this reason, your pornography literature is truly a blasphemous desecration of your SOURCE of BEING – it is a sexual scourge deliberately whipping up sexual appetites, releasing through lustful men's minds, untold suffering and misery on the bodies, minds and emotions of female young. What you have perpetrated and are presently doing has helped bring your 'civilisation' to its present edge of destruction. Rest assured, the day of reckoning will come for you who publish and distribute the 'printed sickness' and it will come for those who use it to arouse themselves.

You, in the Western world, have earned the contempt of the East due to your decadent foolishness. You will not escape what you have sown.

And you of the East will not escape your foolishness in your callous attitudes towards your women who bear and raise your sons and precious daughters.

Some of you, in ignorance of Truth, for your own selfish purposes and gain, have made a mockery of the **Truth of Muhammad!**

You have shrouded your women in heavy garments, denying them freedom of movement and of Allah's fresh air as they venture out amongst other people.

To what kind of man will your beliefs and your irrational, ego-centric behaviour appeal? Only to men who have no kindly feeling for women. Is it such followers that your Prophet Muhammad would have attracted when he was on earth? No, indeed, he appealed only to the most spiritually minded of people.

What kind of imagery or picture of your Prophet are you sending out to the rest of the world?

I will tell you – of a man demented and obsessed by the lowly state of the female sex, who regarded a woman as a man's possession to be imprisoned from the world.

A man unaware of a woman's true needs to be happy, a man oblivious of her misery **in the captive, subjected state.**

This man has nothing whatever to do with the true Muhammad, the Prophet of Islam. **When on earth, he revered and respected the female sex.**

It was from the female of the species he derived the means to move forward on his spiritual path to enlightenment. He owed them much and knew that, although they were different in body, they were equal in spirit.

In fact, it was no accident that he came to earth, poor and deprived, to meet a lady of extreme virtue, material wealth and spiritual insight to help raise him up to the stature of Prophet when he was fitted to fill it.

That was the purpose behind Muhammad's coming to earth – to restore woman to her rightful place – as equal partner of dominant man.

Consider this well. After enlightenment, I, in the person of Jesus, became celibate because I chose to do so but this in no way interfered with my love for the women who ministered to my needs.

But Muhammad, after enlightenment 'knew' many women and his ministry was of one who was called upon to learn how to live and deal with women equitably and with love.

Just as expediency caused my followers to report my doings and teachings selectively to promote their own purposes, so has the selfishness of certain spiritually blind individuals caused them to distort Muhammad's original teaching with numerous additions and interpretations never intended by Muhammad. In such a way is every great **spiritual Teacher's work** overlaid by the misinformation of human thought until the Truth is so shrouded in fallacies that people are led seriously astray and even caused to sin in ignorance.

Because you and certain other religions have strongly adhered to the belief in Adam and Eve created to live in happiness in the Garden of Eden, of Eve's temptation by the serpent, her fall from grace and her temptation of Adam, man has been encouraged to perceive woman as the great temptress.

The imagined origins of human kind are not true. They are merely allegories. Neither is it true that woman is the great temptress.

For eunuchs, the woman has no appeal. Why is this? Because that which impels a man to lie with a woman is removed. Therefore, in whom is the tempter? In man himself – and can be physically removed from him – or in the woman who remains herself despite all?

Man has been made expressly to plant the seed. **Therefore, to plant the seed he must – wherever he sees the opportunity.**

Woman has been made to receive the seed. In past years, before the 20th century, women were sexually dormant until seduced by men. Where then the tempter? In men, the arousers and seducers or in women, the seduced, and aroused?

Man has been hiding from his own masculine nature in the name of purity and placing the responsibility for his downfall on woman. Is this a sacred activity? Is it worthy? Should it continue?

WE speak to those of you who profess to adhere to the Muslim faith and who believe you are 'sinless' or of 'pure mind' because you have shrouded your women in heavy clothes to protect yourselves from temptation and prevent other men seeing your 'possessions'. How greatly are you misled by your own passions.

By being protected from the exercise of your human desires, they only increase until they break out in some virulent, brutal form.

I – We – say to men and women everywhere – true Purity is only attained when you can be surrounded with every form of temptation and yet remain untouched by desire, unmoved by earthly feelings, untainted by earthly lusts, free of craving and longing for possession.

Purity in its every form transcends all earthly physical hungers. Purity is the ability to see temptation for what it is – grossness of thought and feeling which traps the senses of men and women into doing unclean things. A truly pure person desires only the clean and honest environment suited to their innate longing for spiritual love and beauty of self expression in every facet of their lives. That is true Purity.

However, true purity cannot be achieved unless there have first been the long years of temptation. It is a necessary part of your spiritual development; unless you have been sorely tempted at times, and have eventually come to understand that there is a higher road to walk, a road of self-denial, and of sincere concern and caring for a good woman, you will never attain a state of true purity.

You will be enslaved by desire and will be in a constant turmoil of inner conflict.

Therefore, do not avoid temptation by covering women and living in artificial conditions of pseudo purity. Rather – men and women, remove your clothes, revere each other's bodies as the outer visible beautiful forms of the inner **DIVINE CONSCIOUSNESS** and **experience** the release that true spiritual purity will bring you.

Suffer grievous temptation – and overcome! Take your conflict to **Divine Consciousness** and seek **Its power** to help you overcome your physical longing, for only in this way will you find the freedom, the peace of mind, you are basically seeking.

If, at the moment, you seek relief and release of your craving by giving way to it, that is no freedom or release. The self-same craving will return in due course – and once again you will know the searing conflict. If again you give way – again the conflict, even more intense, awaits your decision to stand firm in the power of **Divine Consciousness** until the craving is finally

135

subdued by perceiving the sacred beauty, the *Reality* behind and within all physical form.

The highest spirituality between the sexes is when man and woman can be together naked and at peace together, in a state of mutual reverence of soul, mind, heart, and body.

In such spirituality, all they feel for each other is love and regard for the well-being of the other. Out of such LOVE and compassionate tender CARING will come a union of ecstatic being that few have experienced – and, if intended, a child of incomparable beauty of body and mind will be conceived.

In the centuries ahead, when people have begun to evolve spiritually on every level of their humanhood, such a love between partners will be normal – and the kind of selfish sex, seeking only physical satisfaction, as indulged in at this present time, will be regarded as utterly degrading – as abhorrent as rape.

At the present time, the highest spiritual way to follow in regard to the sexes, is to acknowledge and abide by the perception, that:

Men and women were created to perform special tasks in life suited to their underlying natures.The man impregnates the woman. Without the woman's good will and help, the man would go to the end of his days – childless – without a human being to carry on his name.

Therefore the man should treat a woman as wholly equal but born to carry different responsibilities. He should give her the highest respect, and love and care – at all times – to enable her to carry her burdens with greater ease, for it is she who gives visible form to what is first conceived in mind.

When a woman receives a sperm which unites with her ovum within the recesses of her body, a miracle is wrought to which you, the man, have done nothing to contribute, other than your sperm in a moment of delight – in which is your reward.

You can only contribute to the continued health and normal development of the 'miracle' you have given life to in your partner's body, by your unfailing, caring love for her well-being and health, and protecting her from all emotional and external harm. This is your masculine responsibility.

Only in this way do you deserve to remain at her side as father of her child.

If you fail in this, you have no value as father to the child – and have no value to yourself as a man born to manifest your spiritual **'Divine Consciousness Father'** within your physical life.

A man who harasses a woman carrying his child, who treats her with contempt, who offers harsh and brutal words and physical treatment is breaking the most fundamental **Law of Existence** in which male and female should be united in equality of **Divine Beingness.**

Women who are respected and loved and protected should equally respect and love and offer refreshment of spirit and body to her partner, nurturing his capacity for giving of himself to her. A woman who does not nurture her partner with caring, tenderness asnd love, is depriving his masculine spirit of the will to endure in face of difficulties he encounters in the external world.

He will seek his solace from another source – men or women – drink or drugs – or by isolating himself within the household, of use neither to partner nor children. Therefore, men and women have an equal responsibility to cherish each other.

Just as the **Man** must learn to channel, daily, the **'Father Aspect'** of **Divine Consciousness** towards family and work, so must **Woman** learn to express the **'Mother aspect' of Divine Consciousness** in her daily life.

Those who deny this Truth will be denied access to the Celestial Kingdoms until they have increased their spiritual perception, and prayerfully changed their attitudes. Only when their vision is lifted above the earthly human perception of 'male and female' – and beyond their earthly desires and ego drive – to the Reality out of which they have drawn their 'being', will they escape the wheel of re-incarnation and find entrance to the ultimate Joy and Glory.

If, within a culture, a woman is regarded only as a 'possession', an object of a man's desires, and not treated as a woman, absolutely equal with a man, such a culture has not understood the true nature of man and the true nature of woman.

Man and woman are two equal halves of one whole.

When single and alone the man is manifesting but one aspect of his **SOURCE OF BEING** and when woman lives alone and single, she also manifests but one aspect of her **SOURCE of BEING.**

The **DIVINE INTENTION** of **UNIVERSAL CONSCIOUSNESS** was to express **ITs** own wholeness through creation by individualising, in physical form, each of the two equally balanced aspects of **ITSELF** and then bringing them together again in physical form, to experience the unity and wholeness of **DIVINE CONSCIOUSNESS** from which they originally took their individuality.

As they come together in love and unity of spirit and body, they discover the joy and ecstasy of **UNIVERSAL CONSCIOUSNESS in equilibrium.**

(This entire process is clearly set out in **Letters 5 and 7.**)

Therefore, the combination of the masculinity of the man and the femininity of the woman is essential to make a 'whole' drawn from the **SOURCE of BEING.** Out of this combination is formed a whole child.

When I was in the desert in Palestine, I first perceived that the over-riding **nature** of **UNIVERSAL CONSCIOUSNESS Creativity**, our **SOURCE of BEING** was **INTENTION.**

The Intention to create, plan and design – and then to bring forth that design by growing it, feeding, healing, protecting, and fulfilling its every need in a disciplined manner.

Both male and female have been evolved in physical form and consciousness to experience – **INTENTION and express it in all ways possible in their lives. This is the very first act of creativity. Without INTENTION there would be no CREATION.**

INTENTION is the origin of – and permeates – the whole of existence.

INTENTION defines the nature of the deed – loving or destructive.

138

The **male and female** have been individualised to experience and formulate **INTENTION** in their lives. This is the very first impulse of creativity.

Male and female have also been individualised to experience and express **WILLPOWER.**

WILLPOWER in the **MALE** is experienced and expressed primarily as **Activity**. In primitive forms – he moves out into the environment to fulfill his intention. Therefore, he dons the robes of the leader and quester. He was individualised to think and work to fulfill his purposes without the encumbrance of emotions.

WILLPOWER in the **FEMALE** is motivated and experienced primarily as **Feeling** – the **Need to Nurture** the **original INTENTION** and bring it, purposefully to full term – fruition – through the process of caring, feeding, clothing, repairing, teaching, protecting.

PURPOSE is entirely different to **INTENTION** since **purpose** comes down from the mental plane of intention and becomes an emotional drive, a desire to formulate 'a means to achieve the intended end'.

A **'powerful INTENTION to do something' becomes a PURPOSE behind continued existence**. In this way, thought and feeling are married to perform the work of creation.

The **male** is constantly roaming seeking new ideas, new ways to fulfill his intentions to give him purpose in life.

The **female's intentions** are 'purpose personified', sensitive and stable, prepared to make sacrifices for the loved ones.

Therefore, the two basic **IMPULSES** within the **SOURCE of BEING** – **expressed in physical form as male and female** – are inter-dependent. One could not survive without the other. Both are needed for the continuity of creation.

Because of his masculine mobility, his leadership drive, the male has considered himself superior to the female. This is because she remains stable, creating security for the male. **But the feminine drive is the drive of unconditional love, the drive worthy of the highest respect and consideration to enable her to flourish and perform her innate purpose within the household in peace of mind and joy.**

The man's role is to provide physical security and material means of subsistence for the family.

The woman's role is to provide emotional security and the emotional means of personal fulfilment and joy within the family environment.

In the past, in the East and West, the male has exercised his role of dominance within the home, making the woman subservient and obedient to his will. In so doing, he has bent and distorted the energies of **Divine Consciousness** and channelled them through his mind and heart into a bent civilisation.

He has also distorted the woman's consciousness by instilling in her a deep resentment of her sub- servient role which she knows intuitively she should not be expected to endure.

Therefore, he has created a degraded and degrading way of life for himself and partner, entirely in conflict with the **NATURE** of his **SOURCE of BEING.**

The fact that the female has had to exercise her masculine drive of aggression to express her equality of being, to achieve the respect due to her within society, means that your civilisation has become thoroughly destabilised and unhealthy. The woman is usurping the male role out of desperation but in doing so, she is defeating the intention behind creation.

Male and female have lost their way completely. In under-developed countries, people are only half alive, trying to solve the division between male and female through casual sex. As a result, man and woman become ever more divided and unfulfilled. Conflict in the family unit creates stress, misery and separation, even though they may live under one roof.

In 'developed' countries, psychiatric offices are filled with unhappy people and children who say they do not know who they really are or what their purpose is in life. They are asking the 'experts' who do not know the answers either.

It should be remembered also, that each person, male and female, have lessons to learn in life which can only be learnt in the sex – and the race – in which they find themselves. Therefore, a woman must accept her role in life as the provider of emotional love and security to her mate and children, with self-respect and dignity and perform it to the very best of her ability. She must recognise that the role of provider of emotional security is absolutely vital to society. She provides the 'glue' of love and well-being which holds families, cities, countries together. When she understands her true place and goals in society, and seeks to perform and achieve them in the highest way possible, she is moving forward rapidly on the path to unconditional love and the highest rewards in personal fulfilment and happiness. She will also move on to a higher level of consciousness – perhaps as a male in her next life, who will bring great benefits to mankind.

Similarly, spiritually evolved males – even spiritual teachers – return to life on earth to learn true humility and to put all their high principles of existence into daily practice as a loving woman who mothers with wisdom and nurtures all who have need of what she can offer. Where then, is the inequality?

Remove the scales from your limited sight and intellect and see with clear vision that there should be no inequality – only shared INTENTIONS to express all that you have both drawn from **Divine Consciousness** in the most spiritual way to achieve the highest happiness possible on earth.

In years to come, when a man and woman have evolved spiritually, if or when divided in **intention**, they will together take their intentions to **'FATHER-MOTHER-DIVINE CONSCIOUSNESS'**, asking: 'What is to be created in our circumstances? What is our best way ahead?'.

When they have received answers, they will accept them with loving heart and pool them. Any differences in answer will be respected and again taken to **Divine Consciousness** with the same request until they reach sincere consensus.

Together, man and woman will then return and ask of **Divine Consciousness**: 'How may we best achieve our purposes?'. And again, they pool their answers and continue asking until they finally arrive at a working plan which has been conceived, not in the human brain alone, but in the highest dimension of creativity – **DIVINE CONSCIOUSNESS.**

Working together in this way, they will eventually experience the 'bliss' of true unity of soul, mind, heart and body.

Finally, the male could not exist comfortably without also experiencing and manifesting some of the feminine drive. He needs emotion to bond with his wife, children and other relationships – school mates and workmates, colleagues and friends. Without some warm feelings, he would be a cold monster. Frequently, if an old soul, he brings through much warmth and caring from previous incarnations as a woman. The more spiritually evolved he becomes, the more equally are the two sexual impulses balanced within his nature.

This also applies to women.

Equally, the female could not exist comfortably without some of the masculine drive. Without a capacity for intelligent planning, her household would be a disaster zone. There is also the possibility that she has been a strong masculine character in her past incarnation and is uncomfortable in the feminine role of sacrificing herself for others. Such a one must ask of **Divine Consciousness** to clarify her vision that she may see that without love for humanity, leadership is a dangerous exercise.

When men and women are nearing an equal balance of male and female natures within themselves, their task in life is to transcend their sexual drive through achieving unconditional love for all people and directing the drive itself into pure creativity – such as the arts. Of such people are 'Masters' made, masters of themselves, masters of creativity, masters of human consciousness, masters of 'matter'.

Unfortunately, at this present time, your men and women who are nearing equal balance of 'male/female natures' within their one nature, have no guideposts as to what their true goals should be. They have lost their way and have created a spurious society amongst themselves in which the joy and personal fulfilment they seek is negated by their pre-occupation with bodily functions rather than with spiritual achievements. They will remain unhappy people, torn with conflicts, until they discover the truth regarding 'who they really are'.

In speaking about the feminine role in life, it must also be said that many of your modern women in developed countries, have achieved a high degree of masculine drive in the past 100 years.

They must choose their priorities in life carefully. They do not have to sit at home, stagnant and bored but they will become happier, more fulfilled people if they turn their intelligence and abilities to creating new modes of constructive life for the whole family. At the moment, they may not know how to do this, but meditation will draw into their minds, the necessary inspiration on the best way to use their powers of leadership and talents for the happiness of all.

Men who have developed greater capacity for empathy with women and their fellow men, will also, through meditation followed by inspiration, find higher ways of expressing their capacity for leadership in their work, bringing happiness to others.

Why have **I – We** – dealt with the matter of the sexes in such depth?

This has been absolutely necessary since the battle of the sexes – both in the East and West, is creating unhealthy conditions on earth. It fosters aggression and festers as anger and hostility. Sexual freedom has brought the world to a crisis point of extinction by the impregnation of AIDS. All viruses are created within destructive consciousness forces.

You must understand that human beings have created their own viruses! Every virus is a destructive living consciousness impulse made visible. It targets what the impulse of destructive consciousness targeted at the moment the virus took on form.

I was very clear about this aspect of existence when I was on earth in the persona of Jesus. The Jews had the rigid tradition of washing cups before drinking from them. I told them explicitly that they should not be worried about what went into their mouths. They should be concerned about what came out of their minds and hearts – then out through their mouths. At that time, science had not discovered the presence of viruses but it was agreed that disease came from eating and drinking from dirty utensils. But I knew that the disease had originally come out of the minds and hearts of savagely angry people. Thereafter, it was propagated by the division of the cells but it carried within itself, forever, the instinct and consciousness which initially brought it into being.

AIDS has been no accident. It has emerged from the consciousness forces of self-indulgence and destructive emotional reactions between sexual partners. Submerged hatred and anger can drive people into a sexual act, leaving a residue of sickness behind it in mind, emotions and body.

Because emotional attunement has not always motivated the sexual act between men and women, they have known severe disappointment and lack of release and fulfilment. When this happens, the male sexual energy dwindles. It has to be rekindled by images of sexual perversions.

As a result, pornography has become 'big business' in some countries. It panders to the body instincts alone. Out of pornography have come a lack of respect for women, and a mechanical non-emotional sexual act, together with rapidly increasing rape and child sexual abuse. People giving way to these abominable   acts of depraved   cruelty will surely reap the consequences either in this life or a future incarnation.

Therefore, when followers of Islam condemn the West for their lax sexual behaviour and perversion, they are right to believe that it is bringing down unhealthy conditions on earth.

These unhealthy conditions are not sent by 'Allah' – but are a natural consequence of their breaking the **LAWS of EXISTENCE.**

Similarly, the followers of Islam are breaking the **LAWS of EXISTENCE** because they, like the Jews, hold to the tradition of an eye-for-an-eye and believe that there is such a thing as a Holy War. There is no such thing as a Holy War – there is only the *Reality* of **Holy Forgiveness** and **Holy Reconciliation,** treating your 'brother', be he your enemy or friend, with love and understanding.

None of you may break the LAWS of EXISTENCE and hope that you may enter into the kingdom of heaven or paradise. Your behaviour has no place beyond the mayhem you are presently bringing on yourselves.

WE will leave you with these thoughts which **we** beg you will receive deeply into your consciousness and make good use of them in your daily lives. We strongly urge you to band together, irrespective of religious beliefs, in small groups to use the **Letters** as guide lines for your daily lives. Shed, if you can, your conditioning, and come together in true humility, as people willing to agree they know little of true spirituality – but are strongly desirous of learning how to enhance and spiritualise their lives.

As many of you are aware, you are entering a new phase of world history, during the course of which it will be realised that no longer is the great divide between the wealthy and the poor.

The great divide will be in **consciousness**. The divide will be between those who have been able to find entrance into the higher spiritual consciousness and radiate love and acceptance equally to all – friends and foes – and who make it their goal to radiate **Divine Consciousness** into every facet of their daily lives – and those who remain encased within their ego-drives, seeking domination of the weak. They may appear to succeed for a while – but eventually they will fail and their suffering in their self-created darkness will be great.

These **Letters** will be the means of your moving out of darkness into **LIGHT**.

As you seek to raise your frequencies of spiritual consciousness through radiating love to all unconditionally, so will you be going through a slow ASCENSION in CONSCIOUSNESS which will dynamically affect your physical health and your earthly conditions.

On you brave people will rest the upliftment of world consciousness. You will emerge from the coming conflict, strong and purposeful, and will proceed to build another type of world consciousness. You will introduce the beginning of spiritual and technical and economic progress and world peace for centuries to come.

I, the CHRIST, have spoken – WE – the BROTHERHOOD of MASTERS – speak to Christians, Muslims, Buddhists, Jews, Hindus, Sufis, and to every religious persuasion of the world. You are all encompassed in our love. Believe this – for this is true.

LETTER 5

I, **the CHRIST**, am writing this **LETTER 5** to clearly define the hidden **REALITY, which I will also refer to as the 'UNIVERSAL' and 'DIVINE'** to help you stretch your minds to understand that whilst you are an 'individual, **THAT WHICH HAS GIVEN YOU 'BEING' AND 'INDIVIDUALITY'** is ITSELF Universal – Eternal – Infinite – Everywhere without beginning or end.**

For the sake of those people who have chosen to read Letter 5 before my earlier Letters describing my life and true teachings on earth, I will make a further statement that my true 'Jesus' CHRIST self must not in any way be confused with the 'Jesus' recorded in the New Testament.

Since my original teachings, in the form of the four Gospels, have been distributed world-wide and grossly misinterpreted, it is my intention to begin teaching **TRUTH of EXISTENCE** by explaining the true meaning of my original terminology as quoted in the Gospels. This is necessary to dispel and eventually eradicate from people's consciousness the misunderstandings which have persisted and misinformed generations of spiritual seekers since my life on earth.

When on earth, to describe the **Reality** behind and within existence, I deliberately coined the term the **'Father'** when referring to 'God'. This was done for two reasons.

Firstly, as I explained in **Letter 1**, when I received enlightenment in the desert, I was enabled to see that the concepts describing the Creator of the universe as 'revealed' by the Jewish prophets were completely wrong.

Secondly, I was given to perceive clearly – and fully understand – the true nature of the Creator and I realised that it was a nature of parenting – of fulfilling the needs of creation in clear-cut, specific ways which were synonymous with those of a father-mother. Indeed, I saw that the parenting impulses present in all living creatures had been drawn directly from the Creator, and that the origin of all love and parenting drives was also the origin of life and existence itself.

I also 'saw' that creation was a **visible manifestation of the Universal Creative Impulses of Being**, and therefore humankind could be termed the offspring of the creator.

147

For this reason, it was quite natural for me to speak of the '**Father**' when referring to the Creator, since, to me, this is what the Creator truly is in every way – more especially '**Father-Mother**' but having regard to the Jewish insistence on the woman occupying a subordinate position in their daily lives, I referred only to the '**Father**' to avoid Jewish resistance and to gain their acceptance of the new terminology.

I also coined the term the '**Father**' to help the Jews realise that their concept of Jehovah and the rigidity of Jewish laws were totally erroneous. Also by using a new terminology – the '**Father**' – to describe the Creator – **the Creative Impulse** – behind and within existence, I made it clear I had brought an altogether new teaching in opposition to the accepted belief in a 'God' which rejected certain people and sent disasters upon them as retribution.

I want you to understand fully, that nowhere has it been made clear in your New Testament that I brought a teaching completely opposed to the teachings in the Old Testament and therefore the New Testament as a true record of my life and teachings cannot be trusted or accepted or believed.

A true and accurate record of my personality, enlightened nature, emotional attitudes and teachings themselves, would have made it abundantly clear that the old Judaic forms of religion and my enlightened teachings were diametrically opposed in every way.

The Judaic religion was one of extreme materialistic concepts. There are certainly writings from which spiritually enlightened Jews drew, and continue to draw, a mystical perception of our **SOURCE of BEING**.

They are to be greatly honoured and respected for their transcendent states of mind.

But as the prophets reached the average man and woman, their writings transmitted a different, controlling message which is purely human and false. No control for 'good' or 'evil' is exercised from a 'God above'. If there were, the world would not be in such a shocking state of upheaval and misery.

I brought a new teaching which was directed exclusively at making people aware of **universality and love – the indwelling nature – as well as the transcendent nature of ...**

'THAT' ... WHICH BROUGHT ALL CREATION INTO VISIBLE MANIFESTATION.

It is my purpose to make this abundantly clear to enable seekers of Truth to rid themselves of any remnant of belief that I was merely a prophet in a long line of Jewish prophets; that I continued preaching their themes of an almighty Jehovah possessing ambivalent feelings towards his own creation.

Fear of Orthodox Jews kept my disciples in line with what they had decided they would tell the public about me. You must remember that to gain new Jewish adherents to Christianity, they were afraid to discard the Old Testament since it had held the Jews together for centuries; therefore, they extracted and added on from my teachings whatever was compatible with the old religious beliefs. My genealogy was listed to re-assure Jewish people I had descended from King David. Why should they bother with this unless they wanted to make it clear that I was very much a Jew of ancient lineage and therefore could be a candidate for Messiahship?

If they truly understood what I had come to earth to do – to break away from the past and lay the foundations for an altogether new future of understanding and activity – they would have made valiant efforts to make certain that people understood the true purposes which drove me to the day of my death. But they did not do this. They obscured much of what I tried to teach.

A strong-hearted disciple of mine, Stephen, was less afraid to speak out about my true teachings, although these had also been embroidered, but even so, he was stoned to death.

You must understand that life for my disciples was precarious and it is little wonder that my true teachings were covered over with traditional thinking to make it more palatable to the public.

Even so will there be fierce disputations when I say that 'Christianity' only presents a record of some of my statements and healings which are not in too much conflict with Judaic teaching. It is a religion coined by my early disciples and by Paul, after his induction in Antioch, to keep the Jews together as far as possible and to bring gentile converts into the fold. Expediency then became a facet of Christian thought.

This is the truth of my life and death on earth. Disputations will arise because people hold on to cherished beliefs and surrender them only with the pain

149

experienced by those who lose their dearest possessions. Nonetheless, dear as the beliefs may be to people – they are only **beliefs.**

They are not a sure foundation on which to build new lives.

Now that I am returning to you through the medium of these **Letters**, I am again making every attempt possible – **within the parameters of your human perceptions** – to describe for you the *Reality* – **your Source of Being – which initiated the universe and existence itself.**

Exactly as 2000 years before, **I have now come through the medium of these Letters to lay the foundation for future spiritual evolution during the next millennium. Your spiritual development can only arise out of your deeper perceptions and understanding of the nature of existence and of**

... 'THAT' ... WHICH BROUGHT YOU INTO BEING.

For what you clearly **perceive** creates the conditions under which you live.

Because you have not understood your true spiritual origins, humankind is continually embroiled in wars and has spawned earthly conditions which are both a disgrace to human consciousness and a source of human suffering of every kind.

For this reason, I am **SENDING – RADIATING – THE FULL POWER OF MY CHRISTHOOD CONSCIOUSNESS** to bring the **TRUTH of EXISTENCE** to you in the kind of modern understandable terminology to enable you to construct a new consciousness and realisation **'of Truth as it really is'** – rather than allow you to continue adhering to those false beliefs you have been taught, or have been brought to you by tradition.

With usage and understanding, the terminology will come to arouse in you the same – **or more** – reverence and love and spiritual insight as you previously felt when using the word 'God'. Loaded with universal meaning the more appropriate terminology will eventually fill you with spiritual power when you use and visualise the meaning of the words.

I am here to tell you that when you have purified your consciousness of the gross human thoughts and feelings pertaining to the ego-drive, and persevere in meditation and a lifting up of your consciousness to the **Universal**, you will begin to feel the spiritual power invading your mind and eventually your whole body.

Therefore, my teachings are **exclusively** directed at assisting you to open your consciousness to newness of life, vitality and spiritual power that you may abandon your old way of limited and dis-satisfied living and find a new source of inner joy and fulfilment of your every need.

Think about this statement. I have not brought you any 'should's' or 'should nots' or frustrating restrictions you, yourselves, do not want to impose on yourselves. I have certainly come to tell you how your 'consciousness forms' have life within them and eventually manifest in your world but I leave it to your good sense to choose the healthy thoughts, the loving actions, and the right path leading to joy and fulfilment when you realise the true nature of creation.

I have also come with the full force of my **Christ Power** to help you realise that there are no barriers between you and ... **'THAT'** ... **WHICH BROUGHT YOU INTO BEING** – only those you have created yourselves through ignorance of the **Laws of Existence.**

I have come to help you remove the barriers by enlightening your present ignorance and teaching you how to open your consciousness – your entire being – to the inflow of **THAT WHICH BROUGHT YOU INTO BEING.**

Therefore, I REPEAT: in the final analysis, my teachings are **exclusively** directed at assisting you to open your consciousness to newness of life, vitality and spiritual power that you may abandon your old way of limited and dis-satisfied living and find a new source of inner joy and fulfilment of your every need. **I long for you with Divine Love to reach this supreme state of being before you pass into the next dimension, that your passing may be painless and your transition one of sublime anticipation.**

This is the sole motivating purpose behind the **Letters.**

The above statement is a more compelling and powerful re-phrasing of the statement I made when on earth: 'Seek first the Kingdom of Heaven and all good things will be added to you.'

I did not make this statement to entice people to be 'good'. I stated a fact of existence.

You must also understand fully and clearly – that ... '**THAT**' ... which you call 'God' and I refer to as '**UNIVERSAL**', possesses none of the *human* attributes attributed to *IT* by many religions.

The human characteristics of anger, threats and punishment, for instance, only pertain to the human condition.

Again, I repeat: I, the **CHRIST**, have come down to dictate these **Letters** *expressly* to disinvest people's minds of the former 'human word pictures' coined by prophets. It is my firm intention to replace them with descriptions of the **POWER – the UNIVERSAL CONSCIOUSNESS** which really creates, moves within, and supports the visible universe and all other dimensions beyond your present perception and comprehension.

I am also here to tell you these further universes or dimensions, will be opened and will become accessible to your consciousness when the knowledge outlined in these **Letters** is absorbed and made the very fabric of your individualised consciousness.

Eventually, death will come to mean a happy transition from a limited dimension of existence to a brighter and more powerful one. You will know that when you are adequately spiritually cleansed and the time is ripe to emerge from the capsule of your body, you will leave, relieved to be free of physical limitations to enter a dimension of love and beautiful and wondrous beingness.

You will perceive death to be what it can be – really is for enlightened souls – a glorious transition – a gift of greater life, greater creativity and an experience of 'ecstatic being' you have not yet dreamed of.

I also want to make it clear that many, many people believe that they can live fruitful and fulfilled lives by following the hundreds of various teachers of 'positive thinking'. Changing your consciousness, they say, will change your lives. This is true to a limited extent but, for spiritually evolving seekers, such a change in consciousness still leaves a dryness of spirit and a yearning for something more.

That 'something more' that the soul craves is the true contact and re-union with its **SOURCE OF BEING**. Whilst you may have drawn a certain amount of spiritual growth by following the path of perceiving only the good, the truthful and loving, you remain an entity functioning alone in your own earthbound domain, unassisted by the **eternal, infinite Universal**. Once you realise the **nature of the Universal** and turn your thoughts to making true contact with It, you begin to realise you are no longer alone – you are supported by the **Reality** which supports the universe.

And when I say: 'making true contact with It', I mean that the prayer of supplication for this benefit or that is not making true contact with your SOURCE OF BEING.

Your prayer is certainly received into the **Source of Being**, and an answer is frequently received swiftly and the need is fulfilled, even as you have asked. But true contact with the **Source of your Being**, is only experienced when you have sufficiently cleansed your consciousness of the gross human ego-drive and have spent some time in meditation and a regular **emotionally powerful** 'reaching out' in consciousness to your Source seeking contact and renewal and refreshment of spirit.

This is the true purpose behind existence. **A constant and mutual** reciprocation of communication between the **Source of all Being** and creation.

Here I would remind you that when I lived on earth, I made it abundantly clear every day to the Jews that: 'of myself alone I could do nothing'.

I constantly stated that 'it is the 'Father' does the work, not I'.

I have come at this time to enable you to make the transition from the earth-bound human consciousness to that of enlightenment when a person **knows** that he or she finally **knows** the **Truth of Being.**

Undoubtedly, deeply religious people, indelibly indoctrinated with religious dogma and theology – Jewish, Christian, Muslim, Hindu or belonging to any other religious persuasion – will find it difficult – even painful

– at first, to accept and make good use of these **Letters** – for: A conditioned and programmed mind is like concrete. Cherished beliefs, used as talismans, emotional supports and affirmations to give strength in times of crisis, are emotionally imprinted in the sub-conscious, and usually incorporate in them a fear of 'offending God' when contemplating moving on to some higher Truth. Unless there is a sincere longing to know the **TRUTH of BEING** rather than traditional beliefs, these mental patterns are almost impossible to annihilate in the mind and emotions and they block true spiritual progress.

I have come expressly to help those who have the will to do so, move beyond these barriers to true enlightenment. Therefore, if you feel intuitively that the words on these pages are **TRUTH** and you feel drawn to them, have confidence you are ready to begin the spiritual journey outlined in these **Letters** and I am at hand to give you the courage to pursue it until you reach your goal – true spiritual enlightenment, newness of life, strength of will and a finding of what I termed the 'Kingdom of Heaven'.

Daily, sincere meditation and prayer will enable a mental cleansing to take place and gradually **TRUTH and UNDERSTANDING** will replace the old myths which once were so dear to you.

At the outset of the following teachings, *I*, the *CHRIST*, must remind you that yours is not a solid universe. As you probably know, according to your scientists, solid 'matter', the visible substance of the world, is really composed of energy particles.

The **TRUTH of BEING** of your earthly dimension rests on this fundamental reality of creation.

To understand my teachings regarding the Truth of Being, it is necessary to grasp this fundamental 'seeming emptiness' underlying all your created world.

The majority of you know this fact of existence intellectually, but it has not yet even remotely filtered through to your consciousness to give you a new perspective of the world and existence itself. You continue as you have done for millennia, thinking that your world is solid and the conditions of the body and all other external phenomena are beyond your control. You believe you are the victim of existence. Instead of which, the reverse is true. And your daily lives reflect these beliefs. Therefore, it is absolutely necessary for me to return and help you move on to a higher perception of Truth.

As I said in **Letter 1**, after enlightenment in the desert, I came back into my world of Palestinian towns and villages and immediately began to control the 'elements of matter' wherever I saw the necessity to help those who were deprived or suffering.

I have come to show you exactly why I was able to do this.

As I revealed to you in **Letter 1**, during the time I received full illumination in the desert, I was shown that 'matter' was not really solid. I was not given to understand exactly how the electrical particles which I termed the 'shimmer of motes' took on the appearance of visible 'matter'. I only knew that these 'motes' were moving at high frequencies of speed within 'GOD MIND' and 'GOD MIND' was therefore universal.

I perceived that 'GOD MIND' was both the creator – and substance – of all things within creation itself. Of this, I was absolutely certain.

I also 'saw' very clearly that human thought, when fraught with conviction or emotion, radically affected this process of materialisation of visible forms.

Therefore the human mind could – and did – interfere with the true intention of 'GOD MIND'.

It was a thrilling and exalting realisation since the myths taught me by the Jewish rabbis were clearly false and were immediately swept out of my mind. I embraced the truth with excitement since I now realised why people experienced misery and suffering. This emanated from their own thought processes.

I was also given to 'see' the '**communities of living particles'** which science has named 'cells' at work within every living thing. I was aware of **the Divine Harmony** controlling the work of the cells, which were busily building and maintaining the various parts of physical bodies of all living creatures and plant life, big and small. This is why I drew heavily on the countryside to give examples of the immanence and activity of the **'Father'** within the least of wild life – such as plants and birds.

As I have clearly explained in **Letters 1-3**, I called 'GOD MIND' the '**Father'** because I was enabled to 'see' – perceive – the true **nature** of the 'GOD MIND' and was determined that when I returned to the people of Palestine to describe the revelations I had received, they would understand that their beliefs imbued in their very consciousness by the rabbis were entirely false.

155

I saw that the true **nature of 'GOD MIND'** was the very highest form of **Divine Love** and this could be seen consistently active within every living thing.

As I mentioned above, out of this knowledge, I was able to perform 'miracles' and control the elements where appropriate and necessary.

Just as I longed to explode the myths which possessed the minds of the Jews in Palestine, so do I yearn to show you that many of the theories put forward by your scientists have been prompted by a strong reaction to the church dogma and doctrines in years gone by.

To understand this statement, you must realise that until the time of Darwin, whilst the various Christian Churches held dominance over the minds of the populace, it was generally accepted that the universe had been created exactly as written in Genesis in the Biblical Old Testament.

When men of science attempted to announce their discoveries and theories, they were forced to describe their new beliefs in the presence of enormous religious opposition. Consequently, they found it necessary to concentrate much of their mental energy on proving the Prophets' pronouncements wrong. In doing so, their agenda caused them to lose clarity of vision and they also became ego-driven. Thereafter, **any intuitive perception** proposed by the scientific fraternity was derided and rejected out of hand by other scientists. Because of this mental climate, the pendulum of the search for 'Truth' swung solely to an undeviating belief in reason and logic, thus imprisoning the human intellect in materialism for the answers to the origins of life and existence.

Therefore, it is absolutely necessary for me to refute some of the 'scientific theories' and show them to be as erroneous as are the so-called 'truths' of Christian Doctrine. In arriving at some of these 'theories', scientist and churchman alike have dipped into the realms of unproven preposterous suppositions to answer questions which have previously been unanswerable by the earthly mind only.

Having told you that the substance of your material world is basically electrical particles agitated at high speed within 'space', your science is unable to tell you **'why'** such 'energy particles' take on the density and form of 'matter' except to speak of forces of fusion which happen to create the elements.

Science cannot tell you what is the '**Motivating Force**' which draws particles into the form of elements.

Neither can science tell you from whence such energy particles originally came except to say that they were released during the time of the Big Bang which they believe gave the first impetus to creation.

Why a sudden 'Big Bang' – of what? What was the Motivating Factor behind it?

Science speaks about electromagnetism but cannot say from whence come such energies which appear and disappear. Where do they go? Why do they come back? From the human perspective, there appears to be no intelligible activity within or behind its work.

Science says that electromagnetism 'just is' – a simple fact of existence – yet it produces highly purposeful and intelligent work in the form of millions of billions of substances of which your universe is made. How does this happen?

There is nothing that electromagnetism has brought into visible being which the human mind can deem to be lacking purpose or meaning.

Science ignores this most basic and vital level of creation. Without an answer to this question, as to why everything which has been brought into visible manifestation by the activity of the twin energies of electromagnetism is invariably purposeful, successful and rational – nothing of any value in the search for your origins will be discovered.

Until science can probe and discover the '**Reality**' of the '**space**' in which electrical particles of 'visible being' are supported, science will forever remain behind locked doors of materialism. It will be barred to eternal Truth and universal wisdom and imprisoned within the bondage of reason alone – reason which is solely the product of the finite activity of brain cells.

It is to the **true nature** of the **SPACE** I intend to introduce you – but before proceeding to this, I must first bring many highly pertinent questions to your attention.

Down the ages, much of the work produced by electromagnetism has appeared to the mind, vision and touch of living entities as being solid, unchangeably durable. Metals, wood, rocks, living entities were all believed to be composed of solid, inanimate or living 'matter'. With such a belief in a solid universe it is only natural that the mystical prophets of old should have envisaged a 'Mighty Individual' possessing enormous powers in creating all the solid substances of the universe. In visualising such a 'Mighty Individual', it was only natural they should perceive a 'Kingly' figure of universal control, possessing a retributive nature when confronted with the behaviour of mankind which created a turbulent society. Neither Prophets of old nor science of today has been near to the Truth of Existence.

Both have completely missed the truth.

Science says that life began when in some unexplained way, a **correct** combination of chemical reactions produced a molecule capable of making copies of itself by triggering further chemical reactions. Such a description of the enormous and teeming complexity and power of the **LIFE FORCE as being discernible because it is 'capable of replicating itself',** reveals the basic impoverishment of scientific perception and thought which produced such a theory!

Furthermore, the suggestion that such a combination of 'inanimate' chemicals could get together in a specific way – accidentally – to produce such an astounding result of 'self-replication' remains unquestioned scientifically.

This is because the finite human mind, even though scientific, cannot deal with such a strange eventuality of uninitiated 'self-replication'. It is too suggestive of a magical occurrence – of some intervention from an unimaginable source which scientific men dare not contemplate for fear of ridicule.

This sheep-like acquiescence is considered more scientific than producing 'inspired' theories blocked by the materialistic laws science has established for itself. This block to future scientific progress will prevent science properly investigating the realm of mind and spirit until some enlightened scientist defies convention and dares to cross the borderline between the 'seen and the 'unseen'.

Prophets of old, if presented with the theory of molecular self-replication would have no difficulty with such a 'magical occurrence' and would say that 'God' made the chemical combinations and imbued them with life. That would not be the right explanation either.

It is this old religious concept of a 'God on High' 'creating from afar' which is blocking the man of science from moving forward to more spiritually aware reflections. Therefore, despite science's seeming emancipation from age-old doctrines, it is still as mentally bound and hindered by fears of ancient shibboleths as in the 19th century. It adopts its ridiculous theories because it has not yet perceived the '**Reality**' of **Our Source of Being** behind and within the living molecule.

Continuing its story of creation, science states that after the 'self-manufacture' of living molecules capable of replicating themselves, they 'formed themselves' into a living cell, (so small it cannot be seen by the naked eye), which became the building block for all the multiplexity of living organisms, including plants, insects, reptiles, birds, animals and man himself. Therefore, all living things have a common ancestor – the first living molecule.

Science cannot explain why the self-replicating molecules combined themselves into a living cell. It remains a mystery to science to this day.

The living cell, your science tells you, is endlessly repeated in a billion-billion-billion differing forms. It is the building block of the visible universe. How can this be? What impulse motivates such replication? Science cannot say. Entrenched in its own blindness, it has dragged people down into materialistic blindness with it.

And now – the first living cell deserves the undivided attention of anyone seriously seeking the spiritual dimension and the '**Mainspring of Existence**' – because the first living molecule and the first living cell are the very first evidence of some **intelligent activity** within 'matter' – within the universe.

The foremost feature displaying sense and sensibility is the function of the membrane which covers the cell, giving it protection and individuality. Think about this 'miraculous' phenomenon.

The cell takes in, from the environment, only selected nourishment through the membrane.

Not only does the cell take in the right nutrition but – having utilised the nutrition – the cell rids itself of the waste through the permeable membrane.

You should ask yourself how the 'purely physical' membrane of the cell, invisible to your eye, can 'distinguish and select' the correct nourishment to enhance its well-being and then exercise sufficient discernment to rid itself of unwanted toxic matter?

Do you not see a high degree of **purposefulness** within all this activity and can you believe that such purposefulness is accidental?

And is not **PURPOSE** the very hallmark of **Intelligence?**

Not only this, the membrane of the cell continues to do this work of selection of nutrition and discarding of waste in a billion-billion different circumstances and conditions relating to survival within differing species and differing environments. Is this not evidence of **PURPOSEFULNESS** displayed within every single action of every single species be it insects, plants, reptiles, birds, animals and human beings?

Could you not describe the universe as being the consistent and undeviating **IMPULSE** of **PURPOSEFULNESS** made visible within the realm of visible 'matter'?

Is the spirit of **PURPOSEFULNESS** a physical element – or one of 'consciousness'?

And if you can accept that **PURPOSEFULNESS** is an undeniable creative impulse behind **EXISTENCE**, then can you move on to the next perception of your universe as being the visible manifestation of **'an INTELLIGENT APPRAISAL of cause and effect'** clearly evident within living 'matter'. For – if the living cell can select the right nourishment **and also provide for the elimination of toxic waste** – this simple activity displays an awareness of the need for digestion and also foresees the resultant build up of toxic waste, and the need for the elimination of such waste to ensure the continued health of the cell. Is this not a clear indication of **an INTELLIGENT APPRAISAL of 'Cause and Effect'?**

Furthermore – Science says that the cell contains a 'nucleus' which might be likened to the brain of a human being since it conveys messages and its most important function is the storage of information, the 'library' which contains not just the details relating to one cell but of the whole body in which its resides!

In fact, on investigation by science, it would appear that the cell itself is a system of chemical 'messages' carried out in a purposeful, intelligent and intelligible way. How could this happen if the **origins** of the cell's molecules were only inanimate chemical elements? Would you dispute that behind every 'messenger with a message to convey' there is intelligent thought or consciousness? And behold how accurate are the messages transferred from cell to cell to ensure the accurate replication of certain species for millions of years?

At what point in creation then, did 'consciousness' creep into living organisms? And how did intelligent thought which weighs and decides come into the field of unconscious inanimate matter?

Without inherent consciousness, how can so much informed and informing activity take place in a cell invisible to the living eye? Is not such activity the **product** of **consciousness/awareness, proving the presence of 'intelligent' life in its lowest denominator?**

Furthermore, a single living cell, in the form of a bacterium, can move about on its own and live its own specialised, frequently exciting life within the environment – or – as a virus doing its deadly specialized work of attacking specific targets within living organisms. Alternatively, the cell may be fixed within an organism, carrying out its own highly important work of construction and maintenance of some part of the organism. Such work produces 'living material' exactly suited – and necessary – to the living organ on which it works – be it parts of the human body or of animal life, or plant – such as human toes and spleen, or animal fur and tusks, or fish scales and feathers of birds, or bark of tree and foliage on branches, or petals and stalk of flowers, or antennae of butterflies and their gauzy wings, the reptilian skin of crocodiles and their teeth, the eyes of squid and their skins which change colour according to need of camouflage. Each of these completely diverse and seemingly unrelated physical phenomena are created by the individual, specialised work of billions and billions and billions of identical living cells.

On contemplating the magnitude and diversity of the work accomplished by a simple living cell invisible to the naked eye – can you believe in a mechanistic universe?

It would be possible to do so, if the 'matter' produced by such cells, was illogical, offering no plausible purpose behind or reason for its existence – devoid of personal consciousness.

But this is not so. These identical living cells work together in harmony within man or beast, **to make a liver** with its multiple duties within a body, **to create an intricate eye** having its own specific purposes of putting the entity into direct and intelligent touch with its environment, incorporating the assistance of the brain, **or strong bones** expressly and intricately designed in conjunction with tendons and muscles, to unite with others in such convenient ways as to enable full and supple movement of the entity. Furthermore, the cells never intrude on each other's work.

When creating a kidney, they do not suddenly make an ear.

When creating hair they do not suddenly launch into making skin. No, cells create the scalp and the selfsame cells create the hair. The only difference between   skin and hair cells is the work they do, second by second, throughout a lifetime. Why?

What is the 'Motivating and Inspiring Factor'? Accident?

What organising **intelligence** set the entire process of creation in motion from the most fundamental level of the formation of simple elements out of free electrical particles within 'space',

 the combining of elements to form chemicals,

the correct combination of specific chemicals to form a living molecule,

the correct combination of living molecules to make a living cell which can take in nutrition, excrete waste, build according to clear-cut specifications, move about, and **sustain** this enormous edifice of creation consistently through billions of years?

Not only this, but what is the '**Motivating Force**' which has designed and successfully evolved within living systems and entities, billions and billions of different ways in which to fertilise seeds of every kind – whether they be those of plants, insects, reptiles, birds, animals or human beings, evolving for each an intelligent system of procreation suited to climatic conditions, the production of vegetation in the environment, in order to ensure survival?

162

Is not SURVIVAL also evidence of intelligent purposeful activity?

And having accomplished this great feat of creativity, should you not question how it is that every living species has its own individualistic way of rearing its young and protecting it as far as possible until the young are capable of **SURVIVAL** on their own? Is this not **LOVE FOR CREATION** active in its highest form?

You cannot move on from this analysis of what the human intelligence has to say about the origins of life and creativity, without mentioning the '**all important molecules DNA**' – which are said to carry the 'plan' for the whole organism – plant or baby. Furthermore, these DNA molecules give the instructions to the cells, informing them they shall build according to the chromosomes deposited by the seed.

Yes, indeed, in place of **Intelligence** – science has given you the **DNA molecules** as your source of existence, your supreme leader, your director of creation upon which materialistic, flimsy cells, the whole of creation must depend for its survival. Behold the glorious **DNA – Lord of your creation!**

From whence did the DNA cells draw their **intelligent directional powers?**

Science is quite satisfied now that it has been able to satisfactorily explain why the various species of every kind replicate themselves so accurately and consistently. **Science would have you believe that you live in a purely mechanistic universe; that the phenomenon of evolution arises out of chance mutations and the 'survival of the fittest'.**

If you study the various organisms of creation, the multifold and differing activities of related species, can you truly believe in such an unlikely materialistic concept?

It has been no mere co-incidence that, to-day, to enable you to discover the vast **Intelligence** behind creation, you have numerous creative people who embark on difficult journeys to explore, determine and photograph the habitats and habits of wild creatures and plants. You are entertained – and instructed – by a feast of facts and photographs of the **wonders** of your universe.

In my time on earth, I had no such marvels to refer to in order to teach the Jews the universal **Truth of Existence**. I only had domestic animals and birds to use as examples of the marvellous inventiveness and intelligence and **awareness** apparent in every living thing. Nowhere has it been written in the gospels that I referred to a High and Mighty Jehovah as Creator as was customary with the Jewish Leaders.

No, I turned to the countryside, the flowers and birds and tried to show my fellow countrymen that they were surrounded by a marvellous and miraculous creation. Two thousand years ago in your dimension, we lacked your modern scientific background to be able to intelligently observe and explain the activity of what I termed the '**Father**' everywhere around them.

To discover your true **SOURCE of BEING**, I ask you to take stock of the unimaginable and indescribable complexity and diversity of purposeful work plainly evident in penguins and pigs.

Can the human mind replicate any of the most basic of activities within – say – the digestive system, which swiftly summons up the requisite enzymes and hormones necessary for digestion.

How dare the finite mind, which is incapable of perceiving clearly the true creative process governed by instinctual knowledge, presume to state unequivocally – defying contradiction – that it understands the true origins of creation and the forces out of which creation took form?

What arrogance! These men can only think according to what their eyes tell them.

I view the present scientific ignorance with loving compassion, a degree of amusement, and a great all consuming passion to puncture their pride. For, until someone can penetrate their self-satisfaction and position of infallibility, a true mating of Eternal Verities and human scientific knowledge can never take place. But it must take place; otherwise human spiritual evolution will remain at a standstill.

The scientific mind is too full of 'finitely' devised book lore, accepted formulas and equations, and the need for their fellows' approval, to permit mystical penetration by Higher Intelligences.

On my behalf, I ask readers of these **Letters**, to form an association to challenge Science and ask 'at what point in the evolution of the 'material' world' is **CONSCIOUSNESS** first discernible?

164

I repeat and mean what I say: Ask the scientist at what point in the evolution of the world is 'consciousness' first discernible. In the living cell? If in the living cell, ask whether it was discernible in the living molecules which combined to make a cell and encase itself in such an intelligently designed membrane, permitting the intake of selected food and excretion of toxic waste? How does it recognise toxic waste? And if it should be conceded that consciousness might be present in living molecules, should you not ask whether the chemical properties which became a living molecule might not themselves have possessed 'consciousness' which eventually impelled and propelled them into the life-giving combination to make a molecule? And having gone back thus far into the origins of existence – the chemical properties – you must still question why 'consciousness' should only become a viable presence within the chemicals – why not within the elements in which individuality first took shape, and if in the elements why should it be denied that 'consciousness' propels the electrical particles to form the elements? Is it rational to deny such a possibility?

And having reached such a possibility, should you not go further and ask from whence comes electromagnetism? **What is the 'reality' of electricity more than streaks of fierce light now described by science as photons and electrons?**

And what is the 'reality' of magnetism more than two-fold energies of 'bonding and rejection' – energy impulses which have brought stability and order into chaos?

Ask science: "From whence comes electromagnetism which is responsible for the most basic steps in the creation of an ordered and orderly universe of an unimaginable complexity and diversity?"

I will now attempt to put into your words **THAT WHICH** is beyond all words and presently beyond all 'individualised earthly comprehension'. Therefore, the intellect, although it assists the brain to understand, intellectually, the spiritual realities I am putting before you, it also creates a barrier to true spiritual perception and experience.

For this reason, regard the following references to the *ULTIMATE UNIVERSAL DIMENSION* as only guidelines – ideas, 'shadow consciousness forms' of the **REALITY** behind and within your universe. ((Take each IDEA – one by one – into meditation))

165

What I am about to explain is entirely within and of CONSCIOUSNESS without parameters and boundaries. If you are sufficiently spiritually evolved to follow me there, beyond the words, you will begin to understand 'spiritually' all I am trying to tell you. The words will guide you towards – and then unlock new 'vistas of being' for you.

Persevere! The **LIGHT** will gradually, perhaps imperceptibly, penetrate your mind and you will have little bursts of insight.

There are many who have experienced a little 'burst of insight', have briefly felt a touch of 'Divine Consciousness' and then, hardly daring to continue to believe in such a transcendent moment of awareness, have begun to question, doubt and finally dispel the little inflow of 'Divine Consciousness'. Beware you do not do this. Disbelief will set you back, enmesh you in the material plane of existence more than you will ever know.

Whatever you are given and able to receive – hold fast to it and do not doubt.

Doubt destroys steady progress because it creates its own 'consciousness forms' which will suppress and even eradicate the insight you had gained previously.

Therefore, your choice of thoughts – belief or disbelief, doubt or faith – construct or destroy your progress in your search for TRUTH.

Any denial erases from your consciousness the progress which has been previously made. Furthermore, the higher you ascend in spiritual truth, the more powerful do your thoughts become. Therefore, create and hold fast to your own spiritual momentum and allow no one to intrude and undermine that momentum. Hold firm to your former perceptions. In times of doubt, cruise along in positive thoughts, using enlightening affirmations, clinging to earlier inspirational guidance when your consciousness frequencies of vibration were higher. By use of your willpower, choosing affirmations containing 'golden nuggets' of spiritual Truth, return to this higher level of consciousness again and again. Do not, through mental laziness, wholly surrender to the ebb and flow of spiritual consciousness energies and become a spiritual 'see-saw'.

I cannot emphasize this danger of self-obstruction strongly enough. Become actively aware of it.

If you know anything of the accounts of my life in Palestine, you will recall that I, too, suffered the phenomenon of ebb and flow of spiritual consciousness and found it necessary to absent myself in the hills to pray and meditate and renew my spiritual strength.

Therefore, understand your 'dry' periods, but do not give way to them by yielding passively to an undesirable change in your attitudes and mental/emotional patterns. As you conscientiously draw upon your **Source of Being** for new strength and the upliftment of your consciousness frequencies, so will these negative periods be greatly reduced in strength and duration.

I repeat, at all times beware how you use your minds! Let your mental activity always be constructive that it may contribute to your own spiritual growth rather than its constant hindrance.

****

Having said all the above and proceeded to dictate the rest of **the Letter, the recorder of my words,** began to question the likely public reception of this **Letter,** because it seemed to her too pragmatic to appeal to people who are accustomed to picturing some magnificent Power or Being or 'Utterly Other' which has given birth to the universe.

Indeed, I have made numerous efforts to describe the immensity of the Power out of which all things have come but as I have said, it is impossible for me to describe in human terms the **Reality** of the **SOURCE of your BEING.**

Those spiritually evolved souls who have been lightly infused with Divine Consciousness report the experience to be utterly beautiful and glorious and entirely unforgettable – but still not fully describable in human terms. This mystical experience is possible when the frequencies of vibration of the mind are already raised and the entire consciousness is suffused with rays of Divine Consciousness. It is a condition that involves the 'feelings' more than the intellect and brain cells.

In this case, where I have to _infuse_ my recorder's mind and brain cells with a description of the *Reality* of your **SOURCE of BEING** and she has to interpret in words, I have to take care not to interfere too forcefully with the frequencies of vibrations of consciousness in which my recorder's brain cells are working. There have been occasions when it was dangerous to proceed any further and I have interrupted the working of her computer to break the contact.

Before you begin to study, meditate and absorb the following pages, I want to make it clear to all who read these Letters that my purpose in coming through them is first and foremost to dispel the myths which have surrounded my human persona and teachings. It is my intention that religious dogma and doctrines should eventually die a natural death, world-wide – as complete a death as the animal sacrifices in the Temple of Solomon.

Secondly, I have also come to help the churches let go their archaic notions of 'God' and 'sin.' No true spiritual progress is possible until the dawning of a clear realisation that each person is responsible for the way his or her life develops.

Thirdly, I have come to remove from your minds the pictures of an 'Almighty God' of magnificence and grandeur and unlimited active power, who rewards the virtuous and punishes the 'wicked'. These beliefs are wholly erroneous – albeit comforting.

Fourthly, I am explaining the Truth of Being for you, to finally dispel the old concept of 'God' sitting aloft somewhere in heaven where He is said to have created the world and all that is in it in a relatively short while.

Fifthly, I have come expressly to help science bridge the gulf between UNIVERSAL CONSCIOUSNESS and the appearance of electrical particles. Without this bridge between the Unseen Spiritual Dimension and the Seen world of 'matter', science will remain rooted in old ideas and concepts instead of moving forward into new realms of spiritual/scientific research for the betterment of mankind.

I have also come to show you the TRUE NATURE of ... 'THAT' ... WHICH BROUGHT YOU INTO BEING – gave you INDIVIDUALITY. For, without this knowledge, which will reveal to you the 'nature' of your 'dual, yet fully inter-related being', Spirit and body, you will also remain rooted in the same level of consciousness as you are at this moment.

I want to make it manifestly clear that:

'Nothing ever comes from Nothing.'

This is a well-known saying amongst you, and a perfectly true one.

However, there is an eternal, infinite, consistent FOUNDATION of BEINGNESS – and THIS I am going to reveal to you.

You have not been 'created' – you have drawn your 'being' from **IT**.

Obviously, you could not have come from something entirely foreign to your own consciousness. I am asking my recorder to choose some mundane understandable examples:

You could not draw a filling for tarts from a vat of treacle and discover they were mince meat.

You could not squeeze an orange and make ginger beer from the juice.

You could not fill a balloon with air, pop it and find it was dripping jelly.

All the above examples chosen by my recorder are instances of logic.

I want you to realise that your entire universe is a manifestation of logic and consistent logical effects arising out of related causation.

Your universe is CAUSE & EFFECT made visible.

This is an undeviating principle of existence. If there are instances of deviations such as paranormal experiences or instantaneous healings, the average person exclaims in astonishment and science refuses to believe that such a thing is possible. As my explanation deepens, you will eventually understand how such deviations take place – logically and effectually. In other words, these deviations occur according to natural spiritual laws and always serve a necessary purpose. Nowhere is there any mindlessness in creation – even in the ant or gnat – unless the mind of an entity has been born defective or been damaged.

Therefore it is clear: you live and operate in a physical universe which displays the highest degree of intelligence and purposeful activity within the creation of 'matter' itself, in the physical bodies of all individual entities from plants to human beings. Unfortunately, this high degree of

INTELLIGENCE and PURPOSEFUL CARING is only minimal in the consciousness displayed by the **created entities themselves from plants to human beings.**

In other words, the BODIES in which you conduct your lives, in which you think and feel and do whatever comes to mind, manifest within their physical organs and working parts a very much higher order of intelligence and loving purpose than does your human consciousness.

Human interests are mostly wrapped up in the problems of personal daily survival, enjoyment of pleasures, and emotional/physical satisfaction.

To achieve these purposes, the majority of people use only the commodities manufactured out of 'matter'. Even the minds of scientists cannot fully unravel the hidden secrets of earthly existence and despite all their scientific expertise are as bogged down in the changing fortunes of existence as are those who have no learning at all.

Therefore it is a logical conclusion that '**THAT**' out of which you have **drawn** your physical being, is one of **IMMENSITY – not only of size, but IMMENSITY of WILLPOWER: the Will to self-expression and creativity.**

Visualize for a moment – the size of the material universe, the SUN and its heat, the Moon, the earth planet and solar system, the galaxies of stars, and the fact that all this visible material is totally interdependent yet also dependent on the movement of the planetary bodies and subject to Universal Laws of consistent function and movement. This vast universe has had its origins within – and has been drawn out – of the **FOUNDATION of your BEING** – and the entirety of **LIFE FORCE/ENERGY** in the universe has been drawn out of that same **FOUNDATION of BEING.**

Therefore, do not be dismayed, if, in my efforts to analyse for you the **SPIRITUAL COMPONENTS of YOUR SOURCE of BEING**, you find that you recognise what these components are, and to a very, very, very limited extent, possess the same spiritual components of consciousness yourself.

170

You have drawn all that you are – spiritually, mentally, emotionally, physically, from your **SOURCE of BEING.**

Before I explain to you how this could be, I want you to take certain steps to help your minds absorb the immensity of ... **'THAT'** ... out of which you have drawn your being.

After you have read the next pages to the end of my **Letter**, take each paragraph individually into meditation and visualisation, for only in this way will the 'words' begin to grow in realisation and take on the **spiritual reality** of their **true meaning.**

ALL (spiritual, unseen/seen/imagined) is
CONSCIOUSNESS/AWARENESS
The primary comprehensive nature of CONSCIOUSNESS
is AWARENESS.
It is not possible to have consciousness without possessing awareness.
All that you see, all that you touch, hear, feel, know is
CONSCIOUSNESS/AWARENESS
made visible.

There is nothing in the universe that is _not_
CONSCIOUSNESS made _visible_.

CONSCIOUSNESS/AWARENESS is infinite and eternal

There are TWO DIMENSIONS of CONSCIOUSNESS both beyond and
within your own earthly plane of existence – the plane of heavy 'matter',
'solid form'.

The ULTIMATE UNIVERSAL DIMENSION of
CONSCIOUSNESS/AWARENESS

can never be fully or truly known by an individualised spirit.

IT IS INACCESSIBLE. IT IS IN EQUILIBRIUM. IT is the ONLY
SOURCE of all POWER, WISDOM, LOVE, INTELLIGENCE.

The UNIVERSAL DIMENSION of CONSCIOUSNESS/AWARENESS
in equilibrium is a state of SILENCE & STILLNESS

out of which come sound, colour, individualised form, and all visible creativity within the visible universe.

Out of ULTIMATE UNIVERSAL DIMENSION of CONSCIOUSNESS/AWARENESS in equilibrium has come all of creation – all the various unseen dimensions of existence descending in order of spirituality from the very portals of the UNIVERSAL DIMENSION down to the most ponderous vibrational frequencies of inanimate earthly substances and beyond into unspeakable horrors of consciousness perversions and anti-Truth.

This ULTIMATE UNIVERSAL DIMENSION of CONSCIOUSNESS/AWARENESS

is not only in space

IT *is* ALL SPACE

IT is undetectably everywhere. For those who think in terms of atoms – you can say IT

is the SPACE in the atom – therefore, IT is 'in silence and equilibrium' within the 'space' of all elements and 'matter'.

The NATURE of UNIVERSAL CONSCIOUSNESS is:

INTENT inactive and in equilibrium.

Therefore, Universal Consciousness is an infinite, eternal, limitless, boundless, state of POWERFUL INTENT – pristine, pure, beautiful.

This INTENT is to EXPRESS Its NATURE.

UNIVERSAL CONSCIOUSNESS NATURE INTENT

is the ALLNESS of WILL & PURPOSE

always locked in 'embrace'

The Universal Will is: to move out and create.

172

The Universal Purpose is: to give individual form to creation and experience it.

Within the ULTIMATE UNIVERSAL DIMENSION OF CONSCIOUSNESS/AWARENESS INTENT

UNIVERSAL WILL is in a state of mutual restraint – with UNIVERSAL PURPOSE

both in perfect equilibrium within SILENCE & STILLNESS

UNIVERSAL WILL is UNIVERSAL INTELLIGENCE UNIVERSAL PURPOSE is UNIVERSAL LOVE universally in equilibrium – in mutual restraint out of WHICH all things visible and invisible and human impulses have taken form.

If you could receive the fullness of UNIVERSAL REALITY into yourself, you would be disintegrated by ITs explosive power and dissolved into formless consciousness/awareness IT as far transcends the individual humanhood as the heat and light of your sun is billions times more powerful than the light of your fireflies flickering in darkness

....

When I was on earth, I made a distinction between

'Your Father in Heaven' and 'Your Father within you'.

When I spoke of

'Your FATHER in heaven'

I meant

UNIVERSAL INTELLIGENCE.

Because of the Jewish attitude to women, I only referred to this **aspect** of **UNIVERSAL CONSCIOUSNESS.**

Now, to you who are so aware of the equality of genders, I speak of:

'FATHER-MOTHER-CONSCIOUSNESS'

in equilibrium

173

within UNIVERSAL CONSCIOUSNESS/AWARENESS where

'Father Consciousness – is – Universal Intelligence'

'Mother Consciousness – is – Universal Love'

the TOOL of 'Father Consciousness' creative energy – electricity

is in a state of mutual restraint – equilibrium with

the TOOLS of ' Mother Consciousness' creative energy – magnetism

Because 'FATHER-MOTHER' tools: electro-magnetism is in equilibrium within

UNIVERSAL CONSCIOUSNESS

IT will never be detected within SPACE by scientists no matter how they may probe space.

The IMPULSE: 'Father Consciousness WILL' is INTELLIGENT ACTIVITY

– in equilibrium with –

The IMPULSE: 'Mother Consciousness PURPOSE' is NURTURING for SURVIVAL

'FATHER-MOTHER CONSCIOUSNESS'

is a powerful impersonal FORCE – yet IT is personal for you even before you seek to make contact with IT.

As you evolve spiritually, you will feel IT – for IT is the REALITY of BEING

IT is everywhere and within everything .

FATHER CONSCIOUSNESS is

the INTELLIGENT LOVE Which gives intelligent energy and momentum to the world of complex forms – expressed physically as electricity

MOTHER PURPOSE is

the LOVING INTELLIGENCE Which gives purpose and the impulse for survival to the individualised complex forms – expressed as magnetism – bonding & repulsion.

These are the **UNIVERSAL PRIMAL IMPULSES of ALL BEING of**

UNIVERSAL CONSCIOUSNESS

your **SOURCE OF BEING – INTELLIGENCE-LOVE** This is the **STATE OF BEING** before creation. **CONSCIOUSNESS/AWARENESS within a STATE OF EQUILIBRIUM.**

I want you to move again into an inner state of conscious equilibrium, where all thought is stilled and your mind resides in silence. You are in interior control, your mind and emotions no longer divided into activity and feeling. You may feel a build-up of power within you, strength, peace, and contentment. This, expressed in you, in individual form, is the **STATE of BEING** out of which came creation.

I want you to notice that the equilibrium is impossible the moment that thought is introduced.

I want you to REALISE that the UNIVERSAL DIMENSION is a DIMENSION of unformed IMPULSES. It contains no blueprint of creation. It is in a state of UNDIVIDED FORM.

The equilibrium – the restraint between opposing **IMPULSES** – **'to move about'** and **'remain bonded'** creates an **infinite spiral of self-contained energy. The SELF-CONTAINED ENERGY of MUTUAL RESTRAINT** is beyond the power of individuality to even imagine.

As I have told you before, were individuality able to enter the **UNIVERSAL DIMENSION** of the **MUTUALLY-RESTRAINED IMPULSES** of 'Movement & Bonding' – the individuality would be immediately dissolved and returned to the equilibrium of **UNIVERAL CONSCIOUSNESS**. Ponder the unimaginable immensity of Power

175

contained within the **MUTUAL-RESTRAINT** of the **TWIN IMPULSES** in **UNIVERSAL CONSCIOUSNESS** which are primarily

CONSCIOUSNESS/AWARENESS

INTENT

WILL >>><<< PURPOSE

INTELLIGENCE LOVE

combined as

Intelligent Love   &   Loving Intelligence

Impulses of: Movement   Bonding-Repulsion

ELECTRICITY........in equilibrium........MAGNETISM

The above describes the UNLIMITED UNIVERSAL DIMENSION before the BIG BANG!

You now know that the **Father-Mother Creative Process and the tools of physical creation** are all in a state of **equilibrium** within the **Universal Dimension,** but now that **equilibrium** is to be exploded to bring about

INDIVIDUAL FORM.

You know, too, that since the **Infinite Eternal IMPULSES** are contained in a state of **mutual restraint**, these **IMPULSES** are of an unimaginable intensity of energy – against which your atomic energy contained within the splitting of an atom is a mere 'pouff', an infinitesimal twitch of no importance.

I want you to fully realise all the foregoing, since your realisation of what happened at the time of the Big Bang will give you a glimpse of what happened at the time of the **sundering of UNIVERSAL CONSCIOUSNESS** to permit the creation of individual form to take place.

UNIVERSAL CONSCIOUSNESS was RIVEN!

WILL & PURPOSE

'Father' INTELLIGENCE & 'Mother' NURTURING LOVE

were exploded to work independently and also jointly.

Their respective 'tools' were

Electricity & Magnetism

Out of the explosion of EQUILIBRIUM came the

GREAT INTENT of SELF-EXPRESSION

'The Universal Awareness of BEING' became

the Impulse of individualised 'I' awareness demanding self-expression

LIFE and 'I'ness are synonymous in the dimension of 'matter'

They became the consciousness of 'matter'
What is the consciousness of   **LIFE?**

It is: **Father-Intelligence   And   Mother-Love**

          Impulse of Movement   Impulse of Purpose-nurturing
– survival.

          Seen as Electricity   Seen as Magnetism in **Matter**

Can you begin to imagine the explosion of **CONSCIOUSNESS!** of **AWARENESS!**

To help you fractionally visualize what happened at the moment of the Big Bang, try to recall a moment when you also experienced an explosion in your consciousness.

This takes place when you have set your entire 'being' on achieving some very important goal.

About to embark on your plans, in a state of excited anticipation, some trivial circumstance or insensitive person prevents you from achieving your 'heart-felt' purposes. How would you feel?

Your **concentration** would be split and you would explode. Here again, I must call on my recorder to think up some examples of my meaning in human terms, for the '**least earthly consciousness**' is drawn from **UNIVERSAL CONSCIOUSNESS.**

You are at the Airport, excited and ready to fly for an unexpected holiday overseas. On reaching your Travel Bureau counter, you discover there are no documents or tickets, and no record of any reservations for flight or holiday accommodation **although you have already paid for them by credit card.** How will you feel?

You are dressed in a very expensive outfit, wining and dining important customers**, and are about to clinch a big contract worth millions**. The waiter drops a plate of hot casserole on your head. How will you feel?

You go shopping and come out to the Car park to find the wheels and doors of your car have been removed – **in broad daylight!**

Sympathetically, you open your purse to give a whining crippled beggar all your silver, but the man straightens up, forcefully snatches the purse from you and runs like an athlete. How will you feel?

In all these instances you would have a strong **consciousness enterprise** to the very front of your mind.

Your head would be filled with a plan to move out and do something to achieve a certain purpose – peacefully. **Your intent would be interlocked with your purpose** – therefore in equilibrium – but note that there would be mounting tension of anticipation as you neared your goal. The greater the tension – the greater the explosion.

You would, in fact, be in the same state as

UNIVERSAL CONSCIOUSNESS
/AWARENESS INTENT

'Father' INTELLIGENCE in equilibrium with **the 'Mother' PURPOSE**

to give being and form to the plan you intend to create.

After your explosion – can you imagine the ensuing mental/emotional chaos, the inability to think straight, the thoughts which would come, one after another, demanding expression – none of them sensible or logical?

Try to realise that YOU – individualised form – are the microcosm of the macrocosm.

You are a **pinhead** expressing **UNIVERSAL CONSCIOUSNESS / AWARENESS** either in equilibrium when you meditate in stillness of thought – or as active consciousness, when you think and feel, plan and create.

Therefore, if you can relate your tiny consciousness explosion to the explosion of the 'heavens', you will gain some small idea of the ensuing chaos both – **momentarily** – within the **UNIVERSAL DIMENSION** – and in aeons of time within the newly created expanse of the dimension of 'matter' still in its formless state.

Therefore, many of you will have to wholly re-arrange your thinking in regard to creation.

It started out as a condition of utter chaos. The UNIVERSAL IMPULSES were divided. There were no blue-prints to direct or control the beginning of individuality. The IMPULSES were still without any 'conscious form' or direction. They were **NATURAL IMPULSES** to perform certain distinct impulsive functions in **CONSCIOUSNESS** but they were not intelligently directed into specific movement or bonding by any higher **Directing Force**. They were on their own .Separated and lost **IMPULSES** of **CONSCIOUSNESS / AWARENESS** able to receive impressions – but – there were no impressions to receive other than those of interior chaos of 'movement-activity' of electricity and 'bonding-repulsion' of magnetism.

And this CONSCIOUSNESS CHAOS was manifested within creation as chaos of particles.

Within this expanse of chaos of electrical particles, however, there was the over-riding awareness of **'I'ness.**

No matter what the chaos, the **'I'ness** came through in **the 'Father' intent to move about, to take control, to create.**

The 'I'ness took initial form in a positive charge of electrical energy.

179

It became the dominant 'I' force as a proton with its satellite of negative electric charge – whereupon 'Mother' Purpose of bonding was activated in those conditions of a positive electrical charge meeting a negative electrical charge.

They 'took to each other' as one might say of the evolved male and female in living species – and bonded.

'Mother' Purpose of repulsion was also activated when two positive or two negative electrical charges looked likely to meet and react negatively – she stepped in and pushed them apart – just like her evolved female mother counterpart would separate two unruly highly-charged ruffians about to engage in a fight.

This was the only form of consciousness awareness within the chaos for a very long time – since time is of no consequence within the realm of matter itself. **Time only becomes of importance when there occurs an impinging of conscious awareness between electrical charges resulting in bonding or repulsion, a progression of adjacencies and events taking place and purposes to be fulfilled.** Otherwise, time is meaningless.

Creation is the product of **PRIMARY IMPULSES** working individually and together – making impressions upon the other, fulfilling inbuilt needs imprinted within consciousness – these needs being, at the outset to increase and experience self-expression leading to further separation then – to restore a sense of inner security and comfort – to be re-united within the harmony of **UNIVERSAL CONSCIOUSNESS**. Out of this driving force for a re-united harmony of being, came the male-female drive for re-union to recapture the bliss which is buried in the soul consciousness.

You could make an analogy of the foregoing paragraph with the habit of fathers going out to work in the morning and returning, hopefully, to the comfort and re-union with family in the evening where he regains the strength to venture forth the next morning to do battle with the world. Therefore the process of creation of UNIVERSAL SELF-EXPRESSION took billions of years within time to accomplish.

After the Big Bang, the **Father-Mother Creative Process** was divided into two different energies, continually working apart and together, independent yet mutually constrained to work together having individual characteristics or 'natures' – and different functions. Therefore, their work load was/is different yet indivisible.

You already know, and by a process of meditation, should have fully understood the 'nature' of the **'Father'** and the 'nature' of the **'Mother'** within the **equilibrium** of the **Universal Dimension.**

Briefly, the 'nature' of the **'Father'** is to be active, creative, and perform the work of creativity.

It is also the 'I'ness of individualised existence. Everything living from a hornet to a hippopotamus has a strong sense of 'I'ness and the need to protect that 'I'ness.

The 'nature' of the **'Mother'** is to give form to the electrical consciousness 'plan' initiated by **'Father Intelligence'** by bonding the electrical particles together.

'Father' and **'Mother' consciousness – PRIMARY IMPULSES** – are both within the equilibrium, and of the **NATURE of the UNIVERSAL DIMENSION** and consequently as they create **individual form, they carry out the work** of the **NATURE** of the **UNIVERSAL DIMENSION** which is: **Growth – Providing Nutrition – Nourishment – Healing – Protection – Fulfilment of Need within a consistent system of Law & Order ......SURVIVAL.**

'Father' and **'Mother' Consciousness energies** are **IMPULSES** both restrained within the **UNIVERSAL DIMENSION** and when they have been released from **equilibrium** they powerfully perform the work of creation. Furthermore, consider the magnitude of their work within creation throughout the world. The

'Father/Mother' impulses prompt every level of creation from the formation of elements, the living molecule and cell – to the magnificent Mammoth. They also work instinctually within parents to prompt them to unify, to conceive, bear and rear their young.

Some fathers absent themselves after the birth of their progeny be they: eggs, puppies or humans. These are the fathers whose sense of **'I'ness** is greater than their inborn fathering instincts.

It is at this point that you must become fully aware of the meaning of IMPULSE.

You may think that this seems a very 'nebulous' 'form of creativity', but if you reflect for a while, you may eventually realise that no human or animal or insect or even plant, undertakes any activity within the material dimension without an inner 'consciousness' coercion – which is an 'impulse'. It may be to turn to face the sun, to run, to eat, to work, to sleep, to go shopping, to have a baby. Always – the 'impulse' precedes the activity – even the flick of an eyelid.

Furthermore, there is no impulse prompting any activity which is not directed by a purpose:

Plants turn flowers and leaves to catch the rays of the sun for growth; people run to get fit; eat to satisfy hunger; work to earn a salary; sleep to escape the tensions and recharge the energy; go shopping to buy food – all directed at survival and personal comfort.

Therefore, the **IMPULSES** are the **REALITY** behind and within all creation.

If all matter were to return to its original form of electrical particles, the **Universal Impulses** would remain intact and would eventually give form to another creation. The **IMPULSES** are forever. However, electrical particles within living 'matter' are here today and gone tomorrow – but the soul moves on.

You **think** with electrical impulses in the brain. You **feel** with magnetic impulses in your nervous system. They center and bond the electrical impulses into a cohesive whole.

Without the 'magnetic bonding' in your system, you would be all 'go-go' and no 'know-know'. Now is the moment to take you back to my desert experiences, described to you in **Letter 1.**

You may remember that when I went to the River Jordan to be baptised by John, I was a rebel, my face set against the teaching of the Jews, who stated that Jehovah punished men for their sins.

Intuitively, I felt that this was a false and cruel concept and rejected it.

182

After I was shown the Truth concerning creation, I could not understand why **Perfect Consciousness** did not create perfect beings **made in the image of their Creator Intelligent Love.**

I asked the Creator – '**Universal Consciousness**' – why mankind endured so much suffering and evil.

I was then shown very clearly that all the problems experienced by humans arose from the '**central point**' of the self, (science now calls this the 'ego').

It manifested itself in the 'personality' as a **DRIVING NEED** to defend the self from criticism or emotional/ physical attack and a similar **DRIVING NEED** to push aside other people, in order to arrive first in the race of life. It also manifested itself in the 'personality' as a **DRIVING NEED** to take all that was best for the self, despite the opposition of others and a similar **DRIVING NEED** to hold on to personal possessions, be they relatives, friends, material goods or achievements, despite any opposition.

I was also made to understand that without these **TWO** fundamental, eternal, undeviating '**impulses of creative being**' there would be no creation.

This is the secret of creation – and the secret of existence and of 'individual being'.

By working together as a team, separately but inseparable, in the visible world, these **twin impulses** were the means by which **the substance of 'matter' itself** has been created out of the sublime

'UNIVERSAL CONSCIOUSNESS'.

One **impulse of creativity is:** the '**I'ness** of ACTIVITY.

This **impulse of activity is universal and stems from only one source.**

'**Activity' is a movement in CONSCIOUSNESS, and CONSCIOUSNESS in movement.**

The other **creative impulse** possesses (figuratively speaking) **two faces** looking in opposite directions. They are:

BONDING – REJECTION

Pull towards >>>>>>>> the self <<<<<<<< Push away

otherwise known as

ATTRACTION – REPULSION

Attract >>>>>>>> to – THE SELF – from <<<<<<<< Repel

within **CONSCIOUSNESS.**

These are the ONLY means by which earthly existence has been achieved.

The entire universe is a manifestation of the 'Creative Power' active within these Twin Impulses of PHYSICAL BEING – creating 'matter' and individual form. This is one of the fundamental 'secrets' of the universe.

I saw that the 'core' of the '**Personality**' or '**ego**' as it is now called, had been created

'GUARDIAN of PERSONALITY'

and was irresistibly imprinted with the **magnetic impulse** to ensure

PRIVACY and SURVIVAL.

For the protection of the individual **'I'ness**

This was accomplished by using the two faces of the second Impulse of Being

BONDING – REJECTION to secure individuality.

The **face** of **BONDING** drags, draws, attracts, demands, pulls, buys, grabs, clutches, clings to the people and possessions it craves. This **IMPULSE** creates an illusion of security in togetherness and possessions. It is the **'tool' of 'MOTHER CONSCIOUSNESS'** inspiring the building of families, communities and nations. It can be productive of beauty, joy, harmony and love. It can also wreck lives and destroy communities when it is 'Ego' driven.

184

The **face** of **REJECTION** repels, thrusts aside, pushes away, evades, everything – people, animals, possessions it does not want. Thus the **IMPULSE of REJECTION** creates an illusion of privacy and security.

It is the **IMPULSE** that urges rifts in families, relationships, communities and nations. It is supposedly geared to saving lives, ensuring protection and privacy but is a destructive force when it is 'Ego' driven.

Without these **TWIN IMPULSES OF BEING**, all things would have remained forever merged into one another within the eternal timelessness of **'UNIVERSAL CREATIVE POWER in equilibrium'**.

Without these **TWIN IMPULSES**, there would be no interplay of **'give and take' and 'pull and push'** necessary to the creation of the millions of personal experiences out of which 'personality' grows and evolves.

Therefore, the problem of 'personality' and the 'ego drive' endured by all living things and mankind was/is an irrevocable, unavoidable fact of creation. Any other explanation is pure myth.

I saw that what men called **'SIN'** was the direct result of the inter-play of the **Bonding-Rejection impulses** within human nature.

The **Bonding-Rejection Impulses** constituted the emotional/mental mask worn by all created individual entities, including birds and animals. You see these impulses at work within all of nature – even within plant life.

The **Bonding-Rejection Impulses** directed/directs the behaviour towards survival of all entities in creation.

There was no escaping the **Bonding-Rejection Impulses**.

These Twin Impulses were the ephemeral source of all 'worldly' comfort, pleasure, 'happiness' – and also the source of all sickness, misery and deprivation in the world.

However, added to these – transcending, underlying and interpenetrating all – was/is the

LIFE – born of the EXPLOSION of UNIVERSAL CONSCIOUSNESS

is the very foundation and source of earthly consciousness –

therefore, even as the **'Father-Mother' Consciousness** is creative –

so is man's **THINKING** creative

for human 'thought and feeling' are both the exercise and union of

the **twin tools** of **'Father-Mother' Consciousness.**

Therefore, these **Impulses of Bonding-Rejection** in the individual

personality also become highly creative in that they determine –

and **make visible** – the 'consciousness forms' of

'things desired' and 'things rejected'.

This is the second fundamental 'secret' of the universe.

I saw that **'SIN'** was an **artificial concept** expediently devised by men to describe any human activity causing pain to others. Because of their natural make-up of 'grabbing' from other people, and of rudely repelling them, in order to get what they wanted from life, it was inevitable that all human beings would, at some time, cause other human beings some form of distress or suffering. This human propensity to hurt others in no way caused 'offence' to **UNIVERSAL CONSCIOUSNESS** (God) – as was affirmed by the Jewish and 'Christian' religion.

Only mankind understood the meaning of the word 'sin' since only mankind and all of 'creation subject to mankind', 'would ever know the pain, deprivation and misery caused by the two fundamental **IMPULSES of INDIVIDUALITY** – **Bonding-Rejection** active within the human 'personality'.

Man's inbuilt impulse to protect his own individuality had made him set up rules and laws for human society. **The 'Universal Creative Power' – LOVE – had absolutely nothing to do with the setting up of human restrictions, limitations, laws and judgement.**

I also saw that:

The **'Father-Mother-Creative Power' – LIFE – continually flowed through all the universe and was the life in my mind using the twin impulses of thought and feeling.**

186

Hence any powerful 'imperfect thinking and feeling' could disturb and change the 'CONSCIOUSNESS pattern' of created things.

Conversely:

My 'thinking' when fully cleansed of the twin impulses of 'ego' – and fully receptive of the 'Father-Mother Creative Power' INTELLIGENCE/LOVE would re-introduce the condition of

'PERFECT INTELLIGENT LOVE'.

Therefore, a condition previously made imperfect as a result of 'imperfect thought' could be brought back into a condition of 'wholeness' again by changing ego attitudes and thoughts to those of UNCONDITIONAL LOVE.

My mind was a 'tool' of the whole creative process originating in the UNIVERSAL.

Now that I **knew** this was so – **knew** it <u>spiritually</u>, **intellectually, emotionally**, I realised I could and **must** take steps to overcome the **TWIN IMPULSES** of **EGO** previously governing my mind, in order to allow the <u>**DIVINE REALITY**</u> full scope through my mind and brain.

This is why there was a struggle between my humanly entrenched Ego and my **'Father-Mother- Consciousness'** during the very strident temptations I experienced at the end of my enlightenment in the desert. **Satan had nothing to do with the tug-of-war which took place within my consciousness.**

The war was waged between the

TWIN IMPULSES OF INDIVIDUALITY – Bonding-Rejection
and the <u>**DIVINE REALITY**</u> which had made <u>**ITSELF**</u> known to me as
<u>**INTELLIGENT LOVE-LIFE**</u>

transcendent, yet within me and which would gradually take over my **individuality** to an ever greater extent if I continually meditated and cleared my consciousness of selfish impulses.

The foregoing is a description of the powerful knowledge I returned to Nazareth with.

Therefore, my physically healing time spent with my mother whilst she nursed me back to health was also a time of prayer and meditation, from which I drew the inspiration and strength to consciously and conscientiously **live** the **NATURE** of the **DIVINE** or **UNIVERSAL REALITY.**

As you know, the **NATURE** of the **DIVINE** or **'UNIVERSAL REALITY'** **is LIFE.**

When **IT** is active within creation – or we can also say – within the 'individuality' of creation, **IT grows, nourishes, provides nutrition, regenerates, heals, protects, ensures survival, fulfills the needs of everything created – all within a system of perfect harmony, co-operation and law and order. This is the 'nature' of LIFE. All its work in creation is done in accordance with UNIVERSAL NATURE – the promotion of the highest good of all living things.**

If you can understand these words, you will realise why I returned from the desert – a man filled with joy, with a new awareness of the beauty of the world, a feeling of absolute confidence, and KNOWING it was possible to control the appearance of 'matter'. You will feel with me, my own elation that I could now offer the Jews the glorious news that the 'Kingdom of Heaven' was in their midst. All they had to do was 'find' it with my assistance, and their lives would be changed forever.

I leave you with the same knowledge which, prayerfully used and fully understood, can change the course of your life.

As you read, your consciousness will be lifted and as you seek inspiration – it will come to you.

I long for you to understand, aspire, grow and achieve. Relax in my **LIGHT** for whilst you read, reflect, meditate, and pray, you are drawn into my **CHRIST CONSCIOUSNESS** which will become ever more apparent to you, as you evolve within this **Divine Knowledge.**

My love and faith in your growing wisdom enfold you.

LETTER 6

These Letters present knowledge which people down the ages have longed to know but have not received since their worldly scientific knowledge was not sufficient to enable them to understand. So was it when I was in Palestine in the person of 'Jesus', again and again I explained the TRUTH OF UNIVERSAL EXISTENCE in various ways, but no one understood.

As most of you must realise: I have NOT come to you at this time to bring you a new religion, a better moral code, or a new 'God' to worship. Nor, like your metaphysicians, do I preach 'positive thinking'. Your humanly conceived 'positive thinking', magnetising to yourselves your human needs and desires, and the means to fulfill your ambitions, only strengthens your ego-drive.

All things blest and bountiful will be manifested in you and your life as and when you realise that: the entire universe is transcendent **UNIVERSAL CONSCIOUSNESS** made visible when **IT** takes on material form through the activity of the ego.

Your true purpose in your spiritual journey, is to break free of the bondage of the ego and make ever more **pure** contact with **DIVINE CONSCIOUSNESS. It is your eventual destiny to recognize ITS omnipresence both within yourself and throughout your daily activities.**

Your highest spiritual goal is to come to that spiritually exalted moment when you finally realise that your human mind and its desires are only finite – and therefore, can never bring you the happiness and fulfilment you will experience when you lay down your selfhood and come to DIVINE CONSCIOUSNESS asking *ONLY* for the Higher Way, more Abundant Life, and the true spiritual PURPOSE which you alone can accomplish in your earthly state.

However, to help you reach this high point of realisation, I am about to enlarge on the origins and function of the EGO.

As I contemplate your world, I see a dimension presently controlled by EGO FORCE.

Every evil thing **IN YOUR PRESENT DECADENT SOCIETY** in your vast soulless cities, arises out of Ego Force. It is the source of every wicked, lying, perverted activity presently in operation on your planet. It controls the media, your TV, your families, nations. It is productive of wars all over your globe. It creates a foul miasma of low consciousness energies perceivable by Higher Spiritual Entities – but too horrible to contemplate.

If your present consciousness is permeated with love of possessions and an inability to share with others, devising ways and means to become rich at the expense of others, stealing, failing to perform your work conscientiously or give good value for money, snapping, snarling, indulging in criticism, sarcasm, judgementalism, rejection, denigration, enmity, intolerance, hatred, jealousy, aggression, violent impulses, thieving, falsehoods, double and devious dealings, slander – you are ego-driven. Your ego is in control and you will find it difficult to move through the miasma of ego-consciousness to be able to see *Reality*.

For this reason, I have come through the medium of these Letters to help you understand exactly what is binding you down in your present conditions, the horror of which was unimaginable by the human mind a century ago.

I am now about to explain more fully the

EGO

AT THE TIME OF YOUR CONCEPTION, during intercourse, as your father's consciousness rose, via his spine, ever higher to the top of his head, and tension mounted towards its climax, your father's consciousness briefly touched **DIVINE CONSCIOUSNESS** creating a flash point, a small explosion, which he experienced as orgasm, and thereafter an injection of

DIVINE CONSCIOUSNESS

was infused in his semen

to give life to the mother's ovum.

The moment of union with woman and explosion of tension in a man at the time of orgasm, re- enacts the time of the Big Bang, when the UNITY of 'Father-Mother-Consciousness' exploded into separate energies and the first electrical particles and random 'matter' took form. 'Father Consciousness' provided the energy of 'activity and momentum', and 'Mother Consciousness' provided the 'bonding' to give form and substance to the electrical particles.

These are PRIMAL IMPULSES which give life and form to man and woman.

I want you to understand that creation is not a creation of 'matter' imbued with consciousness. Creation is the visible form of PRIMAL IMPULSES drawn and bonded into individual shapes and entities all *expressing* differing facets and combinations of the PRIMAL IMPULSES in a myriad of ways. Therefore, the PRIMAL IMPULSES are the Reality which your eyes, ears, smell, touch, tell you are solid 'matter' but are really CONSCIOUSNESS IMPULSES individualised in order to be experienced, intellectually understood and appreciated emotionally.

At the time of conception when semen unites with ovum and a mating takes place, male consciousness chromosomes bond with female consciousness chromosomes. This is a physical union of your father's own consciousness of semen and mother's own consciousness of ovum powered by the Divine. Thus, do the male and female consciousness chromosomes carry the imprint of genetic DNA from both parents. The moment of physical union of semen and ovum is conducted on two levels of creativity.

The injection of DIVINE CONSCIOUSNESS became your SOUL embodied within the human consciousness union of semen and ovum. Physicality was created, powered by 'Father-Mother-Life Consciousness' which controlled the activity and bonding of conscious cells, producing the gradual growth and development of your physical body – which is really consciousness made visible on every level of your being – and nothing else.

Your soul remained as an inviolate 'flame' (metaphor) of 'Father-Mother-LIFE' deeply enmeshed within the physical drives of:

ACTIVITY – BONDING/REPULSION

These became your earthly individuality and personality.

Incorporated within the transcendent **LIFE IMPULSES of 'Divine Father-Mother Consciousness'**, these consciousness **impulses** now took over the process of your physical consciousness creation and became the driving force behind your personality. Together, **'Activity-Bonding'** laboured to build conscious cell by conscious cell according to the consciousness specifications contained in the consciousness DNA molecules. Both personality and body are the product of these human impulses of 'Activity-Bonding/Repulsion'. Whilst **UNIVERSAL CONSCIOUSNESS** remains forever within equilibrium in the **space**, and therefore, undetectable – in that self-same **space**, in **frequencies of vibration,** the primal impulses of 'Activity – Bonding/Rejection' work together in the visible dimension appearing to your senses in the form of electro-magnetism.

Both **UNIVERSAL CONSCIOUSNESS** and your soul remain undisturbed within the silence and stillness of equilibrium in space. The earthly consciousness creativity takes place within space and time and varying frequencies of vibration of materialised consciousness.

Therefore, you take on living form and continue to exist within two dimensions. One dimension is Unseen, the **DIVINE CONSCIOUSNESS** – and the other visible dimension is all that the living human being can sense or comprehend until spiritual development lifts its human consciousness frequencies of vibration to the spiritual plane and a glimmer of understanding enters its earthly consciousness. As this process of gradual enlightenment proceeds, the uplifted human consciousness then works **consciously** both within the **Unseen** and the visible dimension.

The higher the frequencies of vibration of individualised consciousness, the higher and more perfect are the forms created in the mind – the lower the frequencies of vibration, the more divorced from **Universal Perfection of Love** are the forms created in the individualised mind wholly possessed by the ego-drive.

The **EGO** takes over control of your developing foetus from the time of the union of the semen and ovum. The new little being became an 'I' immediately feeling satisfaction and dissatisfaction in the womb depending on its sense of comfort or discomfort and what was happening to mother.

When you were born, your instincts of survival imprinted with the deep primeval knowledge of 'created beingness' buried in each living cell of your body, prompted you to breathe, and become aware of an emotional emptiness and deprivation at your separation from the comfort of the confining womb, which was then felt as a physical emptiness and need for physical nourishment.

Thus was your ego cry born.

When you cried you were given nourishment by mother which was deeply satisfying – both physically and emotionally. When your needs were fully met, you could slip back into a state of equilibrium within sleep.

When you woke from your equilibrium, you felt a sense of insecurity (the equilibrium now divided into mental and emotional awareness), you remembered that mother and milk created a fulfilment of needy insecurity, and so again, you cried. Your needs were fulfilled.

So did your **ego-drive** develop.

Sometimes, you cried and it was humanly decreed that it was not yet feeding time and you were left to cry for a while. This built up an awareness that needs were not always satisfied immediately and you would have to adapt. You either chose anger and cried more vigorously – or lapsed into acceptance. Your choice of reaction depended on the characteristics of '**ego-drive**' imprinted in your consciousness at birth.

Neither forms of ego-drive were to be condemned or judged. They were the natural result of the **Creative Factor** of **Ego** which ensures **INDIVIDUALITY.**

As I have explained in my last **Letter, EGO** is the:

GUARDIAN of INDIVIDUALITY

If you did not have this inbuilt impulse to 'cry' for what you want to make you happy or reject what makes you sad, you would be in a limbo of nothingness.

If you did not run when faced with danger or did not call for help when in danger – you might die. If you had not cried – 'demanded' food – when you were born, you might have starved.

If you had not welcomed mother's milk and nuzzled her warmly, you might never have developed a close caring bond with her.

Without the **EGO DRIVE** there would be no creation, no individuality, no fulfilment of need, no protection, no warmth of response and no human love.

Without the **EGO DRIVE** there would be no self-defence, no self-protection, no survival.

However, the **EGO DRIVE – primarily the 'I' of the individual**, is imprinted only with the need for **SELF- SATISFACTION** and **SURVIVAL**.

In childhood, the 'I' of the ego is governed by likes and dislikes, wants and rejection of what is not wanted and by habits formed by a constant repetition of feelings. Bad habits in the form of unacceptable ego responses to personal experiences and the environment are formed and these are, in turn, imprinted in the unconscious – or sub-conscious mind – and remain hidden. However, they erupt into repeated behaviour patterns when the 'memory' of previous circumstances and modes of behaviour unconsciously bring them to mind.

Now, the sub-conscious mind and the conscious mind begin to work together to develop the personality. Much of the behaviour becomes 'conditioned behaviour' and very difficult to break. When the person is unconsciously programmed with strong self-centred ego habits of thought and behaviour – and finds it difficult to live with others in harmony – that person then goes to a psychologist for help in unravelling the complexities of the mental/emotional problems.

Until my **Truth of Existence** is fully understood and the life-giving principles become the consistent guide lines of habits of thought and responses to life's experiences, the pain and suffering arising from the ignorant indulgence of the ego-drives will persist.

The church describes this human difficulty as being a 'temptation by Satan'. It is no such thing. It is a natural process brought about by the **uncontrolled reactions to life** powered by the **Ego-Drive, whose only purpose is to bring the individual happiness and contentment, fulfilment of need – or – privacy, independence, security, peace ..... all directed at SURVIVAL.**

It must be understood that there is nothing evil about the ego-drive. **It is the necessary tool of creation.** It is the individual himself who brings about the imbalances in life by allowing the ego drive full control in his personality without thought or consideration for other people.

This, too, is not to be judged or criticised, since the person possessed by ego-drive knows no other way to think or operate within the earthly dimension.

The child knows nothing about self-control other than that taught by parents and school teachers. Therefore, the mistakes it makes in responding to life and its ups-and-downs, can only be accepted in good spirit by parents and teachers, since the child has no understanding of what is driving him.

If he wants something – he WANTS something right away and wonders why he shouldn't have it.

There is nothing more in his mind than this. He sees something he likes – he wants it.

It is cruel to tell a child roughly, 'No, you can't have it', his entire system is insulted and assaulted. From earliest babyhood, the training process must be initiated by logic and reassurance – affirming his right to feel secure within his environment. **His sense of security should be developed by explaining the right way to express his wishes. LOVE – not irritation or anger, must choose the words which tell the child why he cannot have what he wants**. The child will hear the message when given in love. When delivered in anger, it arouses his deepest ego-drives and begins to take form as resentment – overt or hidden or a sense of deep seated frustration which taints the ego, reducing the child's natural sense of inner validity. A child needs to possess this sense of personal validity and should not be subdued or destroyed.

It requires parents or teachers to point out, very clearly, that other people in the world also have their needs, their rights to their possessions, their desire for peace and pleasure. No one, not even a child – or adult – has the right to upset another person in order to obtain their own satisfaction!

If another youngster hits the child and makes him cry, it is only natural for the ego-drive to want to fight back – he is programmed to defend himself against the other child.

It calls for parents and teachers to point out that a 'pay-back', revenge in conflict, only **escalates**, bringing more pain to each child, and for this reason, 'pay back' is entirely pointless.

Better to **LAUGH** and turn away. And rather than allow the irritation and hurt in the mind to continue, better still to take the problem to **DIVINE CONSCIOUSNESS in prayer** and ask for the hurt to be removed from his consciousness, and seek a means of reconciliation.

A child should also be taught to take time to understand that he and the other child are equally children born of the Divine Moment. When a child is spiritually receptive and can make this procedure of recognising his spiritual kinship with other children and all living things, and the 'rights of others equal with his own', into a habit, he will have been given the greatest spiritual gift possible. In such a way, is the ego-drive weakened by the practical daily application of inspirational love, whilst the central 'I'ness of the child remains strong and self-confident.

The child should be taught the benefits of laughter which I will describe and explain in a later **Letter**. Therefore, skilled and insightful **teaching** is absolutely necessary to steer the child into an appreciation of the rights of other people – **EQUAL WITH THEIR OWN RIGHTS.**

This is the spiritual law which should dominate the home and the classroom. Any other law by which to judge circumstances is faulty and lacking in balance.

The best teaching will rely – not on the will of the teacher – the 'because I say so' attitude – but on a systematic reference in every circumstance to 'brotherly love' and the equal rights of others.

At the same time, a child should not be indoctrinated in 'self-sacrifice' since this type of **caring must be willing and born only of the individual's spiritual perceptions and goals.**

Self-sacrifice is born of spiritual enlightenment, of a higher road to follow, of denial of the little self to remove the ego barriers obstructing attunement with the universality of **Divine Consciousness.** True enlightened Self-sacrifice brings a spiritual consciousness to the heights of joy. There is no sense of loss in any form.

To better describe the reality of **the soul** and the **ego**, I want you to cup your hands together, finger tips touching finger tips and wrists together, leaving a space between your cupped hands. Your hands represent the '**human consciousness shell**' of a person – the ego.

196

The **SPACE** correctly represents the **SOUL** born of the **'Father-Mother-Conscious-Life'** at the moment of your conception. Whilst to human senses it appears to be 'nothingness', it is, in fact, an **off-shoot** of the **ALLNESS & WHOLENESS of DIVINE CONSCIOUSNESS** out of which all created things have taken form. **Your hands with the space between represent the 'I'.**

Your right and left hands represent two potent forces of the magnetic ego-drive. They represent forces of 'bonding-rejection, but at the same time, quite rightly, they are the physical representation of the physical energies known to science as magnetism – 'Bonding and Repulsion'.

Bend back your right hand from the other one and visualise that you use this right hand to 'get what you want out of life'. It represents, also, what your human consciousness perceives as the 'grasping' attitude to life.

Give time to this exercise and fully realise your right hand represents the magnetic pull, the bonding, the attraction, the gravity evident in all of nature. It is the source of all 'wanting' and 'desiring'. It is the **magnetic impulse** which is always directed at getting what is necessary or greatly desired and pleasurable in life. This **magnetic impulse** is '**spiritually intended**' to be directed towards constructive purposes. Gaining, holding, building, achieving.

Were there no other people or living things in the world, the magnetic impulse could have full sway in a personality and no harm done.

It is only when 'other people' or living creatures or other people's persons and possessions have to be taken into account, that the uncontrolled '**magnetic impulse to attract, draw, bond, hold, possess**' becomes a sickness of the personality, if it is not equally balanced with the needs of all other living things.

Return your hand to its original place – cupped with the left hand.

Now pull back your left hand and visualise that this hand represents the 'magnetic impulse' to repel, push away, slap, or defend yourself from any unauthorised encroachment on your property or possessions or any attack on your character, family, or work. This left hand represents the '**magnetic impulse of rejection**' which is '**spiritually intended**' to ensure your privacy and save your life. It is a legitimate weapon when your physical or emotional survival is at stake – always providing you remember that your every action is an electro-magnetic/activity-binding/repulsion blue-print in consciousness which rebounds and externalises eventually in the form of a similar attack on the self.

The unpleasantness may be criticism from your parent, teacher, employer, and the words of self-defence which spring to mind and jump out of your mouth are ego-words wholly given to self-defence, expressing the magnetic drive of repulsion and rejection. And as your ego words of attack flare up into angry speech, so is the ego of your critic similarly threatened and it also rises up in him/her as words of self-defence against you. What may have started out as a necessary and adult action of 'pointing out some error and a better way to do', is frequently immediately seen **by a self-centred sensitive ego**, as a personal attack. What should have been a **moment** of growth, develops into a **time** of conflict, anger, possibly tears, ongoing resentment and mutual hostility.

In such swift unexpected **unnecessary** ways, conflict is generated in the mind, expressed in words – even actions, and perpetuated through resentment and hatred.

Remember that every activity of the mind – the mental thought and the emotional reactions of attraction and repulsion are all **consciousness energies of creativity.** These consciousness energies not only create the unpleasant rebound forms, but they develop the direction of the character and even affect relationships generally and the environment ... and they reduce the life vitality of the body, leading directly to a sense of physical malaise, viral infection or long term disease.

The higher way, when under attack of any kind – a way having only constructive repercussions – is to remember you can instantly call upon **DIVINE   CONSCIOUSNESS** from which you   will draw   instant protection in any eventuality. But this is only possible if you can move beyond the **'magnetic ego drive of resistance'** in the perfect assurance that **DIVINE CONSCIOUSNESS** meets your every need.

Now return your left hand to its original position with the right hand.

Realise that throughout this exercise, the **SPACE** between your hands has remained the **SPACE.**

It has not been involved in any of the activity of the hands. And so is it with your **SOUL** when your ego is busily at work, second by second, always and forever on the alert to fulfill your needs and defend you from any unpleasantness. The **DIVINE CONSCIOUSNESS of your SOUL** remains hidden although It is always within you.

When I was on earth, I spoke to the people about 'the Kingdom of Heaven'. I said it was within you. So it is. It is your soul. It is the haven of equilibrium of the **DIVINE CONSCIOUSNESS** which gave you being as a future man or woman.

I greatly long to be able to put into your minds a broad view of your **SOURCE of BEING** to enable you to perceive a little more clearly your beginnings – from whence you have come.

You must also understand at all times that when I speak a word of description of **THAT WHICH IS TRULY UNKNOWABLE**, I am, myself, standing in the very highest, infinitesimal frequencies of vibration on the very edge of the **GREAT UNIVERSAL EQUILIBRIUM** out of which all things have drawn their being and taken on their form.

If I speak of a mountain, a picture will come to your mind, but you will not know the immensity of its structure, the endurance of its rock, its ravines and peaks and caverns, the snow which caps it in all seasons, the waterfalls cascading into pools when its glaciers melt. For you to gain a glimpse of the grandeur of the mountain, I would have to go into a detailed description of its every nook and cranny. Even after the most detailed **verbal** explanations, you would still have only imagined mental pictures to draw on. You would still not **KNOW** the mountain.

If I speak of a hurricane, I can bring to your mind – trees bowing to the ground, bent by the tremendous winds, walls crumbling, rafters broken, bricks and roofs flying, windows shattered, cars overturned, great trees uprooted, but you will never know the force and the noise of that wind, the crash of falling masonry, or the terror it generates in people's hearts who have to endure it, until you have experienced it for yourself. And so is it when I try to describe for you, **'THAT' WHICH BROUGHT ALL CREATION INTO BEING. You can only guess, not KNOW.**

It will only be after you have experienced all I have spoken about – for yourself – that you will begin to gain some idea of what I am trying to tell you. Therefore, let no one who reads my Letters dispute with another or deny the truth of what I am teaching you – or refute my words – for I tell you truly that you cannot fully know what you have not experienced.

It is only those who will follow me in acceptance and faith into daily meditation, the cleansing of consciousness, and impassioned prayer for enlightenment, who will eventually gain ever deepening glimpses – then experiences – of what creation **itself** may access – **Divine Consciousness.**

You may ask what is the difference between **Universal Consciousness and Divine Consciousness? UNIVERSAL CONSCIOUSNESS is the UNIVERSAL REALM of SPACE which none may enter or access, since IT rests in a state of equilibrium and self-contained energy.**

DIVINE CONSCIOUSNESS is the re-union of the original IMPULSES within UNIVERSAL CONSCIOUSNESS which were released to become both the *activity and the substance* of creation at the moment of the BIG BANG.

These IMPULSES were explosively divided and then came together in a state of mutual restraint. They were also destined to work forever in the created realm either separately, manifested as energies, or together restrained in equilibrium. It is only this realm of DIVINE CONSCIOUSNESS that science may penetrate.

Perhaps the following paragraph will explain this more clearly:

UNIVERSAL CONSCIOUSNESS

embodiment of

UNIVERSAL IMPULSES

IMPULSE of: !   IMPULSE of :

The WILL to create in mutual restraint with The PURPOSE to experience Itself.

INTELLIGENCE   "   "   "   "   LOVE

IMPULSE of INTELLIGENT WILL equilibrium IMPULSE of LOVING PURPOSES

Having given you this intellectual word description of **UNIVERSAL CONSCIOUSNESS,** you will not be any closer to an appreciation of the sublime magnificence and grandeur of the Power, nor of the beauty, joy, harmony, ecstasy contained in colour and sound beyond your dimension. It is only we who have ascended in consciousness frequencies of vibration to the very portals or edges of the equilibrium of **UNIVERSAL CONSCIOUSNESS** who experience and can **radiate the rapture of self-awareness of true potential without desiring to fulfill it – the wondrous joy of personal fulfilment without 'lifting a finger'.**

I use this last term metaphorically, since, although I retain my individuality, I am active in consciousness only and am, in no way, physical any longer and have not been since my continuing spiritual ascension in other dimensions after my death on the cross.

You may wonder how it is possible to have such enormous UNIVERSAL IMPULSES within a state of equilibrium. They are in a state of equal and mutual restraint, the bonding, nurturing LOVE IMPULSE holding, binding the creative, active WILL under control.

I can only explain this phenomenon in the following simple terms.

If you place the palm of one hand on top of the palm of the other, with finger tips of each hand touching the wrist of the other hand and then try to separate them but still keep them tightly flat on each other, you will gain some idea of the meaning of 'equilibrium' or 'mutual restraint'.

Furthermore, you must realise that although your hands are apparently expressing a physical phenomena, they are actually governed by and expressing IMPULSES emanating from your brain. In addition, your brain may be the vehicle of expressing conscious ideas – impulses – but in fact, the IMPULSE is the reality of all movement of any kind – not the physical brain which is only an instrument of expression of such impulses.

I have given you only an intellectual account of UNIVERSAL CONSCIOUSNESS. How can I describe for you the latent power, the magnificence of reverence, the rapture, the radiant joy, the state of utter contentment and peace and harmony of Its Being?

Even if you can contemplate and realise that out of this IMMENSITY of CONSCIOUSNESS the entire universe has drawn life and form, you cannot perceive more than an electron of the vast, immeasurable Joyous Reality of UNIVERSAL CONSCIOUSNESS.

To fully understand the **nature of creation**: the reasons why the ego functions as it does, why created entities feel the urges they feel, it must be understood that the **NATURE** and **QUALITY** of **UNIVERSAL CONSCIOUSNESS** is **RADIANT JOY – FULFILMENT – HAPPINESS.**

THIS IS WHAT I TERMED THE 'KINGDOM OF HEAVEN WITHIN YOU' – WITHIN YOUR SOUL – WITHIN THE DEEPEST RECESSES OF YOUR PSYCHE, which is the intermediary between the radiance of your soul and the shadow self of ego.

To return to this transcendent state of glorious, beautiful, happy, harmonious being is your soul's deepest longing!

It is this enduring longing, this inborn unconscious recollection of equilibrium and peace, joy and harmony, which, through the psyche, prompts the EGO to manipulate the environment on your behalf. Its consistent purpose is to bring you back to your primal original state of glorious ecstasy out of which you drew your soul, being and form.

But the ego can bring about your desired joy and pleasure, **only** by means of the two magnetic/emotional 'Bonding-Rejection' impulses – which are only materialised impulses to give you your individuality.

Therefore, the inborn **longing** to rejoin the **SOURCE of BEING** is experienced in the electromagnetic parameters of thought and feeling as 'More, more, more' of what gave you a pleasurable feeling, previously. More friends, more house, car, clothes, etc. Each time the 'more' has been achieved, there is a little glow of satisfaction, perhaps a showing off to the neighbours to heighten the happiness, (gaining one up on them, and another little glow), and then the novelty dies away, the new possession becomes mundane, the senses are again at rest – in equilibrium – mental tiredness sets in, routine becomes dull and boring. To generate some life, the ego finds another goal to be achieved to provide excitement and pleasure. Thus, life is an endless chase for personal satisfaction of various kinds leaving the hidden soul, starved, unsatisfied, still longing for something 'More' – but what is it my deepest self is craving? You ask in desperation.

When a person reaches an understanding of the true source of emptiness and continual inner craving for 'more of what made me feel good before', and begins to meditate to make contact with ...'THAT'... **WHICH BROUGHT HIM/HER INTO BEING**, a little of the **Divine Equilibrium** filters through the human consciousness. The emptiness begins to recede.

If indeed such a person catches a true glimpse of the **ETERNAL** and the true goal in life, the longing for more possessions will eventually die a natural death. The desire for 'More' possessions will be gradually replaced with a sincere appreciation of what you already have and a sense of consistent contentment. Through experiences of the miraculous interventions or activity of **DIVINE CONSCIOUSNESS** within the daily life, the human consciousness is greatly uplifted and learns that its daily needs are met in the very best way. Faith is increased and joy enhanced.

This is why I have said to you: I have not come to teach you positive thinking to draw into your orbit the things you want and need. I have come to you expressly to lead you back into the **Kingdom of Heaven**. However, it is not only in the matter of desiring more possessions for yourself that your soul is bound down within its secret dwelling place. The ego also uses the magnetic emotional drive to 'repel – reject' to ensure your individuality, privacy, and safety. This impulse takes on numerous forms designed to give you a feeling of superiority, or elitism, or protecting you from people whom you consider to be undesirable, or having less social status than yourself. This ego drive is practised continually and was thought to be perfectly acceptable even by the churches. The truth is: when the soul begins to gain a little control over the ego drive, it will chide the human personality for its selfishness and exclusivity. It will urge the psyche towards the adoption of unconditional love and a belief in universality and Oneness of all people, no matter who they may be.

Perhaps, now, you can more easily understand how and why the creation of your individuality through the medium of the ego, formed the great 'physical impulses' capsule which produced and enclosed your human consciousness – creating both your physical form and your human personality. Since it governs your mind and emotions, thoughts and feelings, it prevents you from making contact with the **SOURCE of your LIFE** and your **SOUL**.

YOUR TRUE PURPOSE in life is to gain the mastery of your ego by reaching out in thought and feeling to ... '**THAT**'... **WHICH YOU SENSE**

IS BEHIND CREATION and consistently asking for enlightenment. This is the very first step a person must take towards that glorious moment when he/she will make contact with the **DIVINE** and then move forward by means of continual cleansing of the ego-drive, to the re-entry into that 'heavenly state' out of which your soul was born and took its individuality.

And how did this CREATION of INDIVIDUALITY come about?

As I said before, **UNIVERSAL CONSCIOUSNESS** reached a high point of mutual restraint and an explosion took place which tore apart the:

****

IMPULSE of CREATIVE WILL from the **IMPULSE of LOVING PURPOSES**

which separated and became active within creation as:

Father Intelligence : Mother Love

seen as

Electricity : Magnetism 'Bonding – Repulsion'

Life

!

Re-unified in equilibrium as

DIVINE CONSCIOUSNESS

!

L I F E

Therefore, far from being solid and imponderable 'matter', – in reality – the visible world is:

Mind/activity working always in conjunction with emotional/magnetic Bonding – Repulsion. Also known as '**Attraction – Rejection**'.

Father Intelligence: physical electricity
and
Mother Love: physical magnetic 'Bonding – Rejection
together produced a child – the EGO.

This IMPULSE of INDIVIDUALITY

was born and took undeviating and consistent form within the energies of creation to ensure that the various electrical forces expressed as protons and electrons and the rest of the 'particle gang' excitedly discovered by science, should not fly off uninterruptedly into a distant 'formless state' but should be restrained and controlled by the magnetic 'bonding rejection' IMPULSE of Mother Love to bring about manifested form.

Science may dispute the foregoing paragraphs, since it has been at great pains to describe the various 'bonding processes' by applying differing word-terms to the 'bonding' energies.

Science is welcome to call the 'bonding or attraction energies' by any term they wish, but the fact remains that these energies have taken on form from the grand and primal IMPULSE of MOTHER LOVE, whose PRIMAL CONSCIOUSNESS function is to give form to individuality.

The IMPULSE of 'Father Intelligent Life' gives electrical momentum to creation.

The IMPULSE of 'Mother Loving Purposefulness' gives the 'bonding' to restrain the electrical momentum and bring it under control within the individuality.

The IMPULSE of 'Mother Loving Purposefulness' gives the 'repulsion-rejection' impulse to ensure the survival of the individuality.

That – is the process of creation.

Science can only approach creation as a spectator. Although its ambassadors are human and experience life for themselves, the human mind can only observe what has been created. It cannot enter into the intimate processes of creation hidden within 'matter' and the most basic fields of energy.

Science will never be able to pinpoint the **MOTIVATING FACTOR X** which gives rise to the energies which are in control of the creation of individual form.

But what science has to say on the matter of creation is of little moment to you as an individual.

Science will not change your life-style, health, environment, personal feelings and achievements one iota. What you need to know – and what I have come expressly to tell you – is how to escape the selfish **possessive-protective drive** given you by the **EGO** to ensure your individuality and survival and your inbuilt longing to return to the joy and happiness out of which all creation took **LIFE.**

This provides you with the reason why I originally came to earth and am coming to you at this present time – to do something that no scientist can ever do for you – help your soul emerge from the confines of your ego-drive and embark on a new programme of 'thought-emotional-living' which will directly express the 'Father-Mother-Consciousness Life' injected into you and all humanity at the moment of conception.

Because the ego itself possesses the electric momentum of Activity-Creativity and the emotional magnetic impulses of 'Bonding-Rejection', whatever is born of the 'ego-drive' by its thoughts, feelings and actions, is charged with physical electro-magnetic life which will produce replica life forms and will be eventually materialised within the life of the ego-creator.

These created forms not only manifest eventually as experiences but also disturb the functioning of the physical processes of their creator and are the origin of physical discomforts or viruses or disease. Therefore, is it a great cause for rejoicing when the soul emerges from its encapsulating human consciousness of the ego, for the ascending spiritual consciousness will create the harmonious life-giving conditions it holds in consciousness. Conversely, it is a cause for sorrow whilst the human consciousness is submerged in ego control, producing upsets, trials and tribulations both in life experiences and the physical condition itself.

Therefore, I tell you: if you do not like your world, you have it within your power to change your 'conditions of existence', right where you are – if you have the faith and consistent will to do so. I repeat in another form to gain your attention:

If you continue in your present level of human functioning and thought, you will only experience your present level of human existence.

You will be bound down to working hard for a paltry living, beset by numerous problems, such as poverty and ill-health, addictions, immobilised by prostrating fear, and exposed to illintentioned attacks of all kinds.

You will be burdened by present conditions until you understand how to change them.

This is your golden opportunity to take control of your lives as never before, by getting control of your thoughts and emotions – **your electrical and magnetic impulses** – the blue-prints of your future experiences.

For – you are like potters possessing clay and daily shaping pots and utensils for your use. **CONSCIOUSNESS** is the clay – the substance with which you make your lives – and every condition pertaining to it. You, alone, shape your lives into the forms you experience.

By your thoughts, you can change your personal future, if you will but heed my words, understand your true origins, believe in them and use this knowledge in your daily routine.

You can affect your environment, your homes, families, work, the people you associate with, and even plants, animals, and climate.

Whatever you hold steadfastly in mind externalises.

Therefore, it is crucial to your spiritual and your personal human development to fully understand all I am trying to teach you.

Do not think that these Letters presented to you are too difficult to understand and then move on to some more easy way of finding happiness.

Believe me – there is no TRUE and more easy way for you to find the equilibrium and happiness you seek – because my words describe the UNIVERSAL TRUTH OF EXISTENCE and the LIFE with which you are presently building or destroying your lives.

At the same time – rest assured that you will never be able to create new conditions for yourself until you discover WHY and HOW you have been creating destructive and negative conditions in the past. Everything you are presently experiencing, you have created and set in motion by former thoughts, words, actions in the past. So do not resent your present circumstances, for you yourself have done whatever was the cause of your present conditions.

Be sensible, therefore, and read these Letters and devote all your strength and will to discover the means you have used (in former ignorance) to spoil your life in days gone by.

Then take the necessary steps to clean out your consciousness.

You may ask: Why should I clean out my consciousness?

I tell you – YOU would never plant a field of mealies without first putting in the plough to turn the ground, and then the equipment to make a fine textured soil and scatter the fertiliser. In ignorance, you could plant amongst the existing weeds in lumpy ground and omit the fertiliser and your crop would be thin and patchy. So is it when you muddle along in your earthly self-centred thoughts and live entirely in your own human knowledge, strength and will. You are limited in everything you do. And, all unknowingly, you create the very circumstances which will limit the harvest of your endeavours.

The moment that you realise from whence you have truly come, Seek the Power on which you may draw to accomplish every single thing in your life, and take urgent steps to clear out the weeds, thus purifying the soil of your consciousness, you will draw on the POWER which will imbue and prosper your daily experiences and activities.

You could say the **POWER** is your fertiliser but this would be completely inaccurate and false.

Fertiliser is inanimate chemical food for the plant – whereas the **POWER** on which you can draw through daily meditation, is the **LIFE** which will invigorate your entire being, your life and even your plants, and the bricks of your houses and your equipment far beyond your present belief. People who have given their entire willpower to living this Truth, see the undeniable fruitage in their lives and the 'seeing' increases their faith and determination. Thus do they enter a circle of blessedness. They marvel that other people can resist this truth and choose to remain outside the spiritual and earthly harmony in which it is possible to live.

If you are prepared to listen and ponder and meditate on the following pages, **you will begin to understand what has been hidden from the beginning of creation**.

CLEANSING THE CONSCIOUSNESS

Whilst doing all of the very necessary work of mental/emotional cleansing, use my words in the foregoing pages, describing ... **'THAT'**... **WHICH HAS BROUGHT YOU AND ALL THE WORLD INTO VISIBLE BEING** to build up an awareness and contact with **ITS** powerful **DIVINE CONSCIOUSNESS.** Out of that contact will come the inspiration and strength to accomplish the cleansing more swiftly. As the cleansing takes place, you will experience new found happiness and fulfilment in every area of your life.

You will also receive inspired directions in regard to your daily lives, either during your meditation or like a ray of light in your mind when you are at peace and thinking of some mundane matter. If you do not discount or reject these directions but follow them – faithfully and carefully – you will be taking your first steps to becoming, eventually, a great and successful planter and reaper of creative ideas in your environment. Everything connected to you will blossom, flourish and prosper. Everything will respond and bless you with newness of life.

If you discipline yourself in meditating daily with undeviating devotion, you will eventually begin to feel a response and inflow of **THAT WHICH BROUGHT YOU INTO BEING**, and the words you are using will take on new meaning. The words will be imbued with **UNIVERSAL LIFE.**

You will be filled with joy and will rejoice exceedingly, because you will then **KNOW** the power is real and active in your mind and life.

You will come to rely ever more confidently on the power beginning to be manifested in your affairs. **You will want to draw others into your state of blessed harmony for other people will be aware of It and ask you about It. Not only this – you will be experiencing a new kind of brotherly love and will want to share what makes you happy, with other people**.

I cannot emphasize this Truth enough, this need to meditate, since so many people give up the search and the self-discipline of daily listening before they have fully cleansed their consciousness and arrived at that state of inner

purification so necessary to making perfect contact with the
UNIVERSAL CONSCIOUSNESS – the Source of your Being.

When you do make contact – seeming miracles happen! This is the commencement of the Universal Power taking on form and shape in your soul, body, mind, heart, and circumstances.

I tell you truly – you may trust my words implicitly – if you persevere, there will come a moment when you actually feel the contact, and know that you have made contact.

You have then reached a most crucial time in your spiritual/human development!

For a few hours so many souls feel uplifted and joyful but then the daily cares intrude into their minds, and they intellectualise the experience. They explain it away in human terms.

Do not do this – for you will lose what you have been given! You will greatly delay your spiritual progress.

If you read these words and are afraid to believe them, or believe they are foolishness, or feel you will lose prestige if you believe them – you are making a creative form in consciousness which will negate any constructive response you may have originally had to this Letter.

So I say to you – cherish your moments of belief, preserve your special times of contact with ... 'THAT'... **WHICH BROUGHT YOU INTO BEING,** believe in them, and hold them fast in your consciousness and gradually you will move forward on to the heights of 'spiritual' consciousness – to great insight and joy.

Again, I say, do not put these Letters to one side. I cannot sufficiently emphasize your need to think about them, recall what they have to say. If you cannot remember, then return and read them yet again, and yet again, and yet again, until they have been absorbed into your consciousness.

The more you meditate on them daily, so will they be clarified in your mind and will come to have ever greater meaning for you. Eventually, you will find that they have been like food and drink, building up your morale and determination to help change your present conditions into those of harmony, widespread growth, prosperity and peace.

Great inspiration & joy will be yours when you come to realise that the immensity of '**That Which Brought You into Being**' is radiant, rapturous ecstatic Power – beyond your present capacity to dream and imagine – It is Reality – **IT** is the **SOURCE of BEING** – the SOURCE of everything that you see in your natural living world and in many levels of existence beyond the one you presently inhabit.

When you are abundantly receiving **Divine Consciousness** into your mind, yourself, into every facet of your existence, then you will begin to see the enormous difference, you will look back at the times of stress and unhappiness and see that gradually the limitations of your life will have yielded to greater blessedness. **This becomes an ongoing process in your life.**

Be of good heart – It is truly I, the Christ, who is reaching out to YOU and the world through the medium of these Letters.

I particularly want to impress on your minds the way I have deliberately made statements in the past pages to lift your thoughts to a higher level of consciousness, depicting the benefits to be derived from working to elevate your consciousness by ridding it of the negative traits mentioned on page 1.

I want you to realise fully that I have only come to help you rid your self of the undesirable ego-driven thoughts and emotions presently controlling your mind. I am also here expressly to encourage and 'help you' – yes, 'help you' – develop within your mind and heart all the love- based thoughts and emotions which will bring you into harmony with Divine Consciousness. It is my most urgent and loving purpose to bring you out of the grey shades of existence which you presently inhabit – into the 'sunshine' of spiritual enlightenment that awaits you when you have conquered the ego-drives, become unified with your soul and 'Father-Mother-Life' and moved into the harmony of unconditional love for all.

Therefore, I will repeat the list of negative characteristics set out on page 1. I want you to read them carefully and watch your own reactions and feelings as you go through them slowly. Criticism, sarcasm, judgmentalism, rejection, denigration, enmity, intolerance, hatred, jealousy, aggression, violent impulses, thieving, falsehoods, double and devious dealings, slander –

How do you begin to get rid of any of those you know to be part of your consciousness?

Do not be too ashamed to face up to them, since you are a human being and have been born under the influence of these characteristics of the ego. So do not be too afraid or too downcast to face up to them. Take the first step in total honesty – and write them down.

The second step is to take the sheet of paper and lie down and place it on your chest. Close your eyes and reach out in thought to the **Divine Reality – your Source of Being, which you should now realise is your Loving Procreator – your true 'Spiritual Father-Mother' – which radiates unstintingly and continually and consistently – UNCONDITIONAL PARENTING LOVE.**

Give time to quietening your mind until you feel that you are moving beyond your own consciousness. Then ask, in perfect faith, and expect an immediate answer, since you are operating in consciousness, for help in removing, dissolving, overcoming the false and unnecessary rejection ego-drives in all the days to come.

Emotionally, you make it clear to your 'Spiritual Father' or 'Divine Reality' – and therefore to yourself – that you want no more of these ego-negatives in your consciousness. You ask for the inspiration and strength to make every effort to avoid or deny them, from that day forward.

By following this course of action, you are creating a **NEW CONSCIOUSNESS FORM** which now begins to infiltrate and take over your present consciousness.

YOUR INTENTION

now becomes your reality.

The former negative characteristics written on your piece of paper and taken to your 'Spiritual Father' are now in a limbo of rejection in your consciousness. This conscious rejection is also the means of drawing Divine Power into your consciousness to help you strengthen your resolve and remembrance to discard any impulses which may erupt from the rejected characteristics.

Therefore, as you can probably see – the surrender and meditation have set in motion unseen work in consciousness of which you will probably be unaware until you later wake up to the fact that the characteristics have disappeared.

I would earnestly urge you to take the paper of characteristics into meditation several times. Each time you do so, you draw into your own consciousness, a further injection of **'Father-Mother-Consciousness Life' power** into your purpose of overcoming and ridding your consciousness of unwanted consciousness forms and forces.

When they have been dissolved, they will no longer draw into your circumstances the negative and unhappy shadows which plagued you before. You will be travelling a higher path to freedom.

As you progress, you will come to perceive little faults of consciousness in your mind and heart which never seemed to be wrong before, and when this happens, you must go through the same procedure of writing them down and taking them in utter faith to your **'Spiritual Father'**.

Now, there is one more thing you must do to complete this re-building of your consciousness. In place of **criticism, sarcasm, judgementalism, rejection, denigration, enmity, intolerance, hatred, jealousy, aggression, violent impulses, thieving, falsehoods, double and devious dealings, slander** – you must write down on a piece of paper – **in gold letters** if possible, to give you a sense of beauty and glow about the attributes – the golden qualities of **Divine Consciousness** of which you want to be possessed by – and to express – in future.

To be in perfect harmony with your **'Divine Reality'** – your **'Spiritual Father'** – each attribute will be founded on unconditional love and will promote the highest good of others.

For no longer will you seek to put others down in order to make yourself feel greater and more self-confident. Your entire consciousness will be directed to affirming other people and building up everything within your orbit. You will seek to nourish, nurture, teach, protect, maintain, fulfill the needs of others, and seek to lovingly establish order out of chaotic mindless actions.

Having written **your golden aspirations** on your sheet of paper, again lie down and reach out to your **'Divine Reality'** and ask that the beautiful impulses – the **nature** of the **Divine** may gradually spread through your mind and heart and become your own consciousness. When this happens, your soul

213

will be like a baby chick pecking and pecking, breaking its shell to emerge into the wonder of the great big world to be united with mother hen, patiently waiting for her child to re-join her. This is how it is with me and all other Christed souls. We wait and watch and help the people who long to find out the cause of their emptiness of spirit, who set their hearts on transcending earthly occupations, whose minds are being drawn to higher purposes in life, and who dream of coming into perfect attunement with their own souls and their **DIVINE SOURCE OF BEING**. We yearn with love over the spiritual travellers more than the travellers even suspect. This means that we yearn with love over you who are reading this **Letter**.

When you are again united with your Source of Being, you will have achieved your true purposes on earth. You will have accomplished your true mission in eternity. And now – let your REAL LIFE begin! You will have entered the Kingdom of Heaven!

I will not tell you what qualities to write for your new consciousness – these must come out of your present perceptions of the highest and best. Again study the **Divine Nature of Divine Consciousness** which I perceived so clearly in the desert and described for you in **Letter 1**.

Let this Divine Nature become your own nature.

I want you to know that when you embark on this journey in true sincerity, I will be at your side in every eventuality. It is my dearest wish that you will come to know that I am with you and that I am sending you support and strength in your quest to become unified with your '**Divine Reality**'.

ABOUT 'CHRISTIANITY'

I am now about to speak to you about more mundane affairs and as you read the following pages, I want you to review what is happening to your mood or feeling of well-being.

This is still an exercise in the recognition of what is happening in your consciousness as your thoughts change and you employ a new set of words.

Please read the next pages very carefully, whether or not you are a professing Christian, even though you may be strongly tempted to skip them. Write down your responses, ideas, feelings – particularly any changing feelings of depression or pleasure.

Make a note of the number of the page when the words begin to lighten your mood and lift you on to a higher plane of peace and happiness.

This is a most important exercise, for, unless you do it, you will continue to read about 'consciousness' for ever, but will never reach a deep understanding how it is the basic energy of your existence, of 'matter', your body and environment, your life events, your MOODS and your spiritual aspirations.

You will not begin to realise that CONSCIOUSNESS is the be-all and everything in your existence and experience – until you notice how 'ideas and opinions' can raise or lower the frequencies of vibration of your consciousness.

I want you to become aware of the words you use in your daily lives, the quality of life they create for you, and the impact they make on others – either lifting their moods into peace and joy or leaving them depressed and depleted.

Furthermore, it is my earnest intention to reach those of you who are presently adherents of the Christian religion and are struggling with past or present religious conditioning, thus finding it difficult to extricate your perceptions from dogma in order to move freely within the finer frequencies of vibration of higher spiritual knowledge.

You may be fearing damnation if you even read these pages – and yet they have a drawing power for you and you intuitively feel that you are reading about the **TRUTH of EXISTENCE** which you have not been taught by your ministers. You are torn by your pressing need to know the Truth and your fear of displeasing 'God' in whatever form you presently perceive 'Him' to be.

• **I, the CHRIST**, am well aware of the distress these **Letters** are causing to many sincere people and I long to bring you through your disquiet to perfect peace of mind and joy.

For this reason, it is an absolute necessity to first analyse your present beliefs and the origins of church doctrines before continuing to teach you the deeper Truth about the 'nature' of the Universal and the nature of man himself.

To fully understand the origins of Christian doctrine, you must travel back in time to the beginnings of Judaism and there find the 'rationalisations' of the human mind which struggled to define in words what was felt intuitively to be a probable source of being.

Those of you who are struggling to free yourselves of past myths and erroneous beliefs, must now come to clearly perceive for yourselves – and **understand** – the fundamental difference between 'church belief' and the **TRUTH of EXISTENCE** I am presently attempting to explain to you.

Until you can clearly discern the 'origin and form of your present beliefs', you will not be able to shake yourselves completely free of the illusions of your past conditioning within the church. You will have a 'foot in both camps' – a dangerous position to be in. This state of mind will give rise to great mental conflict and may cause you to abandon the search and return to the old, comfortable, emotionally secure religious forms which are leading you nowhere. So beware and do not allow yourselves to be intimidated by threats of displeasing 'God' and likely damnation.

ORIGINS OF A BELIEF IN A 'SUPER INDIVIDUAL GODHEAD'

Therefore, we will begin with a description of the origins of a belief in 'God', a name which has meant many different things to mankind. This belief began when the ancient Hebrews walked the desert plains and questioned the origins of creation. It was imagined that in some way the **SOURCE of CREATION** must surely be a 'superhuman man-god' invisible and far transcendent to earth and human kind. Some of the ancient prophets were mystically aware that the Source of Creation was diffuse and present – in some way – throughout creation and was also sited in the eternal dimension but this mysticism was not available to the average human mind.

You must also understand that, despite the present 'seeming reality' (in your minds) of such a 'God' from your readings in the Bible, no one has ever glimpsed such a 'superhuman man-god' in any form whatsoever, except, perhaps, Moses who claimed he saw Him in a 'burning bush' and described Himself as 'I am that I am'.

All that people have known of such a super-human 'god' has been derived from reading the colourful descriptions of 'God' given by prophets during their sojourn on earth. It is a hallmark of how illusory are religious beliefs that religionists return only to the ancients for their 'truth' since they cannot believe that 'God' is truly real, eternal and equally able to speak to people in your day and age.

216

Your ministers are terrified of any beliefs which do not meld into the old ones. They never consider – or are afraid to consider – that perhaps spiritual knowledge within the earthly dimension – is evolutionary!

I want you to 'see' that a 'fabric of belief', a mixture of rationalisations and beliefs has been concocted to make a web of mental/emotional security with which to enmesh and trap the minds and hearts of people. All that people are taught in the Christian faith is emotionally-based and emanates from 'hearsay', derived from early reports of my life and death on earth. Yet these are believed fanatically.

Christians are taught that: 'God is Love – and God is aware of your sin and punishes, disciplines, rewards the doers of good and sends misfortunes to the evil-doers'. This is an exact description of human activity and consciousness!

Christians are taught that **I, the Christ**, in the persona of Jesus 'died for the sins of the world'.

I was the 'unblemished Lamb of God sacrificed to pay the price for people's sinning'! I made a supreme sacrifice of myself to accomplish this strange feat of 'payment of sin' down the ages.

I again entered my body after death by crucifixion and appeared many times in the body to comfort and teach my mourning disciples. I even ate food during my appearance to them.

After forty days, I ascended out of sight of my disciples, taking my body up into 'heaven'.

As I asked in **Letter 3** – what would I do with a human body in 'heaven' – in the life beyond?

Because I said at my last supper with my disciples that they should remember my last meal with them by breaking bread and passing it to each other, and should each drink from the same cup of wine, and remember that my body was crucified and my blood spilt to bring them truth of being, this incident was converted into the bizarre belief that with pomp and ceremony at the altar, my body was transferred to wafers which communicants should swallow with all due reverence.

217

My body! What good would my 'body' – spiritualised or not – do for the communicant?

Can you see how the mind can be conditioned into accepting illogical nonsense which can endure almost two thousand years because it was backed by a great hierarchy of Pope, Cardinals living in palaces, immense wealth, and upheld in earthly pomp and ceremonious prestigious circumstances?

I want you to know the truth about that fateful night – what you call my Last Supper.

Though painful to do so, for the sake of greater clarity, I have brought myself down in consciousness frequencies of vibration right into the conscious recollection of my thoughts and feelings during my last meal with my disciples.

Although a strong man, enlightened, and certain that I had a destiny to fulfill which I could not avoid – did not want to avoid – I was also deeply sorrowful as we commenced our meal – the eating of the Passover. My disciples had been my friends and had stood by me during some difficult circumstances. I was sad to be leaving them and fearful for their well-being.

What would happen to them when they found themselves alone without my guidance and protection? They had depended on me more than they knew.

I recalled my years teaching the people. I felt a deep sense of irony as I remembered my return from the desert – dirty and unkempt but literally possessed by my joyous concern for my fellowmen, and intensely excited that I could now put their feet to the right path, implant in their minds the truth concerning existence, show them how to overcome their fears, their sickness, poverty, misery. I was going to conquer the world!

But how differently it had all turned out! Tomorrow I would hang on a cross!

It was true, however – I had achieved much success. I mused over the instances of healing and the people's joyful acceptance of the 'Loving Father'. I could understand why the High Priest and the Council hated

me. Instead of fear, punishment, and animal sacrifices, I had brought the people the reality of the 'Father Love', proving it by healing terminal cases.

I brought my attention back to my disciples who were talking to each other whilst eating. They were still unaware of the challenge that lay ahead of me – my crucifixion. Although I had repeatedly warned them, they refused to accept my words as truth. They thought I had become frightened of the Chief Priest and wondered why.

I had extricated myself from threatening situations before.

As was customary at the Passover, they were speaking about the circumstances surrounding the escape of the Israelites from Egypt. John, who was highly imaginative, was giving them a colourful account of Moses calling together the Israelites and telling them that, at last, they would finally leave Egypt and escape from their life of slavery into freedom in the desert! For this reason, Moses directed the head of each family to kill an unblemished lamb and with handfuls of herbs, paint the blood of it on the door posts of their dwelling. Moses said that angels would come at night and fly through Egypt killing the first born of all Egyptians and stock, leaving only the first born of the Israelites who would be saved by the blood on their door posts.

As I listened to them, and saw their smiles and nods of acknowledgement of this 'wondrous' happening, I realised with a pang of anguish how little they truly understood my description of the 'Heavenly Father'. I heard John's words concerning: Blood, blood, blood – blood of the unblemished lamb, blood on the doorposts, blood of the Egyptian children and livestock. As ever, I marvelled at the centuries old Jewish preoccupation with blood, and briefly remembered that Abraham was even prepared to sacrifice his only son, intending to slaughter and offer him as a sacrifice because he believed God had told him to do so. I then thought of the daily animal sacrifices in the Temple! To me, the entire concept of 'blood-letting' as a way of paying for 'sin' was an absolute abomination.

But I remained silent and did not argue with the men. I realised that their minds were filled with these traditions, as solid and enduring as rock.

This was our last supper together, our last meal all at one table. It should be a time of peace between us and a loving farewell.

Doubly momentous for my disciples because the Passover was so sacred an event for their Jewish minds and this I would have to accept in the spirit of love and understanding.

Previously, I had not celebrated the Passover since the tradition sickened me. I preferred to go into the hills quietly to meditate, leaving my disciples to eat the Passover with their families. Because of my previous attitudes, they did not wonder at my present silence.

Now, I half lay, half sat, unable to relax as I usually did – tense, wrought up, compassionately warm towards my disciples – yet half annoyed with them.

I wondered how I might leave these confused, somnolent followers an effective token of remembrance – some ritual to bring back to their muddled minds all that I had tried to teach them. I wanted to shake them out of their sanguinity.

As I listened to their talk about Moses and his various miraculous activities, it came to me that if they were so pre-occupied with blood – then blood I would give them to remember me by.

I bent over the table and picked up a loaf of bread and broke it into several pieces and said quite roughly: 'I am like your Passover Lamb. Pass it around, take your share, eat, and do this in remembrance of me who has brought you the only real TRUTH the world has ever heard.

Let this bread be a symbol of my body which is about to be broken on the cross.' They stopped talking and stared at me. 'Go on, eat!' I told them.

As in a dream, they quietly took some bread and passed it around, chewing a little of it.

I then picked up the large goblet of wine and told them to drink from it and pass it round.

'This wine is a symbol of my blood. I came to give you the TRUTH. Truth about God – Truth about life. But I have been rejected. My blood will flow for you.'

Again, in silence, they drank from the goblet and passed it to the next man. Their faces were strained but they said nothing. It was obvious that all were shaken by my words and did not like them.

I knew that Judas had been given money to point me out to the Chief Priest's soldiers when the moment was right. I knew, also, that the night of the Passover was to be the night. I said to Judas:

'Go quickly and do what you have to do.'

Judas looked at me for a long moment and I saw the pain and indecision in his eyes. He was having second thoughts but my time had come and I wanted to get it over and done with.

'Go,' I said harshly. Judas got up and left the room.

The disciples were amazed at the way I had spoken and asked what it was he was going to do?

'He is going to the Chief Priest to tell him where to find me. They are going to crucify me – just as I've told you.'

I looked at the various expressions on their faces, doubt, shock, horror, with a degree of painful cynicism. Then there was an outpouring of resentful interrogation. What would happen to them? They had left home and family for me. They would be losing a life of freedom and security if I were crucified like a common felon.

I said they would abandon me. They vehemently denied such a thing – but they did.

I was too tired to argue with them, and I had grown so strong, so secure in the knowledge that the 'Father' was within – and with me at all times, I could afford to forgive their disloyalty.

And, at the end of it all, I would be released from my body and able to ascend into the realms of Light I had so often sensed but never fully seen with earthly vision. It was a thought bringing me deep comfort and a happy sense of expectation.

So I smiled at them and said: 'It is good you have done what I asked in commemoration of me – and of my death yet to come. Continue to break bread and drink wine together, remembering I have ever loved you and will remain with you in spirit until you join me where I go. Do not fear, you will be guided, you will be inspired, you will be made strong, and you will speak with clear, clear voices.

'My only warning is this. In the future, much that I have taught you will be forgotten. Much that I have told you will be reasoned away by human thinking or distorted by human myths.' Then there was panic and a clamour: 'How will this be?'

I smiled and raised my hands. 'I have told you what will happen in the distant future.

'Meanwhile, be true to all I have taught you and do not doubt any word I have spoken.'

Then it was time to go to the garden of Olives, the place where the Chief Priest's soldiers would seek me.

My disciples wanted to ask more questions – but now I had reached the end of my speech with men. I wanted only to prepare myself in total silence for my ordeal, moving in spirit into a state of secure, consistent attunement and communication with the 'Father'.

We walked to the garden and I retreated to my favourite rock. Sheltered from the wind, I sat down and pulled my cloak around me. Closing my eyes, gradually I felt myself moving into a great inner stillness of spirit and a powerful silence. Then the Power Itself descended and pressed in on me and possessed my mind and heart. It filled me with such supreme love that I knew I was supported and sustained in love, and could retain my love for all, no matter what happened to me. That was all that mattered now that my hour had come.

That is the truth behind the breaking of bread and drinking of wine in commemoration of me, my life and teachings. And as you, who are reading this **Letter** know, all that the 'Father' gave me to know my last night on earth, has come to pass.

Because I spoke of the 'Father', the 'Son' and the 'Holy Spirit', the church decided at the Council of Nicene that I must have been referring to 'Three Persons in One'. Consequently, people pray to the 'Father' to ask for benefits, implore the 'Holy Spirit' to instruct them spiritually and pray to the 'Son' to save them from their sins.

Can you begin to 'see' how 'earthy and humanly conceived' are these beliefs? Can you also see how 'emotionally based' they are?

Because of the emotionalism and the promise of a 'free trip to heaven on the heels of the Saviour', the beliefs have become a humanly conceived religious structure to enshrine an empire of Church within earthly empires – Rome, Austria, Spain. They have been the excuse for wholesale torture, and death by burning and execution of dissidents. They have inspired wars between nations.

But the 'spiritual perception' and 'creativity' arising out of some of the beliefs have also contributed much to existence in the past two millennia.

These beliefs have been the reasons for building of cathedrals and churches, monasteries and convents, giving people a stable purpose, the ability to express their artistic gifts and provided work for the less talented. The beliefs have also directed millions of people's consciousness towards the higher realms of beautiful thought and love. They have even been the impetus behind mysticism and enlightenment when spiritual souls have come to see the **Reality** previously hidden by the beliefs.

Whilst this has been happening, the beliefs have also created the conditions for the development of echelons of religious superiority and immeasurable grandeur and wealth. These are humanly conceived and created edifices of 'ego-impulses' and are therefore, from a spiritual standpoint – entirely spurious.

THE TRUTH REGARDING 'SIN'

It must also be understood that down the centuries, people perceived that facets of human behaviour were detrimental to the welfare of others. They witnessed killing, stealing another's wife and possessions, causing much pain and grief in the community, making life difficult and at times, intolerable. It was reasoned that surely this behaviour must be contrary to the will of what they termed 'God'. They gave this behaviour the name of 'sin' and termed it 'evil'. Eventually, their prophets reasoned that such aberrant behaviour must emanate from an 'evil' force opposed to 'God' and they called it 'Satan'.

They threatened and punished each other in the belief that 'sins' were evil and that their 'God' would punish men for their wrongdoing against each other. This behaviour is practised to this day in the churches. Ministers try to control people by fear.

THE CONCEPT OF 'SIN' against Jehovah, the Eternal and infinitely Mighty Creator, was a clever and powerful method of controlling other people!

The church beliefs are a tragic travesty of all that I tried to teach the people in Palestine.

Moses first enshrined the belief in 'sin' and 'punishment' in the form of the Ten Commandments.

Moses said that they were given to him by 'God' and that if the Israelites broke them they would have to suffer the penalty – in some cases, this meant death by stoning. They were taught that by breaking the Laws, the Israelites would be sinning against their 'God'.

The exact truth is, Moses went to the mountain to pray for a means by which to control the unruly Israelites. In answer to this prayer – the Ten Commandments were inspirationally given to him to help him in his task of bringing the Israelites safely through their desert sojourn with the least degree of trouble-making.

Religionists are happy to accept and wholeheartedly believe in a 'God' which reputedly instructed Moses to engage in aggressive procedures and massacres when conquering the 'promised land'. A beautiful and productive land was callously grabbed from hard working people who were slain in their thousands. This was regarded as the right thing to do since 'God' had promised them a beautiful land in which to settle. To this day, religionists believe that since 'God' spoke to Moses, it must be 'God' who decreed the ensuing bloodshed. There are many similar horrific descriptions of war and bloodshed in your Bible considered permissible – just and right – because it was believed that 'God' had instructed them to go to war – against Gentiles.

Can you not see in the history of the Jews, the rampant **EGO-DRIVE** in which even 'God' is 'used' to exempt them from blame? In the moment of self-aggrandisement, it became permissible and **equitable** to ignore the Ten Commandments and indulge in wholesale massacre.

They believed no sin was involved because the killing had been ordained by 'God'. What a 'God'!

Can you not also perceive why it was necessary for me to be born in Palestine to live amongst the Jews in an effort to help them see that their traditional beliefs and practices were all contrary to the very **Nature** of the **DIVINE CONSCIOUSNESS** which had truly given them being?

Since then, down the centuries, men have battled with the concept of 'sin' and many sincere people have grieved concerning the way they offend 'God' and they beg for forgiveness. Long ago, they sacrificed animals beyond number in the Temple in Jerusalem, to appease 'God' and to hopefully escape the effects of their sinning. Since that time, innumerable books have been written on the subject, expressing grief and horror at the condition of men's souls, seeking ways to change their behaviour, beating themselves with whips to torture the flesh and make it pay for its wrongdoing in thought, words and deed, and many of these books have been applauded by 'Christians' throughout Europe and housed within the archives of religious institutions.

They bind people to my age-old persona of 'Jesus', preaching the 'salvation of man from punishment for his sins' by my death on the cross. As I have explained elsewhere, these beliefs are physically impossible and contrary to the facts of creation. No payment is extracted for 'sin' by any superior 'Deity'. This is a human concept entirely – and pagan. All blood-letting of any description for the purpose of religious rites is paganism. The Christian church has presented its followers with nothing less than a 'glorified' version of paganism.

When people make other people unhappy in any way, they are creating their own future 'comeback'. Not as retribution but as a 'consciousness activity of creation'.

Therefore, it is a matter of urgency that these beliefs in 'sin' and 'salvation by my death on the cross' should be strongly combated – and replaced – by the spiritual understanding given you in these **Letters.** Before leaving this subject of religious doctrines, I want to make it clear that some spiritual seekers within the Christian church, down the ages, have sufficiently purified their consciousness to become strongly aware of '**Power**' they have called 'God' and have come to recognise that the '**Source of Being**' is not as taught by the

Church. But only a **few** people have been sufficiently spiritually evolved to move beyond the parameters of religious beliefs to feel the full inflow of 'Power' since the vast majority of people can only conceive Truth within an earthly terminology.

I, the CHRIST, have to tell you that to this time, not one of all the 'saints' has even glimpsed the reality of creation and the truth behind human behaviour as I am presenting it to you now.

The time has surely come when you must now be told the truth concerning 'sin' and human behaviour and what people are presently doing to the world and to themselves – providing you have fully abandoned the age-old myths of religious doctrine and are presently eager, receptive, and gladly opening your hearts completely to the realities of existence. If you are none of these things, then what I have to say will have no meaning for you.

Believe me – you cannot mix your old religious beliefs with the **Truth of Existence**. If you try to do so,you may be sure that you are not seeing **Truth** but only your own adaptation of what you believe you have gained from these pages.

If you continue the search for Truth of Existence but remain in a divided state of conviction, you may continue the search at great cost to yourselves, torn by indecision, fear, and a continuing inability to perceive the true meaning of the new teaching. Your developing perceptions will be partially obscured by 'messages' arising out of the old conditioning of your conscious and subconscious mind. You may not realise the enormity of such a problem at this present time, but it is a tremendous problem because your present deep beliefs are your present truth on which you construct your daily lives. They are **your** reality. Your convictions and strongly-held beliefs may be completely illusory but if you fully believe in them in your sub-conscious, they become absolutely real for you. No matter how compelling of your attention may be any new ideas contradicting your beliefs, your consciousness will be split and will give enormous discomfort – even anguish to you.

Remember – your consciousness is the fabric out of which you make your lives.

This consciousness fabric is the ground of your every response to every single thing which happens in your mental, emotional and physical lives. **Your** consciousness is **your** reality.

This statement may be expressed in two ways, both of which are the truth of your existence.

Your consciousness creates **your** reality, irrespective of what the actual facts of your earthly life may be. When people believed the earth was flat, they were afraid to venture too far over the ocean lest the ship should fall over the edge. The people who believed in a flat earth, lived according to that belief.

When Galileo said the earth was round, he was considered a heretic but his perception of the 'roundness of the earth' enabled sailors to take a new look at the world and set out to discover what lay the other side of the ocean. It required a change in their belief to make this possible.

You are in a similar position in regard to these **Letters**. Those people who discount and ridicule them are like the people who believed in a flat earth and were afraid of falling over the edge if they sailed too far to the west or east of their known environment. Their horizons were severely limited by their false beliefs.

So are the horizons of those people who believe the world to be solid, also severely restricted.

Day after day, they lament and grieve over the misfortunes which have befallen the world, believing there is no escape from them.

But the people who can grasp and welcome the Truth of Consciousness I am presently giving the world, are like those who perceived that travel on the oceans could be limitlessly undertaken in all directions, providing they had the will to set out on such a journey.

Therefore, your state of consciousness is the most important consideration in your life ... not your relationships or possessions or your position in life. Tend to your consciousness and the blessedness in all aspects of your life will follow.

By your consciousness you feed yourself with inner love and harmony, joy and beauty, even in the backstreets of a slum.

With such a consciousness, you will find yourself being removed from the streets of the slum into an environment in keeping with your inner self. So do you climb out of unpleasant circumstances.

From the foregoing, you should now be able to see that only you create the 'quality' of your internal world, whether you find yourself externally in prison or in command of a battleship! And you can enhance your surroundings by radiating to them the life-force which animates your thinking.

And again, your **consciousness** is your reality, – not your husband or wife, children, home, garden,possessions, qualifications, workplace, friends. For whatever place your people and your possessions occupy in your consciousness – good or evil – this 'place' is only your personal perception of them. The 'reality' of these people is not truly known to anyone. No one has access to the innate goodness hidden in an apparently negative character. Conversely, no one may suspect the hidden drives and desires of a seemingly personable human being.

Your external life only impinges on your consciousness. It does not – cannot – create or determine your conscious responses. You are the 'creator' of your responses. Your type of creation depends entirely on your deepest perceptions and beliefs regarding existence.

Furthermore, you can, at any moment, choose to gradually dismantle your past inner world in order to create a more harmonious inner kingdom of increasing love, vitality, and joy, although your outer 'objects' – people or possessions remain the same. The spiritual power of the 'fabric of your consciousness' will be radiated outwards and absorbed by the people, plants and bricks and mortar in your immediate vicinity. There will be definite changes and improvements in all that comes within your orbit. It is your destiny in this life – or future lives – to arrive at this full and complete realisation. When you do, you will put your foot to the path of self-mastery and then gradually move forward to becoming a true master of your human consciousness world interpenetrated and assisted by **DIVINE CONSCIOUSNESS.**

I, the CHRIST, commend this Letter to you. I have put you in full possession of some of the important facts of creation which will enable you to transcend the ego – the guardian of your individuality – and to return to the **UNIVERSALITY of BEING** from which you have really come. You have within your hands, the means by which you can move into unconditional **Love, Joy and Personal Fulfilment.**

Remember that I have said that I yearn over the spiritual traveller's progress. As you move along the path I have outlined for you, there will be times of confirmation that I am indeed with you on your journey. You will see them- retain your faith in them.

At all times, I uphold you in Divine Love for I am Divine Love in action. Believe this and find rest in my Consciousness enfolding you.

Introduction to LETTER 7

Recorder: There is a strange – miraculous – happening attached to the following **Letter.**

When **Letter** 7 was completed, the recorder was clearly told to use the parable from Matthew 13.v3. as opening paragraphs.

A little later, it came over her powerfully to add a paragraph on p.2 marked with **.

Letter 7 was printed out. When collating the pages she was astounded – shattered – to find that half of page 1 was now taken up with the words:

I am the LIFE, the TRUTH, and the WAY

which had not been typed into the computer.

It appeared to be a 'footer' for a page. But such a 'footer' could only be typed in by using the precise and specific Word Perfect instructions to create a 'footer'.

Furthermore, only two lines are normally allotted to a 'footer'. A half-page would not be a 'footer'!

Still shocked by the event, the recorder searched every file in the computer to see whether, at any time, she had used such a footer and forgotten it – but found nothing.

A computer mechanic was called in, shown the text on the computer and the print itself but was unable to explain how it could have happened. To this time, no one has been able to explain it.

For those who may not be aware of it, this statement **I am the LIFE, the TRUTH, and the WAY,** was made by **JESUS CHRIST** when describing himself during his mission in Palestine.

The text had already been quoted and explained by **Christ** on p.8 of **Letter 7,** but he had used the words in a different order.

When you read the paragraphs marked** on p.2. in conjunction with the 'footer' on p.1.they will undoubtedly take on new meaning for you because they are obviously linked.

First of all the wording of paragraph ** was energetically dictated and typed on the computer, and at some time immediately afterwards, the **'footer'** was added to the bottom of the first page. Another mystery! How it that this 'footer' was not noticed at the time of printing?

The recorder lives alone. No one else could have had access to the computer.

The recorder regards this intervention – and contravention of Word Perfect procedures, as **CHRIST's own personal signature ... something he might have done when on earth.**

LETTER 7

Again, this is **I, the CHRIST, who has come to you through a Letter to whomever can receive my words.**

The following parable is as applicable to your modern era as it was to the times of the Jews, 2001 years ago. I commend its truth to you who reads these Letters.

'A sower went out to sow. And as he sowed, some seeds fell along the path and the birds came and devoured them. Other seeds fell on rocky ground, where they had not much soil, and immediately they sprang up, since they had no depth of soil, but when the sun rose they were scorched; and withered away. Other seeds fell upon thorns, and the thorns grew up and choked them. Other seeds fell on good soil and brought forth grain, some a hundredfold, some sixty, some thirty. He who has ears to hear, let him hear ...'

'Hear then the meaning of the parable of the sower.

I am the LIFE, the TRUTH, and the WAY

When anyone hears the message regarding the kingdom and does not understand it, the evil one, (the selfhood) snatches away what was sown in his heart; this is what was sown along the path.

As for what was sown on rocky ground, this is he who hears the message and immediately receives it with joy; yet he has no root in himself, but endures for a while, and when tribulation or persecutions come on account of the message, immediately he falls away. As for what was sown among thorns, this is he who hears the message but the cares of the world and the delight in riches choke the message and it bears no fruit. As for what was sown on good soil, this is he who hears and receives the message and understands it; he indeed bears fruit, and yields, in one case a hundredfold, in another, sixty, and another thirty fold.' Matthew 13. v.3

My purpose in sharing this knowledge of the **Truth of Being with you in these **Letters**, is to enable you to grow in spiritual love and wisdom and bring forth the fruits and blessings of such spiritual love and wisdom in your every moment of evolving consciousness. I long for you to be **richly** joyful.

Therefore, let us, together, plough into your human soil of consciousness, turn it over, get rid of the stones of despair, break down the clods of non-comprehension with deepening wisdom, pull out the weeds of your negative mental/emotional patterns with my help, fertilise your soil of consciousness with ever increasing faith. Then sow ever more beautiful seeds born of your evolving spiritual perceptions and unconditional love. My joy will be your joy in this endeavour – and your joy will be added to my joy. In this unity of purpose and achievement, you will eventually feel that you are indeed of my spirit and my spirit is being poured into you. In this way, we will experience the oneness of **THAT** out of which we have both taken our individuality. My thoughts will become your thoughts untainted by your former ego-consciousness. **

I have described the process – the path – along which you will travel to achieve your most sublime and perfect heart's desires.

And so I say to you, although this **Letter** may be difficult to accept at first, and will require time and effort to fully understand, it is a strong link between your consciousness and mine.

In my transcendent state, I can do more for you when you call upon me than I could if I were to return to earth in a physical body when you might see me with your eyes and hear me with your ears, but your understanding of **Truth of Being** might be limited.

In this mode of contact with your consciousness, you can receive me direct into your mind and heart when the pre-conditions to such contact have been fulfilled.

For I tell you truly, the more time and meditation you devote to these **Letters,** the more will it become possible for you to receive higher inspiration and instruction from me, personally, because with every reading of these **Letters**, the more will your own frequencies of consciousness be raised towards my spiritual consciousness frequencies – and eventually we will be able to reach a true meeting place of consciousness. Then – abundant will be the fruitage in your life.

To explain why this is so – I must tell you that my **consciousness** descends through many differing planes of vibrational frequencies of consciousness to meet the needs of those seeking help and inspiration. The many differing planes of consciousness, my **consciousness** passes through, are all distinct from each other.

Each level of **consciousness frequencies creates and manifests as different conditions of existence**, since the highest and lowest vibrational frequencies of consciousness are produced by the highest or lowest spiritual/mental/emotional patterns or forms of consciousness. By high and low patterns, I mean those which are closest and furthest from **Divine Consciousness Intent.**

As you know, each frequency of vibration of sound waves produces its own unique and individual note and tone. Similarly, habitual mental/emotional thought forms produce their own vibrational frequencies in consciousness and these in turn, produce the outer conditions in which that consciousness resides.

The higher the frequencies of vibration of consciousness, the more beautiful, harmonious, joyous and fulfilled are the lives of those who reside within those frequencies. The lower the frequencies, the more harsh, bitter, acrid, and miserable are the lives of those who resonate to such frequencies. Their lives are punctuated with disasters, deprivation, and brutality.

The higher the frequency of vibration of consciousness, the more spiritually loving and beautiful are the thoughts, the creative imagination, the ideals and beauty of colour and life forms, for they are rising closer and closer to the dimension of UNIVERSAL CONSCIOUSNESS where the frequencies have become so heightened as to level out and enter into powerful equilibrium – the **ALL POWER of UNIVERSAL CONSCIOUSNESS** – the **Source of All Being – LOVE.**

To you, the outer conditions may appear to be those in which the **body** resides but the truth is, it is the **consciousness** which dwells within, experiences and responds to the outer conditions. The body is but a vehicle making the human consciousness visible to others, and the condition of the vehicle itself is a manifestation of the level of spiritual/mental/emotional consciousness which inhabits it.

Therefore, as I said before, as an observer of individual need and in response to pleas for help, my **consciousness** descends through the various levels of existential consciousness to reach the sincere suppliant, for, to give the answers, I must first receive the need. And, as I said on the second page, these

Letters are a link, a means of your communication with my **consciousness** to enable you to be spiritually drawn to, and made receptive – and then deeply understand and use all the knowledge I wish to share with you to bring you up the ladder of spiritual consciousness to its ultimate heights of the **CHRIST CONSCIOUSNESS.**

Because I am in near perfect equilibrium myself, I have the spiritual power of **UNIVERSAL CONSCIOUSNESS** to a near perfect degree. I am imbued with the nature of **Universal Consciousness**. Therefore, my entire consciousness – irrespective of other people's thoughts or words, belief or non- belief, love or hatred, acceptance or rejection of me, remains that of pure unconditional **LOVE.**

It never falters or changes. My attitudes are consistently those of pure LOVE, CARING and COMPASSION which I experience as a profound yearning to uplift, heal and prosper. Therefore, it is perfectly possible for some people, if sufficiently sensitive to consciousness vibrational frequencies, to become aware of my presence, or love, or extra life-force, when they are in a state of conscious yearning, seeking, praying to know me better or evolve spiritually.

As I speak of the lower frequencies of consciousness which cause trouble on earth, you will be aware of my wholly compassionate acceptance of them, for these are but a manifestation of people's painful struggles and suffering whilst trying to find their way towards the LIGHT of their SOURCE of BEING. I am coming to people – not to condemn – but to uplift and strengthen them.

I radiate my **Christ Consciousness** towards you by receiving and holding your name and spiritual form in my mind when you appeal to me for assistance. And according to your receptivity and freedom from magnetic 'bonding-rejection' impulses, a little of the Divine Nature of Being is absorbed by your present consciousness vibrational frequencies which then experience a strong sense of upliftment.

Therefore, it should be clear to you that as you unload your earthly consciousness of its emotional bondage by mentally/emotionally rejecting the patterns of emotional thought you perceive to be out of harmony with Divine Love, so will you become more and more aware of higher inspiration invading your mind – even your solar plexus – giving you guidance in times of need when you are unable to perceive the right course of action or unable to clear yourself of emotional ego-thinking when reacting to a troublesome situation. With my help, you can live in two dimensions – that of the physical world in which your body resides, bringing you your experiences – and that of the higher standpoint of Christ Consciousness which will enable you to transcend the ego-thinking and radiate thoughts and feelings into your situations from that state of being I termed the 'Kingdom of Heaven'.

I am not alone in this work. There are innumerable most highly, transcendent, spiritual, beautiful, lovingly- intelligent souls, possessing entrance to the dimension of Christ Consciousness, working with me to help people. Although we are in the dimension of Christ Consciousness, we are all individuals. We are not replicas of each other. We all express the Christ Consciousness in differing glorious ways – the emphasis of our activities placed on differing facets of creativity. We have powerful imaginations and are able to create and bring into visible, individual form within our own dimension, those things which are way beyond your present comprehension.

You will hear that all over the world, people are receiving inspiration, and are aware of the Christ Presence. My inspiration radiated to the world at this time, is received by different natures and different minds. Due to their prior mental conditioning, the inspiration will lead each person along a different path. The messages I am able to insert into their consciousness will wear differing faces. In some cases, the messages will be grossly distorted by the recipient who is psychically receptive but possesses an **orthodox mind** which clings to the beaten religious tracks of yesteryears. Any message will be interpreted according to the beliefs already in control. Any message received which might contradict accepted beliefs will be hurriedly pushed out of mind and authorship attributed to Satan. For this reason, it has been possible only to reach the mind which is open and eager for truth rather than traditional teaching. **You can be certain, however, that my personal message will always awaken people to the urgent need to move away from the restricting and erroneous tenets of all dogma and institutionalised religion. The message will open up channels of consciousness leading to the growth of spiritual awareness. It will be leading people into ever higher and higher dimensions of celestial thought, as opposed to earthly and materialistic concepts. It will impart a**

more vivid appreciation of the true nature of your Source of Being and the universe in which you presently live.

I prophesied, when on earth, that the time would come when I would return as 'lightning flashes from east to west across the sky'. This was a graphic description of the way in which I am presently working. Perhaps, after the foregoing paragraph, you will accept the 'lightning' has struck world-wide in such a form as to reach those who are eagerly hoping for my return. **My Truth is intended to uplift and illumine the minds of those who are seeking to waken people to the many causes of misery and future destruction of the planet. Countless 'old souls' are acting selflessly in hundreds of different ways to alleviate the suffering of people in need, devoting all their energies, time, earthly status, to the promotion of love for nature, animals and their well-being and protection, and the future health of the planet itself. Although these lovely souls may not be aware of it, none of these concerns arose out of earthly human thought, exclusively geared towards selfish needs, but from the dimension of Christ Consciousness where all living things are seen to be an expression of the Love/Intelligence of the Source of All Being.**

In this **Letter** I want to explain clearly that I have come through the medium of these words **to** assist **receptive** people in all stratum of society – labourer to General, clerk to President, to work entirely from the standpoint of **LOVE.**

There are spiritual/scientific materialistic reasons why it is absolutely imperative that people should devote all their mental and emotional energies and sensitivities to bringing their actions and reactions into perfect alignment and harmony with unconditional **LOVE – DIVINE CONSCIOUSNESS.**

To remain within the world-wide state of consciousness as it exists at this moment is to remain on the steady downward slide into countless diseases, misfortunes, upheavals, and deepest suffering.

Men and women can live in two dimensions of existence in your world – either exclusively from the level of ego-impulses which are the controlling forces behind and within all the daily phenomena which comprise the human daily experience – or – mentally/emotionally poised within **Divine Consciousness** whilst their bodies are still living on the earthly plane.

The fruits of the ego consciousness are discords, disruptions, climatic upheavals and abnormalities, wars, addictions of every kind, poverty, diseases, murder, robbery, lying, cheating, slandering, backbiting, low miserable thoughts, envious thoughts, angry thoughts, bad humours, judgementalism, criticism, sarcasm, rejection of other people, etc.

These consciousness frequencies are forever bringing forth 'mirror reflections' of the circumstances and feeling reactions which gave them birth – and are continually subject to the 'highs' and 'lows' of fulfilment of expectations and disappointments, swinging between happiness and misery.

Those who, through prayer, meditation, self-discipline and determination, manage to purify their consciousness of ego and lift it by defining and entertaining ever more sincerely loving thoughts towards other individuals and the world generally, gradually ascend in consciousness to the vibrationary frequencies of the realm of **Divine Consciousness – the Kingdom of Heaven,** where they live comfortably and at ease in harmony with the **Universal Laws of Existence.**

Such people find that no matter what may be the troubles and uproar in the world around them, they are nourished, healed, protected, cared for, and maintained in perfect peace of mind – providing they remain within the spiritual frequencies of vibration.

When they allow themselves to be drawn down into selfish disputes and any negative human condition involving any of the attributes of ego, the peace abruptly disappears and they find themselves trapped in the consciousness frequencies of vibration which are fed by similar consciousness frequencies of other people in their environment.

They are like a fly caught in a spider's web and the ensuing battle to extricate thoughts from the lower frequencies of consciousness vibration can be exhausting and painful.

At such times, constant meditation and prayer, a plea for help, strength and guidance in achieving the 'right emotional attitudes' are the only means by which a spiritual traveller can find his way back from the entrapping lowered energy fields, to a state of harmony with the heavenly consciousness frequencies of vibration.

You may think that the foregoing is too difficult to understand and not necessary in your search for spiritual upliftment. On the contrary, this understanding of the nature of your consciousness is highly important. If you should find yourself descending into lowered consciousness frequencies of vibration and experiencing the conflict between what you are 'feeling at the moment' and what you know you ought to be feeling or would like to be feeling – you will experience more control if you realise you are suffering because you have allowed your normal spiritual consciousness vibrational frequencies to drop. Pinpoint the reason and take it to **Divine Consciousness** for a resolution of the inner conflict. In time, guidance as to the correct attitudes and affirmations to clear the problem will be given you swiftly in response to your prayer.

Furthermore, as you lift your level of 'consciousness frequencies', you will find that you are inwardly strengthened in spirit and life force – and the opposite occurs when you find yourself entrapped in lower consciousness vibrations either through a personal descent into lower thought frequencies or by being emotionally drawn into them through communication with a negative or egotistic personality. When this happens, you will experience a loss of energy. **This loss of energy results in a depletion of physical energy in your body cells.**

Therefore, when deliberately setting out on a spiritual journey, you should visualise yourself as being like a traveller boarding a train bound for the destination of your choice. If, when travelling, you leap out of the window on glimpsing verdant valleys or exciting cities offering pleasures of some sort, and go wandering into highways and byways far removed from the journey you had originally undertaken, you will find it very difficult to resume that original journey. First of all, you will have to go through a cleansing of the lower consciousness energies you absorbed during your jaunts into other areas of interest. This may take a long time and you may have to go through other painful experiences to enable you to go through the necessary cleansing of your consciousness again. Everything you do in life, you are either moving forward spiritually, or moving into areas of consciousness detrimental to your search and long-term journey towards higher levels of spiritual consciousness. You never escape the processes of consciousness nor from the inexorable working of the **Laws of Existence**. You cannot put your life on hold as you dodge off to have a little fling which you think won't matter since no one will know. Whatever you do is an action in consciousness and whatever it is – promotional of your well-being or contrary to your highest good – will have its repercussions of a like nature.

240

Everything in your life is related to some other activity in consciousness. Nothing is isolated from everything else. People think that what they do today is in a compartment. They think that 'to-day' becomes yesterday and is past, it can have no bearing on their 'to-day'. But – unfortunately for them – they will find it cropping up in their experience as 'reaping time' in six months, a year or even ten years ahead – when the consciousness energies have attracted what is necessary to bring about their visible manifestation. Then people wonder – why did this happen to me? Why me?

You must understand that when you embark on a spiritual journey, you have set foot to a path which will lift your consciousness vibrations to higher levels. Carelessness and inconsistency will lead you into a condition of swinging between levels of vibrationary frequencies. These times of inconsistency are fraught with emotional pain. As you swing, the original momentum of spiritual energy which previously lifted your spiritual vision, dies away and eventually you complain it is hard to get back to prayer and meditation. It is difficult to make the contact with **Divine Consciousness** that you were able to make before you went off on some pleasurable jaunt which led to a dropping of your consciousness frequencies. In this way, by giving in to overpowering impulses, you make life difficult for yourself, you walk a more rocky path.

At the same time, the impulses within your consciousness indicate that certain areas of your human consciousness need refining. The impulses become the necessary means to teach you some important lesson. In fact, no one can move on to the narrow path leading to the 'Kingdom of Heaven' and remain there without divergence or deviation until they have thoroughly experienced the fruits of their hidden impulses. By fully experiencing all they have to offer, people eventually arrive at a clear understanding that they were false enticements – not worth the pain and tremendous effort involved in getting back on the spiritual path again. Only when the deeply ingrained impulses have been indulged and the results imprinted in the consciousness, can a deliberate mental and emotional choice be made to live life on a higher spiritual level. When this final decision is made decisively and positively, the former impulses are then erased from the consciousness.

But I have to tell you that when you do make the choice to live your life on a higher spiritual level, you have not necessarily come to the end of your problems. In ignorance of what is real and false in higher spirituality, you may

241

find yourself attracted to different cults which will lead you further into a wilderness without ending.

I, the Christ, have come, through the medium of these **Letters**, to show you how to choose the highest goals in your human existence and your **true final destination** on your earthly 'train' journey.

In your spiritual quests, you are like people being presented with many beautifully coloured travel brochures depicting the pleasures and luxuries of various exotic holiday resorts where you can relax and renew your strength. One spiritual teacher holds up the enticement of a journey leading to a specific goal – the resolution of some mental/emotional problem, whilst another teacher offers another goal and another path to follow. Each of these spiritual teachers are offering alleviation of some kind of human pain and suffering which they, themselves, have experienced in the past and overcome. Each one has eventually found relief in their own unique way. **There is no doubt that they all have some valuable message of one kind or another to share with people who are bewildered by the problems of living and do not know which way to turn for help and comfort in their difficult existence.**

But I have come to you from the highest vantage point of spiritual, universal existence, through the medium of a mind carefully cleansed and impregnated with spiritual life and dedicated to the work, to carry this message to people who are ready to receive it.

I have come to you to show you who you really are in the deepest recesses of your individuality ... and who and what you can become.

Just as importantly, I have come to show you the means by which the transition from the human consciousness to the higher realms of spiritual consciousness may be achieved.

When I was on earth, I said: 'I am the Truth

The Way

And   the Life'

And so I **was – and am.**

In these **Letters** I am giving you the Truth.
I am showing you the Way
To achieve Abundant Life.

It is weakening to the soul to need another agent as a spiritual 'crutch', therefore, to depend even on myself must be recognised as a temporary measure. For this reason, I am making every effort through my recorder, to enable you to realise that your true support, mainstay, **'SOURCE OF LIFE & BEING'** are drawn directly from the all-powerful dimension of **Universal Consciousness in equilibrium.**

I have come to YOU – you who are reading this **Letter** – to help YOU find **LIFE more abundant** and what I termed, when on earth, the **Kingdom of Heaven.**

What did this statement mean in human terms? What did I mean when I said 'Life more abundant'?

It is easier for me to describe my meaning to yourselves in 2001 than it was to spell it out clearly to the people in AD.1, but I know that for many people whose inner spiritual perceptions have not yet been opened, what I am about to say will be deemed fantastical.

Therefore – to help you understand – I must remind you and ask you to fully realise – that you are not bodies possessing consciousness – you are:

'Divine Consciousness individualised into separate 'consciousness beings' and made visible on your earth by means of electrical particles drawn and bonded together into elements, to give you visible living form according to a fundamental physical pattern'.

To understand the **Truth of Existence** and the origins of your physicality, you must make daily efforts to rid yourselves of the limited earthly perception that the body receives its 'beingness' and is conceived and developed entirely – and only – according to unchangeable physical/scientific laws.

In place of your old limited human beliefs, you must make daily efforts to develop a strong, clear realisation that your 'personal reality' – your soul – is drawn directly from All Reality – SOURCE of BEING.

Your physical body also draws Life from All Reality at the moment of conception, but it is also tempered by the initial plane of 'consciousness

243

vibrational frequencies' out of which your body was conceived. It is constricted and encapsulated ever more strongly as the years pass, by the magnetic emotional 'bonding- rejection' impulses which control the human consciousness.

 What do I mean by that?

What I am going to tell you has enormous implications for the future of mankind – that is, if those of you who are capable of doing so, will make every effort to understand it.

In fact the way you view these Letters will determine the course of your future lives. They will mean to you the difference between remaining stuck in your present parameter of consciousness vibrational frequencies or gradually moving forward yourself to higher levels of consciousness and producing children who will benefit from the exercise of the knowledge I am about to give you.

When I was on earth I made the oft-repeated – but never understood – statement:

'What is born of the flesh is flesh – and of the spirit – spirit.'

I meant that some people have a natural spiritual ability to return to the original frequency of spiritual-emotional consciousness in *which they were conceived* – and, in later years, can be reborn – take on new spiritual mental awareness in the same spiritual frequency of vibration of conception, and thereafter *live, and evolve, and work from it.*

The original frequency of spiritual-emotional consciousness of conception will become the platform for the child's spiritual journey.

Those conceived only of 'fleshly lustful desires' find it difficult to perceive any 'truth' beyond the evidence of their ears, eyes, touch and smell.

If you doubt the foregoing, pause and reflect on the undeviating principle of existence: ALL CREATION is CONSCIOUSNESS made visible.

Every living thing only thinks and acts out of that level of spiritual or ego-consciousness in which they reside.

Before conception takes place, the sperm is imbued with the total consciousness of the male, the future father, and the ovum is imbued with the total consciousness of the female, the future mother.

During intercourse, changes take place in the mental/emotional consciousness of the man and woman. They may sense a deepening of love, caring, and drive to express their longing for greater closeness and harmony of spirit – this is a true spiritual/physical union. Alternatively, as their desire for union with each other changes to an ever stronger desire for self-satisfaction – this becomes an ego activity – reaping only ego reactions. However, whatever the condition of consciousness of the participants in the act of union, their consciousness of desire to achieve the ultimate climax, strives and drives the physical organs to move in a rhythm producing psychic/physical energy which gradually rises up into the brain, creating a higher and higher momentum of vibrational energy to reach a peak of near-delirium and delight, bursting into an explosion of momentary ecstasy and glorious fulfilment – and then follows release and a gradual descent into human consciousness again.

At the very moment of delirium/delight, the human consciousness rises to touch the **Divine Life Force** which ignites the sperm in the male and the ovum in the woman. Conception may not take place, and both sperm and ovum return to normal physical consciousness.

When conception takes place, sperm penetrates the ovum and they are united in the highest vibrations of **Divine Life**, in spiritual and physical fusion. In united consciousness, they too ascend into their own moment of equilibrium and joy to become one both within **Divine Life** Itself and human father/mother consciousness.

This moment of '**consciousness union**' takes place within the very highest dimension of **Divine Life Consciousness** and is a moment of unimaginable rejoicing and joy, for the two elements of male and female are again conjoined, united and merged in equilibrium to become one to produce a child. This moment of union is a re-enactment of a person's return to the glorious and ineffable ecstasy of the **Divine Consciousness of Universal Equilibrium.**

When intercourse is prompted by pure heartfelt love between man and woman, the united human consciousness ascends, during intercourse, into higher and higher levels of 'consciousness vibrational frequencies'

until they are caught up in the vibrational frequencies – of Divine Intelligence/Love Consciousness. Such a child, conceived in such circumstances, is born of spirit.

Lovers know when they truly love and come to each other in pure tenderness and love because such intercourse is a moment of union of mind, emotions and body, and lingers in their consciousness afterwards, making it difficult for them to draw apart from each other. They are aware of transcendent beauty, a renewal of emotional love instead of satiation, and an all encompassing harmony. These men and women are joined by **Divine Consciousness.**

Sadly, their personal **EGO-CONSCIOUSNESS** can eventually taint the love they felt for each other and gradually largely replace it, leaving them separated and alone, sad and emotionally/physically weakened, wondering why such a beautiful, exalted state of love could ever dwindle and die.

These Letters can be the means of their overcoming the ego drive and re-discovering their previous love on an even higher and more spiritual level. In which case, man and woman will become more whole than ever before. This may or may not bring them together in a new sexual attraction transcending all other depending on their state of consciousness – whether it has itself transcended the desire for physical fusion.

Physical union undertaken in any other emotion leads to a condition of 'flesh entering flesh' and is but a receiving and giving of earthly – frequently negative – vibrational frequencies producing like-minded progeny of such a union. Even if a child is not conceived, such intercourse is detrimental to both partners, since there is an exchange and absorption of each others' consciousness energy into the body, which, if negative – hostile, or critical – can be damaging to one another. Remember that 'consciousness energy' is compounded of **'Father-Intelligence'** and **'Mother-Love'** electro-magnetism.

The energy exchange between sexual partners is of the same energy out of which the mental/electrical and emotional/magnetic fields of the body are formed. All is consciousness. Therefore, when consciousness energies within body fluids and mental/emotional attitudes and thoughts are exchanged and absorbed, you are each of you affecting the mental/emotional/physical condition of the partner.

Intercourse should, to be healthy and life-giving, only be undertaken in true heartfelt love, where the good of the loved one is more important than the good of the lover.

It should never be used to heal emotional rifts or wounds.

Intercourse may be a joyous act undertaken after a difference of opinion and anger, where there has been sincere mutual forgiveness and a full restoration of – and renewed love for each other – but never to cover the hurts and effect a false sense of emotional receptivity in the other partner.

No doubt such intercourse will give them a temporary sense of well-being and transient goodwill since their consciousness energies will have been lifted into higher vibrational frequencies – but this is a **TEMPORARY ALLEVIATION OF THEIR PERSONAL CONSCIOUSNESS ONLY.**

When partners go to each other still bearing hidden resentment or critical denigrating thoughts about the other, those negative **consciousness forms** are transmitted into the electro-magnetic fields of the partner and create a sense of inner disturbance of which the partner is not fully aware. Nevertheless, the relationship is being gradually eroded without either partner being fully aware that this is happening. **This is the reason why the physical attraction between partners dwindles and dies. It is destroyed by hidden negative critical thoughts and feelings which little by little, affect each other profoundly on every level of their being.**

As their frequencies of vibration drop, they will find themselves being drawn into the thoughts and feelings which previously drove them into arguments with other people and consequently the problems will be repeated day after day. When people use sex as a panacea – it becomes a frustration and disillusionment sets in, leading to a loss of respect and love for each other.

Therefore it is essential for people to realise that fights and quarrels arise out of their own hidden ego- consciousness drives which gain control of their loving feelings – and the ego drives must be healed before couples can reach a new level of mutual understanding, consideration and consistent love for each other.

Not only this, but the condition of consciousness of each partner eventually affects their environment, living conditions and success or lack of it in their daily lives. It also affects the children, creating a family of mutual co-operation, and healthy mental/emotional patterns – or the dysfunctional family where no member is in true sympathy or acceptance by the other.

You may say that the successful or dysfunctional family conditions arise purely from their innate characters and the way they perform in their daily roles. It is perfectly true that the family life is a product of character and performance, but I want you to consider the dysfunctional family which breaks up, the partnership and sexual cohabitation ends, parents move away from each other – and move on to entirely new lives because they have managed to disentangle themselves from the unhealthy or critical consciousness they were absorbing during the sexual act. If strong enough to do so, each partner discovers a 'new self', builds a new environment and goes on to new success.

However, those partners who live truly in love with each other, considering each other's needs together, giving and taking in equal balance, offering emotional support when needed, or loving counsel (not advice) when this is asked for, will find that the family is glued together by the absorption of each other's dynamic consciousness energies.

In the light of the previous paragraphs, it may now be understood that prior to intercourse there should never be a sense of grievance, buried hostility, contempt, denigration. Any such feelings must be fully resolved before sex is resumed. In a relationship where discussion and freedom of speech is accepted as normal, each partner should resist the act of sexual love until a powerful inter-force of responsive love has been built up, and the consciousness of both partners is in a state of pure equilibrium.

As for rape – this is the most heinous act against another and will draw to itself its own just rewards at some time in the future. It proceeds out of an especially warped and distorted ego- consciousness. The frequencies of consciousness vibrations of such people are so low and ponderous as to be personally destructive.

In the olden days, society was continually taught and sermonized. In western countries, the Ten Commandments were rightly presented as being the true foundations of a civilised and humanised culture, teaching self-control and readily acceptable to all religions world-wide.

Today, with the strengthening of the ego-consciousness due to the influence of the entertainment industry and media, ego lusts have control.

You must also understand – and accept – that consciousness energies are **energies** as real and active as are the energies of heat and sound. Just as sound waves can penetrate certain substances, so do the consciousness energies of one person infect **like a virus** the consciousness energies of another mind with their own brutal tendencies. These energies may not be expressed in exactly the same way as the rapist, but rest assured that transmitted consciousness energies do implant a new idea or a new feeling within an innocent party. Your scientists are not prepared to believe in telepathy, but telepathy is a fact of life, although dull conscious activity may be so self-oriented as to not recognise that new impulses have originated in someone else's mind.

I will say no more on this subject, except to warn those in high places of church, law and government who fail in their responsibilities towards people at this critical time. They will eventually perceive the enormity of their lack of moral performance whilst undertaking their earthly duties. They will feel the imprint of the lives of those who have been harmed and destroyed due to their moral negligence, rebound upon their own lives. EVERY action has its like repercussions.

Perhaps you will now realise why the present sexual trend in the world is causing the most dire conditions world-wide.

For you to fully understand what I am talking about, I want you to strive to VISUALISE & REALISE that the Nature of Divine Consciousness of Universal Equilibrium is limitless Power, since the equilibrium-harmony arises out of equal constraint between the universal impulses of the:

the male and female,

intelligence and love,

the will to experience and the will to remain acquiescent,

the yearning to be active and the yearning to hold back and maintain the status quo, in order to form bonds and stability.

These primal **IMPULSES of Being**, as I explained in **Letter 4,** are the **'Reality'** which has given life, form, shape, being to all visible things.

This dimension is a state of beauty, joy, harmony, rapturous ecstasy, reverence,intelligence, love. It is all that the earth can demonstrate – but on a scale beyond your even remotest conception.

Try to take into your consciousness the **meaning** of the two foregoing paragraphs. Understanding and making the **meaning** your very own, will change your whole perspective of your Divine origins and of existence itself. In these paragraphs directly above, I have described to you – **the nature and essence of LIFE** – which comes into action within the sperm and ovum when they are united in giving form to a child.

This is your truth, your reality, your soul, psyche, your deepest state of being.

Instinctively you are aware of this. The baby is the embodiment of joy. The joy it expresses as it develops consciousness of its relationships and environment, comes out of the deep well of Divine LIFE Which has grown it cell by cell, according to genetic instructions, into its present form.

What is the difference between the soul and psyche? I am now going to explain the difference which your earthly psychologists may dispute, but nonetheless, this is the truth. The Soul is the 'Divine Flame' – a metaphor used to describe the **essence of Divine Life** which is drawn into individual being at the moment of conception. **LIFE FORCE** takes on personal form and releases the energy of 'electrical force of activity' and the magnetic impulses of 'bonding – rejection' to embark on the intricate work of construction of the body.

Therefore, you have, at the core of your being,

your soul – Divine Reality

this is   **Divine Intelligence/Divine Love**

Which is the powerful Divine Impulse to create, grow, nourish, nurture, heal, protect, fulfill every need, within a system of perfect law and order.

This is the **Reality** which is your **soul**.

Therefore, when you have overcome the ego impulses and invited the SOUL to hold dominion in your thoughts and feelings, you will be driven

to express all of the Divine Impulses described above. **You will be possessed by a desire to only promote the highest good of all living things and the universe itself. You will have become a true messenger from Divine Consciousness, expressing all Its qualities of Being.**

Until that time of soul re-unification with **Divine Consciousness**, the psyche occupies the deepest recesses of your **human consciousness** and draws its awareness from your soul. It is the hidden instinct within you which knows right from wrong.

The ego is also formed at the moment of conception.

As the baby develops, the ego begins to make itself felt. It is the foundation of your human selfhood which gives you individuality. **It is the energy of your human consciousness.**

It makes you distinct and unique from everyone else.

In order to preserve your individuality, the ego must protect you from outside attack of any kind and it must give you what you need to help you prosper, flourish, grow and be happy.

This is Divinely ordained and not to be treated with contempt. The ego constitutes an 'all-important' and very necessary nucleus of consciousness of creation, development and growth.

The ego is exclusively governed by the electrical current of activity consciousness – the 'Go-go' impulse apparent in **all** living things, even in plants which turn and display their foliage to catch the sun in the best possible way. This is a movement conceived in the 'go-go' electrical field and in the 'bonding-desire' emotional field in the consciousness of the plant to enable the plant to grow and enjoy the warmth of the sun. The ego in every living thing is the seat of the 'earthly consciousness' only. In no way does it resemble in any shape or form the **Divine Reality** which constitutes the soul. The ego-drive, the drive which is directed exclusively at getting what it wants to make the individual entity happy and to protect it from attack to ensure its survival, and will trample on other entities or species to achieve its purposes, pertains to the earthly dimension only. This ego force is active within every living thing from the least amoeba to the mightiest king.

You could call the **Ego-Drive** the Protector and Dictator of the living Universe.

It is at this point that the majority of people in your world to-day become confused when contemplating the possibility of the existence of a 'God'. They review the activities of various species driven by their ego-consciousness, the one feeding on another to obtain sustenance and these people decide that this 'savagery' must be the working of the creator.

How then can the creator be a 'God of Love'?

This is one of the misapprehensions and beliefs I would like to sweep away. It is my purpose that all people should come to realise that: the entire universe has, at its basic core and foundation in all things, the **Divine Life Force** which inspires and respires through all of creation. **It** is the hidden but powerful **Equilibrium** out of which all things have taken being, form and shape.

It is the 'scientists' space' **in which** is conducted the 'Movement and Bonding of the Electrical Particles'. It is both the impenetrable and forever unknowable 'ground of existence' and also the hidden Source of all substance of all things in the universe.

The **Ego** is the *tool* of **Divine Creativity** to produce *individuality* out of the **UNITY OF ITS OWN BEINGNESS.**

What I am about to say will be hotly disputed by your scientists – nonetheless, I am about to refer to the souls of those 'earthly' beings whose intellect is sufficiently evolved to debate and decide on a course of action and – with even only partial understanding – respond intuitively and intelligently to what is happening in the environment. These entities of all more advanced species are the genius of their kind. Do not judge the inner development of any species, human or otherwise, by their outer physical bodies. All living things are individualised out of the same **Divine Life.**

Some psyches are enabled, by their increasingly spiritualised mental/emotional fields to peer through the ego consciousness and embark on neighbourly, caring acts which can only proceed from the promptings of the soul drawn from the **Divine Reality.** Therefore, the greatest respect and consideration should be accorded to all living things.

Where the species has evolved to the point of formulating clear ideas and thoughts and putting them into sounds and words – and the spiritual development of the psyche can penetrate the ego consciousness – the psyche begins to question:

'Is this all there is to life? What are our life purposes?' etc.

When this happens, the soul is beginning to impress the psyche with an urgent need to reach out to its Source of Being which it instinctively knows does exist and is its true home and resting place. The soul's hidden but continual longing to be re-united with its Source of Being can now be felt by the psyche.

If there are people who never reach this vital development in their lives, it is because their ego mental/emotional processes are so strongly geared to the exercise of intelligence and reason that when other people ask questions such as : 'How did life begin? Is there a God?

'How has such a wonderful universe been designed and created?', the ego of the non-seeker and non- believer is conscious only of its own omnipotence, and sets out to disprove there is any higher dimension out of which the earth could have taken form. It argues away the voice of the soul relayed through the psyche, and with each argument entombs itself more firmly within the perceptions of the material and visible world which represent their only security.

Therefore, the soul remains imprisoned within the ego mental/emotional electrical/magnetic chains, and the human mind remains convinced that there is no soul – that the earthly dimension of existence and the physical life force are the only realities.

If such people's minds are determined to reject any inspirational whispers from the psyche/soul, the body suffers minor ailments, relationships are strained and life generally is stressful; a disease may follow. This is because such a person is drawing only on the limited resources of energy drawn from the food they put in their mouths. This energy proceeds from a chemical process and not from the Source of all Life.

Whilst you have drawn your life initially from the Divine Reality and It has given you being, you also draw your physical energy from your food and the digestive processes which manufacture enzymes to break down the food into a usable form which feeds the physical cells throughout your body and mind. This is the life of the body.

Many people live and die drawing exclusively on the energy derived from their physical processes.

The type and amount of energy drawn from physical processes is greatly affected by the mental/electrical and emotional/magnetic fields of the living entity.

These electrical and magnetic fields surrounding every living thing from an amoeba to an elephant and human being, are the personal **Life Force** radiations from the soul, combined with the personal 'consciousness-awareness' radiations of the entity's mental/electrical 'go-go' activity and its emotional/magnetic 'bonding-rejection' impulses. These electrical/magnetic fields are profoundly affected by all the thoughts and feelings which pass through the minds and emotions of the entity. In turn, the 'fields' profoundly affect the physical processes of the body itself. They raise or lower the health of the body according to the state of the personal consciousness – whether it is in harmony with the Life Force radiations of **Divine Intelligence/Love** or in conflict with them due to selfish ego-drives.

A miserable entity dwindles and dies. A happy entity flourishes. This is a basic fact of existence. In the final analysis, each living entity feeds upon its own inner state of contentment or frustration.

You can see the truth of this statement in the physical and consciousness development of a baby.

A contented, happy child flourishes, laughs easily, is filled with joy. Contact with a loving mother, enhances the child's well-being. The loving, contented radiations from mother to baby feed the little one's consciousness radiations, and in turn, build up strength in the tiny body.

As the child develops, its developing personality begins to 'colour' its soul radiations with bright or dark consciousness force which either re-inforce the child's health or depletes it.

A person with a strong psychic sense can see the electro-magnetic fields becoming dim when an individual or animal is being depleted of field energy although at the time, neither individual nor animal may be registering physical dis-ease. It may be a day or so before the body itself begins to manifest the consciousness energy depletion in some form of exhaustion or illness.

You have on earth, people who have developed equipment to record this phenomenon, and in years to come, this will be the recognised method of diagnosing and treating an oncoming ailment. Furthermore, as the technology of spiritual-scientific knowledge evolves, **the exact mental/emotional state responsible for the physical depletion will be first revealed under hypnosis and recorded electronically in frequencies of vibration on screens. This will be followed by an electronic investigation depicting the frequencies of vibration of the various parts of the body on similar screens. This process will involve colour changes, for every pattern of consciousness is first manifested both in frequencies of vibration and colour. By comparing the mental/emotional frequencies of vibration with the frequencies of vibration of the body parts, the organ depleted of energy – together with the mental/emotional cause will be pin-pointed.**

No longer will psychiatrists delve into past experiences, probing, pigeonholing, producing pronouncements as to the likely origins or causes of mental/emotional/physical disorders and then providing human rationalisations with which to combat them.

The truth of the spiritual state of the 'inner man' will be clearly revealed and will lay the sure foundation for the necessary spiritual instruction and meditative, mental work to be done to enable him to regain health, vitality, new perspectives and goals – and a deepening capacity for unconditional love.

Naturally, drugs will no longer be used to raise the consciousness radiations of the sufferer, since the depletion of **Divine Life – soul energy** is responsible for the illness. He or she will be taught how to deliberately, systematically raise the frequencies of vibration of the affected area of the body and how to deal with the personal circumstances causing the psychological discomfort and depletion of **soul energy**. The patient will also be dramatically assisted by an inflow of Divine energy from the hands of those who are true channels of pure spiritual life. With the re-vitalising procedures, new perceptions and control of the ego-drives, the physical condition will be quickly cleared up within days – if not immediately.

However, on reading these **Letters,** you can begin to effect your own healing. Paramount in your self- treatment must be these instructions regarding the **Divine Reality** powering existence, and the right way to tune into **It** and draw **Divine Life** into the healing process.

When you begin to draw on the **Life** of the **Divine Reality** by means of your spiritual search, asking questions, meditating, reading and praying, you begin to open your psyche up from its enclosed ego- consciousness   earthly dreaming; you draw into mind and emotions the nature of the **Divine Reality Itself.** All that passes through your mind and emotions is passed into the   electro-magnetic   fields surrounding you. These contribute to your strength. As your electro magnetic fields are energised by the power you draw from **Divine Reality,** so is the power passed back into your physical body and each organ becomes ever more healthy and any dysfunctions are gradually cleared up. It is vital for you to remember these physical/electro-magnetic field processes because the knowledge will both inspire and encourage your daily meditation and attunement with the **Divine Reality**.

If your sincere search and meditation are directed towards the **TRUTH of BEING** and not at some earthly religious forms of belief, or superficial, spurious 'spirituality' or any material objects you believe to possess 'powers', you will find that, gradually, your own nature is changing and you begin to be aware of otherness and their needs as you never did before. You become more empathetic, understanding, caring, compassionate and gentle. In fact, the soul qualities of **Divine Life** now begin to control your natural ego impulses for satisfaction and self-defence.

I want to warn you that you will have now entered a new and difficult time – an era of conflict between the ego-drive which has habitually insisted on fulfilling its 'wants', perhaps at the expense of other people, and the psyche-soul which is beginning to realise that 'love is the law' and the rights of other people have to be balanced equally with the rights of self – the ego. As the psyche absorbs more and more of the **soul – Divine Reality** into its consciousness, the old ego drive begins to release its grasp and the inner daily conflict becomes even more intense.

The psyche-soul, now working through mind and heart, discovers it is balancing the needs of other people against the validity of its own needs and it becomes weighed down and weary of the endless internal struggle of self-questioning and self-judgement. When the psyche is reaching this point of perception, it indicates that the pull of the human consciousness is thinning to such an extent that the soul is now drawing close to and becoming re-unified with the **Divine Reality.**

The **soul** acknowledges through the medium of the psyche, that it loves the **DIVINE LOVE** that is the **Divine Reality** more than it loves anything earthly and longs to be fully united with its **SOURCE of BEING.**

The psyche finally surrenders the ego-consciousness drives to Divine Reality and begs that it may be enabled to yield the 'ego' – to go through the death of the self-hood. This happens when people are truly reaching the apex of their spiritual life and they usually need a spiritual master to guide them through it.

This 'death of the self-hood' should never be undertaken as a means of achieving greater spiritual insight. It is highly dangerous and will not succeed in achieving greater spiritual or earthly life. It will be greatly destructive to the psyche and ego before due time.

It will hinder the whole process of soul-psyche-ego-physical development.

No one should entertain such a thought in order to be more advanced in spiritual perception and truth. Such an act of 'will-power' will be self-defeating since it is born entirely of the ego-drive to be more important spiritually.

When this experience of ego-mastery takes place at the right time – in the right way – the soul, through the medium of the psyche, is free, to a large extent, to commune direct with the Divine Reality since the continual chatter of the 'ego-consciousness' is stilled. The pull of the earth is no longer paramount. Self- centred ambition fades; the desire for personal possessions dissolves.

Peace reigns in the mind. The soul, now speaking clearly through the psyche, longs to uplift, nourish, contribute to the growth of other souls, educate, uplift, and nurture with understanding and tenderness without any desire for recompense or self-aggrandisement.

As the soul is drawn into ever closer contact and attunement with **Divine Reality,** it's only earthly goal is to treat the neighbour or other people with the same kind of concern and consideration it needs for itself to flourish and be content. Giving becomes as easy as breathing – eventually it becomes a privilege to work for and with other people for the promotion of their highest good. This is **Divine Love** in action. **However, there is no sentiment in Divine Reality.**

The intention behind individualisation was to enable **Divine Reality Itself** to experience **Its** own **Nature of creativity, joy and personal fulfilment.**

Therefore, when I was on earth, I drew the lines between giving and receiving quite clearly when I said:

'Do unto others what you would have them do to you'. This statement was a loving warning that as you sow so will you reap. It was also a guideline to behaviour. If you do unto others what you would like done to yourself, then you can be sure that you are acting only from the standpoint of love. If other people do not want what you would like done for you – then you live by trial and error; you have taken a positive step towards fulfilling an act of true love and if it is rejected, you have given yourself an opportunity to find out what would be more greatly appreciated in the future. In this way do you grow in the act of love. I also said: 'Love your neighbour as you love yourself'. This meant that you should have equal concern for your neighbour's comfort as you have for your own.

It also means that whatever you wish on to other people you would be happy to have wished on yourself in like manner.

It means that you must think the thoughts about others which you would be happy for them to think about you!

It means that your entire consciousness should be directed at caring, concern for others, no matter what they may be doing hurtful against yourself. All human beings are living in a jungle of human desires, goals, frailties, disappointments, anger and frustration. Out of this war-torn consciousness come many weak and ill-judged responses and actions.

Therefore, behold the frailty, forgive the unkindness, and let it go back into the nothingness out of which it came. The only **TRUTH** and **REALITY** in your life is *Divine Consciousness Intelligence/Love*. Hold fast to this realisation at all times.

To find the **Kingdom of Heaven, in which the soul is in harmony with Divine Reality,** there must come a time in your development when you no longer want to be drawn into the earthly perceptions and consciousness of human beings towards each other. You long to withdraw entirely and focus on spreading your own contact with **Divine Reality** to others. Beware that you do not force your spiritual way on others, irrespective of whether or not they are on the spiritual path themselves.

At the same time, you must preserve your own serenity by not allowing others to take advantage of your good nature. You must clearly draw your lines of right and wrong – prevent the selfishness of others encroaching on your privacy which is likely to destroy your peace of mind.

To ensure this, there is no need for your ego-consciousness to assume dominance again. You can guard your privacy peacefully. You have been given the intelligence to achieve this necessary purpose with the highest degree of **LOVE**. Remember that the spiritual edifice of consciousness vibrations which have been constructed out of your contact with **Divine Reality and your daily mode of thought, feeling and living, should be sacrosanct** and you have to take care not to become entrapped again in the lower vibrations of others' thoughts and reactions.

At all times, your highest purpose on earth is to **promote the highest earthly and spiritual GOOD of every other living entity – human and lesser. Not by descending to the vibrationary level of those in need but by reaching out and offering the wisdom which has brought you into your sanctuary – your holy of holies in mind, emotion and living conditions – if there is a willingness to listen and accept. Otherwise, hold your peace.**

Sympathy and compassion should be detached. Empathy will drag you down and embroil your spiritual consciousness vibrations in the human vibrational level. This will possibly create conflicts where you had sincerely only intended to uplift and heal. Avoid this since it will deplete your energies and defeat your spiritual purposes.

Pure LOVE is concerned only with upliftment and spiritual progress, healing and achievement of the 'Kingdom of Heaven'.

Divine LOVE is a warm compassionate feeling – primarily charged with the longing to enable the loved one to: grow, create, be nourished and nourish others, to be healed and to heal others, to educate and educate

259

others, to protect and protect others, to fulfill his needs and for him to fulfill the needs of others, all within a clear system of law and order.

This is DIVINE LOVE/LAW in action.

When your highest purpose has become the **Divine Purpose in action**, the ego, the nucleus of your individuality, is now controlled by your soul. The ego-drive becomes your true defender and true protector of your personal comfort – but it now works entirely in harmony with the directives of your soul which draws its nature from **Divine Reality.**

I repeat – there is no sentiment in Divine Reality, no removing any boundaries ensuring law and order, to suit the demands of the egoist, no weak 'giving in' and yielding to the obstinacy of others.

At all times, it must be borne in mind that ALL PEOPLE should respect one another. They must respect the rights of others to privacy, safety, peace of mind and harmony. If differences arise, they can be dealt with, with mutual respect. The more spiritually evolved you are, the more will you respect the highest and the lowest of social stratas, accounting them to be equal – 'not in the sight of God' as human beings like to say, but within **your own spiritualised perceptions of the fundamental equality of the souls within all beings.**

Respect and **DIVINE LOVE** belong together. True *LOVE* is highly respectful of the beloved. Where there is respect between two people, this frequently leads to the highest form of love.

If you have found this **Letter** difficult to accept, remember that **the human mind is limited in its understanding of dimensions beyond the earthly plane. Do not let the reasoning of the ego hold you back from your soul's journey.**

In my next **Letter**, I will develop the theme of **DIVINE LOVE** and will enlarge on ego self love showing you exactly how the magnetic emotions are presently controlling your thoughts, feelings and lives. I will outline the steps by which they can be overcome and eventually dissolved from your consciousness.My purpose is to lead you along the path of self-discovery and spiritual advancement that you may enter immediately into **Light** not only when you pass on into the next dimension of existence but also whilst you are on earth.

At the moment you are living in a shadowy burdened existence instead of consciously living within and entering into the '**Divine Consciousness**' and allowing **_IT_** to permeate and gladden your thinking and your life experiences.

Know that my Christ Consciousness is with you always and you can have immediate access to me when you call. Let this be a comfort to you – but not a crutch. I am but your gateway to your own illumination and your own ascent into Christ Consciousness yourself.

LETTER 8

I have come to you again to speak of:

THE TRUE NATURE OF EXISTENCE

The TRUTH OF BEING is this: YOU who believe only in the material world, live entirely in the earthly, finite world. You live within a dimension of the manifestation of your beliefs.

Those whose spiritual perceptions and lives have been raised in frequencies of vibrations to merge with the spiritual frequencies of vibration of the spiritual dimension can perceive that they live in two dimensions. They are fully aware of this truth. And they live according to this truth, and evolve into ever higher frequencies of being.

They are no longer bound by human belief but live within the realisation that they live within infinity in which are no limitations. The higher their vibrational frequencies of consciousness, the more aware they are that they live within infinity and that only they themselves set the limits on what they can aspire to. Those whose perceptions have been heightened in this way whilst still in their bodies, have seen that there is only one dimension of actual 'individual being' and this dimension is '**Divine Consciousness Activity**'.

They may also come to fully realise there is the further dimension of **Universal Consciousness** in which the Universal resides in perfect equilibrium and may be penetrated by none, because within this dimension any individuality would be immediately drawn into the Unity of Being.

When a soul reaches, in understanding and realisation, the topmost level of the frequencies of vibrations of consciousness – **Christ Consciousness** – the soul can look down and review the levels of vibrations ascending and descending to those of humanity on earth and know, with love and compassion, humanity is trapped in the lower vibrations of Divine Consciousness hidden within the Ego-drive, wholly unaware of the Truth of Being, the soul's true identity and the earthly truth of the ego. Neither does it have the slightest awareness of the immense purpose behind its existence and the eventual mission it must embark upon.

The task of the newborn soul is to experience, through means of its sheath the Psyche, all that these lower frequencies have to offer and grow as a result of the mental/emotional events and experiences arising out of their thoughts and feelings. The soul must learn, through trial and error, the state of consciousness which makes it immensely happy or burdened with grief and sorrow which initiate various physical limitations.

The purpose of life on earth is not to discover a means to experience undeviating joy and bliss, although this is what each soul longs for.

Such bliss and joy would hinder the soul's progress into the higher spiritual vibrations of consciousness.

Eventually after many lifetimes of 'highs' and 'lows' of comfort and sorrow, the psyche will wake up to the truth of its being and will realise that it has within itself the potential to draw on **Divine Consciousness** for insight, understanding and knowledge and to raise its spiritual consciousness vibrations to those of health, well-being, protection, inner growth, spiritual nutrition and to radiate to others the nature of **Divine Consciousness** Itself.

As I have said before **CONSCIOUSNESS is LIFE** and **LIFE is CONSCIOUSNESS.**

Where there is LIFE – there is CONSCIOUSNESS. Where there is CONSCIOUSNESS there is LIFE. EVERYTHING in existence is defined by vibrational frequencies of consciousness. Light, Sound, Colour, all physical phenomena both living and inanimate. If you can change the frequencies of vibration of any single thing, you change the appearance of that thing – be it sound, colour, gas, liquid, physical organs.

When physical organs present an appearance of ill-health, it is because the normal frequencies of vibrations of that physical organ have been reduced and the LIFE within the organ has been depleted. Science presents the universe as being 'matter' possessing consciousness but the truth is:

The universe is CONSCIOUSNESS which has taken on the appearance of 'matter' as a result of a descent into the lower frequencies of vibration of consciousness.

This is the true reality of existence – nothing else.

Your existence is all a matter of frequency of vibrations. The higher the spiritual perceptions and the adherence to spiritual thought, the more swift are the personal vibrational frequencies in the body, the vitality is raised and illness eventually disappears.

The scientific fraternity believes you live entirely within the human dimension comprising the solar system, and the galaxies of stars. Science believes the human intellect is the highest point of intelligent reference at any time, having evolved in response to changing environment and climatic conditions and is purely the product of brain activity. According to science, your emotions are wholly real and valid and what you think and feel is beyond all dispute, these constitute the only 'reality' of existence. Normalcy is computed according to the 'average' thoughts, actions, and responses to the environment. This is perceived as the human 'reality'.

Any talents which transcend the 'average' output of 'average' minds is reckoned as being 'genius' arising from unusual mental powers. The 'below average' output is said to be due to retardation due to some physical cause – genetics, birth trauma, etc. Science believes the physical dimension is the beginning and the end of existence. Science is so set against any possibility of self-delusionary beliefs that it will accept as being 'real' any phenomenon provided it can be computed, estimated and proved by instruments.

If you think about this carefully, you will come to realise that what science holds fast to as fact is, in reality, only belief created by drawing conclusions through the exercise of their five senses.

So is it with every other facet of your existence. In your earthly dimension, facts take place second by second but the moment they have happened, they become memory-beliefs and memories are not always accurate. Whatever feelings and thoughts you have about the past are not facts but points of view, beliefs, and are, therefore, not facts – nor the **Reality** behind them.

This applies to every facet of your existence. The **Truth** is: you live in a worldly dimension composed entirely of your beliefs arising from your responses to what happened a hundred, thousand or ten thousand years ago.

At one time, people believed the world was flat. Therefore, for them, they lived in a flat world and were afraid to sail the seas too far in one direction, because they were in danger of falling off the edge of the world. For the people, a mere 400 hundred years ago, their world was flat. Today, with knowledge, your world is accessible in every direction.

People, in the past, and also in the present time, directed their lives according to 'old wives' tales', the power of the ancestors and other legends. They believed in them so implicitly, the limitations imposed by these beliefs restricted people's actions and activities.

Dancing was believed to be sinful and wicked by certain 'Christian' sects for instance. Therefore, many people who would have derived great happiness and release from stress when dancing, were wrongfully denied this pleasure.

Religion comes under the same heading. Beliefs are the very substance of religion. They are founded on age-old happenings which are nothing but belief. The beliefs may have been relevant to the general mindset of those times, but they have long since become irrelevant in a constantly changing world, yet they are strictly adhered to and become the focus of worship, festivities, celebrations, mourning – and more destructively – they become the reason for men killing one another and causing horrific misery to women and children.

Certain religions claim that 'God is everywhere and in all things' but also affirm dogmatically, that no one knows the 'mind' of 'God', or the reasons why people kill one another – it may be in God's plan, they say. With mindsets composed of a conglomeration of illogical beliefs, where can mankind, at this present time, find any certainty of beauty, joy, health, well-being, love?

Religious ideas present a 'God' whose 'will' can bring life and healing or death and destruction. In such beliefs, there is no certainty of anything other than uncertainty.

With such a belief, any sickness or abnormality can be excused as being 'God's Will'. It is your **BELIEFS** which control all your expectations of what life may hand out in the future.

Healthy agnosticism, the kind of mindset which accepts it does not know the nature of 'God' or whether there is any 'God' at all but is perfectly open to the conviction imparted by enlightenment, is preferable to fanatical beliefs in half-truth or non-truth.

How blind is the human race generally!

People are like moles living within their tunnels, convinced they are capable of 'sizing up' the entirety of their existence by using their senses of hearing, smell, very limited vision and touch.

Thus may you descend the scale of life forms and witness thousands of species living lives entirely defined and limited by their senses. What they can perceive as 'real' constitutes their personal 'reality', their particular world. Every strata of existence experienced by various species of living things, is distinct from every other within the earthly dimension. This includes the human mind which is literally **possessed** by religious doctrines and dogmas and imprisoned in scientific theories and mathematic formulas.

Religious doctrines have been conceived by human reasoning in an effort to explain the teachings of spiritual Masters, whose minds have moved beyond the human sphere of intellect into the heavenly spheres of inspired perception of *'Universal Reality'*.

Scientific concepts are also the product of the human senses rationalising and giving names to phenomena viewed by human sight during experimentation.

When, therefore, the human intellect is able to set aside such limited beliefs and ascend into contact with the **'Reality'** beyond the 'highest human reasoning, logic, and rationalisations' which are termed 'knowledge', such a mind enters the higher spheres of *'LIFE-CONSCIOUSNESS'*. It is imbued with **'universal truth'** which is literally beyond the scope of the 'normal' human mind to perceive or accept or understand. The human mind cannot understand any experience beyond that of the electromagnetic parameters of earthly existence and the functions of the brain – until **Divine Consciousness** enlightenment enters the entire human system of mind, emotions and sub-consciousness – then the underlying unity and harmony is revealed.

When altogether new spiritual perceptions are presented to a religiously indoctrinated mind, these are perceived as being from 'Satan' or sheer lunacy or imagination. This is natural since when the emotions are severely aroused and challenged, as happens when deep beliefs are contradicted, the magnetic-emotional **'bonding-rejection'** impulses of the ego-drive immediately come into action. **Any thesis or proposal which causes the conditioned mind**

acute mental discomfort, dismay or puzzlement, will be rejected instantly and a whole barrage of 'proofs' will be summoned from the beliefs in the conditioned mind to back up such rejection. But the proofs are merely beliefs.

This is an entirely natural mental-emotional process within the purely human dimension.

Therefore, if this **my TRUTH** is offered to those whose mindsets are firmly established and conditioned by fear or strengthened by the human will to adhere to such programmed beliefs, it is only natural that the **TRUTH** will arouse unruly emotions and be quite violently, possibly virulently rejected.

The foregoing is a description of normal mental-emotional activity within the human dimension.

It should not be criticised since a conditioned mind is made to feel completely insecure and 'adrift' or 'all at sea' when confronted with an entirely new concept. These human idioms describe exactly what happens when an indoctrinated mind is challenged by an entirely new perception of what was previously held to be so dear, so safe, so right!

When first reading these **LETTERS** you can determine for yourselves where you stand mentally and emotionally. Are you blocked from spiritual progress by your stubborn adherence to present beliefs?. Are you able, after due thought, to realise that all you are so sturdily upholding **is** only – **'belief'** – irrational belief?

It is absolutely vital to your spiritual development that you should, at long last, fully understand the principles of your human mind and emotional functioning. You think you do, but you do not understand it at all. You can only understand it by coming out of it entirely, transcending it, moving into higher dimensions of perception and experience – entering into **TRUTH ITSELF.**

Only then do you begin to perceive that you and every other person in the world, have lived and directed your lives almost entirely by human 'beliefs' – not **TRUTH.**

There are many people who believe wholeheartedly that if they pray for a certain object or experience or the bestowal of the right guidance

in a certain situation, they will truly receive the right object, experience or guidance which will enhance their well-being.

They believe that when (if!) their prayer is answered, they will wholeheartedly rejoice and immediately follow the lead, irrespective of present conditions, because, coming from the Divine, it can only be the right answer conducive to happiness.

However, when faced with the arrival of the longed-for object, or experience or guidance – the recipient of Divine Grace sometimes becomes so disturbed and disoriented, unable to accept that there has been an intrusion of Divine Consciousness exactly as asked for, that he/she does not know how to deal with it.

If minds are so disturbed when what they have asked for, is actually given them in an unexpected way – where is the true FAITH and BELIEF which they were so certain they wholly possessed in abundance? Do you not also see that belief, not Truth – has orchestrated the whole symphonic movement – with the exception, of course, of the Divine Consciousness intervention – the answer to the prayer. This intervention is the only 'reality' in the whole procedure – the rest is belief and hope – mental gymnastics using past experiences by which to measure the present. Your only TRUTH is Divine Consciousness which leads only to growth and perfection – if you fully trust it to do so.

Pause here and read and re-read the foregoing paragraphs because what goes on in your consciousness is the fabric of your experiences and lives.

So question yourselves: do you really PERCEIVE – REALISE – UNDERSTAND the *Reality as being the source of all knowledge and creativity?* Or do you merely pay lip service and superficial mental acknowledgement to Divine Consciousness?

Do you fully and completely live, minute by minute, in the realisation that UNIVERSAL CONSCIOUSNESS is the only Reality and Highest Intelligence operational within creation? Do you consistently depend on Its supremely effective guidance or do you think that you would rather live by your own finite will and sometimes muddled emotional impulses?

And, if you are given direct guidance to follow a certain lead, but stop to think whether the guidance is leading you where you think you want to go, are you fully surrendered to the Highest Intelligent Authority – Divine Consciousness? Is this not an indication your ego is still in control? Even these **LETTERS,** when circulated as intended, will come to be 'beliefs', not the pure spiritual perception of **'WHAT IS' out of which these words have come.**

Only by taking these words into meditation after asking for spiritual illumination, will the spiritual 'Reality' behind the words eventually come like a shaft of light into the mind. When this happens, you will KNOW that you know.

Those of you who have evolved sufficiently to live in two dimensions, YOU whose minds can move beyond the realm of human intellect into the higher dimension of *'Universal Reality'* will probably encounter many people, in time to come, who will reject these LETTERS as imagination but be not dismayed.

Remember what I am telling you now. YOU are residents of two dimensions and none may pass beyond the dimension of 'mere intellect' until the pre-requisites to spiritual enlightenment have been fulfilled. These are a true *spiritual* awakening leading to deep insight into the activities of the ego and self-hood......followed by remorse......remorse......remorse. This is the ONLY WAY.

For remorse, in turn, leads to the rejection of the magnetic-emotional dimension of 'rejection- bonding' which, in its more virulent forms, humans described as 'sin'.

When a person penetrates the *spiritual dimension* and is imbued with *'LIFE' characteristics*, the person begins to realise and eventually KNOW that the human ego-drive to 'look out for the self' actually shuts the SOUL off from the continuous inflow of *DIVINE LIFE' into the mind, heart, body, relationships and daily experiences.*

'Looking out for yourself' is a human, earthly experience.

Total, sincere, surrender of the self-hood to 'FATHER-LIFE' removes the block between the *spiritual dimension* and the soul. A person no longer has to 'look out for himself', all that DIVINE LIFE is, now flows into the individual's body, mind, heart, experiences and relationships. Such a person lives by 'instinct' and follows hunches which always work out perfectly in the long term.

'DIVINE LIFE' IS ALWAYS THERE TO BE ACCESSED, whenever the person surrenders self-will and turns to IT for every need.

You must remember that I am referring to the time when you **penetrate the human dimension of intellect** and move beyond your reliance on 'intellect' and material means to get you what you want out of life. Many people think they have reached this place of spiritual development but are deluding themselves.

When a person abandons logic – and **knows** beyond all doubt that guidance can be utterly relied upon to achieve inspired goals, your life changes. Benefits flow into your experience when you fully realise that Divine Consciousness is the unseen Reality – the Power – at work behind the outer appearances of your life, moving 'intelligent energy force' to manifest your needs. You do not have to deny appearances, pour thought-power into a condition you are seeking to resolve.

All you have to do is surrender self-will and KNOW that as your limited intellect yields, so does the **Infinite Reality** move in to order your life in an altogether new way, to wean you away from all your supports of the past, bring to your mind a new vision for a new endeavour, and lead you into new areas of activity. But when this happens, you have to be prepared to 'let go' completely.

You have to release your grip on the securities of the past and know that even greater securities of a different nature await you as you follow your inspiration.

Since this state of spiritual/human existence and harmonious well-being depend entirely on a person's ability to make true contact with **Divine Reality,** it is imperative to return again and again to an in-depth study of **Divine Reality Itself** and the way in which the ego-drive is ceaselessly at work within the human consciousness blocking out the intuitive directions of the **Divine Life** within the mind. At the moment you are living in a shadowy burdened existence instead of consciously living within and entering into **'Divine Consciousness'** and allowing **IT** to permeate and gladden your thinking and life experiences. You remain locked within the mental-

271

emotional framework of electro-magnetic impulses until you set your willpower to consciously dissolving the fabric of your humanly conceived beliefs and come to see clearly that your Reality is **Divine Consciousness** – not your family, or bank book. When you achieve this insight, you will enter into **LIGHT** – and the **LIGHT** will abide in you.

Because of the discomfort and the tug-of-war between the evolving soul and the human ego, (which demands to 'look good' rather than **'BE GOOD',** and yet cannot bear the thought that it may ever be imperfect), there are few people receiving inspiration and passing it on to others at this time, who will speak about the need to go through a period of inner cleansing. Modern people are conditioned to instant service, instant light, instant heat, instant food, drink, clothes and entertainment, and therefore are not attracted to a **_TRUTH_** which involves self-sacrifice, hard work and total dedication to the goal. Besides which, many of these teachers are making a good deal of money out of their activities and they must present a 'Truth' that will sell!

If your modern teachers speak of a path of attainment to the highest dimensions by means of the transference of personal mental illumination, it will still be necessary to undergo the inner intense self- examination and purification of the bonding-rejection of 'magnetic emotions'.

If you are truly on the upward path to the highest spiritual dimensions, your road will be characterised by moments of bright clear-sighted self-inspection and self-realisation, followed frequently by self-loathing. This dark and painful feeling is the magnetic emotion in reverse.

Where before, the ego clung to its essential vision of itself as being the greatest and even greater than others, it now begins to glimpse the agonising fact that perhaps it is not only slightly – but very imperfect. Any person reaching this spiritual level of development will find they are now travelling the road to true humility.

Take heart when you find this happening to you. You are now pushing away the debris of past erroneous beliefs about yourself and your illusory self-hood. **Remember that it is your 'intention' or 'motivation' or 'conviction' which gives creative power to do whatever you want to do.**

The moment that you desire with all your heart to reverse your normal trend in your magnetic emotional patterns, you have set this process in motion. If you clearly define the goals you wish to achieve and keep them ever before your vision in writing or in mind, very shortly you will discover that the desired changes have taken place in your consciousness. When this happens, you will feel a lightness in spirit and will have moments of pure joy. You will be proving that the **TRUTH of BEING** does bring 'captive hearts' into the perfect freedom of spiritual living.

At the same time, you have to understand that your ego must, (of necessity to enable you to survive), make you believe you are of value to yourself and other people. Any external serious challenge regarding the value of the self is highly destructive. A desperate fear and internal subsidence of confidence will lead to the conviction that you are without value in the world, and suicide can be the natural outcome. Therefore, your progress will and must be gradual.

No one should ever expect people to be wholly changed by words of advice or times of inspiration. Growth can only take place very gradually – **one insight at a time.**

A true spiritual insight will imbue a person's mind with an altogether new point of view which will enable him to begin to approach certain related circumstances in life differently. This insight must direct the person's actions until it has been absorbed completely into the consciousness for eternity and becomes part of the soul evolution.

For instance, a man may have the idea that he will be successful in life if he enforces his will aggressively on those who come within his orbit. He believes he will be better heard if he shouts.

Then he may wake up to the fact that no one likes him much and he is avoided by employees and 'friends'. He may become more aggressive because he now feels humiliated, or, if he is an evolving soul, he will question what he can do about his isolation. The moment that **DIVINE LIFE** seeps into his consciousness PSYCHE and makes him realise that he, himself, avoids people who shout, he will have a flash of inspiration. He will realize that, to be happy and successful, he should treat others as he likes to be treated. You may argue that this perception is not necessarily inspired but is born of common sense, that he himself was responsible for arriving at this realisation. However, this is not so. Ego thoughts are dictated solely by the 'bonding-rejection' impulses, any new wisdom comes from **'LOVING INTELLIGENCE'.**

This may be the last inspired flash of insight he will ever have, but if he is truly on a spiritual path and seeking the highest dimensions of attainment, he will gradually perceive that this first overcoming of the 'ego' is not enough. He will begin to see other previously unsuspected selfish patterns of behaviour. He will define a further goal just out of reach at that moment, but very shortly, with prayer and meditation, he will have achieved that goal also. In this way, his consciousness frequencies of vibration will be elevated and he will gradually move towards the 'Celestial Kingdoms of Consciousness' – the 'Kingdom of Heaven'.

Alternatively, a woman may only feel secure by not disturbing the present status quo. She is afraid to speak out when treated with a lack of respect. Such a meek person, whilst more comfortable taking refuge in silence, will also suffer deep resentments because people do not respect her passive personality. Such people usually turn to religion for comfort and reassurance and because of non- comprehension of the laws of existence; she will probably remain static in her meekness till the end of her time on earth.

Indeed, because of my words recorded in the gospels: 'Blessed are the meek for they shall inherit the earth', the church has taught that meekness is to be commended, she may feel that her 'meekness' is the way to the **LIGHT.**

However, if the meek little lady should find the **TRUTH** concerning her 'being' and should find the right way to make contact with 'Universal Consciousness' she will eventually be told inwardly and clearly that, spiritually, she is the equal of everyone else. She will be inspired to express herself well. She will be given the strength to speak 'her truth' in a more confident and attractive way.

People will begin to respect this new person and she will be manifesting the inner spiritual development gained during her times spent in meditation.

Remember, you are not on earth to 'please God', as your church may tell you. You are on earth to 'express' 'God' and to make ever closer and closer contact with Universal Consciousness until you become free of the magnetic-emotional bondage.

I must make it clear that my words have been mistranslated in the gospel. I said: 'Blessed are those with peaceful hearts for they will inherit the earth'.

If you contemplate the world, you will see that those countries with 'peaceful hearts' prosper and live in harmony with their neighbours. Where there are upheavals and genocide, this turbulence is the direct manifestation of the 'consciousness' of the inhabitants. Such a consciousness destroys a country and begets poverty and illness.

Sometimes, a country such as Tibet, adoring its own isolation and spiritual rituals and beliefs, may be suffocating under the weight of its own human/spiritual creations. The inhabitants need to be forced out into the turbulent world that they may put their beliefs to the test. They also bring 'what is real in their thinking' to others who are burdened with magnetic emotional responses to life. They have been the means in a small way, of relieving the pain experienced in modern society.

Whilst on this journey towards **LIGHT, the Celestial Kingdoms of 'Divine Consciousness'**, you will undoubtedly undergo rocky and bumpy experiences until you achieve your true goal. You will experience times of wondrous joy and times when your heart is heavy and your emotions dragged this way and that because you feel there is an impenetrable barrier between yourself and **Divine Consciousness.**

You may have heard of these dark times of inner distress when a person no longer knows what he is meant to be doing or where he should be going. Then, suddenly, just when this spiritual isolation is no longer bearable, and the traveller has surrendered his inner self completely, **Light** illumines the mind, and the person will see some marvellously deeper truth concerning existence, will perceive, more clearly, his **SOURCE of BEING**. He will be filled with joy because 'God has spoken'.

Yes, **'DIVINE LIFE' has penetrated his consciousness**, and lifted him safely along the path leading to the attainment of the highest spiritual consciousness of the Celestial Kingdoms – the Kingdom of Heaven.

Therefore, the way forward is through the means of such moments of profound revelations. They must be treasured and remembered otherwise all the spade work of the self will be lost, and the seeker will be continually pushed back to where he began the search.

Faith must be strong at all times. Dithering about avails nothing. When I descend into your planes or dimensions of 'consciousness', I have seen seriously inclined seekers of **Truth** uplifted for a few hours and joyfully telling people of their experience, and then, a little while later, doubting what they were so certain they had received earlier. This slows down the process of spiritual development. These times of doubt should be strenuously resisted and overcome by meditation and prayer. For what is DOUBT but an undermining of what you have known and believed in!

DOUBT is a negative creative consciousness force directed against the very experience of **'DIVINE- LIFE' which lifted your spirit on high!**

You create within yourself a little war between your experience of **Divine Consciousness** and your human blindness. You will probably destroy the memory of that divine moment and erase all vestiges of spiritual upliftment and development it brought into your consciousness. This conflict will leave you feeling jaded and dis-spirited. And you will probably never realise that all alone and unassisted – you have wrought this negative transformation in yourself!

People, on the spiritual path, frequently do this to themselves and hinder their spiritual development, never stopping to question what right they have to relapse in this self-indulgent exercise.

People use their minds recklessly, blighting their lives and the lives of other people with their thoughts and words arising from their ego-drive. For it is only your thought life and emotional upheavals which end in quarrels and mayhem – not your faces, bodies, hands and legs unless the quarrels end in physical abuse. But even bodily conflict has its origins in the frustration of the ego within mind and emotions, and conveyed to the limbs to vent the uncontrollable wrath.

In this way, marriages – and friendships – begin in mutual joy and eventually end in misery and mutual rejection – because people find it impossible to channel their ego-drive into life and love-preserving modes of self-expression.

Parents and children express mutual love until the teen years, and then hatred enters the scene and sours the relationship when children rebel against authority and parents react with self-righteous abuse. Again, there is no need for such conflict. Parents must surely realise that every generation fights to find its feet in the adult world and do things more innovatively than did their elders? How can young people thrive if shackled to youthful bondage?

When children become young adults, this is 'growing time' for parents, who must now prepare for the next stage of their life – the more inspired use of their latent talents, and then old age, acceptance of their past follies and mistakes, and, at last, a peaceful transition into eternal **Light.**

Why quarrel? Why fight? People wholly controlled by ego let fly and hammer away for their 'rights'. Spiritually mature people solve problems by discussing them empathetically.

What does this mean in human terms? It means – listening to the other person with the spoken or silent acknowledgement that the way the other person **felt/feels** in a certain situation is as valid and worthy of respect as were/are your feelings.

When overtaken by a serious confrontation in which neither of you are prepared to yield an iota of ground, go away on your own and take time to realise that what you are engaged in is a 'battle of consciousness'. The battle is not enjoined only as a result of what was actually done and said in a moment of extreme heat – what really took place was the upshot of what you both are – in consciousness.

This involves your backgrounds. The conflict springs from the personality itself, the type of ego drive a person possesses, the basic perceptions of right and wrong, the normal attitudes each have towards other people and life generally. Therefore, when you have conflict or confrontation, tell your opponent you are taking time off to stand still and quieten your mind to be able to listen more helpfully.

Then – be very wise. Call on **Divine Consciousness** for an intervention of **Loving Consciousness** into the situation.

Try to realise – and visualise – that both of you stand in the **Light** of **Divine Consciousness,** equal in soul origins, equal in destiny – equally real, equally human, equally unique.

Until you can fully immerse yourself in this realisation – this state of mind – you are not yet ready to stand in the **Divine Light** to lovingly sort out your conflict and hurt feelings.

Return to your opponent and suggest you should meet and each have five or ten full minutes in which to clearly, quietly, explain your point of view, your perception of what was actually said – what the fight is really about, how feelings were hurt, how the matter should be resolved.

Choose to let the other speak first and again surrender the situation to **Divine Consciousness.**

If there is a great deal of bitter accusation taking place, try to subdue your own ego and remain **absolutely silent** and calm. This will be a great help to the other speaker, since he will feel he is being heard. It will obviate the feeling of frustration. Rationally, realise you are helping your opponent but do not puff yourself up for being superior!

Try your best to see how much of what is being said is true about yourself – whatever it may be, if valid, bite your tongue and accept it. Be glad and rejoice – because in that moment you have had a moment of insight into your own human consciousness, giving you an opportunity to get rid a facet of ego drive. Every time, you are able to rid yourself of a little ego drive, you allow your soul more 'breathing space' and room for more active control of your personality. You also rise in consciousness frequencies of vibration and feel a degree lighter within yourself.

By these means you grow psychologically – and spiritually.

Listen to the feelings of the other person. Try to restrain your own and empathise with your sparring partner's emotions. Feel 'his' hurt, 'his' indignation, 'his' anxieties. **Put aside your own – and feel his.** ('His' represents both genders for brevity.)

Ask yourself – If someone had said or done to you what you have said or done to the other, how would you feel? If you can set aside your ego sufficiently to be able to consider this, then you are on the way to overcoming the kind of ego drive which puts 'self' above every other consideration and is unable to see any other point of view.

Before speaking, calmly wait in silence until your sparring partner's ten minutes are fully up – even if it means he finishes before time and both of you remain in silence for a while.

Acknowledge as pleasantly as you are able, that you have heard what he has said and you can understand why he is upset. In that instant of

self-control, realise that you have gained a modicum of control over yourself and you have taken the first step to healing the situation.

On the other hand – if you have not truly understood what he has told you then you are mentally blocking something he is saying which you do not want to hear or receive. Therefore, again, your ego is in control. Control it and invite him to explain further – and again do your best to put yourself in his place. Feel his pain. Understand his anger.

When you have received the other person into your understanding and acknowledged it, his ego defences will begin to lessen, you will see him begin to relax. Both of you will feel better.

Having done this, quietly, slowly, carefully – you then give an equally clear picture of the way that you felt in the circumstances. Do not use words calculated to set your opponent down and thus upset him. Remember that: you are making an effort to control your ego as a prelude to unconditional love.

You are working to achieve peace and understanding between you – not points.

Your reply should not lead to further conflict because you have used words likely to further upset him.

If it does – then your ego has won the round **against you**. Your psyche has lost.

If you are both living in the spiritual frequencies of consciousness, it will follow that your opponent will accord you the same response of listening, thinking and acknowledging your position, as you gave him, but if he lives entirely in the earthly consciousness frequencies, you may encounter difficulties. He may feel you are trying to score points by being 'holy', 'superior' or 'bigger' in some way. Calm him down; tell him it is painful to have conflict between you. You are only trying out a method to ensure both of you get a fair hearing from the other, and reach a truly mutual forgiving reconciliation instead of a superficial one when hurt feelings are left to fester in the mind and heart and body.

You should each give the other the right to disagree in gentle words – giving valid reasons for the disagreement. Find the fortitude within yourself to recognise that you, as a human being, cannot possibly be always right since you, like everyone else, has been born with a controlling ego-drive which forces you to take up and strongly defend the position of 'top-dog'. Remember that whilst you believe yourself to be 'top-dog', he too believes the same thing. Humanly, he believes himself to be at least on an equal level with yourself if not superior. Whatever his ego causes him to think about himself and his point of view is exactly the same as your ego causes you to think about your opinions and ideas.

When you can bring **Divine Consciousness into the arena of your human consciousness,** you have literally received – with compassionate acceptance and love – the human reality of each of you into yourselves, have dissolved the negativity between you and raised the frequencies of your consciousness vibrations, leaving you feeling lighter and more vibrant. Since this leaves you in perfect peace, no longer in conflict, this is extremely important to your well-being.

If, however, you should refuse to listen and empathise and accept with loving forgiveness, the 'truth' of another person, the rejection creates an emotional 'magnetic rejection' energy which joins and re-inforces other residues of rejection energy force within the consciousness electromagnetic fields of your entire system. 'Rejection magnetism' depletes the 'bonding magnetism' between cells and ill health sets in.

This **fact of existence** is the ground of all psychosomatic medicine. People who constantly blame and judge others and keep a wholly closed mind in regard to their own part in conflict, eventually experience some kind of radical breakdown in their physical or emotional make-up. If they can monitor and work on this tendency to exercise control, judge others and exonerate themselves from blame, and can eventually give their 'soul' full mastery in their personality, the breakdown of whatever kind it is, will ultimately disappear completely.

If, during conflict with another, you give time, space and understanding but only encounter stubborn resistance in the form of a continual statement of personal aggrieved feeling, then you are dealing with ego blindness and the only thing to do is to laugh, concede defeat, and walk away.

Providing you walk away with forgiveness and understanding of their controlling ego, you may have conceded defeat but you gained a victory over self and refrained from introducing negative vibrations into your consciousness field.

The very worst thing you can do to promote discord is to tell a person 'they shouldn't feel a certain way' or 'they do not mean what they are saying'. These two sayings are a gross violation of the dignity and respect due to the other and you have rejected the 'human reality' of the other person.

You may question a person: 'Do you really mean what you are saying?' If the answer is 'yes' then it must be accepted and the discussion should continue from that point.

Never ignore what another person is trying to tell you because you do not want to face up to what is being said. This is cowardice and gives points to your ego. Be brave and listen – with both ears open to receive the truth behind the words.

You must accept the 'reality' of a person – whether you agree with it or not, even if a facet causes you shock or displeasure. Remember, you do not know the full circumstances   out of which that human consciousness has grown into its present form. If you judge, criticise, condemn in any way, you have erected a barrier between yourself and that person which will not be removed, no matter how much you may wish to overlook everything negative in him and become friends in the future. Unknowingly, what you reject in him will remain in your consciousness as a foundation for future discords which will build up and eventually outweigh the affection.

Unwittingly, you will say things in the future reflecting your underlying secret mistrust or displeasure. Instead of accepting his weaknesses with love and helping him deal with and overcome them, you will put him on his guard against you and he will never fully trust you. Your ego and his ego will have had a secret battle which neither of you will be aware of consciously.

Love could turn to hate. Remember – your life is a STATE OF CONSCIOUSNESS in which thoughts and feelings are deposited as in a safety box. Let acceptance and caring be the steel of which the box is made. When you have an encounter with someone to whom you are drawn, if only in friendship, and you discover that there are elements in his past which are contrary to your principles – you have the option:

to remain in contact with him, fully accepting his past, and possibly in future situations pointing out the characteristic logically and lovingly, helping him grow, or if this is impossible, promptly removing yourself from the situation until you can see his problems from the perspective of loving acceptance inspired by **Divine Consciousness** and you find him receptive to your principles.

You must never accuse a person of acting out of an ego-impulse. All human beings are ego driven to a greater or lesser extent. Never take a stance which will humiliate another!

When I was on earth, I urged people to forgive and to abstain from judgment, criticism, condemnation.

The church has misinterpreted this as meaning you must 'please' God by loving others and abstaining from the negative emotions.

This is not what I meant at all. There is no 'God' who needs to be 'pleased' by your behaviour.

You are masters of your fate in that you always 'reap what you sow'. All of the foregoing pages have been directed at giving you details of how to avoid sowing weeds in your vegetable patch, **how to remain healthy, happy, prosperous.**

A time will come in your spiritual development when you will awaken to the enormous gift you have in your head – the gift of creative, intelligent thinking, and you will also become aware of the enormous responsibility you bear towards the way you use it.

There are wonderful people in your world who have used their minds in such a way as to gain insight and growth from the daily challenges in their lives. Step by step, by probing, analyzing, moving on to new viewpoints, higher understanding, they fashion new ideals for themselves.

They adopt these ideals as guidelines for their future behaviour. By these means they are able to purify their thinking, words, actions, in order to re-define their mode of conduct in the world and of attending to relationships.

These are 'self-made' people – but rarely do you find that they have not also drawn strength, insight, inspiration, emotional stability from the higher source – **Divine Consciousness** or their perception of what they may call 'God'.

When on earth, I told the people a story – the parable of the 'Ten Talents'. I said that a Lord of much wealth was going abroad for a while and he left each of his three servants a sum of money.

To one, he gave ten talents, to another – five – and the last one he gave one talent. When he returned, he asked each servant what use they had made of the money.

One said he had doubled the master's investment, and the other said he had gained half again, and the last man said he had sat on it, fearing to lose what he had been given.

The master complimented the first two servants on their efficiency and ingenuity, but he was angry with the servant who had not attempted to make anything at all of the one talent left in his care.

Each one of you in the world have your own amount of 'talent' with which to work. If, on your own initiative, you find it hard to discover the best way to make a profit out of your personal talent and resources – draw on **Divine Consciousness** through meditation, and little by little, the ideas will surely come, and these will be exactly suited to your own personality.

At the same time – consider how you have used your talents throughout your life time. Have you been engrossed entirely in creating happiness and pleasures for yourself – or have you devoted time also to the upliftment or improvement of the life of others?

It is a terrible thing to have been given talents above the average and to end your lives having squandered them in self-indulgent modes of living. Whatever lessons you have failed to learn, whatever growth you have evaded, whatever development in spirituality you have deliberately avoided – are mountains you have created for yourself to climb in your next lives. They will obstruct your path and will have to be dealt with – spiritually – or again repeated in a further life.

It is not necessary to make a great way in the world, achieve advancement or wealth or fame.

You can use your talents as a parent, seeking the best means of becoming successful in your job of promoting your children's well-being. What higher calling is there than to be a 'good loving parent', more especially if you take as your role model the **Divine Father-Mother Consciousness** which is entirely directed at growth, nutrition of mind and body, healing of mind and body, regeneration of mind and body, protection in every form and the fulfilment of **every** need of mind, emotions, body – within a system of Law and Order and Unconditional Love. As a parent – have you measured up to the **Consciousness** of your **Divine Source of Being?**

Some of the people who have made best use of their talents have been servants – those who have looked after other people's children with devotion and love, cleaning the house with conscientious attention to detail, creating a peaceful calm and caring environment for the employer with love and gentleness. These are the great souls, the ones who have made paths for themselves leading directly into the Kingdom of Heaven.

Alternatively, there are people who have used their talents for the purposes of the destruction of others to feed their vanity and the cold emptiness within their own hearts. Ultimately, their use of their minds has led to their own destruction. Think of the people in history and in the present time, who have brainwashed others into rebellion. They have become dictators. Then think about the likely end of such dictators. Such people have abused the privileges bestowed by 'mind power' and they eventually pay the price, but not before they have ruined thousands of lives for no good reason, for there could never be a 'good' reason for turning countries into war-torn wildernesses and ruining a prosperous economy.

Think of families where emotional and mental abuse is rife. This is an abhorrent use of 'mental power'. It rebounds to the abuser in many, many ways – ill-health, sickness, addictions, depression and loss of self-esteem.

However, do not use your brains, intellect, insight, knowledge, education as a platform from which to criticise, judge or condemn others who do not measure up to your own standards of efficiency or goodness in any area of your life.

At the same time – since to criticise, judge and condemn is as natural as breathing to the human ego, **do not attempt to deny your perceptions of what might be improved.** To do so is to deny the reality of the evolutionary process. The purpose behind existence is to experience – and improve upon your experiences. Therefore, do not judge or condemn or reject the deficiencies you observe in others but take your perceptions immediately to **Divine Consciousness and continually ask for a Divine Resolution of the problem.** Hold fast to the realisation that wherever, whenever, **Divine Consciousness** is drawn into a problem the end result is always growth and development for all concerned.

Try to bear in mind always, you are on earth to bring Divine Consciousness down into your daily life, relationships and circumstances. You are there to use your minds for this special purpose.

When I said I have come to help you find _**'LIFE more Abundant'**_, I meant that I have come to help you work through your magnetic-emotional bondage and to find and make true contact with **_DIVINE LIFE_** – the **Source of your being.** Out of this contact comes increased **_LIFE_** which far transcends the 'physical life' you draw from your food alone. Out of this contact comes spiritual direction, protection, and a **Divinely Inspired Path.**

You could call this 'The Path of Christ Consciousness'.

When you have perceived some deeper truth previously hidden from your consciousness, you must accept and rejoice that **Divine Consciousness** has penetrated your human consciousness and spoken within your mind. Give sincere thanks and treasure this gift and reverence it. Never take it for granted, otherwise you will block further entrance of **LOVING INTELLIGENCE.**

You will wonder why you feel so alone again.

People speak of being transformed by the 'inner Spirit'.

The terminology of 'inner Spirit' is not wrong. I have gone to great lengths to try to rid your minds of old terminology which may have an inaccurate meaning for you. At the same time, I want you to understand that once you have grasped what I really **mean,** (for I have been so grossly misinterpreted in the past that I do not want this to happen again), you must not be bound down by the terminology itself. So long as you **know** what the 'inner Spirit' really is – _**'DIVINE-LIFE CONSCIOUSNESS' operating out of INFINITE UNIVERSAL CONSCIOUSNESS**_ and has nothing to do with the 'spirits of the departed', you may use the terminology which has most meaning for you, provided it is the meaning given you in these **Letters.**

To return to my original statement at the beginning of this new section.

It is frequently said that people can be 'transformed by the power of the Spirit'.

Such a transformation is not possible. There is nothing 'real' in your human self which can be transformed. Your soul has been drawn from **'DIVINE-LIFE CONSCIOUSNESS'** and is therefore perfect. Your human 'personality' is ephemeral and composed only of magnetic emotional 'bonding-rejection' impulses. Consequently, **Divine Life must gradually impregnate more and more of your consciousness to impel you to strip away these gross impulses in order to reveal the spiritual Reality. Perhaps I can best explain this to you by using a parable.**

A girl of great beauty was kept hidden within heavy grey veiling and an ugly face was painted on it. Thus, the truth of her being was kept secret and few ventured near her because of her unattractive appearance. She grew up and realised that the cause of her loneliness and misery, loss of freedom of movement and health, were due to the veils. But she was so accustomed to them that she felt she would not survive without them. However, she was fortunate enough to meet an 'enlightened mentor' from another country, and was ultimately persuaded to discard just one veil. After much searching for the inner strength to do so, she begged her 'mentor' to help her. He lifted her hands and together they discarded the veil on which the ugly face had been painted and she felt much better for having rid herself of it. She began to feel a sense of joy. After a while, she was eager to rid herself of another veil and again her 'mentor' came to her and helped remove it. And so it continued. The more she shed, the lighter she grew, and she gradually glimpsed the reality of nature around her, she could see the trees clearly, the birds on the boughs and listened enthralled to their beautiful songs, she saw the beauty in other people's faces, and began to feel the flow of love in her heart. Life was now becoming a truly Divine gift to be treasured. Daily she gave thanks to her 'mentor' for helping her become such a happy person.

Finally, the time came when she could no longer bear the final veil around her. She knew it was shutting her off from even greater light, beauty, harmony and loving contact with other beautiful people. Although she did not know how she would manage without it, she retired into the silence with her mentor and pleaded to have this last veil removed.

This was a time of agony since the veil appeared to be a part of her being. But she begged and pleaded and in a moment of brilliant **Light**, the veil was burnt off her. The form that was left was her *Reality* – **and she came into perfect inner freedom!**

However, her individualised **Reality** now had to find a way to function in the environment; this was unexpectedly difficult.

Because her perceptions of Reality surrounding and within herself were now so clear and transcendent, the ground of her communication with other people had radically changed. She was no longer at peace in the social and business environment, nor could she remain a member of her community.

People looked at her and said, 'Oh, this is who you are, and you have no veil, how dreadful. We find you very odd – even a little mad.' They turned their backs on her.

What do you think she did? Did she long to go back to the time when she was veiled as heavily as others? No, she had found such peace, joy and fulfilment of need, she left her community and went into a retreat and joined other souls who would recognise her true identity and respond to it with love and joy. Tell me, was her veiling, her personality, transformed? No, **with the help of her 'mentor',** she removed her own veiling when she was convinced by her 'mentor' (*DIVINE-LIFE CONSCIOUSNESS*) it was the right thing to do. As she removed the different layers of veiling, she came closer and closer to intimate knowledge of the *Reality-Soul* hidden by her veiling (the personality).

You can probably understand now that the human 'personality' is like a mental-emotional cobweb, sometimes a dirty veiling of mass inter-actions between magnetic 'attraction/bonding' and magnetic 'repulsion/revulsion'. Spiritually evolved people can see this dirty 'veiling' clouding the skin of people whose language is coarse and their thoughts solely centred around earthy ego activities.

Alternatively, as an individual leaves behind levels of earthy thoughts and responses, the skin begins to clear and a light shines in the eyes. Whilst the 'earth personality' is imperceptibly dying away, the body becomes more 'spiritualised'. This is clearly visible to people who have the gift of spiritual perception.

Do not be afraid of future withdrawal from the earthly mindset. You will relinquish it, little by little, with infinite relief. Your true goal in life will become ever more clear and your determination to reach it will grow ever more strong.

You may argue that you are not often mentally or emotionally engaged in magnetic emotional thoughts and feelings. But when you examine your spontaneous thoughts, you will find that you are completely dominated by magnetic 'attraction-bonding' and magnetic 'repulsion-revulsion' thoughts all day long! Your mind keeps up a ceaseless chatter of comments and judgements, criticisms, wants, don't wants, reactionary feelings verging on resentment or rejection, longing for certain things and fears that the longings will not be fulfilled, striving for success and irritation or anger with those who stand in the way of that success.

When the ego is in control, the one who prays does so with faith and yearning. Immediately, after prayer, on meeting someone, the trauma just taken to 'God' to be dealt with in the right way, is sorrowfully aired to gain the comfort of human sympathy, but – the consciousness form and force released during prayer, the 'asking, the faith and the yearning', are now cancelled by the self-pity.

The mind is usually a bog, a quagmire, of conflicting ideas. During stress, a person may strive to focus on a life-giving affirmation or perception but, like a playful puppy tossing a paper bag filled with air, the thought is soon swept out of mind and the stressful thinking the person was trying to avoid has once again taken hold. And so it goes on in the mind, back and forth, until the person longs to escape the conflict.

Your internal dialogue will probably go along lines similar to: "I don't want to get up. I don't want to get breakfast. I don't want to make sandwiches, I don't want to go to work, I don't want to meet so-and-so today, I don't want to do the laundry, I don't want to do this, that and the other.'

And so the litany of 'rejection of life' continues with thoroughly disgruntled people all day long.

However – instead of mentally complaining, the dialogue may be along the lines of 'I don't FEEL like ...' All these feelings come from ego-drives which rejects such activities since they are perceived to be a bore, uncomfortable or a burden.

Alternatively, you may wake up and say or feel 'It's Saturday, I must hurry and dress and get to the market, there are things I want to buy. I must get some of those strawberries before they are sold out. I must get down to the sales to find some bargains. I'm going to speak nicely to my husband to give me some money. I do hope I see Patrick when I go to his office. I want that new Boss to like me, so I'll work extra hard and I'll look attractive for him. I hope my husband buys the new car. I'm certain I'll find a parking space if I remain positive. I hope I get a bonus.'

All these foregoing ideas come from the ego-bonding impulses. 'I want'. You may also string together several 'bonding' and rejection' feelings:

'I hope my children go to sleep early so that I can relax. I hate it when they call for water and want me to read to them when I'm so tired, but I ought to be a good mother and spend a little time with them.' 'I hope' 'that I can' 'I ought' 'good mother' 'spend time' are all connected by the magnetic attraction-bonding.

These are the things you 'want' for yourself. These thoughts also arise from fears – fears of being asked to do more than you feel you can do at this moment. Fears of failure as a mother. Fear is a direct impulse experienced from the ego which demands that you measure up in order to be acceptable to yourself and other people and yet is very much aware that you do not!

With the development of civilisation, the magnetic bonding-rejection impulses have become so complicated and interwoven that they are difficult to differentiate and discern. 'I hate it' 'call for water' 'want me to read' 'I'm so tired' are all magnetic rejection-revulsion feelings and since it requires more energy to reject and push away than to accept and bond with, the conflict within you will end up by making you feel even more dispirited and tired, even feeling guilty, but unable to find the strength to do what you would really, deep down, like to do: 'spend more time with your children, read to them and mother them.' This would give you a sense of satisfaction and well-being, because, at an even deeper

Letter 8 level you know you would be experiencing and expressing love – whereas all the 'wants' and 'don't wants' are a coating hiding the feeling of love. When you are in tune with your deepest recesses of being and are experiencing and expressing 'love' – you are truly at peace and happy.

At the same time, notice that in this interior monologue which goes on all the time in caring mothers, the little interjection of: 'I ought to spend a little time with them' is an insight drawn directly from **DIVINE-LIFE-CONSCIOUSNESS** but you will probably believe it is your conscience telling you what you ought to do.

Perhaps you are beginning to see that your mind and emotions are like a war arena with conflicting ideas following each other so rapidly that you are completely unaware of what you are doing to yourself. Your mind is a see-saw. Your beliefs, opinions, reactions, change according to any changes you find in relationships and environment – a see-saw of likes and dislikes, resentment and friendship, possessiveness and rejection. All of this hub-bub arises out of superficial understanding of all that is really taking place in your environment at a subterranean level. You are like boats sailing the seas. You can see the sky, but you have no inkling at all of the growth, movement and life activity taking place under your keel.

This means that you may think you are relating to someone in a real way but underneath the surface and behind their pleasant exterior, your friend may feel lonely in your presence and aching to be understood and spoken to on a level more sensitive and empathetic, more suited to their needs as well as yours.

Take for instance, the following example. On the face of it, it appears to be completely harmless both to yourself and other people, but an analysis will show you it is anything but innocuous.

'I hope that bad-tempered woman is away from work today.'

First, to be able to make such a statement, **in your hidden consciousness**, you have reviewed her behaviour and condemned her for the problems she causes by her bad temper. You have hung a label around her neck – 'bad tempered woman'. You have created a consciousness energy force with her name on it. It won't do her any good. You 'want' magnetically (not spiritually) that she should be **absent from work** to make life more pleasant for you. In the above statement you reveal you are in the grip of 'ego' completely, since you did not pause to wonder whether she was subject to any problem of 'character personality', any hidden sickness, misery, financial problem, causing her to be short-tempered. The hope she will be absent is in the nature of a 'curse on her'. If your thinking was sufficiently passionate and powerful, she will probably pick up the

290

negative consciousness energy force and suddenly feel too unwell to go to work!

The same principle is involved in the development of emotional tension into nervous breakdowns.

At the onset of emotional tension, the mind and emotions begin to race with magnetic-emotional 'rejection-repulsion-revulsion' feelings. A person engages in continual thoughts such as: 'I can't cope' which is a rejection and outright denial of any existing energy that the person does have to deal with the crisis. 'I can't bear it' also denies personal strength. 'I hate this happening to me' 'I hate the person doing this to me.' 'I hate having to change my life-style' 'I hate, I deny, I refuse, I object, I oppose, I don't deserve'. A particularly virulent consciousness form (thoughts) 'I'll get my own back' is a mixture of magnetic-bonding-rejection. In reality, the 'consciousness' of such a sentence is:

'I hate him and what he has done so much that I will teach him a lesson. I will do to him exactly what he has done to me. I'll make him pay!'

This is pure revenge. Revenge is a boomerang which magnetically returns, bestowing suffering of some kind on the thinker. If he is on the Path to Christ Consciousness, it will also teach the sender a much needed lesson. All these foregoing thoughts and feelings including the killer resentment bring on nervous – even physical – breakdowns.

There may be some people reading these Letters who will remember my confrontation with the fig tree near Bethany. I was hungry and foolishly looked for figs when they were out of season.

When I found none, I said to the tree 'may no one ever eat of your fruit again.' And the tree withered to its roots and was dead by the following day, much to the astonishment of Peter.

This was a time when I, as Jesus, was thoroughly irresponsible in the use of my 'mind power' and caused damage for which I was contrite. (I explained the true reasons for this incident fully in Letter 3.) However, when speaking to my disciples, I also used it as an example and warning of the power exercised by mind over living things.

Let it be said, also, that on that day, I whipped and drove the money lenders out of the temple, and harshly denigrated the scribes and Pharisees to their faces. All these activities were magnetic-emotional bonding-rejection impulses. **Deliberately, I set the seal on my soon-to-be death by crucifixion**. I knew exactly what I was doing for my time on earth was drawing to a close and to tell the truth, I was eager to leave your world.

When people first come on to the spiritual path and seek a 'Higher Power', many are taught by 'self-help' teachers to engage in magnetic-emotional bonding thoughts to a greater degree, although such teachers have no idea that their instructions are serving to strengthen the power of the ego.

The spiritual aspirant is taught: 'If you meditate, 'God' or the 'Power of my Sub-conscious' will help me get all my needs', 'I'm going to visualise the house I want and I know I'll get it', 'I'm going to buy the clothes I need and have faith that I'll somehow find the instalments'. They concentrate on 'having faith' and on getting what they need or want.

At the beginning of their change in consciousness and the exercise of their faith, they do indeed feel great benefits. The desired objects do come into their lives, they find doors opening, they achieve success. This phenomena reveals that the material planes of their consciousness are becoming more spiritualised and as a result there are improvements in them. Life is less hard.

But your lives are meant to express every level of your consciousness – mind, emotions, body.

When you have mastered the physical realms of consciousness, your next adventure into spirituality is in the realm of your emotions. Therefore, suddenly, in the midst of your plenty, the winds blow and the rains fall upon your previously stable emotional consciousness, creating manifold miseries of every kind. These can be in the nature of loss of family, health or possessions, sudden setbacks of numerous kinds in numerous areas of your life. It is at these times that so many lose their previous faith. 'Positive Thinking doesn't work!' they affirm.

No, positive thinking on its own does not work; neither does the 'power of your sub-conscious' since it is only a facet of your entire spiritual/human being. When your emotions are in upheaval, you are being called to examine your entire consciousness, your beliefs, your feelings towards yourself and others, your faith in a spiritual dimension – even the meaning of death and your life afterwards in a higher dimension. This is an extremely painful time in the lives of people. All are subject to this time of upheaval in one form or another.

It can be a time of tremendous inner growth and a movement into happiness or an ongoing time of bitterness and resentment. This is the time to wake up fully and realise that the outcome of the experiences are entirely up to you – not fate or destiny – but you – either working on your own or devotedly and consistently with Divine Consciousness arriving eventually at the height of felicity.

It is at this time also, that a person is challenged to use the mind constructively, reaching for the highest insights and ideals with which to master the emotions.

The difference between re-active thought – arising from impulsive ego responses to uncomfortable situations – and creative, intelligent, thoughtful thought, will become clear.

When this takes place – and the insight is put into daily practice – self-mastery is close at hand.

Only the teachers who can lead you through all the levels of self-realisation, remorse, awakening, changing mental/emotional patterns, moving ever upward into higher spiritual frequencies of vibrations until reaching true **'God-realisation'** – are the **Teachers of Truth** – who can truly lead you into the Kingdom of Heaven.

If the first level of development, seeking material satisfactions through positive thinking were wholly satisfactory to seekers and brought them all they hoped for, the whole world would, by now, have been converted to the belief in 'positive thinking'.

However, this is the starting point of the previously quiescent soul's spiritual journey and is not to be rejected or criticised. The psyche wakes up to the fact that beyond the earthly dimension there is some spiritual dimension called 'God', a 'person sitting up there' or a 'universal power' which answers prayers. Remember we are talking about 'consciousness'. The psyche is becoming aware that there is more to life than the daily grind and wants to experience 'whatever it is' because deprivation in some area of existence – health, financial means, happiness, love, etc. is causing 'it' to seek help.

Here, we have the same magnetic-emotional bonding at work. 'I want'. However as the awakening psyche becomes an observer of what is going on in mind and emotions, through its filtered contact with **'LIFE CONSCIOUSNESS'**, it will begin to 'see' some of the magnetic-emotional 'bonding-rejection' activities it is engaging in. Eventually, it will be sufficiently enlightened to turn from the 'possessive- repulsion' feelings and will pray for help to overcome them. It is usually at this time that the right **Teacher** for that soul will come into his life. If the soul has travelled the road of life several times, then it will be some **Teacher** who has evolved sufficiently to lead the seeking soul out of the chains and bondage of the ego-drive and forward into *Light.*

Remember, in your approach to others, be careful of their 'egos'. It is their sole means of internal survival until they have gained a real and lasting glimpse of **Divine Consciousness** and they also perceive that they have within – and transcendent to themselves – a source of strength, power and inspiration.

You must also realise that in becoming individualised into bodily form and mental-emotional activity, you are subject to the laws of existence. You have been given individuality and identity and infinite potential of achieving **Christ Consciousness** and there is a price to pay for these.

For, perhaps, many lifetimes, (until you are educated into this rare knowledge of 'self'), you will experience the vagaries and multitudinous complexities of life and relationships. In many lives in the past, you may have done outrageous things considered by others to be 'sin personified' but these magnetic personality experiences will have contributed to bringing you where you are today in spiritual perception. Therefore, you should be able to accept that there is no 'sin' against a 'God' and there is no 'sin' against others. The 'ego' can only have total control and do reprehensible things because the 'soul' is still asleep within the heavy cobweb bondage of the magnetic personality. Where this is the case, there is no possibility of persuading such a person he has done wrong against others. There is no interior illumination from *Light* to show him a better way to live. *IT* is entirely blocked by the ego magnetic consciousness. However, the pain such a person experiences (since everything he does to others will return with full measure and more), will ultimately make him question existence, and asking questions is the means by which to receive answers from **'DIVINE-LIFE'**.

I began this section by saying that people believe they can be transformed by 'Spirit'.

Now, you understand why I said 'there is nothing to be transformed' There is nothing 'real' or 'eternal' in the personality. There is a great need to strip it away **to reveal the Divine within.**

In Palestine, I called this process a 'dying to self' which has proved to be a frightening statement. Because of it, many people have been deterred from stepping on to the path leading to the highest spiritual dimensions. And yes, that last step in the stripping process is indeed like a death. A person loses an essential part of his human/earthly self whilst undergoing it, but the relief and the inner peace experienced when the struggle is finally over, cannot be described. Joy fills the heart. There is true security, rest and tranquillity in the silence of the mind. At last, the struggle for personal control is over. The person becomes a 'master'. There follows a time of spiritual rest and recuperation.

This is later followed by a stepping into a new dimension of 'being'. Nothing in the human scene, 'matters' as it did before.

People criticise you? Previously, the magnetic personality would have made you feel angry because of your insecurity, your driving need to appear perfect to everyone, in order to gain approval. If you do not have approval, the ego argued, how will you survive? What will your life be like?

When the voice of the 'ego' has died away, there is no need to seek security for you are SECURE! You know that you are sustained, maintained, nourished, protected, healed by **'DIVINE-LIFE CONSCIOUSNESS'** no matter what others may think of you. Your joy, gladness, happiness, personal fulfilment and contentment are all inside you. In fact, you no longer need otherness at all.

Except, you are a part of all 'otherness', and when the ***Light*** fills you, you have a driving need to render to others all that **'DIVINE-LIFE CONSCIOUSNESS'** is pouring into you every moment of the day as you keep in constant touch with this beautiful dimension within you.

No longer do you reject the personality of others, everyone is acceptable to you, everyone is in need of love and now you have plenty of that to give. No longer is it a struggle to 'love unconditionally'. It comes spontaneously.

Whatever faults you may have left, whatever mistakes you make in your attitudes to others, as a result of remnants of the 'ego' left behind, these are revealed to you but you do not shy away from self-knowledge but rather embrace it with love and thanksgiving. You discover that recognition and acceptance of the negative human reactions in yourself is both wholesome and healing. You happily accept and take responsibility for whatever mistakes you make and then when you have discerned the 'loving way', you let it go. You will experience inner peace, knowing that you have learnt something else valuable which will stand you in good stead when next you are challenged by earthly experiences. The time for deep remorse is over, since it has now done its work of releasing you from magnetic emotional responses to life which brought you suffering in the past.

You have now entered what I termed 'Kingdom of Heaven' when I was on earth. You will find that all your needs are supplied and you will KNOW that any needs in the future will also be met almost spontaneously. This knowledge keeps you in constant touch with *'DIVINE-LIFE'* and gives you an immense sense of security. With the peace of mind and tranquillity come joy and happiness, and a new sense of youthful well-being. Minor, or chronic or even terminal ailments will be cleared up and you will again enter into a new phase of existence. Each time you learn a lesson, you leave something of the human dimension behind you and move forward into a higher frequency of spiritual consciousness.

I am describing for you the rewards which await you when you have struggled and dealt with the magnetic emotional bondage of 'attraction/bonding-rejection/repulsion'. It is these which initially give you individuality but which become fetters of the soul and from which you must break free in order to get off the treadmill. This treadmill is the span of your present human life, continually turning, continually bearing you into experiences you do not enjoy. When, at last, you are able to transcend, in spirit, your magnetic emotional reactions to life, the treadmill will begin to slow down and then, suddenly, you will find that you are almost stationary and you will begin to experience the beautiful quality of life I have described above. Would that I could remove this burden imposed on you by your earthly humanhood. I know your suffering, your times of despair, your grief in the lonely night, your hours of mental and emotional turmoil. As I descend into your consciousness frequencies to transmit my messages and to understand what needs to be said to you, I become aware of your earthly conditions and these words are my response to your most urgent needs for relief and healing.

Do not doubt these words are from me. Take comfort from them and KNOW that as you study these words they will, in time, bring you deep illumination within your soul which will bring about the longed-for changes in your life and self.

HOW TO MEDITATE

When you meditate, take up the position which is most comfortable for you. You do not have to go into physical contortions. Rest and relax. Tell yourself to relax and release all your limbs, including your head, neck, face, into a state of utter limpness.

I must impress on you that meditation should be – eventually – as simple as slipping into slumber. The purpose of meditation is to enable your entire consciousness to move beyond the boundaries of intellect and reason. There are teachers who will tell you to 'imagine' ... whatever you are told to imagine, you can rest assured you are not being assisted to go anywhere except into new imaginative realms of your own thought processes.

What this method of 'meditating' will achieve for you will be a relief from the thoughts and stress that your ego pressures are creating for you. In the world of imagination, the ego may – or may not – be dormant.

Before commencing meditation, prepare by fully realising you are about to make contact with *'DIVINE CONSCIOUSNESS'* both within and transcendent to your consciousness – therefore *IT* is also out there and around you. Visualise exactly what this means.

Remember, at all times, that what you THINK about is what you are tuning into.

Your thoughts are 'searchlights' making contact with what you seek.

Remember that every 'thought' has its own frequency of vibrations in consciousness. Believe, know this, for this is true. The more spiritual the thought, the higher the frequencies of vibration.

'Consciousness forms' embodied by words are not visible but are 'specific entities of being'.

They have the life of consciousness within them. They are magnetised to like 'consciousness forms'. Like is drawn to like.

Think 'dog' and visualise what you mean, and your thoughts are attuned to the dog species.

Think 'UNIVERSAL CONSCIOUSNESS' or 'DIVINE LIFE' with understanding of what you mean – and your thoughts will be directed into 'UNIVERSAL CONSCIOUSNESS' – DIVINE LIFE.

If you have fully understood all that I am trying to tell you, you will KNOW that your meditation reaches its target.

Know this and you will find your faith strengthening.

Your faith remains weak because you only hope, or wish, or magnetically 'want to' tune into **LIFE- CONSCIOUSNESS,** because you hope you will derive some benefit from the exercise.

Do you not see how 'earthy' is such an approach to THAT WHICH GAVE YOU 'BEING'?

Is it reverent? Does it befit a person who is seeking true contact, and expects to do so?

Whilst *__INFINITE UNIVERSAL CONSCIOUSNESS__* is not the mythical 'God' on high as depicted in the Old Testament,

It is the *Infinitely Powerful Reality* everywhere present, manifesting Its own designing, intelligent, evolutionary, loving caring for all that It has brought into being.

This is what you must realise you will eventually approach, whilst you are still on earth, when you reach the highest dimensions, after your magnetic-emotions have been dissolved not only from your mind, but also your sub-conscious, and solar plexus.

First of all, you will be getting in touch with **FATHER-MOTHER-DIVINE LIFE** which is ever active within your entire system and the universe.

Remember **It** is in equilibrium within the **infinite universal dimension,** and active within the world.

'**Father-activity**' sets the goals. '**Mother-love**' directs the way the plans will be developed to promote the highest good of that which is being adapted, or healed, or protected. (Countless people will say that these statements above are all imagination. They can scoff as they will. Those who manage to make contact with '*Father-Mother-Life-Consciousness*' another name for **DIVINE-LIFE CONSCIOUSNESS** but denoting its double qualities – will verify that the foregoing is an accurate description of spiritual evolution which follows such contact.) To return to your meditation.

First of all, before attempting to enter your meditative state, memorise the following prayer so that the words become your own. When you have become perfectly relaxed, start your meditation with this prayer. Say it slowly and visualise the meaning of each word to enable you to enter into the consciousness of the word and enable the energy consciousness of the word to enter into your deepest self. As you say this prayer, your eyes should be closed and your gaze lifted towards your forehead.

FATHER-MOTHER-LIFE, you are my life, my constant support, my health, my protection, my perfect fulfilment of every need and my highest inspiration.

I ask you to reveal the true Reality of Yourself to me. I know it is your WILL that I shall be fully illumined that I may better receive awareness of Your Presence within and around me. I believe and know that this is possible. I believe that you protect and maintain me within perfect LOVE. I know that my eventual purpose is to EXPRESS YOU.

As I speak to you, I know that you are perfectly receptive of me, for you are UNIVERSAL LOVING INTELLIGENCE which has so marvellously designed this world and brought it into visible form.

I know, that as I ask YOU to speak to me, I am sending out a consciousness searchlight into your Divine Consciousness and as I listen, YOU will be penetrating my human consciousness and coming ever closer to my increasingly receptive mind and heart.

I commit myself and my life into your care.'

(Each time you say and visualise this prayer, you create a **spiritual consciousness form** which will become stronger and ever more elevated in frequencies of vibration as the true meaning of the prayer deepens in your mind and heart and your perceptions heighten.)

After the prayer, relax ever deeper and let your mind go as blank as you can. If thoughts intrude, gently recite **'Divine Life'** or **'Father-mother-life'** to yourself and again quieten your mind. After many months of sincere meditation, you may come to feel that your body is suddenly jerking, like a person entering sleep and then suddenly waking up. If this happens, be thankful as your consciousness is penetrating the barriers of your previously created consciousness forces encapsulating your soul.

When you feel yourself entering a different deep state of consciousness, so deep you are barely breathing, know that you are beginning to attain your goal. At the end of your meditation, always give glad and grateful thanks.

Remember that nothing you can think, say, or do, can in any way reduce all that *'Father-mother-life- consciousness'* is.

However, any disbelief will form a barrier between you and *Father-mother-life.*

I want to warn you: when you are trying to still your mind and thoughts, you may feel ill-at-ease, physically uncomfortable and even distressed. This is because – initially – you will come up against the black wall of your own 'consciousness' and this can be extremely disconcerting – even painful.

Bless the experience and ask *'Father life' to penetrate your consciousness next time you listen.*

Then get up and put the experience behind you.

When you find that you are at last entering into the silence, then rest equably, knowing that you have now entered what one might call the 'holy of holies' because, at last, you are achieving contact with *'Father- mother-life'* within you. It will take time for this highly spiritual experience of the Silence to become a daily routine.

Remember you have a lifetime of ego baggage to discard and dissolve.

No matter what you sense or are aware of during your meditation, when you come out of it, expect to sense a difference in your life. Remember that expectation is a 'consciousness' form and as you 'expect' you are opening the way for that which you 'expect' to be magnetised into your experience, whatever it may be you are needing or dealing with.

If you do not feel any new lightness of spirit, despite your sincere expectations, do not deny changes or doubt the possibility of them.

Remember your consciousness is electromagnetic, of the same substance as your physical body, and it is the foundation of all experiences in your life. Continue to expect – as you do so you are building up the power, the energy of your 'expectations – consciousness forms' which will draw to themselves the manifestation of all that you are expecting. **'Father-mother-life-consciousness'** can only be magnetised into your individual consciousness by faith, sincere expectancy, and the willingness to open yourself to the cleansing of your magnetic-emotional 'bonding-rejection-impulses.

How many of you presently go into meditation in this way and come out **EXPECTING** changes? How many lose heart when they have felt some change and then nothing for a little while?

Bear in mind that I told you that you are subject to rhythms of 'high' and 'low'. When you are in your 'lows', the flow of Divine Life in your system has dropped and the frequencies of vibration of your consciousness also drop. Consequently, contact with **'Father-Mother-Life-Consciousness'** during these times, at the beginning of your search, is almost impossible. In the early days of your seeking **Truth**, during your meditation, you are very much in touch with your subconscious, and you will find that there is an irritating resurgence of all the old negative thoughts and memories you had thought you had overcome.

When you enter your 'highs', you will find a resurgence of your spiritual self and will rejoice in this. Your meditations will be more positive and productive of contact with **'Father-Mother-Life-Consciousness'**. If you will have the courage to persist and exercise self-discipline during the 'low' times as well as the good, you will find eventually, that the 'lows' will get less 'low' and any former depression will be lifted. Remember, that each time of 'prayerful consciousness' brings you closer to your goal, although you may remain completely unaware of this. Nonetheless, things are happening for your ultimate good – believe in them.

When on earth I said:

I have come to give you FREEDOM

I have come to bring you 'LIFE MORE ABUNDANT'!

The secret of your tiredness, exhaustion, inconsistency, instability, fear, despair, depression, lies in your magnetic-emotional   'bonding-rejection' responses to life and the sub-conscious patterns which sometimes take over and project you into situations you never intended to create. Because of these 'natural impulses of individuality', you are certainly not free, you are under the control of the magnetic- emotional bondage both in your conscious and unconscious mind. **You live in the grip of the Ego which has given you individuality and bound you in fetters of emotional responses to life.**

However, the time comes for the sincere and ardent seeker, the person who gladly follows the path of **'Christ Consciousness'** – **THE CHRIST WAY** – when 'he' meditates and penetrates the magnetic- emotional areas of the brain, to receive enlightenment which is impressed within the very topmost areas of the brain under the skull. New cells are impressed with new knowledge.

This is an ongoing process, and you will probably feel this 'opening' taking place in your brain.

You now begin to operate more and more within the super-conscious mind which is in ever greater contact with **'father-mother-life-consciousness'** until the time comes when you can no longer bear the 'ego' thoughts and feelings dominating your normal every day consciousness and you die the death of total self-surrender. When this happens, **'father-mother-life-consciousness'** will fill your vision to the exclusion of all else. You will be entering the 'consciousness frequencies' of what I termed, on earth, the 'kingdom of heaven'. This phase will be characterised by a gradual withdrawal from the kind of life you enjoyed before. Your thought life will become ever more purified, and you will find yourself responding to situations, events and people, in a more dispassionate way. Whilst you may be less emotionally warm or cold than before, you will now be in the first wavelengths of what you term 'unconditional love' and will do everything from the point-of-view of promoting the highest good of everyone, which means: for their growth, nutrition, healing, protection, fulfilment of their legitimate needs within a system of law and order. You will love more deeply than ever before but there will be none of the 'human' sentiment which can cause so many errors in communication and action.

When you have gained true inner knowledge, you will be able to transcend the emotional baggage, you will be able to meditate and draw upon **'father-mother-life'** and you will feel new energy entering your system, giving you new buoyancy. You will laugh, be more playful, find happiness in little things, love the world, feel brimming gratitude for every little blessing entering your life. You will find the blessings multiplying in your experience and showering your daily path.

How does the person behave, who has come through to freedom from the 'ego'?

Eventually, such a person is totally free of fear. There will be absolute conviction that wherever he goes, he is protected. Although he may go through potentially dangerous experiences, he will emerge unscathed. He will know that he has no need of sword or gun to protect him. He is protected against every negative eventuality wherever he is.

He will fear no sickness, since he will know that every built-in device in his system to keep him healthy is fully operative and working efficiently.

He will know that he will never 'want' for the things needed to make his life happy and comfortable. Continually, he will praise and give thanks to **_'FATHER-MOTHER-LIFE'_** for all things already received and will be received in the future.

He knows he will be guided to be at the right place at the right time.

He also knows that he can ask for whatever is needed and the response will come swiftly.

But the asking will come from his spiritually enlightened centre and he will never seek for anything selfishly but will always pray for things within the context of what will be good for his environment, community, family, friends.

He will have an open mind, knowing that TRUTH is infinite and whilst he may know much there is always a further dimension to explore. This is what makes life in any dimension, even the Celestial Kingdoms of consciousness, so exhilarating and purposeful.

In his daily life, the enlightened soul will wake up with a mind empty of all but praise and thanksgiving. Eventually, he will be aware of the chores awaiting him, and giving thanks for the energy and the willingness to perform these tasks, he will go away to do them without any inner resistance or reluctance to start.

As a result of this attitude to daily routine, he does not waste energy on resistance in any shape or form. If there is a special reason to resist some suggestion or coercion, he will do so calmly and reasonably without magnetic-emotional feelings of annoyance or rejection.

He becomes the dispassionate observer, doing the right thing at the right moment.

He possesses his soul in patience, waiting for guidance, waiting for the right doors to open, waiting for confirmation that any plans are indeed divinely willed into being through his mind and heart and energy. He becomes a true man manifesting **'Father-mother-life-consciousness'**.

He also takes on the feminine characteristics of universal love and becomes the embodiment of: Intelligent love or loving intelligence.

She takes on a more masculine characteristic of strength and strong sense of direction.

If instruction is needed by a person, he/she will exhibit loving intelligence and the person will be uplifted by his/her words.

If healing is needed, he/she will demonstrate intelligent love and the person will be healed. This is the goal to which I lovingly commend you.

The Path to Christ Consciousness is outlined in these LETTERS.

When you achieve it, you will rejoice and say it was worth every moment of the rocky and bumpy times which will now be behind you forever. You will be free to climb into higher dimensions, each one bringing you new experiences and joys.

You will become founders of a new order on earth which will form the spearhead of a new surge of spiritual evolution.

When this spiritual evolution spreads to the general masses in many years to come, people will finally learn how to live in peace with one another.

These things will surely come to pass, for the SEEDS of such a future have been sown within these LETTERS. Whoever welcomes them into their consciousness and endures in faith will eventually find them blossoming in beauty, joy and harmony and bringing forth fruit in their daily lives.

Believe – for I, the Christ, have spoken.

****

LETTER 9

I, the CHRIST, have come through the medium of these **LETTERS** because I cannot return in bodily form – or take on human personality again – since I reside in and am, myself, of such fine and heightened vibrational frequencies of consciousness that no human physical form could contain my spiritual consciousness.

My only means of reaching you has been through the medium of a human being – sensitive, clair- audient, obedient and dedicated to 'God', born to be the channel through whom I could watch the tumult of her active, eventful life and world events. I have been able to intimately review the conflict and pain unknown in centuries past because scientific and technological discoveries, and the lessening of moral and conventional values have led to new highly stressful conditions of modern living and new ways of relating to each other. Through the medium of this pliable mind, the modern human condition has, to a slight degree, become subjective for me.

Without this knowledge of the human experience, these Letters could not have been written in a form which is intended to be helpful to the human condition at this time.

The process of partial overshadowing began before her birth, continued in her youth and life.

Beginning with the thorough de-programming of her mind and full cleansing of old concepts, my 'recorder' has been deliberately subjected to every type of human experience, bearing witness to the struggles and sorrow involved in modern living. With my instruction, she has climbed out of her many diverse holes of distress, culminating in the death of her ego and mental/emotional bondage to materialism; she is learning how to move into the consciousness frequencies of universal love and has had personal experience of the Reality of UNIVERSAL CONSCIOUSNESS ... so has she been sufficiently cleansed to receive, ever more clearly, my teachings to distribute throughout the world.

Under my influence, she has withdrawn from social life into seclusion and aloneness and has ultimately become dependent on me for her daily will-to-live, and I work through her total minute-by-minute readiness to receive my words whenever cosmic and her personal consciousness energies enable her to hear and receive me. I rely on her honesty and dedication to

307

wait to hear me accurately and I make it clear when it is I who speak. Until I speak – she is unable to write.

I have told you this that you may understand out of what **CHRIST CONSCIOUSNESS** energies, these **Letters** have taken form.

888

I have come again in this Letter to bring together all the loose ends of my other LETTERS and present them *WITHIN A WORLD CONTEXT*, showing how these teachings are relevant to every aspect of your earthly lives and to all nations.

These LETTERS are meant to be the impetus – the spur – to a personal opening of the mind and heart to your SOURCE of BEING and eventually, to become the means of your perfect understanding of the effects of individual and mass thought and behaviour on every facet of your earthly existence.

Whereas, in the past, the laws given you for national behaviour have been directed mainly at 'You shall not ... if you do – this will be the penalty', true spiritual laws are entirely different.

They are expressed like this:

'Because you and your place in earthly existence have been created in this way ... if you work harmoniously with the **Laws of your Existence** ... you will open your entire system of soul, mind, emotions, body, and personal circumstances to the consistent inflow of **Divine Consciousness, your Life Force**. The fruits of your disciplined behaviour will return to bless and load you with health, harmony and prosperity.

'If, on the other hand, you ignore these **Laws of Existence**, and continue living as you did before you received this message, then your lives will continue to be punctuated by turmoil, difficult climatic conditions, pests in your crops, financial disasters, famines and stressful lives.'

I have spoken through these Letters – expressly – to enable you to reach true, consistent peace of mind and spiritual love, joy, and inner healing of mind, emotions and body.

You should have understood by now that this was also the sole purpose behind my last mission to people on earth – to show them how they themselves were creating their own misery.

You have been taught by 'Christian' churches that you who have been created by 'God' must 'worship and please God' by keeping his Laws.

But this is not truth. 'Worshipping god' is a pagan ritual. When people 'worship god' they set 'god' apart and above them – 'unreachable and to be feared – for who knows what evil he might send on earth if people did not act according to his will'.

But that was not the message I brought to earth. I spoke of the 'Father' which supplied all needs,which answered when called, which healed when requested to do so, which was both transcendent to people and also 'within them', meaning that the Creator was universal.

The Jewish religion taught that only the Chief Priests could approach the 'Holy of Holies' and make supplication for the people. The populace could approach Jehovah only through the priests by bringing birds and animals to be offered as burnt sacrifices to appease Jehovah for the people's 'sins'. By these means, the Jews obtained 'forgiveness of sins'.

I repeatedly taught the people that they would receive the **'Father's' forgiveness of sins** according to people's willingness to forgive others – for it would be done to them according to their own 'sowing'. I also taught the people to approach the 'Father' directly and pray in simple terms, asking for what they needed in life, and assured them that they would be heard and their prayers answered, providing they prayed with total faith – with no doubt in their minds. You must understand that everything I taught the Jews was in direct conflict and opposition to what their Religious Elders taught them, which was why the Priests hated – and crucified me, since I was robbing them of their exalted positions as 'personal henchmen' of the 'Almighty'.

Because, for fear of reprisals after my death, the disciples did not break entirely free from the Old Testament, much of the Old Testament thought was carried forward into the 'Christian' religion.

Instead of animals, the body and blood of 'Jesus' were substituted to be the sacrifice offered by priests upon the altar. After many years and the entry of Rome as protector of the 'Christian' religion, like the Jewish priests before them, the 'Roman' priests dressed themselves in costly vestments and used silver and gold appurtenances for religious ceremonies.

In the time of Paul, this would have been unthinkable. His was a simple message of 'salvation by my death on the cross' which was not the message I brought to my countrymen in Palestine. He was perpetuating a Jewish tradition of 'sacrificing another to pay for one's own sinning'. What shameful cowardice! Yet, Paul also performed a great service to humanity, since he set in motion a movement which would be the means of blessing all races equally. He outlined a mode of thought and daily conduct which would bring harmony into the lives of those who tried to live according to his teachings.

In all probability, some Jewish traditionalists will vociferously reject my words again, the second time of coming, they will resent my constant allusion to the ancient Jewish practice of sacrificing animals and birds in the Temple to please God and obtain forgiveness of sins, but no matter what their objections may be, the historical fact remains that the Temple was a place for offering burnt sacrifices and the smell thereof hung over Jerusalem. And all the while I knew that the whole edifice of the Temple was dedicated to a myth, a figment of man's imagination, a rationalisation of what men's minds could not comprehend spiritually.

I was there! I felt the hot stones under my sandalled feet and the sun on my head. I argued with the Pharisees, bore their mockery and sneers with some amusement and watched them as they dogmatically taught a burdensome way of life of continual obedience to a worthless tradition concerning eating and drinking which was entirely unnecessary!

I was there! At times, my amusement ignited a spark of mischief in my mind and I handed out to the Pharisees the same kind of analytical mockery of their personal habits, their ostentatious clothing and their laws, as they applied to me and my teachings.

'He is a fool!' they said, and loudly ridiculed my statement 'The Kingdom of God is within you'.

'Tell us – how could 'God' be within a person?' they shouted derisively.

Using a barrage of contemptuous arguments, they called on the prophets and compared their concepts of the **Almighty Jehovah** with my descriptions of

310

the simple **'Father'** 'who even had thought for the birds'. How could this be, they demanded, when birds were regularly sacrificed in the Temple for payment of men's sinning? Would Moses have instituted such a holy practice of burnt sacrifices if birds and beasts were of any consequence in the eyes of the Almighty?

I remained unmoved as they launched their verbal attacks at me. They only had the conviction of Jewish tradition to support their statements – whilst my mind had been imbued with the true knowledge of existence itself during my illumined experiences in the desert. I had been given understanding of the universality and creative GOODWILL of the **'Father'** which enabled me to perceive and do things which no Chief Priest or Pharisee or Sadducee or scribe could ever do.

Because I understood the nature of our **SOURCE of BEING**, I could, with confidence, put my hands upon a crippled man and raise him up to wholeness again. Who could measure this knowledge against the ridiculous traditional laws of the Priests? The Priests and Pharisees and all the rest of the religious hocus-pocus knew that none of them could do such things – and for this reason, they hated me for challenging their authority, they loathed me for my strength in the face of their opposition, and they reviled me for drawing crowds of people when a healing was done which no one could deny.

There it was, done in the open, for all to see – an act of love which the Priests averred only God could do and therefore I must be a child of Satan! Furthermore, they did not see the healing as an act of love but rather as an inexplicable blasphemous usurpation of the role of 'God' – they accused me of 'showing off' my magical powers but could not tell me how I came by such magical powers, therefore they decided I must be a son of Beelzebub.

Now that I have explained the situation, it should now be as clear to you who read these words – as it was so very clear to me at that time in Palestine – that the whole hierarchy of Judaism was composed of self-centred, self-important, mixed up men who lived only by rules and laws. When challenged to use their minds, their brains, they could not cope but fell into highly emotional spasms of vitriolic outrage. Was it any wonder that, when brought before their council, I held my peace and refused to communicate with such obtuse minds?

Yes, I was truly there in Palestine, 2000 years ago. I lived amongst the ordinary men and women who had been taught to fear Jehovah in a very real way; who were obsessed with paying for burnt sacrifices to ward off punishment for their sins. I was raised, indoctrinated in the fear of Jehovah – but I had been born to bring the Jews out of their long slumber of myth and fallacies – to set them free of a burdensome history of wars and bloodshed, brawling and arguments, of demanding a head for the loss of an eye, of hidden and secret sinning which counted for nothing if a man was not found out. If he was, then the whole weight of the Mosaic Law descended on his head without compassion or mercy or even a hesitant thought as to the true circumstances surrounding the transgression.

Because I had been born with a mission to open up the minds and hearts of the Jews to the **Reality** which had given them life and being, even from an early age I rejected the Jewish teachings. Some secret depth of spiritual instinct rebelled against the age-old Jewish intention to let some other living thing carry responsibility and 'pay the price' for their own waywardness and sinning. Even more than this, I could not accept that a 'God' who was supposed to have created such a wonderful world would rejoice in burnt sacrifices of his own creation for which he had provided abundantly.

I found it impossible to have respect for such illogical beliefs and practices. After my illumination in the desert, I became passionate in my rejection of Jewish traditions.

Just as I came in human body 2000 years ago, to rescue the Jewish nation from an edifice of artificial and man-made burdensome religious practices, so have I come through the medium of these **Letters** distributed world-wide, to make it abundantly clear that the 'Christian Religion' in no way reflects my true **CHRIST** message either as I taught it in Palestine – or at this present time when these **Letters** will arouse the fury and condemnation of orthodox 'Christians'. The Christian religion, as it stands at this time, is only a hotch-potch of the muddled thinking of my disciples' **selective** recollections and Paul's worthy homilies and other early writings. Much later, when the impact of Christianity lacked the visual effect of the gods and goddesses of the Romans, the Christian religion was adorned with 'theatrical' but 'expedient' nonsense to impress those whom the Ecclesiastical Empire of Rome desired to draw into their fold. This empire later imposed monetary burdens on the gullible people even more iniquitous than the taxes demanded by the secular

Roman Empire on conquered nations. Even Caesar did not demand payment for souls to gain entrance to heaven!

You may wonder why I am so explicit in my rejection of 'Judaism' and 'Christianity'. It is vital to the success of the distribution of my **CHRIST MESSAGE** that people should fully understand the true nature of religions which held humanity in their grip until the twentieth century. Until they do realise the mythical foundations on which they have placed all their convictions, people will find it difficult to let go of their cherished beliefs. Please understand that when I make such statements, I am referring to 'Christian religion', to the 'tenets of faith', to the 'dogma and theology'. I am not referring to those great spiritual souls who have sought – and continue to seek God and Truth beyond the dogma and beliefs. Many of these have received my inspiration into their minds and hearts but are afraid to let go their cherished beliefs. They are hampered by religious practices. The time has come for them to let them go and grow in spirituality and awareness of their true **SOURCE of BEING** and take their congregations with them.

To the 'Christian' Churches of every denomination, I say 'Wake up!' The time has come for you to rouse yourselves from a long unnatural sleep when reason has been suppressed by hypnotic and emotional traditions. These have been handed down through the centuries by a succession of people claiming to be the highest authority on all that I taught in Palestine. Do not be afraid of the consequences if you examine your past beliefs and want to cleanse them from your thinking. Get rid of the cobwebs of illusion and – THINK!

When 'Christian' ministers fully accept that **I, the Christ,** have truly returned to speak to people world-wide, 'like lightning striking from East to West' and are ready to teach my true message from the pulpit – you will find your churches filling again with people eager to find and make contact with the Reality which will lead them to live in total harmony with their **TRUTH of BEING**. Alternatively, you ministers of religion, who wilfully and egotistically continue to teach the dogma of 'Christianity' to save 'face' and your stipends, will watch your religion die a natural death during the next thirty years and will be abandoned by your congregations who are already sensing that your words are only words – in which there is no spiritual life. You will see your churches taken over by those who have realised that I, myself, have indeed returned to humanity to show them the way to find and enter the 'Kingdom of Heaven'.

There will also be those whose positions of authority are threatened by these **Letters from CHRIST – from me.** They will oppose them mightily. There will be vilification of every kind through the services of every type of media – from people who have no scruples in stirring up public wrath to make money from destructive, vindictive sensationalism.

I have to tell you that the greater the uproar world-wide, the more swiftly will my **Letters** reach and convince those people who are weary of the old beliefs, that at last they have heard the simple **TRUTH of BEING**. They will swiftly respond to its love and call to leave the lower levels of human consciousness to start their ascent to the higher spiritual levels where they will begin to experience the first inflow of interior peace and contentment.

There will be conflict throughout the entertainment industry, since more and more people will recognise – and turn against – the violence and degradation with which their entire consciousness of mind, emotions, body, have been fed by **'DEGENERATES'** obsessed by making themselves a fortune. These spiritual ghouls have understood the strange fascination of the unholy and macabre for ignorant people who have been so surfeited with the security, comfort and luxury in the 20th century, they no longer find contentment in them. They need excitement to stimulate their jaded consciousness.

Were the lives of people truly as horrible as is depicted on the entertainment they watch daily, they would turn from their screens in search of something beautiful and easeful to rest their tortured nervous systems. And yet, if you will reflect honestly on the conditions of your present lives, you will realise that they are already becoming a terror-inducing mirror image of all that your entertainment industry has given you in the past 50 years.

People have been fed on the worst scenarios possible by cinema, TV, books and media sensationalism and are now complaining that the former sense of security they previously enjoyed has been whipped away from them. I see you on earth, presently barricaded behind electric fences, high spiked walls, guarded by security men who themselves traitorously murder the people they guard; I see men and women who previously walked the streets and country lanes fearlessly at night, now locked up behind security gates – afraid of the most despicable and brutal attacks. I see races traumatised by their own people. I see genocide, revolutions, bombing, assassinations, mindless killings of every description. The murdered come through into their next existence still traumatised by the shock of their unexpected passing. I see them and minister to them – if they are able to see and receive me. Many, many people are far from ready to move on to a higher form of existence and so they dwell in the shadows until they are released through rebirth. Earthly life has become the hell which you depict on your screens and in your literature. Why? Because your so-called civilised 'culture' permits brutality in all its perverted forms, to enter your homes through the medium of your TV for your titillation and excitement. You wanted it – and now you have it in its most real form – within your own daily experiences. No one is immune from these disasters you have brought on yourselves.

Do you wonder that **I, the Christ,** have returned to you at this time to explain to you what you have done to yourselves?

How would it be possible for any spiritual embodiment of **LOVE** to remain remote from such agony of spirit and fail to reach out to render help when help is possible? Therefore, as I said before, I am not alone in my work. **I speak for every Master as I speak through these Letters.**

Every Master is ministering to those who follow his earthly teachings. Every Master is calling on their adherents to read, heed, pray that they may absorb the TRUTH within these pages and strive to cleanse their thoughts and actions and become the embodiment of love to all.

But these Letters will set in motion a Season of Change.

When people truly wake up to what has been done to their consciousness, world-wide, by greedy, unscrupulous and degenerate tycoons, they will experience extreme anger. The public will begin to recognise the insidious and devious ways in which they have been gradually enticed into the webs of abomination.

And **I, the Christ,** have to tell you that when this happens, you will no longer find the word 'abomination' old-fashioned and out-of-date. You will clearly perceive the difference between wholesome, life-giving consciousness forms – words – and destructive consciousness patterns.

You will rebel and nationally call the destructive 'consciousness forms' – abominations.

Conscientious and truly loving parents will become particularly vocal against the present form of entertainment and will prevent their children from continuing to view the decadence of unpleasant, emotive language, unbridled violence, and promiscuous, emotionally superficial sex, presently on offer on your screens, in books and media. Your society is riddled with these low, despicable consciousness creations which are carried through into human lives and human actions.

Parents will also come to realise that since the **CONSCIOUSNESS FORMS** created within their children's minds are the ever enlarging foundations of their children's future lives as adults, they will begin **to investigate the ETHICAL VALUES taught in schools.** No longer will parents be concerned about the religions taught in school, since these will only be of interest to a minority, but they will be very seriously interested in the kind of philosophies for living, attitudes, arguments, conflicts, statements, encouraged or tolerated in schools in the future – by teachers and by pupils alike.

Groups will band together to start small schools on the foundation of these **Letters,** since the old factual material will be abandoned as obsolete. Emphasis will be placed on languages, the arts, logic, the art of effective inspiring communication, the development of constructive creative imagination, mathematics and science, and manual skills.

The curriculum will be centred around the development of an ability to differentiate between truth and myth, to perceive clearly the highest values to be adopted and cherished, and the most constructive, productive way to use them in life – to improve conditions for the self, the nation, and the world generally. The child will also be taught to become proficient in those sciences and manual skills which will enable him to work joyfully and successfully in his chosen field of endeavour. Children will be tutored within a new aura of concern and love and shown how they can contribute to such concern and love in the classrooms. They will be encouraged to work with joy and happiness. If this does not come easily, the unhappy child will be shown how joy and happiness may be achieved and will be rewarded when successful.

People will be valued according to their commitment to seeking higher levels of spiritual thought and their dedication to serving the interests of the underprivileged and communities generally.

It is a matter of extreme urgency that people world-wide should recognise that the TRUTH is you have been born to individualise and express the UNIVERSAL – the SOURCE of your BEING – in an evolutionary manner, eventually reaching peak

INDIVIDUALISED manifestation of your SOURCE of BEING – CHRIST CONSCIOUSNESS.

AND you have also been created to be cared for, nurtured, provided with your every need in order to ensure your health, perfect well-being, and harmonious prosperity whilst on your soul's journey to individualised re-union with your Source of Being – Divine Consciousness.

Until you do grasp this **TRUTH of BEING**, you will never achieve your true potential on earth either physically or spiritually.

No country, religious organisation, and no single person, no matter how humanly exalted he may be thought to be, will be able to alter the contents of these Letters since

I – the CHRIST

am also radiating the TRUTH of BEING world-wide to everyone who is on the level of spiritual frequencies to be able to receive the TRUTH. Such people will receive, revere and adopt IT fully, without reservation, to be their own guidelines for their thoughts and actions.

If there are those who cannot understand or receive the Letters, it will be only because they are not yet ascended to the necessary level of consciousness to be able to empathise with them. Their growth will come later.

Therefore, I say to those who have not yet experienced the quality of life I have described as being yours by **Divine WILL**, do not ask what is the matter with life or people or circumstances – or with you ...

Look inside your own thought processes, your own attitudes towards life, generally, your feelings towards other people and yourself – and find out what kind of thoughts – and expectations – you regularly indulge in. These create a powerfully creative consciousness energy force which you are emitting throughout the day. It will attract to you exactly what you fear and expect. Sometimes, the negative creative consciousness form is deeply

317

buried in your sub-conscious, implanted there many years ago due to certain circumstances. Or the negative creative consciousness impulse may have come through from a past life. In any event, if you have been subjected to consistently bad experiences, examine your inner state of consciousness and find out what kind of negative expectations possess your sub-conscious. Discover, also, what are your attitudes and feelings towards other people?

Are you consistently living within the harmony of the Laws of Existence? Are you expressing 'unconditional love' on every level of your life – towards every single thing in your experience?

Are you able to see the 'light of the soul' within all living things – or can you see only their ego- drive – their darkness?

Do you realise that for the people whom you may reject or criticise, I – the Christ – have the highest love and compassion for them at all times? Whom you may be rejecting, I am radiating to them my unconditional love.

Bear in mind, at all times, that your **SOURCE of BEING** is in two states – in **equilibrium** and **activity**.

The **ACTIVE** state of your **SOURCE of BEING** is the dimension in which you have been conceived and given individualisation.

The **EQUILIBRIUM** of **UNIVERSAL CONSCIOUSNESS** is the dimension of perfect silence and stillness, in which the underlying **IMPULSES OF CREATIVITY** are locked together in an embrace of mutual restraint.

When you fully realise, accept, understand that in every 'learning session in your school on earth', you always have access to the Divine Loving Intelligence which resolves every problem the perfect way, you are then lifted beyond the reach of panic and pain.

You solve your problems swiftly and smoothly and realise that your own store of wisdom and knowledge are being increased in many ways.

In this way, do you evolve on every level of your being.

Whilst my purpose in coming to you through the medium of these Letters has been to show you the way to live in harmony with the **Laws of Existence**, to help you avoid unnecessary pain, limitations and deprivation caused by your ignorance of the **Laws,** I also want to imprint in your consciousness that everyone is subject to rhythms in their lives. Everyone goes through the high periods when an inflow of blessedness brings you all the things you have wanted and you are on a peak of human happiness and success. You rejoice! Then comes the time when suddenly the rhythm of life changes, resources dry up, relationships become difficult and precarious, your career takes a downward turn, or obstacles occur which keep you static for a long time. You may ask yourself what you have done wrong. Previously, you worked very successfully within the **LAWS of EXISTENCE** but now there are daily challenges and nothing you think or do is truly alleviating the stress of your daily life.

When – if – these times come upon you – be still and quiet within your heart and mind – and know that you are still drawing life and direction from Divine Consciousness, despite appearances to the contrary, despite the superficial agonies. At these times it is essential to withdraw and take stock of the ways in which you may have slipped in consciousness during your 'up' times – and strengthen your dependence on Divine Consciousness.

Without these dark periods of depression, you would not grow in spiritual stature. They have a special message for you so do not give way to despair or bitterness. Although you may feel fragile, this is your winter season of self-discovery and inner renewal which will ultimately prove to be of greater blessing than ever were your 'peak periods'. Take heart and do not lose faith. Hold on patiently until winter gradually yields to your spiritual spring again.

Persevere in relaxing and confidently waiting for the time when Divine Life will again flow into your mind, heart and earthly life and all you had hoped for will begin to manifest in your experience. And throughout this time, realise and hold on to the fact that if you are no longer aware of the inflow of Divine Consciousness during your meditations, it is not because you have been abandoned but because your own cosmic – and therefore your personal consciousness vibrations – are at a low ebb and you are no longer able to rise to experience the vibrations of Divine Consciousness as you did previously. Although you may not feel them, rest assured that always you are enfolded in them and in DIVINE LOVE.

I also want to remind you and impress upon your consciousness that the moment the most impoverished of human beings can understand the true nature of their origins and can make use of the knowledge, they can begin to pull themselves out of their rut and can then rise to any heights they choose for themselves – providing, daily, they tune into the **SOURCE OF THEIR BEING** and draw on **Its Infinite Power, Life, direction, inspiration and guidance.**

You are not victims of fate – you are victims of your own creative consciousness until you realise that your consciousness is entirely of your own shaping. When this glorious Truth dawns within your own consciousness, you will begin to turn your life around and will eventually discover that you can work to become a Master and achieve complete freedom in **DIVINE CONSCIOUSNESS.**

Try to remember that, in your spiritual search, your aim should be to keep your consciousness frequencies as steady as possible within your highest spiritual perceptions. This is extremely difficult for the human mind to do, since it eagerly reaches out for new forms of spiritual/mental stimulation wherever the interest is aroused.

But I have to tell you, it is not enough to read these Letters and then turn to other books, hoping to find some higher, more inspirational truth.

I, the Christ, tell you, truly, there is no higher truth or higher way on offer to you at this time.

You may sometimes feel you have found something higher, because on the level of your present human consciousness you can relate to what is written more easily – but you can rest assured that SPIRITUAL TRUTH of EXISTENCE is the only KNOWLEDGE which will bring you eventually to CHRIST CONSCIOUSNESS which is your true destination and none other.

CHRIST CONSCIOUSNESS is the spiritual consciousness of all the great Masters. There is no higher. To increase your understanding, you may seek out those authors who have already found for themselves and are practising what is written in these Letters, but do not follow those who still follow other writers and quote other authorities and are still seeking a way through human thought into the vastness of spiritual Truth – beyond human thought. They, like yourselves, are still in the foothills of consciousness – they have not yet penetrated the mental/emotional ozone to draw close to the precincts of SPACE.

Do not follow those who are finding pleasure in – and writing of 'marvels' in occult practices and are seeking to lead you into experiencing them also, advocating the use of material substances to increase energy in different areas of your lives. When you use material substances such as crystals, candles, incense, joss sticks, you focus your human consciousness on those things which have human meaning for you and give you pleasure. In this way, do they anchor your human consciousness to the 'effects' of human consciousness, continually leading you back into fixed levels of human consciousness. Whereas, if you want to ascend into true spiritual dimensions of consciousness, your goal is to penetrate and then transcend the earthly human consciousness dimension. The only true energy, true dynamic healing Life Force comes from your consistent contact with **DIVINE CONSCIOUSNESS.** As you journey upwards, you will become acquainted with the finer vibrations of the astral planes but do not loiter in these levels since they are only manifestations of higher physical forms of consciousness and should not be your true goal.

Attunement with Divine Consciousness and total self-mastery should be your reason for living, and your only goal. When you have achieved it, all you have ever wanted for yourself will be yours – in a new, transcendent and eternal way.

You may read these Letters and decide you want to continue as you are – in your ego-consciousness, trusting **Divine Consciousness** to help you through the difficult patches. But I can tell you that life itself will eventually convince you that any other way does not bring the rewards which your soul, hidden and silently waiting for release, is longing to experience – particularly that of full re-union with **Divine Consciousness.**

The greatest gift you can give **yourself – or anyone else** – is to gratefully accept into your own mind – and try to imbue in other receptive minds – the full inspired understanding of **who 'you and they' really are and what can truly be accomplished** when 'you and they' abandon self-will and look to the **SOURCE of their BEING** for help, guidance and fulfilment of every need.

Become a Light to yourself – and whomever can receive it.

321

At the same time, no one can absorb learning on an empty stomach; therefore a certain amount of physical nutrition should be given to help the process of spiritual-physical evolutionary development, if you are trying to teach the materially impoverished. Be willing to give to others and know that as you give, you become part of the 'give-and-receive' system of the entire universe.

It is impossible to give and not receive in return – unless you yourself believe you live only on the supply from your work, your bank account and investments. When this is what you believe, then this is what you will experience.

Until people truly wake up and open their eyes to the full realisation that they are the individualisation of the **SOURCE of their BEING** which is a combination of **PERFECT IMPULSES of Creativity & Love**, they will remain attracted to the enticements of materialism, satisfactions of body lusts, and the desire for self-promotion above all others – which ranges from take-overs and strikes in business and industries, and gross disharmonies in relationships to murder, rape and war. Wherever a person exerts his ego over another, angry discords abound.

This is the very first Law of Existence which must be publicised throughout the world.

How then, should human nature strive daily to live in a world naturally dominated by ego-drive – the overpowering desire for self-satisfaction?

The answer lies in my statement: **'Do to others as you would be done by'.**

This is the first step to overcoming ego-drive.

When involved in argument, let there be full justice rendered by each party to the other. Listen – absorb – heed – make amends as far as possible.

Make certain that in your demands you do not make inroads on the well-being of the other party – be it personal, pleasure, business or industry.

Remember that as you do to others, so will it eventually be done to you. Remember that your thoughts, words and actions of today will take on form in your experience in days, months or years to come. Sometimes, the sowing will take years to grow into its harvest and the sowing will have been forgotten. However, rest assured, whatever you do today will return to you in some related form, although you may never recognise it as such or perceive the connection.

Whatever you would have people say about your mistakes – say those things – and mean them –about the mistakes that other people may make – friends or strangers.

Give the acceptance and forgiveness you would like to receive. What is true forgiveness? It is a state of understanding the other person and their reasons for their behaviour so clearly that you can say in all honesty – there is nothing to forgive.

The loyalty, kindness and generosity you would like to receive when in trouble – give to others when they are struggling with heavy burdens. Never turn to them a cold shoulder.

Learn to look at a person or a situation with the eye of kindly discernment. See them as they are at this moment and then **remember that I see them with compassionate love.**

If you see a real need of improvement in them – for their own good and the future enhancement of their well-being – look at them only with heart and eyes of love and see them as they can be in the future. Take them in thought to their **SOURCE of BEING** and know that your prayer has surely blessed them and opened doors to their development. Seek guidance from **Divine Consciousness** as to whether you can broach the subject of their 'improvement' and ask how this may be done to ensure their happy acceptance of counsel and ultimate success in personal development.

If someone wants to tell you how you have hurt them at any time – stand or sit still quietly and **know** that this is a true challenge to your ego-drive. This is your big moment – your greatest testing-point.

How will you handle it? Will you make excuses and defend yourself, considering, even saying, that your actions should not have hurt the other person – and were fully justified in the circumstances? If this is how you respond, then your ego-drive is still in perfect control of your consciousness.

If, however, you can realise that the great moment of truth is upon you – and because of this awareness – you are able to remain quiet and calm, listening to the other person's descriptions of their hurt at your hands, you are succeeding in the first overcoming of your ego.

The next urgent step is to put your own need to defend yourself firmly aside and sincerely empathise with what the speaker is saying. You will only be able to do this sincerely if you can be self-effacing enough to enter a place of inner silence where you can fully enter into their hurt, hear what they are saying and receive their pain into your heart. If you can do this, you will have got inside their skin. And when you can get inside their skin and feel their pain, you will want to apologise from the very bottom of your heart for what you did; the pain you inflicted ignorantly and unknowingly will become your own pain and you will not rest until you have managed, through loving words, to remove all residue of pain from the other person's consciousness. You will then have healed the hurt and it will also be eliminated from your electro-magnetic consciousness system. You have won a great victory over self. You will have reached that point of inner strength and endurance when you can truly perceive the reality of other people as being of equal validity with your own. You have recognised and accepted that others can be hurt by your actions in just the same way as you have been hurt by others.

After reaching this **great moment of truth** in your life, you will find yourself able to move between yourself and others quite comfortably, able to see events from their perspective as easily as you can see your own. A great balancing between the needs of other people and yourself takes place, and you enter into a state of peace since you are now confident that you treat others fairly and with generosity of spirit. You have now begun to remove the barriers between yourself and other people and are receiving them into your heart.

You have also begun to remove your own defences and because of this, you will find that – at last – **you are achieving true self-esteem and peace of mind.**

This new understanding of the feelings of others will inspire in you a great respect for them. You will always want to deal with them justly, giving them their dues, never wanting to take advantage of their good-nature, never wanting to put them down, reduce their self-esteem, always ready to encourage and pick them up when they're in pain – physical or emotional.

You will find yourself doing these things for yourself also. You will become your own counsellor, support, healer.

You will see each person, no matter what their status, as of an equal basic reality as your own and you will see that you are the equal of everyone else be he King, Pope or President for underneath the externals, you have both come out of the **GREAT UNITY of BEING.**

Therefore, you will no longer feel inadequate in any situation, because you have moved forward in the strength and wisdom drawn from Divine Consciousness, and recognise that you, too, have equal rights with everyone else.

Quietly, calmly, you will not allow others to take advantage of you. You will be able to speak your mind clearly and honestly with due regard for the feelings of the other person. You will no longer want to denigrate another and reduce their self-esteem. Rather, will you make every effort to save their self-respect yet relating your truth in a clear, but loving way.

Remember, when stating your truth to another, it is not within your province to tell them how they should act in any given circumstance or how they should react to your words.

However, standing by UNIVERSAL VALUES of perfect honesty, conscientious work, goodwill towards all, caring for the under-privileged, a person is entitled to demand that these values should take precedence over every other consideration of EXPEDIENCY within a group or community enterprise or national endeavour.

You also have a perfect right to say how you are made to feel by a person's belittling behaviour towards you – **should you be aware of a need to do so. It is probable that your caring honesty may be necessary to solve or clarify a certain situation for the good of all.**

State your case with kindness – gently tell them how you feel in the present unpleasant circumstances and explain what has made you feel that way. Do not say 'You did such and such a thing' because they will feel you are blaming them and immediately you will arouse the ego defence mechanism in the other person. Thereafter, the confrontation will become difficult and unpleasant for both of you. To get through to ego-driven people you must continually speak in such a way as they will never feel threatened. This is the art of loving communication and you can only learn it by trial and error and dedicated practice!

Each time, you conquer ego in yourself, it becomes that much easier to relate to others because you are reaching an understanding of the function of ego in all people.

As time passes, and you are gradually released from the grip of your ego-drive, you will find that, more and more, you can listen to others with soul empathy and love. If they behave in a way which would have hurt or offended you previously, you will feel the welling up of laughter instead. You will then know that your soul is in direct touch with **Divine Consciousness** – for **Its** natural state is that of laughter.

Laughter is a **consciousness impulse** which ripples across your skies, from one planet to another, through your Milky Way and out into the furthest reaches of infinity. As infinite as **Divine Consciousness**, it came into existence at the moment of the **Big Bang.**

What is Laughter? It is a spontaneous consciousness response to a situation where two events or two incidents or two people, do not – in the natural order of things – belong together, they are strangely at odds or in opposition to each other.

It is a **ripple effect** experienced in all living things of higher species capable of certain judgments or perceptions. **It eliminates stress.** The 'ripple effect' is felt over the diaphragm which guards the heart and nervous system.

As you have seen on examining the nature of creation, everything possible has been done in the evolution of design and growth of living bodies to make a perfectly adapted body to suit the environment to enable the occupier of the body to be comfortable and happy and live without stress. Stress is inimical to health.

It is contrary to the **WILL of DIVINE CONSCIOUSNESS.**

A spontaneous and hearty burst of laughter is first experienced as a rush of rippling consciousness through the head, bringing a lightening of the entire consciousness. This is immediately followed by the physical 'ripple effect' of laughter, experienced as a light beating of breath on the diaphragm to break up any tension and to smooth away any residue of bitterness.

Sometimes laughter in an extremely amusing situation is prolonged to such an extent that the person eventually feels exhausted – but also happy and rather sad that the laughter is finished.

Most people will testify that laughter promotes a feeling of well-being, even if there was discord just a minute earlier. If a person can genuinely laugh, seeing the absurdity of a situation, where there has previously been annoyance or hurt, the tension is released and friendly relationships are restored spontaneously.

Laughter is a gift of love for a creation possessed by, and needing relief from their egos.

As the ego drive gradually relinquishes its hold over your mind and emotions, you will find that laughter bubbles up spontaneously and brings a wonderful feeling of release. The 'ripple effect' of laughter raises your consciousness frequencies of vibration not only because it is energy released where you most need it – over your heart – over your diaphragm, the seat of your emotions but because **LAUGHTER** is directly of **Divine Consciousness.**

Therefore, laughter is Divine.

LAUGHTER and your inner child. As you read these **Letters** and meditate and your levels of frequencies of consciousness vibrations are raised, you will discover that old mental patterns are no longer comfortable in your mind. You will seek ways and means of ejecting them from your consciousness. As you move upwards spiritually and are ever more desirous of unloading unwanted **human ego drives,** the conflict in your sensibilities will become increasingly burdensome, and you now long and pray for relief. You will find that when you turn to **Divine Consciousness and passionately ask for Divine Assistance, the help will surely come**. You will successfully get rid of unwanted thoughts and re-actions, and you will then discover that laughter becomes more and more spontaneous.

You will also discover tensions are smoothed away and that you are becoming much lighter in thought, easier in relationships, more caring, much more appreciative, more aware of life itself and all that it has to offer in sight and experience. You will enjoy simple pleasures more, you will be less jaded in appetites, you will need less food, less entertainment, will be more content with your own company, and will eventually begin to rejoice in your **own**

company because DIVINE CONSCIOUSNESS will be infusing your human consciousness with Its own exalted State of WELL-BEING.

Little by little you will be returning to your 'child' condition which views the world with happy, enquiring gaze.

This is not senility. It is a state of greater awareness and vibrance no matter what your age may be.

This is the 'state of being' I meant when I said that 'Unless you become as a little child you shall in no wise enter the Kingdom of Heaven'. I actually said that when you enter the Kingdom of Heaven, you become a little child – a child in wonder and joy.

I have given the world these Letters that those who read and absorb them may eventually enter the 'Kingdom of Heaven' and reach that state of joy which comes of purity of mind and innocence.

SPIRITUAL EXERCISES

If people tell you to enter into 'spiritual exercises' and 'imagine' certain conditions – be sure that if you follow these instructions you will only keep yourself rooted in the material dimension of ego. Imagination has nothing to do with 'spirit'. Imagination is the exercise of your own human consciousness which you should be trying to transcend by entering into higher levels of spiritual consciousness. These levels are not those of imagination but those of 'Reality'– regular spiritual levels of frequencies of spiritual consciousness vibrations. The spiritual frequencies are those of Divine spiritual consciousness not of earthly mental imagination. Therefore, beware whom you would accept as your teacher.

Only absolute 'Stillness' and 'Silence' of your consciousness will open the door to the entry of **Divine Consciousness** into your mind and that is what everyone should be seeking. If you are thirsty and you need a drink – why imagine you are beside a lake? Go to the lake itself and take a drink of pure refreshing water. Again I say, imagination is not spiritual – it is the exercise of your will within your present level of consciousness.

RACISM

For you who have come to understand the truth concerning 'who you really are', I want to talk to you about the world-wide concern regarding 'racism'.

I would have you know that this talk of RACISM arises only out of the ego-drive of those people who have felt themselves despised and rejected because of their racial differences. These feelings are rooted so deeply in the 'self' that no matter how circumstances may change for them and they may be able to progress in life, even becoming characters of extreme importance on the world stage of life, there always remains the feeling of inadequacy and resentment against the people who first made them feel inferior.

It should be understood that such feelings of inferiority are not unique to black races.

These feelings of 'extreme lowliness' are experienced by the majority of people subjected to the caste system in India, class distinctions in the European culture, and in those countries where 'differences' are made into mountains of separation of one person from another. These painful and undermining feelings of 'lesser status' are experienced even by the so-called exalted personages who are never quite comfortable in their positions of authority.

This feeling of inadequacy and unworthiness is endemic to the human race as a whole, no matter what the position, or race, or education of an individual may be.

The feeling of 'worthlessness' arises to a large extent from the deep, deep awareness of the psyche that ego-behaviour is contrary to the highest principles of human existence. When this natural inbuilt drive of 'unworthiness' is re-inforced by proximity with other apparently more prestigious or successful people, then this natural feeling of inadequacy takes on agonising overtones.

The only means of overcoming the ethnic painful feelings of rejection, even when highly successful, is to reach the clear realisation that if there had not been the kind of ethnic upheavals, removals, arrival of strangers and aliens with their different languages, cultures, educational processes and their subjection of your natural states and modes of living, the various races would not now be occupying the positions of responsibility and worldly status as some have achieved at this moment.

Therefore, the only healing and life-renewing course of action is to meditate, ponder, reflect, and ask for Divine Light on the subject until you can, in all honesty say: 'Lord – I am sincerely glad and happy that all those terrible

329

things took place. Because of them, I am where I am today, because of them I have been given an opportunity to test and experience the extent of my endurance, intellect, emotions, talents. I can measure myself against the achievements of other races – and perhaps continue to learn how to rise still further from my beginnings. I thank You for the strength and inspiration to show my basic equality with everyone else – I send out my thoughts of love and gratitude to those who laid the foundations for my present good all those many, many years ago.'

You can also reflect upon the fact that it was inevitable, according to the **LAWS of EXISTENCE,** that those who were connected with slave trading and other tragic events, or were responsible for handing out pain and torture to other human beings, should return in a future life as a member of the down-trodden races and suffer grievously. When born into black races, it is more than likely these people were vociferous in their demands for equality and humane treatment for black people. Such a person may even have been your great grandfather or father – and you may be wondering why life has treated the 'poor soul' so badly. Alternatively, the 'white people' who manacled the black people and kept them in dungeons, at this time, may still be creating mayhem for other people by occupying the stratum of society of all races which are rebelling vociferously against the past. It may well be a past which they themselves had helped to bring into being.

IT IS A FACT that people are re-incarnated into different strata of society in different races to enable the soul to learn some meaningful lesson as it journeys upwards towards CHRIST CONSCIOUSNESS.

Bear in mind the fundamental principle of existence. You, yourselves, create your to-morrows.

You bring into being, also, whatever you need for your upliftment by reaching out for it. Whether you are aware of it or not, as you reach out for an improvement in your life conditions, you are spontaneously reaching into higher levels of spiritual consciousness.

As I have already told you – the DIVINE WILL is to release creation from stress, and therefore, those lessons needed to take you upward towards Divine Consciousness will come into your experience. Therefore FORGIVE – for you have no true knowledge of the journey of your soul through many centuries of earthly existence. You have no knowledge of what you, yourself, did in lives gone past. Forgive the present, forgive the past and accept that much good has come out of it, learn to bless and love those whom you thought injured you or your ancestors.

And you who presently occupy skins which carry the power of privilege – consider other races and their problems, and reflect upon the fact that you may, in a future life, occupy an underprivileged body and come to know, first hand, what it is like to be born with a sense of being a second class citizen. Reflect also on your past lives, ponder what you may or may not have done to bring about your present situation. The truth about RACISM is this:

Every single entity under the sun has descended from Divine Consciousness in one way or another. At the very inmost roots of their being, everyone is united in ONENESS.

Therefore, where do the differences lie?

They arise out of the development of species, genetics, conditioning, traditional teachings, customs and educational and family habits of relating with others and the differences in thought patterns.

It is not the colour which divides you. A small child of every race and colour because of its innocence and spontaneity of self-expression will find acceptance in the heart of most adults. It is the CONSCIOUSNESS which divides you and which is felt on every level of your being – for you are all, despite your materialised bodies, CONSCIOUSNESS FORMS expressing consciousness patterns and CONSCIOUSNESS FORMS receiving consciousness patterns from others. The consciousness of each individual is their reality – not their skin or appearance – and it is the consciousness of people which either attracts or repulses others.

You can rest assured that you will only overcome your sense of racial differences when your mental/emotional thought patterns are in sympathy, and when your VALUES by which you choose to live throughout your day, are the same. Until that time comes, it is useless for people to be angry with one another for experiencing racial differences. They are endemic to the human condition.

If you want to be accepted completely into another race, you have to change your values, your perceptions, your ideas, modes of living and of relating to others to match everyone else's in that race. Racial differences then die a natural death.

If you are not prepared to take on the 'consciousness' of the race you wish to join, then acknowledge, accept and RESPECT with LOVE the differences in consciousness. No one has the right to demand you should ignore the differences.

MOST IMPORTANTLY OF ALL: Choose the highest standards on offer in the world, work to embrace and use them – and then all skin colours will take on a new and inner beauty which none will be able to resist. All people will then willingly bond in perfect harmony.

Physical appearances of every colour will also change and take on new inner beauty.

When these Letters have been distributed throughout the world and groups of people bond together to live within the spiritual laws of existence, such groups will find they are living harmoniously protected lives, although there may be mayhem going on around them.

Everywhere, those who bond together to learn how to enter – and live within – the Wholeness of Being which I termed the 'Kingdom of Heaven' 2000 years ago, will discover that their circumstances are surely changing.

I urge you to meet together on a Sunday to speak of your many blessings, give sincere wholehearted thanks and raise your minds in praise of That Which has given you Being.

Meditate together to draw Divine Consciousness through your minds into world consciousness that the nature of the Divine may, more and more, imbue the nature of the world psyche with Its own transcendent Love.

Your groups will emit spiritual consciousness energy which will influence mind energies around you.

I would have you remember that the world was not in such a dangerous predicament when the churches, world-wide, met on Sundays to worship God.

Those days are now past. You will not worship God.

You will build up a strong awareness of Divine Consciousness universally present. Its universality and scope of creativity will be ever more firmly entrenched in your minds by means of sincere praise. In the silence and stillness, you will all reach out to DIVINE CONSCIOUSNESS and invite IT lovingly to take possession of your mind and heart. Thus, little by little will you become unified, and the Divine Consciousness will, more and more, take possession of the world as was Its earliest intention.

RE-INCARNATION

There are many who will ask how it is that at the moment of conception, a soul can be drawn from **Divine Consciousness**, but the body itself may be used as a vehicle of self-expression in its coming life-span by another soul, who is ready to re-incarnate.

When a soul is ready to enter earthly conditions on its next span of earthly learning, the soul is drawn to the parent – or parents – who can offer those conditions which will enable it to take its next necessary step forward in spiritual evolution. At the moment of conception, the old soul infuses its personal consciousness of past lives and past spiritual progress into the conception process and becomes the soul of the fertilised ovum.

Some mothers are almost immediately aware of an alien consciousness within them. The new consciousness the mother has received in her womb, sometimes deeply affects the course of her thinking, her pregnancy and state of health. Once the child is born, the mother feels that she has been restored to her normal self. Sensitive mothers frequently experience an awareness of the direction their child's life will take and may think that this awareness is really born of her own wishes for her baby.

Re-incarnation is not haphazard or without a consistent plan directing its action.

The purpose is always to provide the journeying soul with many entirely different experiences which will enlarge the soul's hidden store of worldly knowledge. It provides stimulating and necessary changes of scenery and of family and environmental personalities, of characteristics drawn from genetics, but **always** that thin thread of the soul's journey will be buried in the subconscious mind and will surface to influence the present incarnation, although the person may be wholly unaware of it. Therefore, it is possible for characteristics, strongly held views, or passionate ambitions to be perpetuated from one incarnation to another. Sometimes the ambitions are formulated in one lifetime and only brought into a successful manifestation in the next lifetime under entirely different conditions. In such cases, before re-birth, a soul must wait until the world conditions will further the hidden ambitions of the soul successfully.

If you can imagine a soul first plunging into a red pond and coming out dyed red and entering life as a red person with all its natural red racial tendencies and educated in childhood to live 'red' lives, you will understand that the soul leaves that life with much that is red in his consciousness.

Next he will plunge into a blue pool and he will emerge blue with all the characteristics of blueness – and the life style of blue people. When he leaves the world again, he will have accumulated facets of blue consciousness mixed with the red. And so it goes, life after life, the same soul growing through differing experiences of colours, religions, status, marriages, sexes, countries, politics, until finally, he wakes up to the fact that this is what is happening to him and he decides he is tired of all the various colour combinations – he wants only to ascend into LIGHT. Then his true spiritual journey starts – and gradually, by moving into one life after another, he sheds the red, blue, yellow, green, black, brown, purple accumulated in past lives, until at last, freed of all the illusions and false concepts of past lives, his soul steps out into LIGHT and re-incarnation is no longer necessary. The soul is strong, resourceful, creative – but the individuality of the soul is still inviolate and he begins to ascend into different levels of spiritual LIGHT beyond the frequencies of vibration of the world.

As I said in this Letter, I am with you always, radiating the TRUTH of BEING in consciousness. The more you read these Letters, the more you will become aware of my Presence and my Love and through this contact my loving purposes for you will be fulfilled. Only you will be able to break the contact. I am radiating Love no matter how you feel.

I leave you with my LOVE and longing for your speedy journey into Spiritual Light.

■■■

Christs Articles

CHRIST'S ARTICLES

Contents

1 - Cracks in your planet

I have come this time, not to speak beautiful passages of spiritual encouragement to arouse your spiritual yearnings but to reach into your daily lives with your own colloquial language to shed LIGHT on what people are daily doing to themselves – their bodies, lives, relationships and to the planet generally.

It is their thoughts – leading to words – leading to actions with which I am particularly concerned at this time.

People of all races and cultures – heed me!

The majority of thinking people realise that all your scientific technology and widespread industrialisation are slowly killing your planet.

You recognise this.

But when will you wake up to the even more vitally important and compelling realisation that your ego thoughts, words, actions are equally destructive of your planet because these are consciousness energy forms – and consciousness energy forms are precisely what your world is created from – consciousness energy forms.

Your entire world is nothing more than a giant consciousness energy form composed of billions of individual consciousness forms sprung from and based upon the Void of Universal Consciousness which you could term 'God' and have been evolved from apparent nothingness to its present state through the process of your own desires and longings.

Therefore, you must try to understand that when, daily, you pour your ego consciousness through the medium of your thoughts, words, actions, into your world, you are sending out consciousness forms which are entirely contrary to the Laws of UNIVERSAL CONSCIOUSNESS.

You are helping billions of other like-minded people to create a destructive force in direct conflict with your SOURCE of BEING, UNIVERSAL CONSCIOUSNESS which underpins and sustains all existence.

Inevitably, **CRACKS IN THE STRUCTURE OF YOUR PLANET** take place and people experience tornados, earthquakes, floods and blizzards – which are ALL physical manifestations of the breakdown of UNIVERSAL LAW, which is UNIVERSAL LOVE, governing your world.

Does this indicate that 'god' love has been withdrawn from the world?

No! There is no such thing as 'punishment from 'god' – because no such individualised 'human thinking'god exists. This is a myth which should be erased from people's minds.

But your planet and you yourself, have been individualised out of UNIVERSAL CONSCIOUSNESS which ITSELF is a Law which I constantly re-iterated when on earth – the LAW of FAITH in good and evil.

The LAW of CONVICTION.

Whatever you truly believe in – good, bad and indifferent will eventually be manifested in your lives. Therefore, be warned, and use the knowledge on this website to free yourself of the world's most destructive consciousness – ego consciousness.

Going to church will not help you. Sunday worship will not release you.

Your only hope of shaking yourself free from ego and the world's destructive consciousness is to follow the CHRIST WAY.

The Christ Way is the WAY which I, personally followed and lived after full enlightenment in the desert – enlightenment which enabled me to return to Nazareth and embark on a new life of healing, teaching and control of the elements. Because my teaching was in direct opposition to Judaic teaching of retribution, and a vengeful Jehovah, I was eventually crucified. Any other explanation of my crucifixion is spurious and wholly untrue.

Prior to my six weeks in the desert in Palestine, I was an idle non-achiever. After enlightenment, I was sole keeper of the secrets of creation and creativity.

My enlightenment is fully explained in **Letter 1** and my full transcendent perception of the truth of existence itself, is outlined in my **Letters.**

These are offered free to all who have the will and courage to WALK my CHRIST WAY leading ultimately to enlightenment, freedom from ego and entry into the Kingdom of Heaven.

Enlightenment can come in various ways – it can come as a mind-blowing experience which immediately transforms your perception of your SOURCE of BEING and your previous intellectual understanding of your world. True Enlightenment is an inflow of Divine Consciousness into your human consciousness which you will never lose and which permanently transforms your attitudes to your Creator and your life generally.

Or – through persistent study of my **LETTERS**, little moments of extraordinary insight, little times of illumining shafts of LIGHT will enter your mind which will shift the focus of your inner sight – or clear the lens through which you see the world and judge the validity of all its opinions and beliefs.

Gradually, you shed the illusions which previously blinded you and you find yourself gaining mastery of your mind and actions, leading to wholeness in every aspect of your individual being.

Walking the CHRIST WAY – as set out in my **LETTERS** – is a lifetime work leading directly to freedom from anxiety and want.

As you read, you will find in them both my Presence and my Love.

2 - Create wonderful lives

'Create beautiful lives, wonderful sex.'

CHRIST SAYS:

"I have come again to talk, colloquially, about your lives and the way you approach your daily living. You get up in the mornings and have absolutely no idea of what really lies ahead. You plunge into your routine and speak sentences and say words without a second thought of their likely impact on your environment or of what they may do to your listeners or of what you are laying up for yourselves in the future.

You believe you are in control of your life but, in fact, you are all acting heedlessly and in total ignorance of what, minute by minute, you are creating for yourselves.

Just as importantly, you carry around an emotional burden which no amount of interesting events or exciting experiences can wipe from your heart and consciousness. Everywhere you go, the emotional burden lowers your consciousness vibrations and moves down into your nervous system and then into your physical cells, reducing the life force in them and their mode of functioning – including their efficiency in self-repair.

When you encounter opposition, your human ego stands up bristling in self-defense. Your Ego's job as 'Custodian of your Individuality' is to ensure your survival. Therefore, it springs to your defense and you feel that opposition in any form, is intolerable and not to be borne.

As a result, you find your minds and emotions becoming agitated, resentful and heated, and you want to hit back, to make the opposition go away, whether it is justified or not.

This is something that people must understand about the Ego – it is absolutely lacking in insight, objectivity or spontaneous sense of justice.

When you are controlled by the Ego Impulses, the consciousness vibrations you are now emitting are so off balance, so devoid of good sense, that they adversely affect the people around you and create consciousness blueprints of so much disharmony that they begin to affect your future experiences, activities and situations.

It is vitally important to your future welfare and lives that you wake up to the fact that you are not victims of your circumstances and the experiences in your lives – but the CREATOR of them.

For instance, if, during the day, you create a rumpus or argument with work mates or boss, when you return home from your work to your nearest and dearest in the evenings, you may be still controlled by your resentful Ego. If so, you no longer speak from the quietness of your truth or from any spiritual values you may possess – for these will now be discoloured and distorted by the run-away emotions you created for yourself at work earlier in the day.

Equally, in the morning, you may emerge from your home (which should be a place where your spirit is renewed and your heart uplifted in warmth), but you walk through your front door swathed with the disquiet of early morning grumpy reactions to and from your partner.

Perhaps you had a row with your partner over one grievance or another and tried to heal it with sex, only to find that whilst the sex seemed to bring you emotionally closer again, it did not really satisfy, and it did not heal the resentment. You must understand that when you have unprotected sex, you exchange not only your body fluids but also your consciousness.

Many people's consciousness is constantly so reactive, even hostile, towards mankind and life generally, that it not only reduces the physical health of the individual but also adversely affects the partner's physical and emotional wellbeing.

When, after a hurtful row you have sex to 'make-up the quarrel, you are then also infused with the consciousness of your partner's bad feelings. All unknowingly, you take those to work with you as well as your own.

I am explaining to you exactly how your earthly world (which you call solid), but is really CONSCIOUSNESS energy – is fashioned out of bad temper consciousness forms or those of love and good humour – affecting your health and performance in life for good or ill. Whatever kind of consciousness you are creating, you leave your energy imprint on everything you encounter … including your car, your computer and anything else you may be using during the day.

"How can this be?" You will probably ask?

Because the entire universe with all its galaxies, is only CONSCIOUSNESS – LOVE/INTELLIGENCE in Its highest form working through the inter-actions of electromagnetism.

ELECTROMAGNETISM is really the 'stuff' of human mind power and emotional impulses – as they are seen within the field of earthly life.

Read Letters 5 and 6 until you fully understand that nothing is solid. All you see, feel, touch, are really CONSCIOUSNESS IMPULSES made visible through the interplay of electromagnetism.

When you have fully understood this and have seen the true place you occupy in creating good health or non-health, happiness or non-happiness FOR YOURSELF AND OTHER PEOPLE – you may then be persuaded that the only sensible way forward is to WALK CHRIST'S WAY ...... .the WAY of UNCONDITIONAL LOVE

How can you begin to change your normal thought patterns and master your unruly emotions?

You can do it by exercising will-power. But when you rely on your will-power, you are leaning on the same ego consciousness as causes you to lose your sense of emotional balance. This is like using treacle to wipe away a mess of treacle.

Or you can learn to control your Ego by seeking to know and make contact with the SOURCE of your BEING,

Which I termed the 'Father'.

Read Letters 7 and 8

You are not alone. With consistent prayer and meditation, eventually you will make contact with THAT which will prove to be your greatest source of good and comfort in the world.

No doubt, many people will be writing in to as whether Christ approves of or condemns condoms. Christ's vibrant answer to this is:

No new, creative ideas ever come from the human brain cells. People who invent and create something new, receive the new idea from the Universal. Whatever comes from the Universal can be used to benefit creation.

The creation of the condom was one of the most loving and wonderful gifts and blessings to appear on earth both outside and within the bonds of marriage It has brought relief to women sorely burdened by the demands of importunate men. It has been the means of sparing unwanted children the misery of an unloved existence. Countless children may have been born into poverty and died early deaths. With the arrival of Aids, the condom is certainly a means of protecting a partner.

But, it must be understood, there are facets of existence where MORALITY should be exercised.

Letter 9 is very clear on what is TRUE sexual morality, true SPIRITUAL And blessed sex, which the Church knows nothing about.

3 - Is there really a God?

I have returned to speak to you in colloquial language to address various problems which people have to deal with when on earth.

I am doing this, through the mind of my Recorder, because those who have truly embraced the TRUTH contained in my **Letters** and who try to govern their daily lives by this deep understanding of the secrets of creation have eventually found great relief from former burdens.

They have discovered, with joy, that mankind is not born to be a victim of circumstances. They have found that they have a real, reliable 'MEANS' of overcoming difficulties or bearing setbacks with inner strength and even happiness.

What is this 'MEANS'?

It is the SOURCE of all BEING – not the Jehovah type God described in the Bible but the UNIVERSAL LIGHT of BEING which is experienced by true mystics. As time goes by, people with a longing to delve more deeply into spiritual TRUTH (not religion) will discover they have a natural capacity for mysticism. When this happens, such people will no longer ask:

'Is there really a God?'

but will know beyond all doubt that there is a magnificently powerful, universal FIRST CAUSE or UNIVERSAL SOURCE of BEING out of Which all things have taken individualised form; in which magnificent CONSCIOUSNESS ENERGY all living and inanimate things are sustained and maintained throughout their worldly lives … and ever after.

Can you grasp how wonderfully uplifting and gloriously exciting it is to discover that you are not really a burdened soul, a victim of circumstances, born to be stuck in the rut into which you were born or the ravine into which you have fallen in later years?

Can you understand how exhilarating it is to come to the full and clear realization that this UNIVERSAL CONSCIOUSNESS ENERGY has been within you all these years, secretly and quietly maintaining the growth, nutrition, healing, protection from germs, ensuring replacement of dying cells, giving added strength to muscles and tendons when called to do so by extra exercise … all these wonderful activities within your bodies have taken place without any help from you.

Can you see that you are daily, nightly, supported by – what you do not know?

Scientists can explain all these activities but they cannot start to explain what great IMPULSE of BEING impels them into action.

I can tell you – because I was given full enlightenment on earth and because I have ascended through the various levels of LIGHT until I am on the very edge of the ETERNAL EQUILIBRIUM in which our mutual FIRST CAUSE, SOURCE of all BEING resides in a VOID of Stillness and Silence.

I know the true nature of our FIRST CAUSE because I am an almost perfect individualisation of IT myself.

YOU and I, who am the Ascended Christ, formerly known as 'Jesus' when on earth, have BOTH come from the same SOURCE which I called the 'FATHER' because, after enlightenment, I realized that IT is the TRUE FATHER/MOTHER OF ALL CREATION.

Human parents are only the vehicles of creation through which the SOURCE of BEING works.

Trust me, for I know beyond all doubt and tell you truly –

Whilst your human parents may let you down, When you walk MY WAY – the CHRIST WAY You will eventually find that the FATHER is an unfailing SOURCE of supply, healing, guidance, presenting of unexpected opportunities, inspiration and joy.

No matter where you may be on earth, what trouble you may be in, what disgrace you are facing, what lack of money may be dogging you, right within you, around and above you, you have the SPIRITUAL MEANS on which to call with all your heart and mind – and the answer will surely come – IF YOU DO NOT DOUBT.

Many people will disagree with this statement and scoff. But it is also true that they have lived in a state of disbelief.

Those who have chosen to walk, minute by minute, MY WAY – CHRIST'S WAY will agree with my words for they will have learnt how to meditate properly – quietening the mind, experiencing a little of the Stillness and Silence of the Void and the Universal Equilibrium – the very Source of creation – and thereby drawing on the SOURCE of all creativity and perfection.

Let no one dare to condemn or criticize these words, until they, too, have managed to quieten their chattering minds and entered the Silence. After such an experience, no human mind can resist the call of the Divine to seek THAT Which has given them life and raised them up to adulthood.

Go to **Letter 1** to discover what I learnt through total enlightenment in the Desert in Palestine.

When you have fully absorbed the full TRUTH concerning existence and begin to try to put the knowledge into daily action as I did – you, too, will find miracles happening, ever more swiftly, the more deeply and fully you absorb and practice the eternal Verities.

To fully understand your SOURCE and your true relationship to IT – **read Letters 5 and 6** – read them again and again so that you will never again think of your world as being solid matter – but will immediately recognize that it is only composed of ETERNAL CONSCIOUSNESS and the magnificent IMPULSES which comprise the NATURE of all BEING.

4 - Chase the Bogeys

CHRIST explains in colloquial language

'WHY YOU MUST ALWAYS LOOK UNDER YOUR BED before you go to sleep at night'

What does this usually mean in your world? It means that when you are young, you sometimes have a fear of bogey men hiding under your bed and so you must look to see if they are really there.

When you WALK CHRIST'S WAY, you must always examine your mindset before you sleep, to discover what fears you are harbouring. When you have discovered whether you have any and what they are, you must remind yourself that just as your imagination placed bogey men under your bed when you were a child, so do you, as an adult, imagine catastrophes that NEED never happen.

Please note: I say: "Need never happen" – not 'May' never happen.

I say this because no matter what your problems may be, they remain only in your mind as 'problems'

until you have given them enough mind power to manifest themselves as 'apparent realities' in your life.

Problems may be grave POSSIBILITIES according to the way your affairs stand at the moment. For instance, you may be headed for dismissal from work, you may be so short of money you do not know how to manage next week, your child may be falling behind at school or facing expulsion – whatever the problem, it does not become a true problem until it manifests as a reality in your life. In the meanwhile, they remain 'MAYBEs' for the future but already they are making you cringe and walk around with a heavy heart.

But even if the fears should manifest as apparent realities in the future – even on the very brink of disaster, things can CHANGE!

PEOPLE in the world, who constantly WORRY, usually feel that nothing GOOD is sure or reliable, yet the very opposite is true. Oh, you dear, dear people, if only I could lift your consciousness high above the world, take you behind the scenes of visible matter to the unseen dimension of spiritual creativity where everything truly begins to come into being. You could then see for yourselves that the SOURCE of your BEING, your only SOURCE of SPIRITUAL UNCONDITIONAL LOVE has put in place everything to fulfill your every need, but you, because you do not understand the reality behind existence, create your own lack and limitations, sickness and disasters. You create them with your criticism, complaining, being grudging in praise of others' achievements, grudging in affection to all people around you, grudging in generosity to those who are experiencing poverty.

To discover why this is so, read **Letter 1** until you fully understand the TRUE NATURE of your SOURCE of BEING which I called 'the Father' when I was on earth.

When you walk CHRIST'S WAY (MY WAY) you know very well, beyond all doubt, that your absolute faith and conviction in Divine Protection will bring you out of your troubles and will rescue you from possible loss or pain.

To find out just why people who truly WALK CHRIST'S WAY can possess such faith and conviction, read and read **Letters 5 and 6** until you fully realize that the things you can see, feel and touch are really only IMPULSES made visible through the good services of electromagnetism.

When you WALK CHRIST'S WAY, you also know, just as I did when I was on earth, there are just some things you have to go through – because they are a natural consequence of something you have done in the past. It is a result of something you did – it will now return in the form of a necessary lesson which will bring you spiritual growth ...out of which will come spiritual blessings.

BUT ... When you truly WALK CHRIST'S WAY- you accept the lesson without resistance or resentment because, CHRIST LIKE, you too, KNOW ... that you will be given the strength and inner comfort to go through the lesson with the least distress.

Read Letter 3 in which I speak of my time on earth and the few weeks before my crucifixion. You will see that 'mind control' in any eventuality is the only way to face up top life and overcome its obstacles.

5 - Walking in Love

WALKING IN LOVE – BECOMING LOVE

As I said to you in my last article, this series of notes to you will be practical and down to earth, using colloquial language to reach you more easily.

I know that as soon as you hear a message concerning 'love', you may react with a lift of your shoulders, thinking:

"Yes, that is what they all say. Very easy to say Christ has sent a message about Love – but tell us something new, something real!"

The very first thing I want to tell you is this:

There are two kinds of love – both completely different. They arise in two different dimensions of being.

One is Spiritual and unattainable by the human consciousness until it has gone through specific stages of initial ego-cleansing.

The second love is human and has nothing to do with Spiritual Love.

When a person's soul begins to free itself of the Ego, it begins to impress within the person's consciousness an urgent need to get rid of the barriers which shut one person off from another and to feel spiritually at peace with other people. This is an advanced state of the soul which will now meet a personal Master to lead him/her through the various stages of death of the Ego.

If you examine the nature of human love, you will find that it is entirely based on 'a desire for something which will give you pleasure' – whether it be new clothes, different foods, a new house, more opulent car, new partner.

That is why human love evaporates with time. If you come across a man or woman who continue to care deeply about their spouse's welfare after many, many years together, you can be sure that certain aspects of the lover is ascending into the spiritual dimension and absorbing a capacity for unconditional love from higher realms.

When you encounter the mindset: 'I no longer love you and want someone else', you will recognize that this is Human Love, governed by Human Ego speaking, and the consciousness of that person is quite unable to say anything different as that is the level of their personal spiritual perception in your world.

Therefore, they are not in any way to be judged –

Now if you have one facet of your consciousness already in the spiritual dimension, you will be able to reply quietly and patiently to the partner:

"I see. I understand your statement. You must do what you feel you have to do in the circumstances. Go in peace. Would you like me to help you pack and call a taxi?"

If, on the other hand, such a statement is ever made to a HUMAN consciousness, governed by the Ego, he/she will yell:

"I always knew you were a s.. of a b.... I don't want to see your ugly face again ..." or words conveying a similar message of angry rejection.

OR

He/she will scream: "After all I've done for you. Is that the way you repay me?"

OR

He/she will weep and say: 'You know you don't mean what you're saying (although he has made it quite clear he means what he is saying) and you cling to his leg whilst he drags the partner out of the door.

(I told you I would use colloquial language to get through to you. My Recorder is shocked and did not know what I really intended doing before we started these articles.)

I think that you are now beginning to understand 'Ego language'. Because you recognize: 'I WANT.'

or 'I DON'T WANT – SO I REJECT.'

BOTH FEELINGS ARE PERFECTLY LEGAL and LEGITIMATE (according to Universal Law) providing you are not making anyone else suffer by stealing, or running away from them.

If you read Letters 7 & 8, you will come to understand exactly what I mean by Ego Love and SPIRITUAL LOVE. You will learn how to move through the Ego Barrier to make contact with the spiritual vibrations of UNCONDITIONAL LOVE to make it possible for you to feel and express true, spiritual, unconditional Love.

This is essential if you intend to Walk Christ's Way.

6 - You are NOT Alone!

CHRIST SAYS:

'I have come to speak to you in colloquial language as far as I am able, to reach people who have not yet found my **LETTERS** and who, presently, see no reason to read them.

'In fact, my **LETTERS**, explaining what I taught in Palestine and giving further explanation of the origins of creation, will give receptive people the means to overcome every difficulty encountered in existence.

'This may sound like a far-fetched claim but it is nonetheless true. The **Letters** give you the information known to true Masters who showed that they had control of 'atomic states of being' by controlling the elements and creating food and objects from nothing. I also controlled the elements, healed and created necessities and was only able to do so because I possessed the deep and secret knowledge I have shared with you in my **Letters.**

Do not compare my message to you with the messages from others.

Everyone has their unique mission and purpose in life – and mine is EXCLUSIVELY to give you the exact means to lift yourselves out of your present turmoil of existence – nothing else. Therefore, my messages may be repetitive but they are directed solely to inspiring and helping you to make a decision to follow CHRIST'S WAY – MY WAY, no matter how difficult you may find that way to be. You will persevere because along My Way, you will find rewards which will prove to you that you are definitely on the right path.

But you cannot put foot to My Way until you realize fully and completely that the entire universe is CONSCIOUSNESS – AWARENESS made visible through the inter-action of electrical particles and magnetism.

This is fully explained in **Letters 5 and 6.** But reading alone will not make you a Master. A true Master understands that the ORIGIN of all creation is UNIVERSAL CONSCIOUSNESS and that IT is the Divine Source of all Love and Intelligence. To be a true Master, a person has to understand the way the universe has come into being, know, intimately, the true nature of UNIVERSAL CONSCIOUSNESS, and has to so purify himself of the impulses of the Ego, that he is absolutely free of all ego impurities in his mind and emotions.

When he reaches this state of inner cleanliness of thought, feeling and action, never demanding of others but willing and eager to give to the uttermost of all he possesses, because he knows perfectly well that he can have anything he needs, he will be a perfectly open channel of DIVINE CONSCIOUSNESS which is the creative Impulse within this dimension of visible creation.

When he has achieved such a state of inner purity and cleanliness, he will live in a state of inner joy, peace, and unconditional love. He will understand the living world and the difficulties such living things encounter and feel an immediate and spontaneous love and compassion for all.

He will have transcended the world and its millions of self-interests, self-indulgences, experiences of despair, fear, revenge, hatred, slandering, gossip, rejection of others. All these worldly activities will go on around him but he will not experience them himself. He will only feel boundless compassion and love for them. He will only long and yearn passionately, to TEACH the world the TRUTH OF BEING.

He will make every sacrifice with joy, to help people understand the TRUTH and live it in their every thought, word, deed. He will do this, because it will be painful for him to know that as people stubbornly persist in their own way, thinking, feeling, reacting, in any way that their emotions prompt them to do, they are only creating more of the same misery which has driven them to seek a way out of it.

When people eventually find their way out of the morass of their chaotic thinking and emotional reactions, they discover that this is the only true way to happiness and they are exceedingly relieved and grateful that they have managed to surmount their habits of thought and feeling which previously pulled them down into experiences causing them pain and misery.

Do not marvel or question that it is truly I, the CHRIST, speaking to you. I come to speak to you through the total emptiness of my Recorder's mind and heart – and speak those things which are necessary for you to know to start to put behind you the sadnesses and despair of the past, and to give you the courage and incentive to start anew, daily meditating and drawing into your human consciousness the Divine Consciousness which brought you into being in the world.

Above all, I want you to understand you are not alone in your struggle to live comfortably and happily. You are not alone in your battle to change your habits of thoughts and feeling. The more you call upon for Divine Consciousness, even if it is only a momentary connection you set up, you are drawing into your consciousness new life and moments of Intelligence and Love which will inspire you to an even greater degree as you persevere and DO NOT LOSE HEART.

As you call on me, you will make contact with my Christ Consciousness and will eventually be aware of my response and instruction when you have questions to ask.

Remember that it takes time to purify your thoughts and emotions and negative reactions to other people. Until you have got rid of your deep and darkest feelings of anger, vitriolic criticism, rejection, resentment and frustration, you will not be able to hear my Voice.

Remember that to receive even my first whispers in the silence of your meditation or during a moment of inner quiet, you have to make changes in your consciousness, you have to become fully aware that LOVE is the only way to freedom, and this takes patience and time.

You are not alone. We who have moved into highest echelons of spiritual realisation and Divine Consciousness have only love for you and our most urgent desire is for your escape from travail and your progression into Light, wisdom and unconditional Love.

7 - My TRUE Mission

CHRIST says:

'I know how very difficult your life is. As I descend from the heights of spiritual Joy to make contact with earthly vibrations, I, myself feel the changes of consciousness within myself and feel the pressure of the heavy, burdensome vibrations and your thoughts upon my soul.

When I came to earth two thousand years ago, my Mission was to enlighten the minds of people who had taken on and into themselves, a religion part pagan – part mystical. The people, who had so imbued themselves, were arrogant and convinced they were the chosen people of a God – Jehovah – whom they ardently believed in but who did not exist.

Their prophets spoke of their mystical perception of some transcendent spiritual Consciousness. They used imaginative language to describe this GOD. They created mental images of greatness and grandeur. They also produced the desired effect of controlling the people by fear of reprisals from Heaven in the shape of personal loss, disease, deprivation, pests and climatic disasters.

The purpose behind my, Jesus', life in Palestine, was to teach the Jews that their perception of their CREATOR was entirely wrong. But their fanatical adherence to their treasured religious beliefs was impenetrable and consequently, instead of achieving my purposes on earth, I was crucified because of them.

It is not possible for me to return to earth in any form – either as a child, which could not contain my powerful vibrations, or as a Celestial Being. The multitudes would be unable to see me. Just as there are things seen and heard by animals which are invisible to the human eye, so do I remain invisible to people who are on an earthly wavelength.

Consequently, I have had to prepare the mind of an evolved soul who took on human form to bring my message to earth. Those who are sufficiently spiritually evolved to hear – will hear. Those who are not yet ready, will not hear and will not be able to receive – at this present time. But all people are on the upward walk leading eventually to the very highest Celestial kingdoms.

So what is my true Mission this time – through the mind of another?

It is to try to make people fully aware of the way in which their universe has been brought into visible manifestation and being.

This is the most important message ever brought to earth, since it goes way beyond superficialities, to the very basic level of all creativity and deals with the part that humans play in that creativity: in the creativity of their personality, health, relationships, environment, experiences and events in their lives. It explains the reasons for their success in their daily lives – or their lack of it. It outlines the sure way to change persistent failures into success.

This article is to draw your attention to the vibrations of consciousness. As your thoughts change, so do the vibrations because these are responsible for the appearance of all things. When trees are newly felled, they are healthy and their vibrations are of a certain frequency. But when the wood has lain on the ground for many, many years, the vibrations gradually drop – and the wood visibly rots.

You should understand that the appearance of the wood is only changing because the vitality and vibrations are gradually fading away.

Therefore, it should be easy to understand that the reality of everything under the sun is really within the underlying energy which supports it, not in the thing which can be touched, seen and heard.

The same applies to your bodies. In the beginning, vibrations in a healthy body are normal. Later on, through wear and tear and negative thoughts, the vibrations begin to drop to such an extent that the tissue changes and sickness sets in. When you are tired, exhausted, your vibrations in your body drop somewhat and it is no longer so easy to move around. After rest and sleep, the vibrations are restored and you feel able to continue your daily activities again.

Everything in existence is CONSCIOUSNESS appearing as different materials in plants, animals, humans, and in inanimate things such as the elements and stones, earth, metals.

Everything you encounter is really electrical particles vibrating at a certain rate, producing certain appearances. Change the vibrations of a thing radically – and inject it with a new consciousness – and you have a different commodity.

In this way could I, with the powerful use of my visual imagination and belief, draw together the electrical particles to create food. When you visualize what is needed, and believe with all your heart and mind that this electromagnetic blueprint will draw to itself the components to make it real in the world, eventually it will manifest itself.

This revelation has been around for a long time but the even greater revelation has been overlooked.

Beware of what you may be creating for yourself when you have no idea you are doing it.

Beware of those judgemental, critical thoughts which can harm another human being – and can return to harm you also.

Beware those unguarded emotional moments when you wish certain circumstances or events on another. Destructive thoughts bring about destructive consequences.

Have you found that things continually go wrong for you? Examine your attitudes and your thoughts about other people.

Remember that electricity sends out the message and magnetism brings it back – sometimes with interest.

Remember that when you look upon things with grave disfavour, or irritation you are interfering with their natural vibrations which make them what they are.

Beware, lest, unwittingly, you bring your own house down around your ears!

Beware when you contemplate the weather. Don't complain about the rain and say you wish it would stop. It may stop longer than you want it to. Don't complain about the sun and wish it would rain – it may come in floods.

When you WALK CHRIST'S WAY – MY WAY – you will take everything in the world which is posing problems to DIVINE CONSCIOUSNESS – the 'FATHER' and ASK for adjustments or needs which will be entirely suitable for you.

In this way, the 'FATHER' which is intimately connected with you, within you and around you, will respond with the right input of CONSCIOUSNESS to put all things right for you.

8 - When are you going to WAKE UP?

'When I last spoke to you, I was saying as clearly as I could through my Recorder's mind:

WHEN ARE YOU GOING TO WAKE UP, GROW UP AND DECIDE YOU WILL HAVE THE COURAGE TO CAST ASIDE YOUR OLD

WELL-LOVED MYTHS OF A BLEEDING CHRIST ON A CROSS, PAYING FOR YOUR SINS?

When will you accept MY Truth – the truth that I, Jesus, was seen to be a threat to public peace and a THREAT TO THE JEWISH LEADERS because I taught the people about a God of Love. A GOD Which did not need sacrifices!

I taught people that FORGIVENESS was essential to experience a happy and healthy life, whilst the Jews taught 'an eye for an eye' and that their GOD sent them into Holy Wars against the 'pagans'.

I, the true Christ, taught them that they should not be worried about unclean drinking cups but should watch what came from their minds and mouths.

Those who have insight and understanding will recognize that I have returned and am enlarging on this simple theme and explaining WHY I taught the principles of life which people now need so urgently to save themselves and the planet from wholesale disaster.

Read Letter 1 until you fully understand it.

Read Letters 5 and 6 until you fully realize:

- that you THINK and FEEL with the same energy as your world is created from.
- that your thoughts are electro-magnetic blueprints which eventually externalize as events and things you have either longed for – or greatly feared OR as those things which, good and bad, you have done to others.

Don't dismiss these **Letters** as having no bearing on your lives.

They explain exactly why LOVE is the very stuff of which your body has been fashioned. When you live with anger, resentment, and dislike in your hearts, you are actively creating negative forces which gradually undermine your health and destroy your bodies and your lives.

Because the **LETTERS** describe the true NATURE of 'THAT' Which has brought all visible things into conscious being and your exact relationship to IT, with the **LETTERS**' help, you can change your own self.

You can become the kind of person YOU will be happy to live with. Never again, will you have to be told to love and respect yourself

When you have read and re-read And LIVED my **LETTERS** daily, you will respect and esteem yourself spontaneously – naturally– JOYOUSLY.

You will rejoice in WHO you really are and in your limitless potential for creativity.

THIS IS NOT A NEW AGE teaching.

My CHRIST TEACHING remains and will remain the same throughout eternity:

'It is the 'Father' – DIVINE CONSCIOUSNESS – does the work of creativity in me – and will do so equally in you when you overcome the ego.

'When you, too, BECOME Universal Love.'

9 - Human love brings disappointment

CHRIST SAYS:

'LOVE – LOVE – LOVE – is the only way to healing, wellbeing, prosperity, true success, happiness.

'I know that you regard this talk of LOVE as being sanctimonious or sentimental, or advice that will make you 'please' 'God' – or 'pleasing' to 'God' – or that will make you a 'good' person as opposed to a 'wicked' one.

'But this is the way that your grandfathers thought. Never, at any time during or since my life in Palestine, did I ever make a statement to help you become a 'better' person.

'This is a Jewish misinterpretation of my earthly teachings.

Such interpretations must now be discarded as swiftly as possible. They cloud your inner perceptions and spiritual vision.

They prevent sincere spiritual seekers from accepting the TRUTH of BEING.

Knowledge of the TRUTH of BEING enabled me to leave the desert in Palestine a changed man, a spiritual Master and Healer in control of atomic elements.

It is now time for those who are ready, to absorb that knowledge and begin to construct the lives it is within their power to construct.

This is why I have deliberately set up a means of reaching the world through the dedicated co-operation of the Recorder, to try to lift you out of world-wide beliefs taught by Christian Churches – beliefs which are blinding your spiritual vision.

The BELIEF that you were created by the kind of 'God' which views the earth as a schoolmaster views his school, marking up black crosses for bad behaviour and awarding 'golden stars' for good work.

A GOD whom ignorant people worshipped for thousands of years, A GOD who needed GIFTS and WORSHIP to sway 'HIM' from sending punishments in the form of pests, diseases, floods, epidemics, death:

- a GOD who delighted in the sacrifice of birds and unblemished animals:
- a GOD who could only be reconciled to the world he had created, through the bloody death of his so- called only SON.

I, the true Christ, can only say to the Christians in the world: 'What a very exemplary, noble-minded GOD you have fashioned for yourselves! A GOD to be feared – but never revered!

I, the true Christ, can only ask the Christians in the world: 'What is there in your personal nature or character which drives you, in this more enlightened age, an age of evolving' brotherly love, to cling to and violently defend the old Christian Dogma, which, logically speaking, has not a single provable truth to commend itself to your reasoning mind.

You have made for yourselves, a GOD which you, yourselves, would never emulate, whose dictatorial behaviour your countries have legislated against by passing LAWS on HUMAN RIGHTS.

Your Human Laws have outlawed the stick in your schools, yet you cling to and defend a religion which is all about the 'big stick'....

'Believe in Jesus Christ or you'll go to hell.'

Since I, The CHRIST, am Universal LOVE Itself – please stop reading for a moment and try to understand that such a statement could never, ever be made by myself. Try to understand that my intervention by means of your Internet was inevitable.

I will leave you here to give you time to absorb my message. I commend to you **Letters 2 and 3**, describing as best we could, the real persona of Jesus who lived and was crucified in Palestine, 2000 years ago.

10 - Consciousness Energy

'Keep your Consciousness whole, unfragmented'

CHRIST says:

"It is of the greatest importance to your health, relationships, success in life and your happiness, that you should fully understand the true nature of Consciousness (Letter 5 & 6 onward) and of your own unique Consciousness.

"You must fully grasp that what you THINK – and FEEL – and what you DO, is a 'consciousness energy' which forms the entire fabric of your experiences in life. It is the driving force behind all that happens to you and what you do. It is the ground on which you build your life and the reservoir of strength giving impetus to your daily life. It is all you ARE beyond your soul, at this present moment.

It is the full scope of all you can be and do at this precise moment. The state of your consciousness limits or promotes your wellbeing. Therefore, the contents of your consciousness, the degree of your spiritual awareness, insights, perceptions, beliefs, knowledge, standards of behaviour, qualities of nature, morals, are your treasure from which you build your life. You can only build on what you are at this present time. And what you construct will be built of the elements or bricks of your consciousness – nothing else.

"Therefore, as hundreds of thousands of people are finding world-wide – if you want to change your life, you must first change your consciousness.

(**Letter7** describe how to do this, very clearly)

"When you drive a car, you make very certain (if you are wise) that every part of the car is in good working order. Every tiny contributing factor to the trouble-free running of your car must be attended to – the battery topped up and leads connected. Spark plugs cleaned and tuned, petrol in tank, oil in sump and so on.

"Therefore, to create a happy successful life, you must take the greatest and daily care of the various elements and facets of your consciousness.

"You will remember and try to practise non-criticism and non judgementalism for these are destructive of others and eventually, we find ourselves in a similar firing line. You will try to control your anger, searching your mind for reasons why the target of your anger, behaved as they did. This will defuse your anger. You will try to find lovable traits about everyone you meet or see throughout your day, otherwise, you will, all unknowingly, be radiating an offensive consciousness energy which will be picked up and resented by others.

Possibly, all of these facets of consciousness are already known to you. But now I want to tell you about the dangers of fragmenting your consciousness.

You do this even when you tell a white lie. A black lie is a horrendous insult to your own consciousness and to the consciousness of your listener. You may think that it is of no consequence but when you lie you send out a stream of false consciousness on which you expect other people to build their responses.

 Such a hitch in your consciousness, since you know you have lied, creates holes in the fabric of your own consciousness.

Where there are holes in your consciousness there is a hiatus in the life force you expend on activities and goals, and a foul-up in the consciousness which keeps you healthy and happy. Even in your communication, it will cause a lack of the vibrancy and certainty that those with whole and healthy consciousness fabrics, are able to impart when speaking to others or even simply leaving a spoken message.

A healthy consciousness is created when you treat others as you would like to be treated. Therefore, fulfill your promises or make provision that the breaking of a promise will not cause undue frustration or unhappiness or difficulty.

Tell the truth in such a way as your listener will not be offended. Love always finds a way.

Do not 'fabricate' stories to make yourself a hero of heroine or victim.

Do not exaggerate a circumstance in any way since you can send another person away with a falsehood in their minds. This can be more injurious to them than you can imagine. Never ever cause another person to stumble or fall along their daily path.

Let everything you think, say and do, be a harmonious whole directed in your mind and heart by love and concern for every other person's wellbeing. In this way, you create the foundation of a whole, happy life for yourself. You create the type of consciousness which is easily attuned to that of Divine Consciousness.

Then, miracles happen.

If you lack success, examine your consciousness. Do you keep your word?

11 - Christ Consciousness

CHRIST says:

"It is not enough to be concerned about your life on earth. You should be equally concerned about your life and wellbeing when you move into the next dimensions.

"Here, more than ever, you find yourself within the dimension of 'Being' which is the outer manifestation of your own consciousness but to an even greater extent than when you are on earth.

"When on earth, you do create your own unique environment from the fabric of your overall consciousness, but you can also partake of your neighbour's environment when you meet or live together. This means that when you are on earth, you can move into a more pleasant environment, meet more pleasant people than your own consciousness normally creates or attracts towards you. But this incompatibility leads to friction and discomfort.

People either feel out of their comfort zone or stifled by the higher consciousness they encounter and can't wait to get back to the lower consciousness environment in which they feel at ease. Some people are drawn and born into a consciousness strata in which they feel they are aliens and spontaneously begin working, even in childhood, to move away into the strata of consciousness in which they will be able to thrive.

The level of **CONSCIOUSNESS** you die with, is the level you will bring back.

Sometimes, a person with a high level of spiritual perception may be drawn, at birth, into a family of lower spiritual levels because the environment will strengthen their awareness and increase their spiritual stamina as they struggle in their early years to return to their rightful consciousness 'home' in the spiritual stratum on earth – and later, in the next world.

Just as you experience your undeveloped consciousness when you pass over, so do you go into the higher dimensions which reflects your own consciousness when you have re-incarnated several times and worked on gaining spiritual insight. You find that you and everyone else you encounter, is of the same consciousness. You will be magnetised into the conditions which are compatible and by reason of your own creativity, you can perfectly contribute to.

If, on passing over, the consciousness has been ego-oriented and vicious, the individual will quickly re- incarnate, since the feeling of discomfort will be intolerable. Gladly, such a person returns to earth in another identity. At this level of existence, earth conditions seem to be preferable to those in the astral world. It takes many lifetimes before the soul awakens to the fact that escape is only possible when the human mind sets itself to try to lift the perceptions and consciousness to a more endurable comfort zone.

The more spiritual the consciousness of a person before they pass over, the more that they have looked back over their lives, gained insight into the ego control of their minds and feelings, the damage they have done to other people's lives, the unhappiness they have caused, the greater the spiritual progress will they make.

As they experience burning remorse, so does the pain of the remorse eradicate the ego-domination in their minds and hearts, until, little by little, they eventually leave this life fully aware that the PATH of **UNCONDITIONAL LOVE** is the only way to follow.

Such people fully understand, acknowledge and are clearly aware that all misery: – sickness, deprivations, lack of success, unhappiness are derived from lack of LOVE in one's approach to life, people, environment. CRITICISM is the biggest obstruction of all to inner happiness because it is highly destructive. It is reflected in the person's life because when you judge, judgement comes home to roost,as the saying goes.

Criticism of others interferes with their wellbeing and consequently, as we damage others even in the slightest, again, the damage will return with interest.

Therefore, when you undertake to walk Christ's Way, you must understand that it is a path of relentless self analysis and finding the courage to look at your actions in the light of LOVE, willing to see the truth about your thought and emotions.

As you move forward along the path, it becomes easier to move into a perception of the truth of others, of what drives them, motivates them, causes them to make mistakes in their relationships, in their workplace and close family.

The more you can empathise with others, understand what motivates them, perceive the difficulties which push them into ill-considered actions, the higher becomes your own spirituality, your own sense of compassion and love towards those who – you now realise – are really doing the very best they can in the environment and circumstances they have created for themselves.

From this standpoint, it becomes easier and easier to apologise, until the time comes when, seeing the truth of the other person so clearly, you cannot wait to forgive and erase all tension and criticism of them from your thinking.

When it comes your time to pass over, such an illumined person, living in peace and harmony with the entire world, will move into a state of utter blessedness and joy. They move into Light and there is no looking back at earth. At last, they find that they have moved into that dimension of Being where they are content and fully at peace.

After a while, they begin to notice that there are even higher dimensions of existence and they set about preparing , enlarging, expanding their consciousness to absorb even higher vibrations of Divine Consciousness and they become ever more creative and radiant transmitters of UNCONDITIONAL LOVE.

Such people are truly the **CHRIST CONSCIOUSNESS.**

12 - Life more abundant

CHRIST SAYS:

I said, when I walked the earth in Palestine,

'I HAVE COME TO BRING YOU LIFE MORE ABUNDANT'.

'Has anyone in the Christian Churches ever truly understood this statement?

'Life More Abundant in your human minds may mean more energy, vitality, health – perhaps even riches. But from my perspective of having BECOME the individualisation of LIFE ITSELF, I meant something so far beyond your human perceptions at this moment, that I know this is the right time to try to lift your consciousness to the higher levels of spiritual consciousness where you will begin to glimpse the TRUTH I was trying to reveal to the Jews in Palestine.

'LIFE MORE ABUNDANT!!

In the earlier words of this statement, I tried to make it clear that your human perceptions are limited. In fact, unless you have already been on a true spiritual path, seeking the Reality of THAT which gave form and consciousness to all creation, you will be bound down by your ruling 'Sovereign' – the Ego.

'The EGO sorely limits the breadth of your human perceptions and vision, since it forces your consciousness to focus exclusively on your own happiness and survival.

'It is only when the soul of a person first sends out a message to its human consciousness that there is more to life than 'the self', that the individual begins to want to discover more about life and about the Origins of life.

'As the consciousness of the human mind is gradually woken up from its long subordination to the Ego, so does it begin to question much that lies beyond its present knowledge. At the beginning of its quest for greater knowledge of the unknown, it will probably be drawn to a religion, since it would seem, humanly speaking, that the Churches must hold within their wisdom and teachings, the secrets of the Source of Life.

'This Christian subservience to Religious human domination, claiming to know the secrets of the universe, is a good kindergarten for the opening consciousness of Ego directed minds.

'Thou shall worship God; Thou shall not kill; thou shall not steal; thou shall not commit adultery and sleep with your neighbour's wife; thou shall not slander and tell lies; thou shall not envy your neighbour's goods; and so on.

'All these rules belong to the control of the Ego Kingdom. They do not apply to the spiritual realms of the soul. The soul knows nothing of such human impulses.

The very first injunction: 'To worship the Lord thy God' is a pagan concept.

PAGANS put up fetishes to worship. SPIRITUAL ADEPTS move beyond this elementary human practice and begin to experience the Infinite – Divine Consciousness which is transcendent of all forms of consciousness on earth.

'When coming into membership of a Church – especially a Christian and Jewish religion, the first instruction is to remember at all times that you have come from a great SOURCE which has given you individuality and consciousness. Because this is so, you must refrain from the Ego Impulses.

'The Ego Impulses impel you to either grasp those possessions which you believe will make you more comfortable or happy, and to push away, defend yourself, physically if necessary, from those elements and things which make you uncomfortable or are perceived to be dangerous to your life and wellbeing

'On entering a religious observance, your immediate attention is drawn to God and you are taught that to 'please' God and ensure your own happiness, you must avoid all the ego impulses listed above. But this is still an Ego driven precept. Since the unacknowledged purpose behind it is the aim of finding happiness and security.

If you belong to a Christian Church, then there is usually the following:

'Unless you please God – you sin'

'As you may be able to see, this statement places severe limitations on your ability to appreciate life. You are placed in a mental cage imprisoning your mind within these dire warnings that unless you please God, you will sin, and punishment inevitably follows. How this punishment will be recognized is never said, BUT THE THREAT LIES OVER CHURCH GOER'S HEADS. Some people are greatly depressed by this teaching.

'This is a severe restriction of the LIFE IMPULSE which is, in its fullest sense, boundless JOY, enthusiasm, laughter, love, spontaneity, a feeling of wellbeing and an inbuilt sense of optimism – that life will never let you down – that you will have enough to eat, drink, clothe yourself and everything needed to make your lives happy.

'LIFE is an active stream of consciousness having its origins in UNIVERSAL CONSCIOUSNESS.. IT unites – and ignites – dormant SEEDS in plants, animals and human beings, and impels them to grow according to an innate plan which science calls DNA.

'This is the true universal, eternal LIFE IMPULSE which is yours by right of birth into this world.. You can witness it in children, before their little minds, coached by adults, begin to wonder whether LIFE is really so secure and free of pain and misery, as they thought it was. Instinctively, babies lie on their backs and wave their arms and legs and gurgle with laughter. 'BEING ALIVE is GOOD', they are saying. Providing, of course, they have had the good fortune to be born into loving families which cater for all their needs.

'But there is a far deeper ASPECT OF LIFE – which is really UNIVERSAL CONSCIOUSNESS become active within Its own creation of the galaxies and earth itself.

'It is an aspect that was given me to perceive clearly and UNDERSTAND when I was in the Sinai Desert in Palestine. I saw that the ORIGIN of LIFE, the SOURCE of our BEING, always manifested Itself through all living things from the very least to the greatest, from a pansy to an elephant, in a very special way, an intelligent way. It was so consistent, you could call IT the NATURE of THAT which has brought all created things into visible being.

'IT'S NATURE is also the SOURCE of all earthly wonder, joy, happiness, personal fulfilment and creativity.

'No matter where living beings, humans and animals, may go, they are literally supported minute by minute by the indwelling NATURE of our SOURCE OF being. There is no escaping it. BUT – until I came to earth and then, not until I returned through the mind of my Recorder, has this great TRUTH been taught, showing its full significance.

'You do not have to chase happiness, or success, expansion of your dreams, health – because ALL OF THESE are already within you, being impressed in you by your SOURCE of being, your SPOURCE of LIFE.

All these things you so earnestly and rightly long for – are YOURS. But they do not appear to be yours, because they are hidden under all your mental structures, beliefs, opinions, created and handed down by your ancestors and their ancestors before them – and it is high time that you, – as many of you as are capable of taking necessary action, can launch into a wholesale re-upholstering of your mental programme.

'Strip away the myths, strip away your bogey men, your fears, your despair, your frustrations, your anguish, and wake up – STAND UP and REALISE that they are all in your mind, born of your personal mental conditioning, AND GET RID OF THEM.

'More easily said than done, you will not doubt be thinking, but the GREAT TRUTH of BEING is THIS.

'YOU ARE NOT ALONE.'

There are teachers who will preach positive thinking – but I never did that. I told you clearly that the KINGDOM OF HEAVEN IS WITHIN YOU.

What I meant was that LIFE is the source of ALL you could ever want – providing you allow it to work in you by sweeping away all doubt AND by BELIEVING THAT IT WILL BRING YOU INTO PROSPERITY, JOY AND FULMENT to the extent you can rid your minds and emotions of old ego thoughts and feelings.

THIS is what I meant when I said: 'I came to bring you life more abundant'

I came – and I am come now – to awaken you to the fact that LIFE within you, grows you first of all, then it grows your plans, hopes, expectations, it brings to you all the necessary assistance to enable your plans, hopes and dreams to grow in the right and perfect way which will bring life to other people also. IT enters into your difficulties and brings healing where your heart is sore or your bodies succumb to illness, IT mends catastrophes in your life in the same way as IT heals broken bones, it fulfills all your needs as they arise – in the perfect way. And LIFE, unlike human beings, maintains a system of order in all it undertakes to do.

All these are 'LIFE MORE ABUNDANT' – more than you dreamed possible. Put my words to the test.

Make a clear form of your dearest wish in your mind. Take it to Divine Consciousness in silent meditation, ASK, give sincere thanks that you are receiving. The request is now filled with LIFE and must come into manifest being in exactly the same way as a seed grows when put in earth and watered. Wait, give constant thanks for receiving, never doubt, and you will receive a very clear answer.

'It is possible that having read this message, that 'all things beautiful and wholesome, including healing , are already yours', you wonder why it is that you still have your chronic illness or poverty despite your prayer and your belief. You seriously question how much you can really believe.

'I can only say that true belief is a relatively rare condition.

'What is TRUE BELIEF?

'It is a moment of overwhelming transcendent conviction when you KNOW way beyond all negative and fearful disbelief, that LIFE IS more powerful, more transforming, more perfectly in control of atomic elements than any sickness can ever be. Then – as hundreds of chronically and critically ill people have testified down the ages, the longed-for unimaginable miracle takes place, and suddenly there is felt an inflow of heat and power, perhaps a Light is seen, and wholeness of mind and body are experienced where before there was sickness.

'It can be done. Miracles also occur over a longer time span and are therefore discounted but may well be as much a result of ongoing faith as the quick spontaneous healing. Other miracles of 'fulfilment of need', take place far more than you realize they do. Seek to BELIEVE, pray for BELIEF – and when you least expect it, it will be given you. Seek to be absolutely consistent in all your efforts to find and make contact with the Divine – and it will surely be given you.

'It is a Law of Existence that when you ASK you will receive. When you SEEK, what you seek will be revealed to you. When you knock it will be opened to you.

'Take comfort. Believe!'

13 - If you believe...

CHRIST SAYS:

'I am coming down to speak to you colloquially through my Recorder at certain times, to try to awaken in you the realisation that all of your troubles, distress and limitations are already within you.

This is because your thoughts arise from your indwelling characteristics. And all that you experience in your life is the manifestation of your habitual thoughts and words.

Many of you speak of having 'Power' but what I am trying to give you is the most 'Powerful' Truth in your universe.

It literally MAKES or BREAKS your lives, health, possessions, relationships and happiness.

There are very popular talk shows seeking to help people change their perceptions, attitudes, thoughts, words and actions in order to live more constructively and happily in relationships. The human mind is asked to dredge up enough energy and willpower to eliminate its own wrong thought patterns and words.

Since all THOUGHT arises from congenital and planetary vibrations, this is a very difficult thing to do –and few there are who manage to do it.

There is another way which, if followed consistently and faithfully, ensures that people will be successful in their attempts to turn their lives and emotional state around into that of success and joy.

The way is CHRIST'S WAY which I have outlined in my **Letters** dictated through the specially prepared mind of my Recorder.

This website has been almost four years in existence and during that time, people have tried to live according to the Truth contained in the Letters, and have reported great changes taking place in themselves and in their lives and environment.

Following CHRIST'S WAY leads to a great deal more than simply being able to get on better with other people. It leads to an ongoing, yet secret, positive change taking place in a person's consciousness, so that after a while, they find that, all unconsciously, they are reacting easily and happily in more constructive ways to external stimuli.

They find that the things which they have sincerely longed for are, at last, coming into their experience.

They can carry burdens more easily, more certain of an eventual successful outcome. They spontaneously find that they reject old critical thought patterns with distaste. They wonder how they ever indulged in such destructive thinking towards others.

Instead of personal change becoming a daily struggle, they find there is some Super Power – Life Force – Divine Consciousness entering in their minds quietly and silently, enabling them to find new HAPPINESS.

My **Letters** to the world are tremendously important, and urgently required by those who can understand them. They go into the scientific facts already known to scientists – but they go beyond these into the true CAUSATION of scientific facts.

They are vitally important because they explode old myths which HAVE HELD PEOPLE BACK IN THEIR SEARCH FOR SPIRITUAL TRUTH

They explore the so-called mysteries of creation and life itself.

Very importantly, they clearly describe the origins and true nature of the Ego and the right way to deal with it when it hinders the best interests of the self.

The **LETTERS** also describe the origins of creativity and the 'ground' out of which all created things have taken form and being.

If you believe that I ever existed as 'Jesus' in Palestine, hopefully you will be sufficiently open minded to accept that, when most needed in your world, I have indeed returned through the prepared mind of my Recorder to speak to you directly.

If you have no belief at all, unfortunately, I cannot send my spiritual consciousness vibrations to enter your brain cells and switch your thoughts around or open your perceptions. To do this against your will or without your invitation, would leave you permanently brain damaged.

So, until life experiences trim away your mental obstructions, you will remain unable to accept the great TRUTHS expressed in my **Letters.**

But you are as much within the radiance of my Spiritual Thought as are all others who gladly listen, hear, and follow my words.

I am always here for you but whilst you dis-believe – you shut out all spiritual insight emanating from me.

Those who believe can be assured that my Truth is real and valid because the Truth I have set out for you as clearly as I can through my Recorder, was the Truth given me in the Desert in Palestine.

It was as a result of this TRUTH THAT I COULD COME OUT OF THE DESERT AND BEGIN TO PREACH and HEAL.

I beg you, WAKE UP! You can come to me for comfort, spiritual insight and emotional strength. I am very much alive in Celestial Kingdoms.

You can meditate and open your hearts to Divine Consciousness and receive Its healing, guidance, spiritual insight.

But you can only receive – to the extent – that you truly believe you are able to make true contact with me and the Infinite.

But if you BELIEVE, You have but to ask – NEVER DOUBTING – and it will be done for you.

It is my most ardent longing that you may heed these words, download the Letters and really study and practise all they teach you.

I long for you to experience real happiness, real spiritual security, real fulfilment of all your needs in a way which will have no drawbacks.

14 - Urgent message from Christ

CHRIST says:

I am coming through the mind of my Recorder because there is something **URGENT** I have to say to you!

Love your enemies; forgive those who ill-use you; pray for those who speak evil of you, ... and if you cannot do this in your own strength, seek by all possible means to do it in the power of spirit – **Divine Consciousness.**

PRAY and MEDITATE and ask for help. It will be given you if you persist.

If the ego persists in forcing your thoughts downward again to virulence and anger and raising all kinds of arguments as to why you should condemn someone who has deeply hurt and even wounded you physically, go into meditation again and again, seeking insight and relief from your dilemma, asking to have these troublesome recurring angry and vindictive thoughts removed from you...

NOT to please God

as you have been taught by the churches

but to protect yourself from the whiplash of your angry thoughts which rebound in your lives bearing violent upheavals and further rows and arguments to deal with.

FOR – whatever power you give to resentful thoughts, that power will send a direct electrical stream of consciousness to the person who hurt you, –

AND the stream of consciousness returns, zinging its way back to you in due course, like a boomerang.

You must know that every electrical field creates a like magnetic field – the two always work together – so that WHAT GOES OUT EVENTUALLY RETURNS.

This is a scientific law of existence but what science does not yet admit is this:

- Electrical force powers the mind; it is the consciousness impulse of 'Get Going' in the mind.
- Electrical force is a facet of consciousness.
- Two-faced Magnetism powers the human and animal emotions – it 'attracts' and it 'repels'. It is the impulse of human love and the impulse of hatred.
- Magnetism is experienced by all living things as emotion – feeling.

I have described this Truth fully in my **Letters 5 and 6.**

Not only this, scientific medical knowledge has discovered (what I understood so well in Palestine, 2000 years ago) that all the thoughts taking form in your brain descend into your pituitary gland via your hypothalamus, and the negativity and emotional trauma (lowered vibrations) they contain is passed on to your organs, blood and entire body, causing a depletion in energy and eventual illness.

This is the phenomenon producing psycho-somatic ailments acknowledged by the medical profession.

When in Palestine 2000 years ago, I told the Jews not to worry about drinking from unwashed cups but to take note of and be concerned about what came out of their mouths. I have translated what was reported in the gospels in the New Testament into the kind of words I actually spoke to the Jews – who did not have the remotest idea of what I was trying to tell them. And sadly, the various 'Christian' churches are just as ignorant today.

How could they understand – they did not have the enlightenment I received in the Desert which illumined my mind and imprinted in my mind the spiritual knowledge of the origins of creation and laws of existence.

But YOU, who live in your world today, have had countless teachers coming to earth, explaining scientific facts and also mystics who have led you into metaphysical, spiritual truths, preparing you for my Letters which contain the very highest Truth of all – the true Nature of your Source of Origin which you term God, and the Universal Laws of Existence.

I now want you to think about the truly terrible and outrageous works certain people initiate in your world,– despite all these Teachers of facets of Truth.

The ongoing bloodshed in Iraq is a case which should make you all think deeply about the likely boomerang from such destructive actions.

I want you to think of this situation from a spiritual viewpoint which does not CONDEMN but sees the 'truth' inherent in the thoughts and actions involved in the situation.

Here you had a man, Saddam Hussein who was determined to take power in Iraq and bring about peace

and plenty for his people. Unevolved in true spirituality, he used most harsh and violent ways to control a nation, to silence those people who gave him problems. These people used violence in an uprising against him and he poured violence back on them. Here were a tyrannical Dictator and a sect of people of the same mental and moral level – their spiritual vibrations, despite all the prayer and outward religious show, were as dark and dense and low as it is possible to attain in your world today. Hussein and these unruly people deserved each other.

The Iraqi people tolerated him, some even admired and applauded him, because he kept peace for a volatile nation and gave them a chance to live their daily lives as peacefully as their innately aggressive natures would permit them.

He fell foul of the USA, ANGERED ITS LEADERS, and equally governed by ego, the Leaders decided to punish Saddam Hussein by imposing sanctions. Later on, a humanitarian impulse prompted the inauguration of a system 'Oil for Food' which helped the hungry people of Iraq and gave America access to the oil they needed. But this measure was a severe blow to Hussein's pride and did not alleviate the national deprivation of general luxury and everyday goods enjoyed by their neighbours.

I want you, people of the world, to give empathetic thought to the enormous volumes of resentment, hatred, anguish, brought about by this action of a nation strong in their Abundant Wealth, armaments, trained soldiers, sailors and airmen.

I want you to understand that such NATIONAL EMOTION becomes a 'living force' of destruction of huge proportions.

It is certain that NO ONE truly on the path of CHRIST'S WAY – MY WAY – would ever have followed such a sadistic course. Faced with the problem of having to deal with a Saddam Hussein, such a leader, enlightened in the spiritual and scientific Laws of Existence, would have called a session of enlightened people to meet to meditate and to ask for guidance.

My guidance would most certainly have been to call a meeting with Saddam Hussein and to point out the tragedy which would eventually result from the impasse between the two countries. An enlightened Leader, instead of 'lording it' over Hussein and threatening him with war, would have asked him and his advisors to draw up a document, an agreement which both countries could live with in friendship, and which would promote a growth and domestic enrichment programme for both countries.

Such an enlightened Leader would then read Iraqi proposals to establish peace and harmony, would discuss it peacefully with a sincere desire to establish well-being for all. He would call on his enlightened people to meditate and bring back any adjustments WHICH HAD BEEN RECEIVED FROM MEDITATION.

In this way, the people under Saddam Hussein would have been gradually freed from the stranglehold of a tyrant, Saddam himself would have seen the benefits derived from a peaceful approach, instead of an aggressive one, and Arab States would have been impressed by the success of the venture. This would also have caused the Muslims to re-think their present interpretation of the Qur'an.

But what is the acknowledged and generally accepted WORLDLY WAY?

What has the 'Human Spirit' – the Human Ego accomplished today?

Consider whether there can be any lasting benefit from this behaviour outlined below?

A peaceful nation, a peaceful people, already deprived of normal trade facilities with other nations, have been bombed nightly. Their buildings, built with great effort and expenditure of money, and offering various services to the people, are destroyed.

Night after night, innocent people have been subjected to the terror of bombs, asking themselves – 'Where will they fall? Who will be hit? Will they find us in the rubble? Will we lose a family member? Will we all be killed?

What have these people done to deserve such a terrifying ordeal other than knuckle down and try to live as happily as they could under a tyrant whom the USA hates?

Prior to this, in USA, another tyrannical fanatic sent planes to destroy the twin towers of the Trade Centre in New York. A great cry of fury, anger, revenge arose from the American people. They lost many people – loved ones – in the destruction. Every year, there are Christian church services remembering the dead and a great many tears are shed in the deluge of grief thinking of them.

Think for a moment: 'Christian Services' – is there any talk of FORGIVENESS of those who were instrumental in this destruction?

Are Americans shedding tears for the innocents who died under the hail of bombs deposited night after night for no good reason other than a vitriolic hatred of Hussein? Do they hold services for the Iraqian dead? Do they even consider that they have murdered innocents – who had no protection against the USA horrific weapons and had never done them a moment's harm?

Just consider the weight of the emotional distress unleashed by all of this insufferable and arrogant destruction of another country – destruction which has freed all the rebel fighting groups which Hussein had kept in check. Unleashed a most foul mode of killing others – the suicide bombs.

Every time such bombs go off – thus killing innocent bystanders, the Americans who supported war against Iraq, should realize that it was their support which made such suicide bombing possible.

Just consider the unleashing of the gigantic, untold emotional vibrations of horror, hate, revenge, and retaliation that is now directed at America.

How do the Americans think that all this 'Hatred Energy' will be manifested against them?

Because it will be manifested as death and destruction. It is a law of existence. Even 'Christian' churches claim to believe this law.

Where there is no FORGIVENESS there is retribution in the form of Cause and Effect.

FORGIVENESS, complete and total and LOVING, dispels the violent hatred energies. Without forgiveness, they gather momentum from the ongoing resentment of the opponent.

Read the article on 'Cracks in your planet' and then ask yourselves how all this terrifying load of hate will be manifested. Who, in America, will – SOONER OR LATER – be the targets?

Therefore I tell you clearly: In your home, in your community, in your town, in your State, in your country – FORGIVE whoever has injured you in any way – big or small. Let this word ring out across your land through any means you have.

And if you cannot forgive easily because your ego will not let you – then bring your hurt and anger to Divine Consciousness (which I termed the 'Father' when in Palestine) and ask for Its inflow of Spiritual Directing Power to gently ease and remove the burden from your minds.

Will your religions tell you this? No, they did not when I was in Palestine and they will not now.

Indeed, those who occupy the highest positions in the most powerful nations, and cause the most horrific damage in the world are received with pomp and ceremony, smiles and handshakes by the religious leaders of the various 'Christian' religions. The blind grip hands and give blessings to the blind.

To hear TRUTH – YOU MUST COME DIRECT TO ME. I am truly alive and universal in being; COME and I will receive your call and will lovingly respond to it.

Have the courage to join CHRIST'S WAY and to follow the teachings I have brought the world in my **Letters**. They will show you how to remain in tune and accord with the LAWS of EXISTENCE.

They will help you come into harmony with the universe itself. And all things will then work towards your greatest good and happiness and protection.

15 - The True Kingdom of Heaven on Earth

This is the CHRIST speaking, January 2006.

The true KINGDOM of HEAVEN on earth.

'I would that you could see and experience the world as it really could be for you. The living world, the entire creation ringing with joy. Your world has been created by **LOVE**, designed by **LOVE** to meet the personal needs of every single living entity as it has evolved over the millions of years of existence. If only you could become aware of this glorious joy and glowing **LOVE** as you walk in your garden or countryside.

If only you could enter into the consciousness of a magnificent tree as it stands straight and tall, spreading its branches for the birds to alight upon it and make their nest. If only you could enter into the consciousness of a bird as it finds the best nesting place, experience its pleasure and feel its love for the tree which provides a home and shade.

Everywhere, there is reciprocity of love flowing between living things, plants, insects, birds, animals, fish, and their environment. Only the predators put themselves outside this love consciousness.

Study the eyes of the predators, one and all, and compare their fierce intensity with the eyes of the non- violent herb and grass eaters – there you will see the ferocity of the one and the tranquility of the other.

As I said when I lived on your earth: **'The eyes are the lamp of the soul'** And what you have not realized is that all eyes radiate to the world the inner quality of being. They radiate the inner consciousness which blesses what it sees – or shrivels it up with its own bad temper.

When you live entirely in your human consciousness, your thoughts, habitual modes of speech, your continual assessment of people and externals, you are unable to partake in this **JOY of EXISTENCE** which spontaneously wells up in the consciousness of all non-violent living things – felt by all peaceful living things, – unless denied sustenance by drought.

You cannot feel it because your minds have developed along the lines of logic and reason and you act according to your will, imagination, desires and ego – and all of this mental activity blocks your spiritual mind at the top of your head; it prevents sixth sense contact with the beautiful world in which you live and which you do not remotely understand at all. You can see the bodies and the activities of insects, birds and animals, but you cannot enter into the consciousness of their mostly innocent, uncontaminated vitalizing life force.

You may think their consciousness is possibly like yours. But you would be wrong – because all living things other than humans live by intuition – and communicate in a way which is impossible to humans.

Yes, they communicate very clearly – over long distances. Yes, they communicate and rejoice together, more than you'll ever know.

It is the Hermit who sits with his begging bowl and meditates who may soar into infinity and experience the joy and the glory of Divine Consciousness in which **WE**, you and **I, ALL** live and draw our eternal life and being. The Hermit can experience it in the silence and stillness of his mind, and can be uplifted into such ecstasy that he has no need of worldly living – indeed, he runs away from it.

People will say: "How wonderful, he has given up his life for God". But this is an erroneous perception.

He gives up normal daily living to find the **TRUE LIFE of GLORY** out of which all creation has taken its form and being. There can be no greater experience of a glowing radiance and spiritual ecstasy than this.

But – it is escapism offering great rewards and also defeating the purposes of existence in your world.

It is marvellous and wonderfully uplifting to rest in the effulgence of absolute Love and Tranquillity for a while and possess knowledge of this wonderful dimension of eternity for yourself. Here your mind may enter into transcendent facets of universal knowledge.

YOUR HUMAN LIFE TAKES ON NEW LUSTRE, LIGHT AND JOY AND GREATER MEANING.

But it is not your true purpose in life.

Your true purpose on earth is to **EXPRESS** in thoughts, words, deeds and desires the **DIVINITY** in which you have your being.

You can do this through meditation, through cleansing your mind of negative thoughts, by reaching out to others during the day to offer them a smile of friendliness, recognition of their being – that they too are ALIVE and are therefore important – co-existent with yourself, no matter what their status is in life.

What a tremendous joy it is to be able to love the man who has come down to rags, possessing nothing of material things, forced to live by begging – just as much as you may be able to love the man who has made untold wealth, prestige, and lives a life envied by others. This ability to love each and everyone without reservations is indeed **DIVINE LOVE** – pure unconditional love. It is a quality of mind and heart where all sense of superiority or inferiority no longer exists.

'Why should this bring one so much joy?', you may ask.

It gives you joy beyond all imagining because you have risen high above the demands and critical senses of the self which judge and demean others.

What tremendous liberation of spirit you will experience when you can, at last, be insulted or defrauded by another but can still look through his words and actions and perceive his basic divinity. You now rest in a state of pure tranquil acceptance of what the human world may try to do to you and you never cease smiling – because yours is a world of sunshine and spiritual light created by the Divine – and you are aware that those who try to hurt you have not yet managed to find this sacred world conceived and fashioned by Pure Love.

Knowing this so surely, so clearly, how can you **NOT** have only the deepest compassion and concern for them as they struggle, sometimes bravely, with their enmeshing ego?

As you learn to love all states of human being equally, you will come to intuit the actual state of earthly being of each person and will be able to perceive for yourselves what is valuable in life and what is mere ego 'frosting' for comfort and prestige.

You will no longer be led astray – or even moved – by outward show.

If you study **Letters 5 and 6**, you will be able to clearly see exactly why I say the world is made by **LOVE, IN LOVE** and sustained **by LOVE.** When you fully understand why this is so, it is possible that you will go further in realization and will see that to entertain any thoughts contrary to **LOVE** shuts you out of the basic Reality of Existence – it places you in a shadowy world where you can no longer see the world created by Divine Consciousness after the Big Bang – you can only see the **IMAGES** of that living world and cannot feel their joy.

Dwell for a moment on your world as it is today – the average mentality of men and women governed by ego – and then think of the joy and beauty of **WHAT REALLY IS** just beyond your normal vision – out of sight because of human thought – and **HUMAN BEHAVIOUR.**

All of my **Letters** are directed only at helping you lift yourselves out of any present misery you may be enduring and to make genuine contact with Divine Consciousness which will immediately set about rebuilding your health, strength and inner direction towards higher goals of existence. You can come out of your hell – but only YOU can do it for yourself.

YOU must do the work initially but you can invite Divine Consciousness to enter your mind and heart and give you added strength to ensure you succeed.

As more and more people of a like-spirituality and spiritual perception bond together to seek the Kingdom of Heaven on earth, so will there be little pockets of spirit luminescence lighting up that dark world of yours, inviting more and more of its members to join you in your happiness.

How do you cleanse your consciousness? Remember that if you rely **ONLY** on your own human consciousness, you are calling up your ego to drive away your ego thoughts – and this is impossible. Ego cannot overcome ego. You have to wake up to the realization that above the human consciousness is the Super Consciousness of Divine Consciousness described in **Letters 5, 6, 7 and 8.**

You will never be able to enter into the consciousness of plant and insect life, because yours is a world of logical thought. But you can enter into Heaven on earth by learning how to get in touch with Divine Consciousness and inviting It to fill your mind and heart, giving new direction to your thought life – and then to your future life and activities as well.

I long for you to find true freedom from the ego and enter into the transcendent joy of Divinity whilst still on earth.

16 - The Latter Days

I, the CHRIST, known as 'Jesus' in Palestine, more than 2000 years ago, have returned at this most critical time in world history, to speak to you.

As I descend in consciousness vibrations to make contact with your earth vibrations, I see a world of light and shade, of spiritual upliftment and despair … and, most terribly, I see the degradation of the human spirit.

THE WORLD IS MOSTLY IN A STATE OF DARKNESS.

The average person reading my words may feel that this statement is an exaggeration of your modern life, but to understand the full enormity of what is happening on earth, a person must first experience a moment of Light.

First of all, I am compelled to speak about what is happening to your children worldwide.

Do you realize to what extent **that DARKNESS HAS SPREAD RIGHT THROUGH THE VARIOUS STAGES AND CONDITIONS OF CHILDHOOD?**

CHILDREN, – THEIR NATURALLY EAGER, CURIOUS MINDS, ALWAYS LOOKING OUT FOR SOMETHING EXCITING AND NEW TO GRIP THEIR INTEREST, ENTERING INTO EARLY ADOLESCENCE, – and by nature, – OBSESSED BY SEXUAL CURIOSITY, – ARE STIMULATED AND FED BY YOUR WORLDWIDE BOOKS, RADIO AND TV ENTERTAINMENTS.

Yes, you say, we know this. I say, but you still allow this to happen.

If you were Children of Light, you would be so filled with compassion you would rise up as one voice and say to those who are growing rich at the expense of YOUR minds and your CHILDREN'S minds:

'Enough, we will not allow you to do this to us anymore. We will refuse to watch and listen to what you enjoy imagining in your own gross minds – violence, perversions, explicit sex, continual fighting and arguments. We long to return to the PEACE and JOY from which our souls have descended'.

TODAY, UNKNOWINGLY, INNOCENTLY, THE CHILDREN ARE ENTICED BY PEOPLE WITH SELFISH AND SEXUALLY GREEDY INTENT, INTO THEIR WEBS OF SEXUAL PERVERSIONS.

If you were Children of Light, you could not sleep at night, knowing that these innocent little children are being used to satisfy grown men's sexual fantasies and urges.

THESE CHILDREN ARE PLUNGED, EVENTUALLY, INTO EXCESSES THEY DID NOT SEEK, AND INTO HEARTBROKEN DESPAIR BECAUSE THEY DO NOT KNOW THE WAY BACK TO THEIR ORIGINAL INNOCENCE. THEIR CHILDHOOD IS TAKEN FROM THEM AND THEY ARE DEPRIVED OF THOSE IMPORTANT YEARS OF NORMAL, EMOTIONAL DEVELOPMENT.

If you were children of Light, you would feel their pain as though it were your own. Your conscience would give you no rest until you had risen up together and asserted with all your influence and heart and soul that this terrible encroachment on the weakness and innocence of children must stop!

Innocent? Our modern children? – you on the earth may ask. If you were Children of Light you would know they are innocent until they learn the things of darkness which have been spawned by the human mind on earth.

You of the earth say the world is not in **DARKNESS** – that I exaggerate?

You have become so accustomed to **DARKNESS,** you no longer recognize it.

Your world is rife with war-wracked nations. It is heavy, heavy, heavy with gross mental and emotional vibrational frequencies of selfishness and a total disregard for life. Your streets are now thoroughfares of danger, of road rage, of jealous muggers envious of the possessions of others, of stalking predators eager to conquer and control others through use of sexual force.

The numbers of these predators may be fewer than the numbers of your Average Citizens but if you were Children of the Light, such people would never be allowed to prosper. But they do prosper in your midst because your own minds are filled with such events from watching your entertainment. You have become hard and de-sensitized to these horrors and so they are allowed to multiply in your midst like a deadly virus.

AS I DESCEND and enter empathetically **INTO THIS MIASMA** of deadly thought and destructive feelings, I feel the pain experienced by the innocent who fall prey to those who find a thrill and a feeling of power when they terrorize the weak.

These are indeed the '**latter days**' as your world calls the time when life on earth has become so universally gross and separated from the underlying Laws of Existence, that ONLY A FEW of the billions on earth pause for a moment to question;

'What lies beyond the darkness? Is there Light? Where is the Light? Why does it not reveal Itself to us?'

In response to the urgent, most ardent questioning by A FEW people traumatized by the powerful predatory emotions of others, how could I **NOT** return at this time, to reach those who question, those who are sincerely longing for a sure way out of the darkness which now saturates every facet of the majority of people's lives?

Do you recognize that this is indeed **ME**, the **CHRIST** who has come to teach and show you the way out of darkness into LIGHT? How could I NOT come in response to your pain?

Do you not know that **I AM LOVE** and it is the nature of pure **LOVE** to fulfill the needs of loved ones.

Christ Returns – Speaks His Truth 2007 Message

I have again descended in fullness of CONSCIOUSNESS to imprint within the mind of my recorder, yet another message to the world.

Before I could take this new step forward, it was necessary to bring you my LETTERS in handbook form because I would have you realise that your world itself is truly UNIVERSAL LOVE made visible.

How each person perceives it, is born of personal attitudes to the world and life generally. Your view of it is entirely personal and is not the absolute Truth because you do not yet fully understand the processes of creation. You can only fleetingly glimpse them.

Now that you have my LETTERS as a foundation for future spiritual upliftment, I have come to bring greater clarity to your present understanding of them.

I WANT TO SPEAK BRIEFLY TO YOU ABOUT THE TRUE NATURE OF PURE LOVE

of the highest realms of Consciousness and your perception of love in the lower frequencies of your world.

I want you to understand that even though I speak to you with all my transcendent Being of LOVE, I must still speak within the framework of your world thought in order to enlighten you.

Where I reside in the Consciousness of I AM - is PURE LOVE. As I descend in consciousness, my compassion grows and grows and forces me to move down in consciousness frequencies to enter into the consciousness of your plight in your modern world.

How can I help you understand this? Consider how it would be for you if you moved into a place of carnage, would not your loving concern be deeply compassionate? Would you not be passionate in your rejection of the scenes of suffering? Even so am I, although I know it is all part of the evolutionary process of transcending the ego individuality . Only through the lessons of suffering will the journeying soul gain self- knowledge to retain individuality after it has discarded the ego.

I am LOVE - unconditional Love pure and simple, and in my words there is no judgement.

Therefore, if my words seem harsh when you do not expect harshness from me, since I claim to be LOVE personified, please understand that I have not descended at this time to have a loving visit with you, to give you words of comfort to lift your spirit, to tell you how blest you are in Reality but do not yet realise it. I have come to render you a loving service. I have come expressly to give you the worldly facts which cause you pain, illusory as they really are, to show you what you are all helping to create for yourselves.

Just as no loving and successful teacher enjoys the words he must use to help aggressive pupils see and acknowledge the harm they do in the classroom, so must I speak about your present condition in worldly words you may understand to enable you to work to rise above it. But I do not speak the words to condemn the action or the doer of the action. I am LOVE, the embodiment of PURE LOVE, but I speak as the situation demands to people who have not yet managed to overcome their ego frailties. I love all people -

for I am all LOVE - but LOVE dons many masks in its loving attempt to reach out and help those who are seeking relief from present distress.

I speak to you with the words of logic because you have created your world to fit what you deem logical and therefore believable. If I were to approach you with the 'meaning' expressed by Love,you would be all at sea because 'the meaning' would not conform to your logic and you would still refuse to believe that I have spoken.

LOVE transcends and eliminates the need for the Ten Commandments but there are few in your world who can truly understand this.

I WANT TO SPEAK TO YOU ABOUT THE TRUE NATURE OF CONSCIOUSNESS

of the difference between UNIVERSAL CONSCIOUSNESS, Divine Consciousness, and human consciousness. You truly need to understand these differences to enable you to live spiritually pro-active lives within your world... Which is what I have come to help you do.

CONSCIOUSNESS Transcendent and human consciousness!

Consciousness is now a word used widely, even lightly, but is not fully understood by many dear seekers of Truth.

You have drawn your being from Universal Consciousness split into Divine Consciousness at the time of the Big Bang. (See Letter 5)

This is the perfect Consciousness of Loving Intelligence and Intelligent Love. IT is IMPULSES.

These IMPULSES are the very basic energy, the MAINSPRING of all existence. This Consciousness is indeed within you, surrounds you, transcends you and can lift you in ever higher strata of spiritual ecstasy and ephemeral perception,. This Consciousness is what many call God.

It is within you and transcends you.

But what humankind must fully realise is: that it is of such a high frequency of vibration, ...so spiritually refined in meaning.......that it cannot be drawn into your own human consciousness to make Itself known to you, until you begin to overcome your ego and ascend in spiritual perception of Truth.

Your ego is the barrier to Super Consciousness.

Only the most systematic and persistent daily attempt to cleanse your consciousness of ego thoughts and behaviour, will make it possible for Divine Consciousness to SEEP into your human consciousness bringing you new insight and perceptions. Illumined by new insight and perceptions, your thoughts, words, actions will begin to change.

When you SEE things differently, you will begin to ACT differently.

Your human consciousness is imperfect. It is fabricated out of selfish egotistical drives. Let not your ego resist this valid statement. You are in no way to be blamed for this, because the ego is divinely created in order to separate Divine Consciousness into individual people. You need the Ego. It defends you and it draws to you what you need to survive BUT it can overwhelmingly force an individual into behaviour which is sick psychologically speaking. You know that Ego is the impulse behind all the crime in the world.

I would have you know it impels people into such deep-seated narcissism and self-interest that anyone trying to arouse in such a mind any empathy or sympathy, is sadly blocked. No matter what topic may be raised, inevitably, such egotistical, narcissistic people draw the topic back to themselves, how it affects them, how it concerns them exclusively, positively or negatively.

Absorbed self-interest is like a thick dense fabric of consciousness energies sealing off the minds of people of every strata of society in every part of the world.

The degree of narcissism varies. I have come expressly to make you aware of it because such narcissistic people cannot live in harmony with other people as they are incapable of hearing the messages from others. This, as much as your crime, causes your misery on earth.

Here is a parable for you. Behold the little child playing in a sticky mud pit, making pies, covering itself with mud, enjoying every minute. Mother comes, exhorting child to come and bath and get ready to go to a party. The child fiercely resists, crying. Eventually, mother has her way and the child, freshly groomed with hair shining and clad in smart party clothes enters the hall where the party is being held. It stares in astonishment. The glorious lights! The brilliant shrubs and flowers! The tables loaded with delicacies, cakes and jellies. And all the presents and games and fun the other children are having. The heart of this child is filled with radiant joy. Laughter begins to well-up and fill its entire being. This is so much better than its mud pit! All the washing and the scrubbing was worth it. How glad the child is that it listened.

I WANT TO SPEAK TO YOU ABOUT EVOLUTION.

How a study of evolution will enlarge your understanding of the activity of Divine Consciousness within creation. I touched on this in my Letter 1 but you should study the subject yourself and you will be amazed at your discoveries concerning Divine Consciousness in action.

You will discover that whatever evolutionary adaptation takes place in the body is exactly suited to the body's new requirements. This is not a universe created arbitrarily or without the deepest loving concern for the living entities which inhabit it. In every case, a study of evolution will reveal an IMPULSE at work within creation which displays knowledge of the entirety of creation, knowledge of the needs of the least entity and how to perfectly fulfill them.

Therefore, if you can only grasp that you are maintained and supported by this Divine Consciousness which I also term LIFE, and can realise that it KNOWS YOUR NEEDS, and that IT is geared to answering, fulfilling your needs in the very best way to bring you into a stress-free state physically, emotionally, mentally and spiritually - then you can let go your fears and anxieties - and you can trust IT implicitly.

If only you could begin to realise this perfectly, absolutely, completely, comprehensively, compellingly and could stop thinking that your own little finite, limited minds can plan your futures.

I WANT TO SPEAK TO YOU ABOUT YOUR BELIEF IN YOUR OWN SELF-SUFFICIENCY

which is holding you back from achieving true self-surrender and the eventual ascent to Christ Consciousness.

How can you plan anything at all when you do not really know what tomorrow will bring? You don't know! You can only hope! Have you ever truly realised this about your mind power? You can only HOPE you know what tomorrow will bring. You are trapped in to-day, thinking you have stable access to all your environment, but in fact through sheer lack of knowledge of where you really stand in relation to the world, you know nothing, you only hope!

So why do you cling to your belief and trust in your limited knowledge and assert that your limited mind ALONE can make the best plans for your tomorrows when you have within you, DIVINE CONSCIOUSNESS Which is Itself ALL KNOWLEDGE of your tomorrows and the next ten years and even eternity.

IT knows your true purpose on earth, do you?

IT knows what will truly make you happy, what will truly make you healthy, what will truly help you ascend the spiritual ladder of ecstatic spiritual consciousness. So why can you not let go self-will and seek the supreme Love Guidance of THAT which created your world for you to enjoy?

When will you rid your minds of all the old tales of Jehovah's vengeance told you in the Bible, and discover for yourself that the Will of the 'Father' is only JOY, Health, Happiness, Fulfilment of your every need.

I WANT TO SPEAK TO YOU ABOUT YOUR SELF-WILL AND ITS CREATED SELF-DELUSIONS

Earthly Consciousness is a fabric you spin with your thoughts and feelings. If only you had heightened perceptions, you would see it as a kind of dense fog. This is released into the air around you.

When it is not ignited with the powerful drive of desire, intention, purpose, it lies around you like so much waste. But when your thoughts and feelings unite in thought patterns of desire, or intention or purpose, you have created a life- form. That life-form is a blue-print, an electrical outline of your intention and the corresponding magnetic field of emotion draws particles of energy together to bring this driving intention into visible manifestation.

Please realise that this creation in the unseen around you is yours. Out of your limited knowledge of yourself - yes, your very limited knowledge of yourself, what you really believe, how you really react in certain circumstances, how you really impinge upon your environment and affect other people, how truly honest you are in all circumstances - out of this very limited knowledge, you contrive to build these consciousness forms - the blue prints of your desires, intentions and purposes to be experienced in the future.

You do this unknowingly until you realise what you are doing. Then you will possibly join a class where you will be taught to do it deliberately.

Believe me, these are spurious creations. Do not do it. You see with limited vision. You do not know how you can actually distort the paths of others by this belief that you know what is best for yourself or others. This is true error - this is a true trap for the unknowing. Created by the ego drive.

Hundreds of thousands - probably millions - believe that because they say: 'It is so' in faith, that statement will make it so. But they have no idea of what really lies in wait for them because of the various cosmic influences which play a huge part in their daily experience. They do not know what lies in wait as a result of their thinking and behaviour in the past. You cannot create the perfect life for yourselves - until you, yourself, are absolutely perfect within your mind, heart and actions and have worked through a kind of recompense for past hurts you have inflicted. And yet millions of your financial currency are being spent on acquiring the knowledge of how to potently form such consciousness forms as will over-ride all the energy blue-prints surrounding you and make them null and void. You are all going in the wrong direction.

413

All that you seek in harmony and health will elude you until you fully understand that EGO cannot create PERFECTION, until you wake up to the beautiful all -giving nature of Divine Consciousness which is your true Source of Being, the true Source of health, achievement, and inspiration. You are like children in a playground, playing together, making up stories of make-believe and wondering why the make-believe does not work. The children are excited and energised by the imaginative and happy stories they tell each other but when they go home, they have to face the realities of life as their parents live it.

I WANT TO TALK TO YOU ABOUT HEALING AND SENDING HEALING TO OTHERS.

To send any LIFE of lasting value, not just a flash in the pan of physical energy which may uplift another person for a short while, you must first draw IT from Divine Consciousness during deep meditation, and as you do so, re-direct it towards the object of your good intentions. There is nothing in your personal energies which will open the doors of another person's mind to Truth. Only Truth itself can open the doors, can bring insight, can bring healing. The little 'i' mind is nothing but human and finite electromagnetic consciousness, human opinions, prejudices, negative reactions, logical arguments and rationalisation born of previous experiences. Until the little 'i' of ego is able to see the Divine and open itself to receive the Divine in as great a quantity as it is prepared to give time to receiving, it will remain impervious to any Truth which may be presented to it. Indeed, it will vehemently reject it.

So many millions love to pray, love to ask, and hope they will be heard. So many people resist giving time to meditation. Why? Because they do not truly believe they will be in contact with Divine Consciousness. If they believed, meditation would surely be their most fulfilling time of peace and joy during the day. When stresses arise, unhappiness presses down, misery weeps, how blest and wonderful it should be for you to say: 'I will take this to my 'Father' in Whom is all loving comfort and fulfilment of my present needs'.

This is what I did on earth, when perplexed, when happy - I took time to rest my mind and invite my beloved 'Father' to enter in fullness of power to take over and bring me deep peace and the strength and inspiration to continue my mission.

THE ERA of LOVE and PEACE.

I cannot truly explain why I am here with you today if you have not fully understood my Letters. Until you understand them you cannot become the loving creative individual who is needed to bring about the Era of Peace so passionately longed for by people on earth and yet so passionately withstood by people on earth.

I know well that this statement will be passionately resisted by many who will say: 'God is accessible by all'. And they speak truly. But I repeat what I said on earth and I mean it - and I speak the Truth although it may arouse in your hearts, rebellion.

'The path you must walk to reach the longed for Era of Love and Peace is indeed narrow and absolutely straight.'

You may jump the path but when your travels have eventually shown you that you have made a serious, even bitter mistake, you will find that your only sensible way forward is to get on the path again. Since your wanderings may have led you to create many, many blue-prints of agony and sorrow, these will await manifestation in many ways, even as you struggle to master your consciousness anew to regain the path. But they will also cause you to seek *Reality* with greater fervour than before. Therefore, there is no wrongdoing in jumping your path, - no judgement of your choices of your actions, only timely lessons bringing you back to your path. This is followed by the most blessed relief as again you become the recipient of what seems to be heaven-sent blessings and new joy in living.

Believe me, my beloved souls on earth, as you are now, you are not ready to bring about an era of peace. There is much talk about it, longing for it, belief that spiritual evolution has lifted you into a mind set capable of bringing you into an era of love and peace. But a great deal of this thinking is self-illusion, self-delusion. You forgive yourselves your mind sets, your thoughts, words, actions because you are in the world, fettered, blinded by your ego. You struggle bravely to adopt a more loving way to think, feel, respond to every experience but whilst *you* remain the single moving force within your consciousness, the ego will eventually win.

How will you respond if someone enters your home and wrecks it? Will you forgive them instantly because of your deep compassion for their enormous insecurities in life? Because you know that there is no loss when you can draw abundantly from the 'Father' again. You will be able to do this when you have become fully at one with Divine Consciousness.

How will you respond if someone should slander you in public and try to destroy your good name? Will you be able to smile lovingly, peacefully and sincerely bless that person? You will when you enter the ERA of LOVE and PEACE because there will no longer be any ego in you to resist any denigration. You will see the denigrator clearly and will understand the impulse which impels him to harm another. Even more, your good name will no longer matter. You will be joyously in harmony with your Source of Being and that will open vistas of such ecstatic living which will reveal all lesser things to be of no account - mere negative illusions.Can you bear to have your little inadequacies pointed out to you and accept them without needing to pull the cloak of protection around you - the cloak of explanations and excuses? The more you can transcend your ego, the less will your inadequacies bother you. You will accept correction with grace and love and will make up your mind to do everything right in the future. This is true spiritual evolution.

Only the mind set of one who has conscientiously worked through the full process of cleansing of consciousness, and constantly called on Divine Consciousness for help to become the embodiment of compassionate love, will be able to co-create - yes - co-create the kind of existence you would dearly love to experience on earth.

Do you realise how many people there are throughout your world who imagine they have found and practise unconditional love and yet they are ever on the look-out for other people who do not measure up to their standards of behaviour and are exhilarated and happy to judge or chastise them? How can such a mind create an era of love and peace?

A spider spins its web. You spin your environment, health, well being in your minds with your desires, your intentions, your purposes. This is not a process of judgement, you must understand - this is purely a statement of the reality within electro-magnetic energies. This is your truth. Until you fully acknowledge this and decide to seek conscious union with the Divine at all times, - the Era of Love and Peace will escape you.

When you have embodied the transcendent glory of love and compassion within your consciousness, when your consciousness is at rest, peaceful, without the least stain of criticism and rejection of any kind of otherness, you will indeed become a member of the Kingdom of God.

Until that time comes, I would have you KNOW that I am available, accessible at all times, compassionately aware and compassionately understanding of all you are having to endure at this moment. I am available as your love, your comfort and your re-assurance. I am your Life, I am your Way, and I am your Truth. I love with deep compassion and an urgent longing to relieve you of your present burdens. And I will relieve you of them if you will but come to me and let me respond with the warmth of my presence, and guidance and insight to help you rise above your present frailties and sadness.

Therefore, to help all those on earth who are willing to listen and accept my words and seek my comfort, I say to you what I said in my Letters:

It must be widely accepted that, in order to achieve a state of contented peace on earth, there must be a HIGHER VISION to strive to implement in your daily lives. Only by reaching for a higher vision will the physical world be rescued from widespread annihilation when unenlightened people will sadly reap of their present chaotic sowing.

This is not a judgement of criticism or condemnation, dear souls, but a statement born of the Laws of your Existence.

Without the higher vision either for the self or for the world, there can be no spiritual evolution or the achievement of that state of being when Divine Consciousness Itself will be clearly evident in you, your lives, and your circumstances. At that time, you will all have become transparencies of Divine Consciousness and as such you will experience a quality of life previously undreamed of.

THE VISION

Your vision of a perfect world and a perfect life should be of LOVE embracing all creation. A giving and receiving without stint. A shining health and beauty radiating light from all that grows and from all living beings. Ecstatic creativity of every kind. Ease of movement, travelling being merely a matter of desire. Prosperous homes and joyous households. And everywhere, a manifestation of Divine Consciousness in every atom.

I cannot coin a better term for such a vision than Kingdom of God, Kingdom of Heaven to describe the future earthly Quality of Being when Divine Consciousness clearly pervades all living things and they transparently manifest the nature of Divine Consciousness in their every second of earthly existence.

Sadly, millions have not yet glimpsed the Light and they spend their lives in seeking new spiritual experiences through new teachers and new knowledge, whereas the search should be for the experience of Divine Consciousness

within and the spiritual vision arising therefrom. This can only be attained through constant and regular meditation.

MEDITATION

Only through meditation will you be enabled to still and quieten your mind completely. Only then, can Divine Consciousness enter your brain cells bringing Its own knowledge into your mind, Only then can the flaws of ego be slowly dissolved from your brain cells and nervous systems.

I am seeking people who are willing to set aside their self-absorbed search for spiritual felicity, seeking spiritual ways to live a better life, own more possessions.

I am looking for people who will be willing to bond together in a mutual support system to begin to re-build themselves to become fit to join in creating the Kingdom of Heaven on earth, when Divine Consciousness will reign supreme in the consciousness of all Heaven's people.

To achieve this purpose, I will set out clearly what true Members of the Kingdom of Heaven on earth will be willing to accept. The following are the rules that Members must agree to try to implement in their lives daily, followed by the reasons why the rule is so important.

MEMBERSHIP of the 'ERA of LOVE & PEACE' or

'KINGDOM OF HEAVEN' on earth.

Before setting out the rules for Membership, I will refresh your memories concerning your own creative power within your minds.

"But when your thoughts and feelings unite in thought patterns of desire, or intention or purpose, you have created a life-form. That life-form is a blue-print, an electrical outline of your intention and the corresponding magnetic field of emotion draws particles of energy together to bring this driving intention into visible manifestation."

This is a manifestation of your own desires and because your knowledge of yourself and your future is so limited, this manifestation will bring its happy side and its dark side into your experience.

But when you first go to Divine Consciousness and seek the true solution to your problem and take this solution back to Divine Consciousness for its perfect manifestation on earth - then you have the perfect manifestation of Light carrying within it no future disappointments.

Try to make it second nature to first seek guidance from Divine Consciousness. Even though you may feel you have heard nothing from the Divine, I tell you truly - if you remain steadfast in faith, in time to come, you will find the answers in visible form returning to you. Therefore:

1. *As a Member of the Kingdom of Heaven of Earth I will meditate daily, starting with ten minutes, and moving on to whatever time I am comfortable with. I will set aside all thought as much as possible, quieten and silence my mind. I ask Divine Consciousness with heartfelt prayer to enter my consciousness and take over, bringing me Divine Wisdom and Divine Love that It may bless my own life and all I relate to in any way, and the world generally.*

I will use this time of union with Divine Consciousness to KNOW that all matters I take to it for healing and solving will be duly healed and solved.

I pray that Divine Consciousness will give me the grace to KNOW that IT always answers the prayer of loving conviction.

2. *As a Member helping to create the Kingdom of Heaven, I must set aside every thought of envy. I must remember and affirm that as the child of Divine Consciousness, the 'Father', I may ask for whatever needed or wanted and know that, in due time, it will surely be manifested for me.*

3. *As a true Member of the Kingdom, daily I will reject all ego thoughts and replace with those of compassionate love and the unconditional loving thoughts with which I will help build the Kingdom.*

Daily I will repeat to myself. 'I have undertaken to help build an Era of Love and Peace and my every loving thought is a transforming influence on earth'.

4. *I must remember that the Kingdom of Heaven is a place of joy and laughter. Daily I pray that I may become more enlightened and lifted into appropriate spontaneous joy and laughter to help lighten the spirits of those around me.*

5. Daily I must remember that to overcome ego and make deep meaningful contact with other people, I must LISTEN! I must control my ego drive to talk about myself, and must listen, striving to understand and empathise with what I am being told.

6. Daily I must remember that to overcome ego, I must be able to hear any truth about myself without wanting to retaliate or find excuses. In the Kingdom of Heaven is no backbiting, vindictiveness, resentment! By undertaking to help build the Kingdom of Heaven on earth, I must transcend all these ego impulses - exchanging them for unconditional love.

7. Daily I must remember that in the Kingdom of Heaven is only a KNOWING that tomorrow will be perfect because Divine Consciousness fills the minds and hearts of every dweller in the Kingdom. Therefore, I must avoid all alarmist talk. I will not get caught up in retelling the faults of others. I will not indulge my lower consciousness by contemplating the evils of the governments and the world. To build the Kingdom of Heaven I must withdraw from everything which I do not want to see perpetuated - otherwise the Kingdom will never take shape, or others may build it and I will be left behind. I will be shut out by the self-indulgent consciousness I am building every day.

8. I will listen with love to all who seek my comfort and will ask Divine Consciousness to give me the words to say to heal their hurt.

9. Daily, I will visualise and make the following affirmation with love for the world and for myself. I will affirm constantly that because Divine Consciousness illumines my mind, my affirmations are powerful and life giving. I visualise they are the seeds of future events.

AFFIRMATION

'Daily, I open my heart and mind to Divine Consciousness transcendent to help me dissolve all present selfish ego drives.

Daily, I open my soul to receive Divine Consciousness to assist me in building a new ERA of LOVE & PEACE in the world.

'In the KINGDOM of HEAVEN only Divine Love, Divine Compassion, Joy and Laughter and beauty of self- expression will be sublimely manifested always.

Nature in every area of the world will flourish luxuriantly, harmoniously, supplying fruits and food for every single person on earth. All people will be well fed. All will be well clothed. All will be uplifted in spirit and will manifest Divine Consciousness in every way, every day.

I lift this Vision of Felicity to Divine Consciousness where it will be ignited with DIVINE LIFE for its perfect manifestation on earth. I give my loving thanks to my SOURCE that even now it is all beginning to take shape in the unseen.

'Thank you, Father.'

My beloved souls, it is known that at this time there will be clear and unmistakable divisions between the children who choose the Light and the children who prefer the diversions and darkness of the worldly ego. For the Light to lighten the world all must become the children of the Divine.

Lovingly, compassionately, even reluctantly I leave you, having spoken what I would have you understand. My LOVE enfolds you in ardent longing for you to to receive my words as simply as a tiny child listens to its father's well-loved voice, to ensure my urgent message may bear fruit in your lives and the lives of those who surround you.

'This is a true message of powerful creativity of your future. If you will believe and act, you will see it come to pass. Most certainly within your own lives you will find yourselves in your Kingdom of Heaven.

Rest in Love Divine. Rest in Peace. Rest in Light.

A GIFT OF LOVE FROM THE TEACHER OF LOVE HIMSELF.

An impassioned call from the CHRIST to join in the creation of an ERA of LOVE and PEACE - the KINGDOM of HEAVEN on earth - both within and in the environment.

The Membership is for people who are deeply and sincerely committed to ridding themselves of ego; and helping to build a world community of equally committed members.

This is a commitment to Christ and to his teachings in his Letters (1999-2000) and Message 20.10.2007

Membership will carry prestige since it demands: an understanding of and commitment to Christ's Letters and surrender of the 'self' in daily life.

The Rules to be followed daily are:

1. Daily reading of the Christ given rules and explanations of why he has made them into rules

2. Daily Meditation

3. Daily, I will reject all ego thoughts and replace with thoughts of compassionate love and unconditional love.

4. To make meaningful contact with other people I must LISTEN to them and must stop bringing the subject back to myself.

5. I must be able to hear truths about myself without hiding behind a cloak of excuses and indulging in retaliations.

6. I must, at all times, be truthful and straight forward, otherwise my consciousness will be fragmented and I will lack conviction.

7. Daily, I must remember and affirm that in the Kingdom of Heaven - to-morrow is always perfect.

8. I must avoid all alarmist talk. To build the Kingdom of Heaven within and without myself, I must withdraw my consciousness from everything which I do not want to see repeated or perpetuated in the future.

9. I will listen carefully to all who seek my love and my comfort and will ask Divine Consciousness to give me the words to heal their hurt.

10. I will not give way to and jealousy because I know that all the things necessary for my care and happiness can be mine when I ask 'Father-Mother-Love'

11. Daily I will make the following affirmation - visualising the full meaning as I speak:

AFFIRMATION

"Daily, I open my heart and mind to Divine Consciousness transcendent to help me dissolve all present selfish ego drives.

Daily, I open my soul to receive Divine Consciousness to assist me in building a new ERA of LOVE & PEACE in the world.

In the KINGDOM of HEAVEN, only Divine Love, Divine Compassion, Joy and Laughter and beauty of self- expression will be sublimely manifested, always.

Nature in every area of the world will flourish luxuriantly, harmoniously, supplying fruits and food for every single person on earth. All people will be well fed. All will be well clothed. All will be uplifted in spirit and will manifest Divine Consciousness in every way, every day.

I lift this Vision of Felicity to Divine Consciousness where it will be ignited with DIVINE LIFE for its perfect manifestation on earth. I give my loving thanks to my SOURCE that even now it is all beginning to take shape in the unseen.

Thank you, Father."

HOW TO MEDITATE (from my Letters 8 Christ Returns - Speaks His Truth)

When you meditate, take up the position which is most comfortable for you. You do not have to go into physical contortions. Rest and relax. Tell yourself to relax and release all your limbs, including your head, neck, face, into a state of utter limpness.

I must impress on you that meditation should be - eventually - as simple as slipping into slumber. The purpose of meditation is to enable your entire consciousness to move beyond the boundaries of intellect and reason. There are teachers who will tell you to 'imagine'....whatever you are told to imagine, you can rest assured you are not being assisted to go anywhere except into new imaginative realms of your own thought processes. What this method of 'meditating' will achieve for you will be a relief from the thoughts and stress that your ego pressures are creating for you. In the world of imagination, the ego may - or may not - be dormant.

Before commencing meditation, prepare by fully realising you are about to make contact with *DIVINE CONSCIOUSNESS'* both within and transcendant to your consciousness - therefore IT is also out there and around you. Visualise exactly what this means. Remember, at all times, that what you THINK about is what you are tuning into. Your thoughts are 'searchlights' making contact with what you seek.

Remember that every 'thought' has its own frequency of vibrations in consciousness. Believe know this for this is true. The more spiritual the thought, the higher the frequencies of vibration.

'Consciousness forms' embodied by words are not visible but are 'specific entities of being'. They have the life of consciousness within them. They are magnetised to like 'consciousness forms'. Like is drawn to like.

Think 'dog' and visualise what you mean, and your thoughts are attuned to the dog species. Think ' UNIVERSAL CONSCIOUSNESS' or 'DIVINE LIFE' with understanding of what you mean - and your thoughts will be directed into 'UNIVERSAL CONSCIOUSNESS' - DIVINE LIFE.

If you have fully understood all that I am trying to tell you, you will KNOW that your meditation reaches its target.

Know this and you will find your faith strengthening.

Your faith remains weak because you only hope, or wish, or magnetically 'want to' tune into - LIFE- CONSCIOUSNESS, because you hope you will derive some benefit from the exercise.

Do you not see how 'earthy' is such an approach to THAT WHICH GAVE YOU 'BEING'?

Is it reverent? Does it befit a person who is seeking true contact, and expects to do so?

Whilst INFINITE UNIVERSAL CONSCIOUSNESS is not the mythical 'God' on high as depicted in the Old Testament,It is the Infinitely Powerful Reality everywhere present, manifesting It's own designing, intelligent, evolutionary, loving caring for all that It has brought into being.

This is what you must realise you will eventually approach, whilst you are still on earth, when you reach the highest dimensions, after your magnetic-emotions have been dissolved not only from your mind, but also your sub-conscious, and solar plexus.

First of all, you will be getting in touch with FATHER-MOTHER-DIVINE LIFE which is ever active within your entire system and the universe.

Remember It is in equilibrium within the infinite universal dimension, and active within the world.

'Father-activity sets the goals. 'Mother-love directs the way the plans will be developed to promote the highest good of that which is being adapted, or healed, or protected.

(Countless people will say that these statements above are all imagination. They can scoff as they will. Those who manage to make contact with 'Father-Mother-Life-Consciousness- another name for DIVINE LIFE

CONSCIOUSNESS but denoting its double qualities - will verify that the foregoing is an accurate description of spiritual evolution which follows such contact.)

To return to your meditation.

First of all, before attempting to enter your meditative state, memorise the following prayer so that the words become your own.

When you have become perfectly relaxed, start your meditation with this prayer. Say it slowly and visualise the meaning of each word to enable you to enter into the consciousness of the word and enable the energy consciousness of the word to enter into your deepest self. As you say this prayer, your eyes should be closed and your gaze lifted towards your forehead.

FATHER-MOTHER- LIFE, you are my life, my constant support, my health, my protection, my perfect fulfilment of every need and my highest inspiration.

I ask you to reveal the true Reality of Yourself to me. I know it is your WILL that I shall be fully illumined that I may better receive awareness of Your Presence within and around me. I believe and know that this is possible. I believe that you protect and maintain me within perfect LOVE.
I know that my eventual purpose is to EXPRESS YOU.

As I speak to you, I know that you are perfectly receptive of me, for you are UNIVERSAL LOVING INTELLIGENCE which has so marvellously designed this world and brought it into visible form.

I know, that as I ask YOU to speak to me, I am sending out a consciousness searchlight into your Divine Consciousness and as I listen, YOU will be penetrating my human consciousness and coming ever closer to my increasingly receptive mind and heart.
I commit myself and my life into your care.'

(Each time you say and visualise this prayer, you create a spiritual consciousness form which will become stronger and ever more elevated in frequencies of vibration as the true meaning of the prayer deepens in your mind and heart and your perceptions heighten.)

After the prayer, relax ever deeper and let your mind go as blank as you can. If thoughts intrude, gently recite 'Divine Life' or ' father-mother-life' to yourself and again quieten your mind. After many months of sincere meditation, you may come to feel that your body is suddenly jerking, like a person entering sleep and then suddenly waking up. If this happens, be thankful as your consciousness is penetrating the barriers of your previously created consciousness forces encapsulating your soul.

When you feel yourself entering a different deep state of consciousness, so deep you are barely breathing, know that you are beginning to attain your goal. At the end of your meditation, always give glad and grateful thanks.

Remember that nothing you can think, say, or do, can in any way reduce all that *' father-motherlife- consciousness' is* .

However,any disbelief will form a barrier between you and *father-mother-life.*

I want to warn you: when you are trying to still your mind and thoughts, you may feel ill-at-ease, physically uncomfortable and even distressed. This is because - initially - you will come up against the black wall of your own 'consciousness' and this can be extremely disconcerting - even painful.

Bless the experience and ask *' father life' to penetrate your consciousness next time you listen.*

Then get up and put the experience behind you.

When you find that you are at last entering into the silence, then rest equably, knowing that you have now entered what one might call the 'holy of holies' because, at last, you are achieving contact with ' father- mother-life' within you. It will take time for this highly spiritual experience of the Silence to become a daily routine.

Remember you have a lifetime of ego baggage to discard and dissolve.

No matter what you sense or are aware of during your meditation, when you come out of it, expect to sense a difference in your life. Remember that expectation is a 'consciousness' form and as you 'expect' you are opening the way for that which you 'expect' to be magnetised into your experience,whatever it may be you are needing or dealing with.

If you do not feel any new lightness of spirit, despite your sincere expectations, do not deny changes or doubt the possibility of them.

Remember your consciousness is electromagnetic, of the same substance as your physical body, and it is the foundation of all experiences in your life. Continue to expect - as you do so you are building up the power, the energy of your 'expectations - consciousness forms 'which will draw to themselves the manifestation of all that you are expecting.

'Father-mother-lifeconsciousness 'can only be magnetised into your individual consciousness by faith, sincere expectancy, and the willingness to open yourself to the cleansing of your magnetic-emotional 'bonding-rejection- impulses.

How many of you presently go into meditation in this way and come out EXPECTING changes? How many lose heart when they have felt some change and then nothing for a little while.?

Bear in mind that I told you that you are subject to rhythms of 'high' and 'low'. When you are in your 'lows', the flow of Divine Life in your system has dropped and the frequencies of vibration of your consciousness also drop. Consequently, contact with 'Father-Mother-Life- Consciousness ' during these times, at the beginning of your search, is almost impossible. In the early days of your seeking Truth, during your meditation, you are very much in touch with your subconscious, and you will find that there is an irritating resurgence of all the old negative thoughts and memories you had thought you had overcome.

When you enter your 'highs', you will find a resurgence of your spiritual self and will rejoice in this. Your meditations will be more positive and productive of contact with 'Father-Mother- Life-Consciousness'. If you will have the courage to persist and exercise self-discipline during the 'low' times as well as the good, you will find eventually, that the 'lows' will get less 'low' and any former depression will be lifted.

Remember, that each time of 'prayerful consciousness' brings you closer to your goal, although you may remain completely unaware of this. Nontheless, things are happening for your ultimate good - believe in them.

Christ's 2014 Message – A Higher Vision

I HAVE SAID YOU NEED A HIGHER VISION IN ORDER TO BRING ABOUT RADICAL CHANGES IN YOUR WORLD.

But I have not told you how to achieve a Higher Vision and how to bring it into being.Without this more detailed knowledge, you will find this commandment difficult to fulfill. I have seen the many hundreds of people who have taken my words into their hearts and have longed to bring them into manifestation in their lives and for the benefit of the planet.

So much love is being expressed as a result of this call to create a Higher Vision, that it is now essential that I come again, to help you begin to work consciously, intelligently and lovingly to create a new world.

If you look back over the last five thousand centuries of individual human development on earth, with the assistance of your history books, and also the writings of noted Writers and philosophers from different countries and centuries, you can see that the changes in thought and style of living did not just happen, they took place only because of the changing blue-prints of consciousness taking place in the highly intelligent minds of more advanced thinkers'. They presented their thoughts and ideas to the public and as these were absorbed with respect by the public , so did the new ideas take different shapes in the human mind of the populace. Thereafter, gradually, these new ideas appeared manifested as a slightly new mode of behaviour, and also affected national life generally in one form or another. Any and all changes have taken place as a result of someone having a new idea which impacts strongly on public sensitivities and is absorbed by them. You will say this is just common sense. Yes, it is, but we have to build our new perceptions on the ground of common sense, otherwise you will find yourselves rejecting them.

If you look back to what were, in England, the Victorian and Edwardian days, and known by other terms in other countries, 1845 - 1919, you may remember that life in England was very disciplined by the strong traditional rules imposed by laws from Parliament and by members of the aristocracy and Upper Classes. All of these laws and rules were formulated by generations living comparatively roughly but gradually being smoothed and refined by the developing thoughts of the Thinkers in the country. As a result of the visions of these Thinkers, the various appurtenances of civilisation were adopted: sanitation, paved streets, places of refuge to help the underprivileged,

MANNERS BECAME STRICTLY STREAMLINED TO ENABLE PEOPLE TO LIVE PEACEFULLY WITH EACH OTHER. And people went to church and listened to what their preachers had to tell them about damnation and hell fire if they committed sin. You will see that people were able to live tranquil lives as a result of the disciplines voluntarily adopted by the nation on the whole., and this continued until the hidden and subversive elements of human thought and consciousness erupted in wars. All strong emotional thought must manifest eventually. The conflict brought an opportunity to young men to express their hidden aggressive tendencies which had remained hidden. That is why the men and boys flocked to join up in 1914.

But when the war was over, the consciousness of the populace changed again because it had experienced the pain and the anguish of the manifestation of human subversive, aggressive, retributive impulses active in warfare conflict. English people wanted no more war - they wanted fun! The Churches no longer held the respect of the people as they had before the war.

However, the last war, 1939 - 1945 brought society itself into an upheaval. The previously downtrodden masses, directed into the three Fighting Forces in the war, had an opportunity to demonstrate hitherto unsuspected intelligence and skills. As a result, the class barriers were largely broken down, the previously under-privileged people were now given the opportunity to further their education and move up into professional positions.

Sadly, as these opportunities took place, the consciousness, inherited from babyhood in impoverished homes, were not replaced by life-giving thoughts. The old feeling of life not being fair, or being hardly done by, of being rejected by the wealthy, remained, and produced a great deal of negative reaction - Instead of the new opportunities afforded to people generally producing a high degree of an elation of spirit, a belief in success, achievement and happiness,, there was also a very negative, life-undermining consciousness at work in the minds of the population, destroying much of the well-being and joy that should have been built up after the last war, with the advent of a huge amount of Technical skills and discoveries, contributing to the general well-being of human beings.

But, in search of fun and frivolity, the rules for living decent lives were relaxed and gradually cast aside, with the result that the ill-effects of such undisciplined living imbued the consciousness of the masses. They began to experience high levels of misery and despair as a result of emotional upheavals, that these in turn led to abnormal reactions of aggression and hatred. People burdened with these impulses of negative reaction, endeavored to relieve the pain through sexual excesses. These increased as they were talked about and advertised in the media, films, TV. Radio - the more they were talked about, the more they took hold of people's minds and flourished, leading to ever worse crimes against each other.

And this is where you are now. In addition to what has been going on in people's minds and externalising in planetary (?) behaviour and experiences, you have the hugely negative effect of such aberrant thought and behaviour on the 'matter' of the planet itself -because, as I told you in Letter 1, and you probably did not believe me, but when I was in the desert, I was able to see how a change in my consciousness did affect the vibration of motes around me - speeded them up or slowed them down, and thus the appearance would change so very slightly that an ordinary onlooker would never have noticed the changes.

But I was just one man bringing my mind to bear on my environment - what of whole cities, countries, reading newspapers, absorbing all the latest scandals and crime and carrying that around during the day - what of that kind of DESTRUCTIVE consciousness - how would that manifest in your world - would it not go to the areas on your planet which have faults, areas where the composition of rock and earth is fractured, made friable, less packed and stable?

What about the weather? There are those amongst you who are well aware that consciousness does affect the nature of the weather.

Everything in your life is CONSCIOUSNESS. YOU CANNOT THINK TO YOURSELVES THAT THIS IS CONSCIOUSNESS AND THAT IS SOLID MATTER –

EVERY SINGLE THING IS ACTUALLY **CONSCIOUSNESS** MADE VISIBLE and human minds are creating it minute by minute.

Can you begin to see why I HAVE CALLED ON THOSE PEOPLE WILLING TO HEAR, AND THERE HAVE BEEN SO MANY, MANY GLORIOUS HUMAN BEINGS, WHO HAVE RESPONDED TO MY CALL, TO BEGIN TO CREATE A HIGHER VISION IN ORDER TO BRING ABOUT CHANGES AND RESCUE YOUR PLANET?

So how do you set about it?

In the first place, each one of you must go to Divine Consciousness, in meditation.

What do I mean by 'meditation'?

I mean an emptying of yourselves of your Will to be in charge of your life.

I mean a reaching out in your minds to the vastness of space, seeking contact with that which brought you into being. Close your eyes and keep them lifted to the top of your forehead. Surrender your Will, ask to be filled by Divine Consciousness in order to be inspired with new ideas of what the world ought to be. If ideas come to you during your contact with Divine Consciousness, the moment you come out of meditation, write down these ideas in your spiritual journal, which everyone should keep.

Begin to think about the reality of living in unconditional love with everyone. What does that really mean? What will your lives be like? What kinds of feelings are rising within you? Create such a place in your mind for as long as you feel happy within it. Give little parties of unconditional love only. What do you learn from them? Talk about your discoveries regarding your present form of consciousness.

You are having to live in two dimensions at this moment. You are in the world with all its mayhem and unpleasant consciousness - and also it's wonderful drive towards seeking spirituality in mind, emotions and body. You must choose or imagine as consistently as possible that you are within the protection and wellbeing of Divine Consciousness.

This means that when you are brought into contact with the unpleasant consciousness forces in life, you must continually pray to Divine Consciousness to help you ignore the hurt, the disgust, the rejection of offenders which your humanity, your ego would have dragged you into, and instead, rise into an awareness of Divine Consciousness as being the only Reality in your lives. And therefore, you will enter and remain poised in forgiveness and a concerned caring for the erring person's wellbeing and happiness.

At the very beginning of your striving to live in this non-reactive and pro-active way - which requires you to consciously reject the state of ego reaction and enter the second state of pro-activity, you will find it very painful and annoying to have to let go, overcome, the old sense of having been badly treated but as you persist, joyfully, you find one day that you are able to move immediately into a state of pro-active joy, forgiveness, understanding and caring concern for whoever has just that moment upset your equilibrium.

When you achieve this level of loving response to outer dark influences, you have established a framework of Divine Consciousness on earth.

Pause here and try to fully understand that You have created an area of wholeness on the earth and this does not dissolve. Each time, you can retain love in your heart in face of opposition, you have built a little oasis of Divine Love in your environment. You will perceive that as more and more people on earth strive to respond to darkness in this way. The darkness itself will be affected - it cannot be otherwise, and so will the ranks of those striving to create the Kingdom of Heaven on earth, begin to increase and swell, and eventually the voices of the Divine will begin to enlighten the responses of those who are still unenlightened.

And what will be happening on earth whilst individuals are creating their own little oasis of Divine Love on earth? These oases will manifest as long-desired benefits in human society. They will enable human beings to rectify the mistakes made in the past years since the last war. Public services will begin to improve, humanity will begin to take on board new ethics governing their behaviour which will ensure that they treat their fellowmen with loving consideration and compassion. As this happens, prosperity will begin to return, poverty will abate, health will become ever more flourishing, arising from the new loving responses in people's hearts and minds. There will be benefits which at this moment you cannot even imagine because they will accrue from a high spiritual consciousness, beyond your conception at the present moment.

This is how you will create the Kingdom of Heaven on Earth.

I have just one word of warning. None of this will happen until people become aware that their own human thinking only has power over the 'matter' of the world - it is not spiritual.

The ' I ' of each person is not the soul - the soul is hidden within the ego.

Please note well, all followers of Christ's Letters, who have also followed other spiritual leaders.

Your ego remains in control of your consciousness until you have, little by little, drawn into your minds, the transcendent Divine Consciousness to gradually spiritualise your mental processes.

Will you please note: I have to tell you that human seekers of spirit, have been misled by teachers who have only absorbed certain facets of my message.

When water is poured into porridge, it softens the porridge but it is absorbed into the porridge and takes on the consistency of the porridge. So it is when spiritual inspiration flows into a receptive mind. It takes on the nature of the human mind. Very rarely is the inspiration so powerful that it can enter and flash its Truth into such a powerful awareness, that a person's beliefs are immediately changed. This is why inspired people teach many versions of Truth.

The fatal version is when people are told that they are Divine because they have drawn their being from Divinity.

The truth is, they can draw little streams of inspired consciousness into their minds, and very little by little, the darkness of the human ego is dissipated and is illumed by Divine Inspiration. Eventually, the consciousness is fully illumined, and the ego is overcome. When this happens to a person, that person becomes fully UNIVERSAL in Consciousness and is no longer aware of any desires for the self at all.

It focuses on otherness entirely and lives only to experience the rapture and ecstasy of Divine Consciousness and lovingly promote the wellbeing of others.

This is CHRIST CONSCIOUSNESS.

This is why I descended to write this Letter for you.

Study Resources

The Recorder's Short Prayer

Divine Consciousness, the Source of all Intelligence and Love in the world — my LIFE, I open my mind and heart to receive your Wisdom, Love, Strength.

I ask that You may enhance and prosper me and my family, and lead me into doing only what will enhance and bless everyone in my environment. I thank you for your immense Power within me and my life.

Christ says: "I want you to move again into an inner state of conscious equilibrium, where all thought is stilled and your mind resides in Silence.

You are in interior control, your mind and emotions no longer divided into activity and feeling. You may feel a build-up of power within you, strength,peace, and contentment. This, expressed in you, in individual form, is the State of Being out of which came creation..." ~ Letter 5

The Recorder's Long Prayer

Beloved FATHER-MOTHER-LIFE, I am beginning to realize that when I forget and live my life in forgetfulness of my true spiritual identity, I find myself in times of difficulty and tension. I perceive that when I surrender my self-will and yield to the protection and guidance of my Source of Being, I am uplifted on to a higher level of spiritual consciousness and my life flows, taking me into perfect conditions to achieve what is best for me and my family and others connected to me.

I am making this plain as I pray to YOU, because, beloved Father, I want to make my surrender genuine and real, I want it to affect - colour - my daily thoughts and activities. I sincerely want to spontaneously wonder (when doubtful), what is the Father's purpose, what is the right, the loving way which will be of benefit and a blessing for all concerned in this activity.

Beloved Father, I KNOW YOU have taken care of me up to this time of true realization that my will lands me in trouble, and the right way lifts me up from trouble, I pray you will accept my surrender and lift me on to the true spiritual path as outlined in Christ's Letters.

I thank you, Father, I know that you have received my prayer into your Divine Self and that YOU are enfolding me in your loving consciousness of spiritual wellbeing and spiritual growth.

I also pray, beloved Father, Source of all Being, that this prayer may uplift all who have contact and meaning for me in my daily life.

I ask that this prayer may be amplified and radiated far and wide to reach people who are lost in ego and long to find peace and harmony. I pray they may find the Truth of Being and be lifted into a knowledge of Divine Love.

And, Beloved Father, please impress your Divine Love also within my heart that I may respond and love You powerfully because loving you brings me into closer and more perfect union with ALL that YOU are.I thank you with gratitude and joy because I know that my words have been fully received and understood and even now I am enfolded in your Divine Self, we are united, I am part of You, my beloved FATHER.

~ Recorder

The Great Invocation for Christ's Way

My very Dear Friends in Christ, A Prayer Chain is being formed and is already covering many countries.

Due to the very clear developments that are taking place worldwide, everyone is invited to join in the 'chain' with the following prayer, adapted by our Beloved Recorder for Christ's Way followers.

At 22:00 hours (10:00 p.m.), every evening, no matter wherever you are,you will be joined by many souls who are also seeking the Higher Vision that Christ has so lovingly promised us.

"Here is a very powerful prayer for you to use, dwelling on each word and visualising its powerfully IMMENSE MEANING."

This prayer is the Recorder's adaptation of

THE GREAT INVOCATION for CHRIST'S WAY.

"From the radiant Universal Consciousness of Divinity

Let Light stream forth into the minds of men."

"From the radiant Universal Consciousness of Divinity — Father

Let Light descend and irradiate all life on Earth."

"From the radiant Universal Consciousness of Divinity — Mother

Let love stream forth and flood the hearts of men."

"We rejoice that Christ is indeed with us,"

"Christ has returned to Earth — in deed!"

"From the Radiant Universal Consciousness of Divinity —

where is Divine Intent Let Divine Purpose sway the ego wills of men"

"That glorious Purpose known and served by Christ and Celestial Beings."

Affirmation

Daily, I open my heart and mind to Divine Consciousness transcendent to help me dissolve all present selfish ego-drives.

Daily, I open my soul to receive Divine Consciousness to assist me in building a new ERA of LOVE & PEACE in the world.

In the KINGDOM of HEAVEN only Divine Love, Divine Compassion, Joy and Laughter, and beauty of self-expression will be sublimely manifested always.

Nature in every area of the world will flourish luxuriantly, harmoniously, supplying fruits and food for every single person on earth. All people will be well fed. All will be well clothed. All will be uplifted in spirit and will manifest Divine Consciousness in every way, every day.

I lift this Vision of Felicity to Divine Consciousness where it will be ignited with DIVINE LIFE for its perfect manifestation on earth. I give my loving thanks to my SOURCE that even now it is all beginning to take shape in the unseen.

Thank you, Father.

Rules to be Followed Daily

1 Daily reading of the Christ given Rules and Explanations (see Message 10) of why he has made them into rules.

2 Daily Meditation. (see Message 9 and "How to Meditate" in Letter 8)

3 Daily, I will reject all ego thoughts and replace them with thoughts of compassionate love and unconditional love.

4 To make meaningful contact with other people I must LISTEN to them and must stop bringing the subject back to myself.

5 I must be able to hear truths about myself without hiding behind a cloak of excuses and indulging in retaliations.

6 I must, at all times, be truthful and straight forward, otherwise my consciousness will be fragmented and I will lack conviction.

7 Daily, I must remember and affirm that in the Kingdom of Heaven – tomorrow is always perfect.

8 I must avoid all alarmist talk. To build the Kingdom of Heaven within and without myself, I must withdraw my consciousness from everything which I do not want to see repeated or perpetuated in the future.

9 I will listen carefully to all who seek my love and my comfort and will ask Divine Consciousness to give me the words to heal their hurt.

10 I will not give way to jealousy because I know that all the things necessary for my care and happiness can be mine when I ask 'Father- Mother-Love'.

11 Daily I will make the Affirmation (see next page) – visualising the full meaning as I speak.

Meditation Prayer

FATHER-MOTHER-LIFE, you are my life, my constant support,
my health, my protection, my perfect fulfilment of every need
and my highest inspiration.

I ask you to reveal the true Reality of Yourself to me. I know it is your WILL
that I shall be fully illumined that I may better receive awareness of Your
Presence within and around me. I believe and know that this is possible.
I believe that you protect and maintain me within perfect LOVE.

I know that my eventual purpose is to EXPRESS YOU. As I speak to you, I
know that you are perfectly receptive of me, for you are UNIVERSAL
LOVING INTELLIGENCE which has so marvelously designed this
world and brought it into visible form.

I know, that as I ask YOU to speak to me, I am sending out a consciousness
searchlight into your Divine Consciousness and as I listen, YOU will be
penetrating my human consciousness and coming ever closer to my
increasingly receptive mind and heart.

I commit myself and my life into your care.

Each time you say and visualize this prayer, you create a spiritual
consciousness form which will become stronger and ever more elevated in
frequencies of vibration as the true meaning of the prayer deepens in your
mind and heart and your perceptions heighten.

After the prayer, relax ever deeper and let your mind go as blank as you can.
If thoughts intrude, gently recite **'Divine Life'** or **'Father-Mother-Life'** to
yourself and again quieten your mind.

At the end of your meditation, always give glad and grateful thanks.

Printed in the USA
CPSIA information can be obtained
at www.ICGtesting.com
LVHW091303151023
761121LV00001BC/42

9 781941 489390